Lecture Notes in Computer Science 14538

Founding Editors

Gerhard Goos
Juris Hartmanis

T0180538

The series Lecture Notes in Computer Science (LNCS), including its subseries Lecture Notes in Artificial Intelligence (LNAI) and Lecture Notes in Bioinformatics (LNBI), has established itself as a medium for the publication of new developments in computer science and information technology research, teaching, and education.

LNCS enjoys close cooperation with the computer science R & D community, the series counts many renowned academics among its volume editors and paper authors, and collaborates with prestigious societies. Its mission is to serve this international community by providing an invaluable service, mainly focused on the publication of conference and workshop proceedings and postproceedings. LNCS commenced publication in 1973.

Philipp Richter · Vaibhav Bajpai ·
Esteban Carisimo

Editors

Passive and Active Measurement

25th International Conference, PAM 2024
Virtual Event, March 11–13, 2024
Proceedings, Part II

 Springer

Editors
Philipp Richter
Akamai Technologies
Cambridge, MA, USA

Vaibhav Bajpai (ID)
Hasso Plattner Institute
Potsdam, Germany

Esteban Carisimo (ID)
Northwestern University
Evanston, IL, USA

ISSN 0302-9743   ISSN 1611-3349 (electronic)
Lecture Notes in Computer Science
ISBN 978-3-031-56251-8   ISBN 978-3-031-56252-5 (eBook)
https://doi.org/10.1007/978-3-031-56252-5

This Springer imprint is published by the registered company Springer Nature Switzerland AG
The registered company address is: Gewerbestrasse 11, 6330 Cham, Switzerland

Paper in this product is recyclable.

Preface

We are excited to present the proceedings of the 25th Annual Passive and Active Measurement PAM Conference. With this program, PAM continues its tradition as a venue for thorough, compelling, but often early-stage and emerging research on networks, Internet measurement, and the emergent systems they host. This year's conference took place on March 11–13, 2024. Based on learnings from recent years, this year's PAM was again virtual, both to accommodate the realities of modern travel and to ensure the conference's accessibility to attendees who may not otherwise be able to travel long distances.

This year, we received 64 double-blind submissions from over 100 different institutions, of which the Technical Program Committee (TPC) selected 27 for publication, resulting in a program similar in size to previous years. As with last year, submissions could be of either long or short form, and our ultimate program featured 14 long papers and 13 short papers. The 27 papers of the final program illustrate how network measurements can provide essential insights for different types of networks and networked systems and cover topics such as applications, performance, network infrastructure and topology, measurement tools, and security and privacy. It thus provides a comprehensive view of current state-of-the-art and emerging ideas in this important domain.

We built a TPC that included a mix of experience levels, backgrounds, and geographies, bringing well-established and fresh perspectives to the committee. Each submission was assigned to four reviewers, each providing an average of just under 5 reviews. Following in the footsteps of previous years, we established a Review Task Force (RTF) of experienced community members who could guide much of the discussion among reviewers. Finally, 21 of the accepted papers were shepherded by members of the TPC who were reviewers of each paper. As program chairs, we would like to thank our TPC and RTF members for volunteering their time and expertise with such dedication and enthusiasm.

Special thanks to our hosting organization this year, Northwestern University. Thanks to the PAM steering committee for their guidance in putting together the conference. Finally, thank you to the researchers in the networking and measurement communities and beyond who submitted their work to PAM and engaged in the process.

March 2024

Philipp Richter
Vaibhav Bajpai
Esteban Carisimo

Organization

General Chair

Esteban Carisimo   Northwestern University, USA

Program Committee Chairs

Philipp Richter   Akamai Technologies, USA
Vaibhav Bajpai   Hasso Plattner Institute and University of
                                  Potsdam, Germany

PAM Steering Committee

Marinho P. Barcellos   University of Waikato, New Zealand
Fabian E. Bustamante   Northwestern University, USA
Michalis Faloutsos   University of California, USA
Anja Feldmann   Max Planck Institute for Informatics, Germany
Oliver Hohlfeld   University of Kassel, Germany
Jelena Mirkovic   University of Southern California, USA
Giovane Moura   SIDN Labs, The Netherlands
Cristel Pelsser   UCLouvain, Belgium
Steve Uhlig   Queen Mary, University of London, UK

Program Committee

Alessandro Finamore   Huawei Technologies, France
Alexander Gamero-Garrido   UC Davis, USA
Andra Lutu   Telefonica, Spain
Anna Sperotto   University of Twente, Netherlands
Aqsa Kashaf   Carnegie Mellon University, USA
Arash Molavi Kakhki   ThousandEyes/Cisco, USA
Audrey Randall   UC San Diego, USA
Daphné Tuncer   Ecole des Ponts ParisTech, France
Diana Andrea Popescu   University of Cambridge, UK
Enric Pujol   SAP, Germany

Gautam Akiwate   Stanford University, USA
Giovane Moura   SIDN Labs and TU Delft, Netherlands
Idilio Drago   University of Turin, Italy
Jayasree Sengupta   CISPA, Germany
Johannes Zirngibl   TU Munich, Germany
John Heidemann   University of Southern California/ISI, USA
Karyn Benson   Meta, USA
Kensuke Fukuda   National Institute of Informatics, Japan
Kevin Vermeulen   CNRS, France
Kyle Schomp   ThousandEyes/Cisco, USA
Lars Prehn   Max Planck Institute for Informatics, Germany
Lucianna Kiffer   ETH Zurich, Switzerland
Marcin Nawrocki   NETSCOUT, Germany
Marinho Barcellos   University of Waikato, New Zealand
Matteo Varvello   Nokia Bell Labs, USA
Mattijs Jonker   University of Twente, Netherlands
Michael Rabinovich   Case Western Reserve University, USA
Moritz Müller   SIDN and University of Twente, Netherlands
Nguyen Phong Hoang   University of Chicago, USA
Nitinder Mohan   TU Munich, Germany
Olaf Maennel   The University of Adelaide, Australia
Oliver Gasser   Max Planck Institute for Informatics, Germany
Pawel Foremski   IITiS PAN, Poland
Ramakrishna Padmanabhan   Amazon, USA
Ramakrishnan Durairajan   University of Oregon, USA
Ricky K. P. Mok   UC San Diego/CAIDA, USA
Robert Beverly   Naval Postgraduate School, USA
Robin Marx   Akamai Technologies, Belgium
Roland van Rijswijk-Deij   University of Twente, Netherlands
Romain Fontugne   IIJ Research Laboratory, Japan
Sangeetha Abdu Jyothi   UC Irvine/VMware Research, USA
Shuai Hao   Old Dominion University, USA
Simone Ferlin-Reiter   Red Hat AB/Karlstad University, Sweden
Stephen McQuistin   University of St Andrews, UK
Stephen Strowes   Fastly, USA
Taejoong Chung   Virginia Tech, USA
Tanya Shreedhar   University of Edinburgh, UK
Thomas Krenc   UC San Diego/CAIDA, USA
Waqar Aqeel   Google, USA
Zachary Bischof   Georgia Institute of Technology, USA

Review Task Force

Alberto Dainotti	Georgia Institute of Technology, USA
Anna Brunstrom	Karlstad University, Sweden
Georgios Smaragdakis	TU Delft, Netherlands
Jelena Mircovic	University of Southern California/ISI, USA
Mark Allman	ICSI/Case Western Reserve, USA
Oliver Hohlfeld	University of Kassel, Germany

Contents – Part II

Topology

Transport Protocols

User Privacy

Contents – Part I

Network Security

Swamp of Reflectors: Investigating the Ecosystem of Open DNS Resolvers

Ramin Yazdani[✉], Mattijs Jonker, and Anna Sperotto

Faculty of Electrical Engineering, Mathematics and Computer Science,
University of Twente, Enschede, The Netherlands
{r.yazdani,m.jonker,a.sperotto}@utwente.nl

Abstract. DNS reflection-based DDoS attacks rely on open DNS resolvers to reflect and amplify attack traffic towards victims. While the majority of these resolvers are considered to be open because of misconfiguration, there remains a lot to be learned about the open resolver ecosystem.

In this paper, we investigate and characterize open DNS resolvers from multiple angles. First, we look at indicators that likely suggest an intention behind the existence of open resolvers. To this end, we cross open resolver IP addresses with reverse DNS measurement data and show that a relatively small group of open resolvers unmistakably indicate their service in hostnames (i.e., PTR records). Second, we investigate the extent to which anycast technique is used among open resolvers and show that this is mainly driven by hypergiants. Additionally, we take a look at the exposure of the authoritative nameservers as open recursive resolvers and show that a non-negligible number of authoritative nameservers also serve as open recursors. Finally, we look at the persistency of open resolvers over time. We study open resolvers longitudinally over a three-year period and show that 1% of open resolvers persistently appear in more than 95% of the measurement snapshots.

Keywords: DNS reflection · Open resolvers · DDoS · Amplification

1 Introduction

Our daily lives increasingly rely on digital infrastructure and the Internet. One of the persistent threats against the Internet services are Distributed Denial of Service (DDoS) attacks. In a DDoS attack, an attacker directs a large volume of network traffic toward a victim, which causes disruptions to the legitimate services of the victim by overwhelming its resources or those of its upstream networks. One of the common types of DDoS attacks are Reflection & Amplification (R&A) attacks in which connection-less networking protocols are leveraged to reflect traffic toward DDoS targets. Domain Name System (DNS) is one of the protocols that are typically misused to bring about reflection-based attacks.

DNS reflection is possible by sending spoofed queries (typically) to open DNS resolvers. Leveraging open resolvers as reflectors means that attackers need to

© The Author(s), under exclusive license to Springer Nature Switzerland AG 2024
P. Richter et al. (Eds.): PAM 2024, LNCS 14538, pp. 3–18, 2024.
https://doi.org/10.1007/978-3-031-56252-5_1

be in possession of a fresh list of them. This is crucial since open resolvers tend to present a relatively high IP address churn [4,12–14,26,32] and any list of their IP addresses (or at least for a portion of the involved IP addresses) would become outdated rather quickly. For attackers, this means that they need to run discovery scans rather frequently, which might increase the chance that their infrastructure gets detected by network security monitoring systems. As a recent study [8] shows, attackers are selective in scanning networks for exposed services. An alternative solution would involve relying on reflectors that represent a stable behavior, removing the necessity of frequent discovery efforts for attackers. However, it is not yet clear which fraction of the open resolver population is persistent, nor if they are intentionally deployed or what deployment features characterize them.

Open DNS resolvers have been widely studied in the literature [3,4,10,12, 13,19–21,26,27,32]. Multiple previous works focus on characterizing open DNS resolvers, either from the aspect of the legitimacy of responses returned by resolvers [4,12,20,21,27] or by investigating the amplification power of these resolvers [19,32]. Our paper complements prior work by characterizing open resolvers from a persistency point of view and investigating indicators of their intentional deployment. Thus, the goal of our research is to investigate differences among open resolvers that indicate the underlying cause of their existence and contribute to their persistence. The main contributions of our paper are that:

- We cross open resolvers discovery data with reverse DNS measurement data and show that (only) a small set of open resolvers likely signal their service through hostnames.
- We perform a longitudinal study on open resolvers and show that the majority of open resolvers are hosted in networks that exhibit persistence in terms of the total number of open resolvers present.
- We investigate the types of networks hosting open resolvers and show that resolvers with indicators of intentional deployment mostly reside in datacenter networks. Besides, we show that the majority of persistent resolvers reside in user access networks.

2   Datasets

2.1   Open Resolver Discovery Scans

We run open resolver discovery scans through which we collected data over a three-year period between October 2020 and October 2023[1] These scans have a frequency of once per week and target all publicly routable IPv4 addresses (in a random permutation) excluding a minority of network prefixes that have requested to be excluded from our scans. For each IP address, we issue a DNS query (toward destination port 53) using a unique subdomain (to avoid caching)

---

[1]   https://research.openresolve.rs.

by embedding the IP address and a timestamp in the query name. If we receive the expected answer to our query, we consider the IP address in question to be an open DNS resolver. These scans provide us with a list of IP addresses that openly do a DNS recursion themselves or forward it to other recursive resolvers. We include transparent forwarders [18] in our list of open DNS resolvers as well. However, we do not capture responses that arrive from unexpected port numbers (i.e., other than port 53) [10]. We plot the number of open resolvers over our three-year measurement period in Fig. 6 (in Appendix A).

2.2 OpenINTEL

We leverage data provided by OpenINTEL [23], which is an active DNS measurement project that measures the DNS state of 63% of the global forward DNS namespace on a daily basis. The measurement is seeded with domain names registered under a large number of gTLDs as well as various ccTLDs. Relevant to our study, OpenINTEL measures the authoritative nameserver records (i.e., NS) of domain names and resolves nameserver names to IP addresses (i.e., A records), providing us with a picture of the authoritative landscape.

Additionally, OpenINTEL measures the reverse DNS of the entire IPv4 address space daily. In a reverse DNS lookup, an IP address is translated to, among others, a hostname or PTR record (provided a hostname is configured). This can be used for network administration purposes, among others. In this paper, we leverage the reverse DNS measurements to further study the ecosystem of open DNS resolvers.

2.3 IP Anycast

IP anycast [16] is a technique in which the same IP address is shared among multiple devices. Anycast leverages the Border Gateway Protocol (BGP) to route client traffic destined to an anycast IP address to the nearest (preferred) server from the client's perspective. One of the advantages of anycast is that it can reduce latency for remote clients and distribute network traffic over multiple servers.

We leverage Anycast Census data [1,29] to determine if open resolvers reside in anycasted network prefixes. Anycast Census is based on using an anycast testbed network - currently consisting of 20 nodes - to measure anycasted prefixes. It measures one IP address per /24 prefix (which is the minimum globally-routable prefix size) for addresses that are likely to respond to pings. The public dataset of Anycast Census consists of quarterly snapshots.

3 Indicators in PTR Records

Reverse DNS serves a crucial role in network administration and security by mapping IP addresses to hostnames. We begin our investigation by looking at the hostnames of public resolvers to find common patterns that likely suggest an

Table 1. A list of nine popular public DNS resolvers [5], their IPv4 addresses, and hostnames.

Provider	IPv4 address(es)	Hostname(s)	DNS string in hostname	Anycast
Google	8.8.8.8 8.8.4.4	dns.google.	✓	✓
Cloudflare	1.1.1.1 1.0.0.1	one.one.one.one.	✗	✓
Quad9	9.9.9.9 149.112.112.112	dns.quad9.net.	✓	✓
OpenDNS	208.67.222.222 208.67.220.220	dns.opendns.com. dns.umbrella.com. resolver1.opendns.com. resolver2.opendns.com.	✓	✓
NextDNS	45.90.28.0 45.90.30.190	dns1.nextdns.io. dns2.nextdns.io.	✓	✓
CleanBrowsing	185.225.168.168 185.228.169.168	- family-filter-dns2.cleanbrowsing.org.	✓	✓
UltraDNS	64.6.64.6 64.6.65.6 156.154.70.2 156.154.71.2 156.154.70.3 156.154.71.3	rec1pubns1.ultradns.net. rec1pubns2.ultradns.net. - - - -	✓	✓
Yandex	77.88.8.8 77.88.8.1	dns.yandex.ru. secondary.dns.yandex.ru.	✓	✓
OpenNIC	195.10.195.195 51.77.149.139 88.99.98.111 ...	- 139.ip-51-77-149.eu. dns1.dns-ga.de. ...	✓	✗

intention behind their existence. Note that the intention to run a DNS service on a host, however, is not necessarily correlated with running this service openly. We argue that resolvers that are intentionally deployed would likely follow practices similar to public DNS resolvers (i.e., resolvers that are intentionally configured to serve public users) when setting their hostnames. To this end, we consider nine popular public resolvers [5] and the common practices followed by them, which we elaborate on in the following sections. The resolvers under consideration are listed in Table 1.

Out of nine public resolvers, eight resolvers present a similar pattern by embedding the *dns* string in (at least one of) their hostnames. Given the prominent usage of the *dns* string, we consider this a heuristic that likely indicates intentional deployment of an open resolver. However, hostnames do not always reflect services behind individual IP addresses. Many large networks (e.g., cloud providers and user access networks) deploy hostnames in an automated manner by embedding (part of) the IP address of each host as a label under a domain name in their PTR records. To avoid tagging default PTR records that contain *dns* string as an indicator of DNS service running on a specific host, we extend our heuristic by considering two thresholds that we choose experimentally. We tag a /24 prefix with *default PTR setup* if the number of open resolvers that

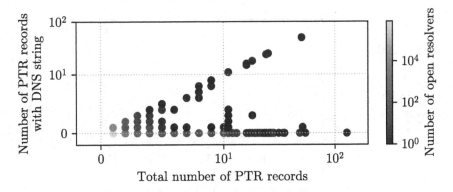

Fig. 1. Number of PTR records (hostnames) including the *dns* string for each open resolver compared to the total number of their PTR records.

have a PTR record containing the *dns* string in that prefix is less than 10% of the hosts in the same /24 prefix with such a string. Furthermore, if the number of PTR records with such a string in that prefix is more than half of the prefix size (127 hosts, indicating a potential default setup), we increase the threshold to 90%. Otherwise, we consider the *dns* string in the hostname of an open resolver to likely be an indicator of its intentional DNS service deployment. We establish these thresholds empirically by investigating their impact on a limited number (i.e., order of tens) of prefixes. Note that our method does not make any inferences on running DNS service openly.

We first investigate the prominence of the *dns* string in the open resolver population by leveraging reverse DNS measurement data from the OpenINTEL project. We observe that the vast majority (~65.5%) of open resolvers on a single measurement snapshot (2023-Jul-31) do not have a PTR record configured. In Fig. 1 we plot the number of PTR records (hostnames) for each open resolver with at least one hostname compared to the number of (their) PTR records containing the *dns* string. The color of each dot represents the number of resolvers for each data point. We observe two interesting patterns among open resolvers with at least one PTR record. First, a diagonal pattern in which all or the majority of the PTR records contain the *dns* string, with the extreme case being a resolver with 50 PTR records, all containing the *dns* string. We attribute this group to hosts that are more likely to be running DNS service intentionally. The second pattern is a horizontal one in which none of the PTR records contain the *dns* string. We attribute this group to open resolvers that are more likely to be exposed due to misconfigurations. This observation indicates that there is a high variability in both the number of hostnames and the way names are assigned among open resolvers, strengthening our observation that names can assist in identifying intentional deployment.

We then investigate reverse DNS data with respect to network prefixes. On 2023-Jul-31, approximately 1.28 B distinct IP addresses over the entire IPv4 address space have a hostname configured. Roughly 32 M (~2.5%) of all host-

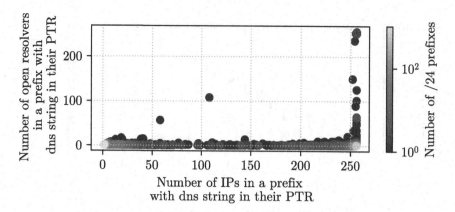

Fig. 2. The scatter plot of the number of IPv4 addresses within a /24 prefix that have *dns* string in their hostnames compared to the number of open resolvers in the same prefix with a similar pattern. The colors show the number of /24 prefixes with the same ratio between the two.

names contain the *dns* string in them. We group all IP addresses with the *dns* string in their hostnames into /24 prefixes. This gives us ∼222 k prefixes. Roughly 51% of these are prefixes in which all of the IP addresses include the *dns* string in their hostnames, likely indicating a default PTR record setup. We then further investigate the reverse DNS data for the open resolvers in the 2023-Jul-31 scan. Out of roughly 2.4 M open resolvers, around 823 k resolvers (∼34.5%) have a hostname configured. Only around 11 k (∼0.46%) resolvers include the *dns* string in at least one of their hostnames, the majority together with their IP address embedded.

For /24 prefixes that host at least one open resolver with *dns* string in its hostname (4.7k prefixes), we plot, per prefix, the number of open resolvers versus the number of IP addresses that embed *dns* string (see Fig. 2). We observe two common patterns in this figure. On the one hand, there is a high number of prefixes in which there are only a handful of PTR records with *dns* string in them as well as a handful of open resolvers with such a string. We argue this group likely indicate their DNS service through their hostnames. On the other hand, there are many networks in which almost the entire block has *dns* string in their hostnames, and in which only a few open resolvers reside. We attribute this group to networks with likely default PTR setups. Alternatively, it is possible that such prefixes are meant to be used as closed resolvers and the limited number of open resolvers in them are misconfigurations. However, we argue that since such networks are typically well-provisioned, misconfigurations in them would be less common compared to CPEs. Using our heuristic with the above-mentioned threshold leaves us with 5.5k (∼0.23%) open resolvers that we suspect to be intentionally running DNS service. Thus, the majority of open resolvers likely do not indicate their service through their PTR records. This suggests that this large portion of resolvers are likely unintentionally open.

Our heuristic will create some false negatives since not all open resolvers necessarily follow such a practice of including the *dns* string in their hostnames. A notable example is Cloudflare public resolver (see Table 1). Additionally, false positives are also possible if a hostname contains the *dns* string as part of an unrelated string[2]. Thus, our results provide an estimate of the number of open resolvers that are intentionally running DNS service.

Key Takeaway: *Although PTR record registration is not mandatory, looking at the open resolvers that have a hostname configured, we observe that the vast majority do not follow a similar pattern to popular public DNS providers. This suggests that most open resolvers are likely unintentionally deployed.*

4 Anycasted Open Resolvers

A common feature among popular public resolvers is to use IP anycast to improve performance for clients in various regions. As seen in Table 1, all but one of the public resolvers in our study are anycasted. The only provider that does not use anycast is OpenNIC, which uses volunteer-provided DNS resolvers. Sommese et al. [28] studied anycast adoption in the authoritative nameserver ecosystem and proved that it is mainly driven by hypergiants, as this is a complex and costly technology. Intuitively, we expect the hypergiants to be the main contributors to the anycasted recursive resolver ecosystem.

We investigate the extent to which open resolvers are located in anycasted networks. We fuse the open resolver scan data (2022-Jan-17) with anycast census data [1,29] from the same month and observe that roughly 9.3 k (~0.34%) resolvers are hosted in 216 distinct /24 anycasted network prefixes. In terms of Autonomous Systems (ASes), this translates to 58 distinct networks. In Table 2 we provide the top ASes hosting anycasted open resolvers. Cloudflare and Akamai together are behind 56% of anycasted open resolvers. Additionally, as one expects, multiple public DNS providers are visible in this table. Looking at the network types, 99% of the anycasted resolvers are hosted in DCH (datacenter/hosting/transit) and CDN networks which are expected network types for anycasted infrastructure. Those findings confirm our intuition that hypergiants are prominently present in the open resolver ecosystem, but the same findings also show that anycast is only minimally present among open resolvers.

Key Takeaway: *While popular public DNS providers hold a large share of the anycasted recursive DNS infrastructure, using anycast is marginal among the overall crowd of open resolvers.*

5 Authoritative Open Resolvers

Authoritative nameservers are meant to serve queries for specific subdomains, i.e., zones. However, there is a possibility to combine an authoritative nameserver

---

[2] A manual inspection shows that this is not common in our dataset.

Table 2. The top-10 origin ASes for open resolvers in anycasted prefixes.

ASN	AS Name	# Resolvers	% Resolvers
AS13335	Cloudflare, Inc.	2636	28.5%
AS21342	Akamai International B.V.	2550	27.5%
AS23393	NuCDN LLC	1022	11.0%
AS205157	Daniel Cid	1021	11.0%
AS34939	NextDNS, Inc.	1020	11.0%
AS45102	Alibaba (US) Technology Co., Ltd.	510	5.5%
AS397213	Neustar Security Services	108	1.2%
AS397232	Neustar Security Services	107	1.2%
AS398962	CONTROLD INC.	32	0.3%
AS3549	Level 3 Communications, Inc.	23	0.2%

with a recursive nameserver, despite the fact that this is not generally considered a good practice [6]. For example, *BIND* DNS software [2] allows configuring a server to act simultaneously as an authoritative and a recursor. This means that there is a possibility for authoritative nameservers to be exposed as open resolvers.

To investigate the degree to which authoritative nameservers contribute to the open resolvers ecosystem, we leverage OpenINTEL authoritative nameserver measurement data and fuse it with the open resolvers discovery scans. We study all domains in *.com, .net, .org* Top-Level Domains (TLDs) as well as all new Generic Top-Level Domains (gTLDs) available through ICANN's CZDS. We create a mapping of second-level domain names in these zones to the IP address of their nameservers. However, domain names may point their nameservers to open resolvers while the resolver is not necessarily the authoritative server for that domain. To investigate the extent to which open resolvers coincide with authoritative nameservers, we issue DNS queries for domain names in our list and send these queries to their open resolver nameserver addresses. If an open resolver is in fact authoritative for a domain name, the DNS answer should have the AA (authoritative answer) flag set. However, it is known [21] that open resolvers might even set the AA flag when they are not authoritative for the domain name in question. Looking at the open resolver discovery scans on 2023-Oct-30 we find 10.6 k of these non-compliant open resolvers. We exclude these resolvers from our study since it is not possible to infer if they are also running an authoritative nameserver using the DNS AA flag.

The mapping of second-level domains to their nameservers gives us 666 M distinct *{domain name, IP address}* tuples. Next, we cross this mapping with the (AA flag compliant) open resolvers list to get a list of domain names for which the nameservers happen to be authoritative and an open resolver. This results in roughly 468 k *{domain name, IP address}* tuples. This involves 248 k unique

Table 3. The top-5 TLDs for domain names that have at least one nameserver address that is authoritative and an open resolver.

TLD	# Domains	% Domains
com	205.9 k	83.1%
net	19.6 k	7.9%
org	10.7 k	4.3%
vip	0.9 k	0.4%
app	0.9 k	0.3%

domain names pointing their NS addresses to 11.8 k unique open resolvers. In Table 3 we summarize the details of our dataset.

Our queries result in 441 k answers concerning 246 k unique domain names. 238 k of these domains have the AA flag set in at least one of the answers from their authoritative nameservers. Approximately 18 k domains have at least one answer coming from a server which is not authoritative for that domain name. Around 10 k domain names use a mix of authoritative and non-authoritative nameservers. Our results indicate that the majority (~95%) of open resolvers that are listed as an authoritative nameserver for a domain name are indeed running the recursive and authoritative services simultaneously. This could constitute a potential security risk since authoritative nameservers are typically well-provisioned and this could make them attractive for being misused in R&A DDoS attacks.

Our methodology to infer the open resolvers that are serving as an authoritative nameserver provides a lower boundary to this number, for two reasons. First, our dataset includes only second-level domains. Second, we cover a subset of TLDs in our measurement. However, it avoids false positives that occur by purely relying on PTR records to infer infrastructure resolvers [22].

Key Takeaway: *Authoritative nameservers are typically deployed with rich resources. Co-hosting these servers with an open resolver might constitute a higher risk of misuse in R&A DDoS attacks.*

6   Persistency over Time

We postulate that resolvers that are intentionally deployed as open should present a persistent availability over time compared to the lifetime of resolvers that are unintentionally exposed. In order to investigate the persistency of open resolvers over time, we look at the longitudinal open resolvers dataset (154 snapshots in three years) and calculate the percentage of snapshots in which each resolver appears among the snapshots that follow its initial discovery. We only investigate resolvers in the first year of snapshots to make sure that the persistency of resolvers is fairly examined.

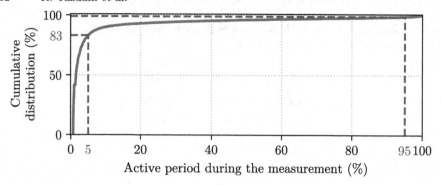

Fig. 3. The distribution of the relative presence of open resolvers during the measurement period.

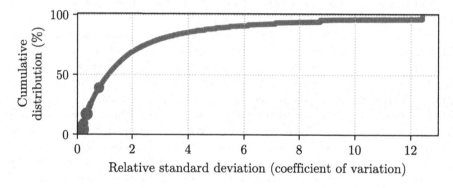

Fig. 4. The distribution of the relative standard deviation (σ/μ) for the number of open resolvers per AS (blue line). We also map open resolvers on a single snapshot to their ASes (red circles). (Color figure online)

We observe roughly 32 M distinct open resolver IPv4 addresses over the first year of our measurement. This number is much higher than the average number of open resolvers (roughly 2.7 M resolvers) per snapshot due to the dynamic appearance of open resolvers (e.g., due to IP churn). Roughly 83% of these IP addresses are visible on less than 5% of our snapshots, while 1% are consistently present in more than 95% of the snapshots (see Fig. 3).

We also look at the persistency of ASes that host open resolvers. To this end, we calculate the Relative Standard Deviation (RSD) of the number of open resolvers per AS and plot a CDF in Fig. 4 (blue line). The RSD (also known as the coefficient of variation) is defined as the ratio of the standard deviation (σ) to the mean value (μ). A lower relative standard deviation means that the number of open resolvers in a network does not change much over time. We also map open resolvers we observed during a single measurement snapshot to their ASes. We plot these as red circles in Fig. 4, where the circle diameter is proportional to the number of resolvers. Figure 4 shows that the majority of open resolvers are hosted in ASes that have a lower RSD, meaning that those ASes show a

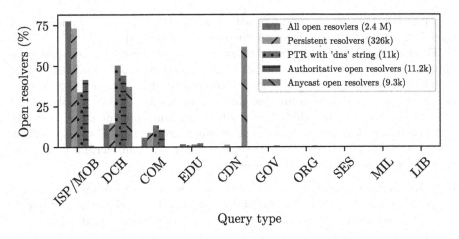

Fig. 5. The distribution of open resolvers in different network categories.

persistent behavior over time in terms of the number of open resolvers in their network.

The persistent concentration of open resolvers in a limited number of networks could have repercussions on the misuse of these servers in R&A attacks, as it could imply that an attacker might not need to sweep the entire address space to find reflectors.

Key Takeaway: *The majority of open resolvers persistently reside in ASes that have a stable number of open resolvers. We argue that this could constitute a security risk, but also it holds potential for prioritized mitigation efforts.*

7   Network Types

Investigating the type of networks hosting open DNS resolvers has been conducted in earlier work. Kührer et al. [12] analyze the reverse DNS records of short-lived open resolvers and attribute them to residential networks. Schomp et al. [26] take a different approach and rely on various metrics such as HTTP probes to infer open resolvers in residential networks. We leverage the IP intelligence data of IP2Location [7] to attribute open resolvers to various network types and corroborate the findings of earlier work. The added value of our method is that it allows us to categorize the network types of all open resolvers even if e.g., they do not set a PTR record.

Looking at the types of the networks that host open resolvers (see Fig. 5), we observe that eyeball networks host the majority (~80%) of general open resolvers, while open resolvers with *dns* string in their hostname(s) are mainly (~50%) hosted in datacenters. Considering the resolvers that are persistently available on more than 95% of the scan snapshots, we see a similar distribution to the generic population of open resolvers, with 72% of these resolvers residing in user access networks. The large share of persistent resolvers in ISP networks is potentially because of providers with a static IP address assignment, even though these resolvers are likely not intentionally deployed.

From a DDoS attacker point of view, there is a trade-off between misusing different categories of open resolvers. While datacenter-based resolvers benefit from a high link-capacity [30], these resolvers are often considered to deploy measures that limit damage in case they are misused in DDoS attacks. Additionally, there is a chance that these resolvers are honeypots deployed to detect malicious network activities. On the other hand, leveraging ISP-based resolvers has a lower risk for attackers, while these resolvers typically have a lower link-capacity compared to datacenter-based resolvers.

Key Takeaway: *Persistent open resolvers are mostly hosted in user access networks. This, combined with the intuition that such resolvers likely exist due to misconfigurations, raises worries about their potential misuse in attacks.*

8   Related Work

Open DNS resolvers have been considered a threat to the Internet for a long time by majorly being involved in DDoS attacks [9,13,17,25] and DNS cache poisoning attacks [11]. Although the number of open resolvers has reduced substantially over time [12,21,32], the remaining ones are multiple orders of magnitude more than what attackers typically misuse in DDoS attacks [17].

Kührer et al. [12] classify the DNS software of open resolvers as well as the hardware of their underlying. Besides, they study the IP churn of open resolvers over time and (by investigating the reverse DNS PTR records) report that a big part of the dynamicity of open resolvers is due to dynamic IP connections. Finally, they look at the authenticity of the answers provided by open resolvers and investigate the intentions behind DNS response manipulation. Similarly, Park et al. [20,21] investigate the authenticity of DNS responses returned by open resolvers and the intentions behind these manipulated responses. Considering the focus of our work being DDoS attacks, we only investigate open resolvers that return an expected answer and thus are more appealing for DDoS attackers.

Doan et al. [5] investigate the performance of popular public DNS resolvers using the RIPE Atlas platform [24]. Although our work does not focus on DNS performance, we base our analysis on the common practices followed by the public resolvers in this work.

Several studies focus on the DDoS potential that open DNS resolvers expose. Leverett and Kaplan [15] estimate a lower bound for the global R&A DDoS potential by leveraging the network speed measurements from the M-Lab project. Nosyk et al. [19] study the packet amplification potential of DNS queries and attribute them to routing loops and middleboxes. Similarly, Yazdani et al. [31] investigate the underlying causes of DNS packet amplification and report directed IP broadcasting to be an additional underlying cause for this phenomenon. The bandwidth amplification power of open resolvers was studied by Yazdani et al. [32], showing that there is a difference in the extent to which open resolvers can return amplified DNS responses.

A common practice among the existing work is that they do not differentiate deliberately public DNS resolvers from open resolvers that are exposed due to misconfigurations. To the best of our knowledge, our work is the first study that investigates the indicators of intentional deployment of open resolvers and sheds light on their dynamics.

9   Ethical Considerations

Our study involves active DNS measurements to discover open resolvers. This introduces some ethical concerns that we have carefully considered when designing our measurement setup. First, we limit the probes that we send to each distinct IP address to one per week. Additionally, the probes were randomized in the IPv4 address space so that remote networks would not receive bursts of queries. We also indicate the purpose of our queries - by using a domain name under our control - both in the PTR record of our scanner machine as well as in the queries that we issue. Finally, we run a Web server for this domain name on which we explain how network operators can opt out of our study.

Additionally, we run measurements to investigate open resolvers that are authoritative for one or more domain names. We follow common good practices in conducting these measurements. For example, we randomize queries for distinct domain names as well as for distinct authoritative nameservers, so that we do not disrupt the tested networks.

10   Conclusions

DDoS attackers typically rely on open resolvers to direct a large amount of network traffic towards victims. Open resolvers, however, present some diversity due to differences in the underlying cause of their existence. Although little is known about the strategies that attackers take to select their set of resolvers to abuse, such diversities can be leveraged to optimize the amount of traffic that is sent to a victim. Our results show that only 0.23% of open resolvers likely indicate an intentional deployment, meaning that there is still ample opportunity to reduce the number of DNS reflectors. Our research also shows that specific groups of open resolvers, namely open resolvers co-hosted with authoritative nameservers and persistent resolvers in user access networks, could enable prioritized mitigation efforts.

Acknowledgments. We would like to thank the anonymous reviewers and our shepherd Ramakrishna Padmanabhan for their valuable feedback on our paper. We also thank Raffaele Sommese for his insightful feedback in the early stages of this research. We gratefully acknowledge the support by ip2location.com, who provided us with an academic license to use their data. This work was partially supported by the GÉANT GN5-1 programme funded by the European Commission.

A   Number of Open Resolvers over Time

In Fig. 6 we plot the number of open resolvers that we observe in our scans. The dip in January 2022 is likely due to a measurement error.

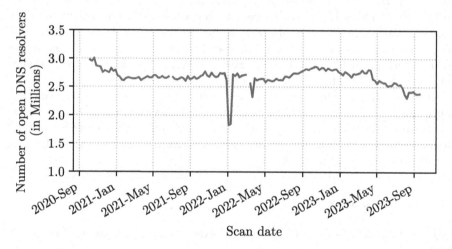

Fig. 6. Number of open DNS resolvers observed in our weekly scans between October 2020 and October 2023.

References

1. Anycast Census, a joint project of the University of Twente, SIDN, and CAIDA. https://github.com/ut-dacs/Anycast-Census/
2. BIND Dns. https://www.isc.org/bind/
3. Al-Dalky, R., Rabinovich, M., Schomp, K.: A look at the ecs behavior of dns resolvers. In: Proceedings of the Internet Measurement Conference, pp. 116–129. IMC '19, Association for Computing Machinery, New York, NY, USA (2019). https://doi.org/10.1145/3355369.3355586
4. Dagon, D., Provos, N., Lee, C.P., Lee, W.: Corrupted DNS resolution paths: the rise of a malicious resolution authority. In: 15th Network and Distributed System Security Symposium (NDSS) (2008)

5. Doan, T.V., Fries, J., Bajpai, V.: Evaluating public DNS services in the wake of increasing centralization of DNS. In: 2021 IFIP Networking Conference (IFIP Networking), pp. 1–9 (2021). https://doi.org/10.23919/IFIPNetworking52078.2021.9472831

6. ICANN: KINDNS (2022). https://kindns.org/guidelines/public-resolver-operators/

7. IP2Location: IP Address to IP Location and Proxy Information. https://www.ip2location.com/

8. Izhikevich, L., Tran, M., Kallitsis, M., Fass, A., Durumeric, Z.: Cloud watching: understanding attacks against cloud-hosted services. In: Proceedings of the 2023 ACM on Internet Measurement Conference, pp. 313–327. IMC '23, Association for Computing Machinery, New York, NY, USA (2023). https://doi.org/10.1145/3618257.3624818

9. Jonker, M., King, A., Krupp, J., Rossow, C., Sperotto, A., Dainotti, A.: Millions of targets under atack: a macroscopic characterization of the DoS ecosystem. In: Proceedings of the ACM SIGCOMM Internet Measurement Conference. vol. Part F131937, pp. 100–113 (2017). https://doi.org/10.1145/3131365.3131383

10. Kaizer, A.J., Gupta, M.: Open resolvers: understanding the origins of anomalous open DNS resolvers. In: Mirkovic, J., Liu, Y. (eds.) Passive and Active Measurement, pp. 3–14. Springer International Publishing, Cham (2015)

11. Kaminsky, D.: Black Ops 2008: It's The End Of The Cache As We Know It. Black Hat USA (2008)

12. Kührer, M., Hupperich, T., Bushart, J., Rossow, C., Holz, T.: Going wild: large-scale classification of open DNS resolvers. In: Proceedings of the 2015 ACM Internet Measurement Conference - IMC '15, pp. 355–368. ACM Press, New York, USA (2015). https://doi.org/10.1145/2815675.2815683

13. Kührer, M., Hupperich, T., Rossow, C., Holz, T.: Exit from hell? reducing the impact of amplification DDoS attacks. In: Proceedings of the 23rd USENIX Security Symposium, pp. 111–125 (2014)

14. Leonard, D., Loguinov, D.: Demystifying service discovery: implementing an internet-wide scanner. In: Proceedings of the 10th ACM SIGCOMM Conference on Internet Measurement, pp. 109–122. IMC '10, Association for Computing Machinery, New York, NY, USA (2010). https://doi.org/10.1145/1879141.1879156

15. Leverett, E., Kaplan, A.: Towards estimating the untapped potential: a global malicious DDoS mean capacity estimate. J. Cyber Policy 2(2), 195–208 (2017). https://doi.org/10.1080/23738871.2017.1362020

16. Mendez, T., Milliken, W., Partridge, D.C.: Host Anycasting Service. RFC 1546 (Nov 1993). https://doi.org/10.17487/RFC1546, https://www.rfc-editor.org/info/rfc1546

17. Nawrocki, M., Jonker, M., Schmidt, T.C., Wählisch, M.: The far side of DNS amplification: tracing the DDoS attack ecosystem from the internet core. In: Proceedings of the 21st ACM Internet Measurement Conference, pp. 419–434. IMC '21, Association for Computing Machinery, New York, NY, USA (2021). https://doi.org/10.1145/3487552.3487835

18. Nawrocki, M., Koch, M., Schmidt, T.C., Wählisch, M.: Transparent forwarders: an unnoticed component of the open DNS infrastructure. In: Proceedings of the 17th International Conference on Emerging Networking EXperiments and Technologies, pp. 454–462. CoNEXT '21, Association for Computing Machinery, New York, NY, USA (2021). https://doi.org/10.1145/3485983.3494872

19. Nosyk, Y., Korczyński, M., Duda, A.: Routing loops as mega amplifiers for DNS-based DDoS attacks. In: Hohlfeld, O., Moura, G., Pelsser, C. (eds.) Passive and Active Measurement, pp. 629–644. Springer International Publishing, Cham (2022)
20. Park, J., Jang, R., Mohaisen, M., Mohaisen, D.: A large-scale behavioral analysis of the open DNS resolvers on the internet. IEEE/ACM Trans. Network. **30**(1), 76–89 (2022). https://doi.org/10.1109/TNET.2021.3105599
21. Park, J., Khormali, A., Mohaisen, M., Mohaisen, A.: Where are you taking me? behavioral analysis of open DNS resolvers. In: 49th Annual IEEE/IFIP International Conference on Dependable Systems and Networks, DSN 2019, pp. 493–504. IEEE (2019). https://doi.org/10.1109/DSN.2019.00057
22. Pearce, P., et al.: Global measurement of DNS manipulation. In: 26th USENIX Security Symposium (USENIX Security 17), pp. 307–323. USENIX Association, Vancouver, BC (Aug 2017), https://www.usenix.org/conference/usenixsecurity17/technical-sessions/presentation/pearce
23. van Rijswijk-Deij, R., Jonker, M., Sperotto, A., Pras, A.: A high-performance, scalable infrastructure for large-scale active DNS measurements. IEEE J. Sel. Areas Commun. **34**(6), 1877–1888 (2016). https://doi.org/10.1109/JSAC.2016.2558918
24. RIPE NCC: RIPE Atlas: A global internet measurement network. Internet Protocol J. **18**(3), 2–26 (2015). http://ipj.dreamhosters.com/wp-content/uploads/2015/10/ipj18.3.pdf
25. Rossow, C.: Amplification hell: revisiting network protocols for DDoS abuse. In: Proceedings of the 2014 Network and Distributed Systems Security Symposium, pp. 23–26. No. February, Internet Society, San Diego (2014). https://doi.org/10.14722/ndss.2014.23233, http://www.internetsociety.org/sites/default/files/01_5.pdf
26. Schomp, K., Callahan, T., Rabinovich, M., Allman, M.: On measuring the client-side DNS infrastructure. In: Proceedings of the 2013 Conference on Internet Measurement Conference, pp. 77–90. IMC '13, Association for Computing Machinery, New York, NY, USA (2013). https://doi.org/10.1145/2504730.2504734
27. Schomp, K., Callahan, T., Rabinovich, M., Allman, M.: Assessing DNS vulnerability to record injection. In: Faloutsos, M., Kuzmanovic, A. (eds.) Passive and Active Measurement, pp. 214–223. Springer International Publishing, Cham (2014)
28. Sommese, R., et al.: Characterization of anycast adoption in the DNS authoritative infrastructure. In: Network Traffic Measurement and Analysis Conference (TMA'21) (2021)
29. Sommese, R., et al.: MAnycast2: using anycast to measure anycast. In: Proceedings of the ACM Internet Measurement Conference, pp. 456–463. IMC '20, Association for Computing Machinery, New York, NY, USA (2020). https://doi.org/10.1145/3419394.3423646
30. Yazdani, R., et al.: Mirrors in the sky: on the potential of clouds in DNS reflection-based denial-of-service attacks. In: Proceedings of the 25th International Symposium on Research in Attacks, Intrusions and Defenses, pp. 263–275. RAID '22, Association for Computing Machinery, New York, NY, USA (2022). https://doi.org/10.1145/3545948.3545959
31. Yazdani, R., Nosyk, Y., Holz, R., Korczyński, M., Jonker, M., Sperotto, A.: Hazardous echoes: the dns resolvers that should be put on mute. In: 2023 7th Network Traffic Measurement and Analysis Conference (TMA), pp. 1–10 (2023). https://doi.org/10.23919/tma58422.2023.10198955
32. Yazdani, R., van Rijswijk-Deij, R., Jonker, M., Sperotto, A.: A matter of degree: characterizing the amplification power of open DNS resolvers. In: Hohlfeld, O., Moura, G., Pelsser, C. (eds.) PAM 2022. LNCS, vol. 13210, pp. 293–318. Springer, Cham (2022). https://doi.org/10.1007/978-3-030-98785-5_13

Out in the Open: On the Implementation of Mobile App Filtering in India

Devashish Gosain[1,2]($\boxtimes$), Kartikey Singh[3], Rishi Sharma[3], Jithin Suresh Babu[3], and Sambuddho Chakravaty[3]

[1] BITS Pilani Goa, Sancoale, India
devashishg@goa.bits-pilani.ac.in
[2] MPI-INF, Saarbrücken, Germany
[3] IIIT Delhi, New Delhi, India
{kartikey17242,rishi17260,jithins,sambuddho}@iiitd.ac.in

Abstract. In this paper, we present the first comprehensive study highlighting the evolving mobile app filtering within India. We study the recent mobile app blocking in India and describe in detail the mechanics involved. We analyzed 220 Chinese apps that were blocked due to official government orders. Our research reveals a novel "three-tiered" app filtering scheme, with each tier increasing the sophistication of filtering. After thoroughly analyzing the app blocking mechanisms, we present circumvention techniques to bypass the tiered app filtering. We were able to access all the blocked apps with the said techniques. We believe our analysis and findings from the case study of India will aid future research on mobile app filtering.

1 Introduction

There are numerous instances of wide-scale filtering in different parts of the globe [63]. While there exist a plethora of studies that systematically analyzed Internet filtering [55,61], a significant fraction of them focused on "Great Firewall of China" and reported its multi-faceted censorship [25,29,34,38,42,51,67,68]. In this paper, we take a different direction and focus on a less studied country India [41,60,72]. Previous censorship studies in India reported different categories of blocked websites [41], the techniques used [60], and a detailed analysis of mechanics employed by Indian ISPs to achieve *web* censorship [72]. However, for the first time, we study a new filtering ecosystem *i.e.*, *mobile app blocking* within India.

Due to the rapid growth of mobile Internet applications, app blocking will become an essential component of any nationwide censorship system. Already, there is anecdotal evidence of banning mobile apps by different countries [3,27,56]. Thus, we conduct a comprehensive study to analyze the mechanics of this less-studied form of filtering. We consider India as a case study where the banning of mobile apps is a recent phenomenon, with 59 popular Chinese apps [13,15] being initially blocked on the orders of the Indian government in June 2020. Since then, India has continued its app-blocking spree, and presently 220 Chinese apps are blocked.

We begin by analyzing the blocking of a popular app *TikTok* (which has over 2.6 billion downloads worldwide [16]). We expected to see traditional filtering

P. Richter et al. (Eds.): PAM 2024, LNCS 14538, pp. 19–36, 2024.
https://doi.org/10.1007/978-3-031-56252-5_2

techniques being used by the Indian ISPs, *viz.* DNS filtering, TCP/IP blocking, and keyword filtering [58,67]. But, to our surprise, we observed no filtering from the Indian ISPs. Instead, a successful TLS connection was established between the app and the actual TikTok server (confirmed via TikTok's legitimate certificate). Moreover, we also noticed that the censorship notification banner was a part of the same TLS session, proving that the TikTok server sent it. *This confirmed that TikTok app blocking is not carried out by the Indian ISPs; rather, it was by the TikTok server itself.*

Our observations were similar for all other filtered apps as well *i.e.*, Indian ISPs were not at all involved in the filtering. Instead, the app servers were themselves selectively filtering the Indian users following the Indian government's blocking orders [5–7]. To identify the technique(s) for filtering, we analyzed traffic footprints (through `pcaps`) and even reverse-engineered a few apps. Our observations were surprising—some apps were even *probing the SIM card* for country information to restrict the user access (see Sect. 4 for details).

The app blocking kept evolving over the course of two years, with some apps changing their blocking mechanisms from just probing the SIM to a combination of inspecting the SIM and source IP addresses (*e.g.,* TikTok). We studied this evolving behavior, and based on our findings, we divided the app filtering mechanics into three tiers, with each tier adding a level of sophistication in blocking criteria.

1. *Tier three* apps are those that are unavailable in the Indian app stores. We found 160 such apps[1]. 136 out of these can be accessed directly after installation. We obtained the *apk* of these apps from third-party sources like `apkmirror.com`.
2. *Tier two* apps are those that, after installation, would still suffer blocking. These app publishers selectively filter Indian clients using geo-blocking [53]. 23 (out of the previous 160) apps fall under this category.
3. *Tier one* apps are those that employ the most sophisticated technique. As already explained with the example of TikTok, not only do these apps censor users by identifying locale information from the SIM cards installed, but they also use geo-blocking. In total, 7 (out of the previous 23) apps employ such filtering techniques. Note that *MICO Chat*, is the only exception that has exclusively adopted SIM-based blocking.

While analyzing the geoblocking of apps, we observed different geoblocking techniques employed by these apps. While most apps employed source IP blocking for geoblocking, there was one app of particular interest (ChessRush) that restricted the content on its CDN edge servers. We provide details of our investigation in uncovering such mechanisms in Sect. 4.3.

In general, our findings on mobile apps shed light on some grave concerns. Following this model, in the future, many app publishers may adopt similar censorship techniques if coerced by authoritarian regimes. Alarmingly, *all* apps could censor users, even without communicating with app servers as the logic to

---

[1] Out of 220 blocked apps, 60 apps were defunct. We couldn't find them in official play stores of foreign countries as well.

extract identifying users' locale (*e.g.*, from SIM cards) can be embedded within the apps' binary[2].

2   Background and Related Work

In this paper, we focus on India, which seems ambivalent about its censorship policies [41]. As already mentioned, two different forms of filtering mechanisms have evolved in the country—*viz.* website blocking and mobile app filtering.

Web Censorship: There exist a plethora of studies that reported Internet censorship across the globe [55,61]. Researchers have reported censorship in various countries like Syria [33], Iran [26], Greece [66], Italy [22], Pakistan [30,54], Saudi Arabia [23], Russia [11,18,58,71], Spain [64] *etc.* Notably, several studies particularly focus on analyzing the Great Firewall of China [8,24,25,34,38,39,44–46,48,52,67,70], owing to its technical sophistication.

In this paper, we focus on India—a country with more than a billion Internet users [2]. In the year 2017, Gosain *et al.* [41] conducted the first (preliminary) study and reported that Indian ISPs follow a "federated model of censorship" *i.e.*, they have inconsistent censorship policies that result in huge differences in the censorship experienced by the netizens. Later, in 2018, Yadav *et al.* [72] conducted a detailed study of web censorship in India and reported its multi-faceted aspects. They confirmed the previous observations [41] and reported the presence of various censorship middleboxes positioned in India. They further demonstrated that using specially crafted web requests, similar to those reported in [43,49], it is possible to bypass such middleboxes. However, Yadav *et al.* did not report filtering of HTTPS websites. But recently, in 2020, Singh *et al.* [60] reported that one Indian ISP has started blocking HTTPS websites using TLS SNI extension.

Moreover, other groups like Citizen Lab [20] regularly assesses Internet filtering in different regions across the globe [8,10,21], study the deployed filtering and surveillance infrastructure [12,17] and report privacy violations [36]. There exist other large-scale measurement projects like ICLab [55], OONI [40], and CensoredPlanet [61] that track and report censorship events across the globe, including India. These measurement projects are extensive in scale and report a breadth of important information about web censorship but do not study mobile app blocking.[3] Thus, in this paper, we devised our own approach and heuristics to analyze the prevailing mobile app filtering within India (Fig. 1).

App Filtering: In June 2020, for the *first* time, the Government of India officially banned 59 Chinese apps in response to growing tensions on the Indo-China border [50]. However, the official blocking order claimed that these apps pose a threat to the privacy and data security of Indian users [13]. By November 2020, the number of banned apps increased to 220 [1]. Banning these apps involved removing them from all the official app stores (*e.g.*, Google and Apple).

---

[2] With regular updates in the app, the publishers can easily introduce such changes.

[3] OONI, in addition to web filtering, also test the blocking of four instant messaging apps—WhatsApp, Facebook Messenger, Telegram, Signal [19].

(a) Web filtering   (b) App filtering

Fig. 1. Types of Internet filtering in India: (a) Web filtering is achieved by an ISP (b) App filtering is achieved by the app publisher themselves.

Moreover, following the ban, even the pre-installed apps stopped working. As described ahead, several of these app publishers go to great lengths to identify Indian users so as to not serve content to them. This departs from the traditional model of censorship, where ISPs attempt to block content rather than the website maintainer itself. Further, we also confirm that the techniques used for censoring apps are quite different from those used in web censorship.

Previous studies also confirmed the unavailability of apps in the app stores in different countries. Ververis et al. [65] reported that many apps (e.g., VPNs) are not available in the app stores of multiple countries (e.g., China, Syria). However, the authors acknowledged that it is difficult to ascertain the precise cause of unavailability, i.e., it is due to commercial reasons or because of the orders from the government. Similarly, Kumar at al. [47] conducted a measurement study to analyze the geo-differences in the mobile apps from 26 different countries. They report that 3,672 apps were geo-blocked in at least one of the said countries. Apps are unavailable in the app stores for various reasons, e.g., takedown by the government, removal by Google due to noncompliance with its policy, and blocking by the developer due to commercial reasons.

In this work, we take a slightly different direction and focus solely on India. Our goal was to identify the *app filtering mechanics* for those apps that are known to be banned by the orders of the government. Our research reveals multiple app filtering techniques at play—almost all banned apps are not available in app stores, many apps are blocked based on the source IP addresses of the client, some apps are not available on select CDN edge servers, and some apps are fetching the locale of the client from the SIM card to restrict Indian users from accessing the content.

Our research shows that it is important to study app filtering and identify possible circumvention solutions. In the future, other censoring countries could adopt similar filtering techniques to censor mobile apps apart from traditional website filtering.

3   Ethical Considerations

Censorship measurement studies often require accessing blocked websites (and mobile apps) that are deemed objectionable by different governments. Thus, accessing the blocked apps may evoke suspicion of the authorities against the individuals involved. Thus, for this study, we carefully devised our experiments following the recommendations given by Belmont [28] and Menlo [37] reports. We applied for the university's IRB approval, and we obtained the same.

We obtained access to Indian ISPs by purchasing their SIM cards. We were extremely careful at this step; only the author(s) of this study (who are citizens of India) purchased the SIM cards. No third person (Indian or foreign) was involved in this. Later, all our mobile Internet connectivity experiments were performed using these SIM cards only. Moreover, throughout the study, we accessed mobile apps from our own infrastructure (mobile phones and servers).

In some experiments, we required sending DNS requests (containing filtered domains) to DNS resolvers. Thus, we required scanning various ISP prefixes for open DNS resolvers. Sending queries for filtered domains to non-ISP resolvers may further force such resolvers to communicate with the top-level DNS infrastructure, thereby putting them under the suspicion of the authorities. Thus, we only selected those that belong to ISPs' infrastructure and avoided non-ISP resolvers.

To do so, from the list of all available open DNS resolvers in the ISP under test, we first performed the reverse DNS PTR lookup for them. We selected those that likely belonged to ISPs' infrastructure. For instance in Airtel, we selected the ones that had a substring `airtelbroadband.in` in the reverse PTR. Similarly in ACT ISP, we selected those resolvers that had `broadband.actcorp.in` as a substring. Additionally, in both the ISPs, we also selected those that were likely authoritative nameservers for some domain. As suggested in [58], we selected only those resolvers whose PTR began with the regular expression "ns[0-9]+nameserver[0-9]".

4   App Censorship Investigation

For the first time, India officially banned 220 apps by the end of November 2020. Our objective was to study how exactly these apps were blocked in the country. More precisely, we attempted to answer the following questions.

(1) Are the apps available in app stores? If not, how can we obtain these apps?
(2) Are these apps accessible/usable once we install them from alternate sources?
(3) After installation, if the apps are not usable, what are the mechanisms used to censor them?

4.1   Experimental Setup

We installed apps on our own mobile phones (running the latest Android version 10 and the iPhone iOS version 14). Likewise, our overseas contact in Germany (a paper-author) used their mobile phones to install such apps and performed tests. For analyzing the app traffic, we required installing `mitmproxy` [9], which helps intercept, decrypt, and analyze TLS traffic. This required the installation of self-signed certificates within the mobile phones. However, the apps in Android versions newer than 7 cannot use certificates signed by untrusted issuers. This is called *certificate pinning* [59]. Thus, to bypass certificate pinning, only when analyzing app traffic, we used an older version of the Android (*i.e.,* 6). The mitmproxy was run on a Linux host running Ubuntu 20.04.1, equipped with quad-core x64 processor and 8 GB of RAM.

Accessing Censored Apps: The mobile apps were gradually banned in India in three stages, first in June, then in September and lastly in November 2020. We began our research by curating a list of the banned apps from the press releases of the Ministry of Electronics and IT, Government of India [5–7]. The banned apps belonged to different categories *viz.* gaming, social media, dating *etc.* (as reported by the app publishers). The gaming category alone constituted ≈ 22% of these apps (see Fig. 2).

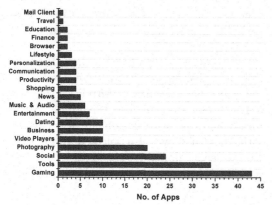

We began by searching for these apps on popular app stores (*e.g.,* Google and Apple). As expected, these apps were removed from them. Thus, to obtain the installation packages of the blocked apps (*e.g.,* apk files), we relied on our overseas contacts in *uncensored* countries where these apps were likely available. Interestingly, 60 among these 220 apps were unavailable even in their app markets, indicating that they were likely not operational.

Fig. 2. Different categories of mobile apps filtered in India.

Additionally, we verified that the installation packages of these apps were unavailable even on third-party sources *e.g.,* apkmirror.com (ref. Sect. A.3 for details). Finally, our overseas contacts downloaded the packages for the remaining 160 apps from their official stores and shared them with us. After installing these apps on our mobile phones in India, we manually tried accessing them. We found that 136 out of 160 apps (unavailable in the Indian app stores) could be directly accessed. After that, we investigated the censorship for the rest of the 24 apps.

Initial Observations: We commenced our research by analyzing a few popular blocked apps like TikTok, PUBG and Vmate *etc.* Upon accessing TikTok, we observed a censorship notification issued in compliance with the government's orders and could not load the content. Next, when we attempted to open the PUBG game, it showed no explicit censorship message; instead, it simply reported a connection error and prevented us from launching the game. It was a "false notification" in the app; through pcap file, we confirmed that, indeed, there was a TCP connection followed by a successful TLS handshake between the app and the server.

In addition, several other apps like Vmate and UVideos neither showed any censorship notification nor any connection error. Instead, they showed no contents whatsoever. This indicated that different apps were likely being censored in different ways. These apps rely on standard web protocols (*i.e.,* HTTP and HTTPS). It is possible that Indian ISPs might be filtering the traffic of these apps, much like traditional web censorship [60,72].

4.2 Investigating ISP Level Filtering

Indian ISPs generally rely on keyword filtering (*e.g.,* DNS, HTTP(S) headers) [60,72] to filter traffic. Thus we began by inspecting the network traffic of the TikTok app via `pcap` files. However, we observed only the standard network protocol messages:

1. The domain `tiktok.com` resolved to public IP addresses belonging to Akamai's own AS. We resolved the same domain from other VPSs in uncensored countries and found that the IP addresses obtained also belonged to Akamai. Thus, DNS censorship was likely not being used as all IP addresses belong to the same hosting service.
2. With the said IPs, we were able to successfully complete the TCP handshake. This largely ruled out TCP/IP filtering.[4]
3. Following that, we were also able to successfully complete the TLS handshake with the same IPs. We observed a legitimate certificate signed by `DigiCert Inc.` bearing the common name as `*.tiktokv.com`. This confirmed that HTTPS censorship (using SNI extension of TLS ClientHello) was also not employed.
4. Eventually, we observed that encrypted data was exchanged between the app and the TikTok server.

We analyzed the network traffic for all other blocked apps, and our observations were consistent—*the responses received by the apps were from the app server itself, and not manipulated by the ISP* (as it usually happens with web censorship). Ironically, this indicated that the app publishers themselves, not the ISPs, restricted the Indian app users from accessing the app content following the government's blocking orders. We repeated the experiments in four popular ISPs that cumulatively capture more than 95% of the Indian clients [2]—Reliance Jio, Airtel, Vodafone-Idea, and ACT network, and observed the same behavior, *i.e.,* no network level interference by the ISPs.

4.3 Investigating Censorship Mechanics Used by App Publishers

After ruling out the role of Indian ISPs in app censorship, our next concern was how app publishers were selectively filtering users from India and not elsewhere.

---

[4] It may happen that we complete the TCP handshake with some transparent proxy (in the ISP). In such cases, one may not detect TCP/IP filtering. But, this would also result in failure of the next steps. However, in practice, not even for a single app, we encountered this case.

We hypothesized that these blocked apps could be using a well-known technique, *IP geo-blocking* [53] for the same. IP geo-blocking involves web servers rejecting requests originating from specific regions, identified through their source IP address. This step often involves looking up geo-IP databases to map IP addresses to countries. However, an alternative could be to filter requests from specific regions. A large number of such app publishers might use CDNs, much like almost all popular web services [31]. In such a case, the app publisher could restrict content from being available to edge servers that serve requests from specific regions (*e.g.*, India). Thus, app publishers might geo-block clients broadly in two ways:[5]

1. *Geo-blocking based on source IP address:* The app publisher would restrict the users based on the IP address of the incoming requests.
2. *Geo-blocking by restricting content on CDN edge-servers:* The app publisher may have the control to restrict content on edge servers that serve requests from India.

Table 1. Filtering mechanisms employed by different blocked apps (before the permanent ban).

Sl No.	App Name	App Type	Censorship Technique Used		
			Client Source IP	CDN Edge server	Client SIM Card
1	PUBG	Gaming	✓	✗	✗
2	ShareIt	Tools	✓	✗	✗
3	Shein	Shopping	✓	✗	✗
4	Baidu	Tools	✓	✗	✗
5	Tantan	Social	✓	✗	✗
6	VooV	Productivity	✓	✗	✗
7	RomWe	Shopping	✓	✗	✗
8	Ludo	Gaming	✓	✗	✗
9	Rangers of Oblivion	Gaming	✓	✗	✗
10	Ali Suppliers	Business	✓	✗	✗
11	Baidu Express	Tools	✓	✗	✗
12	DingTalk	Productivity	✓	✗	✗
13	MangoTV	Video Players	✓	✗	✗
14	Heroes Evolved	Gaming	✓	✗	✗
15	Singol	Dating	✓	✗	✗
16	ChessRush	Gaming	✓	✓	✗
17	TikTok	Social	✗	✗	✓
18	Likee	Video Players	✗	✗	✓
19	Kwai	Social	✗	✗	✓
20	UC Browser	Browser	✗	✗	✓
21	FaceU	Photography	✗	✗	✓
22	Hago	Social	✗	✗	✓
23	V-Fly	Tools	✗	✗	✓
24	MICO Chat	Social	✗	✗	✓

For those apps that do not rely on CDNs, edge-server-based blocking could be directly ruled out. For others (that use CDNs), we would need to distinguish between the aforementioned two possibilities. Thus, we first identified whether the blocked apps were relying on CDNs or not.

Identifying the Apps that Use CDNs: Identifying the use of CDNs requires distinguishing between different types of CDNs. Broadly there are two types of CDNs *viz.* DNS based, and *anycast* CDNs [32]. In DNS-based CDNs [69] (*e.g.*, Akamai), DNS queries for web services are resolved often to the nearest edge-servers, generally identified from the clients' DNS resolvers' locations. However, in anycast-based CDNs [35] (*e.g.*, Cloudflare), edge-serves in different locations use the same IP address, which is announced through different BGP advertisements from different geographic locations. A client's web request is directed to the closest

---

[5] There could be more ways to identify the client's locale *e.g.*, time-zone of the phone. We consider these possibilities where we ruled out the obvious next two.

possible edge server based on the BGP policies of the client's ISP. We explain in Appendix A.1 how we identified the use of CDNs by these apps. Overall, we found that all the 24 app publishers hosted content on DNS-based CDNs. After confirming the role of CDNs with blocked apps, we revisit our problem of how app publishers censor Indian users and the role of CDNs (if any).

Geo-Blocking Mechanisms Employed: Our goal was to identify how app publishers are selectively filtering Indian users—on the basis of source IP or simply denying access to edge servers catering to Indian users. Accessing the apps via VPNs with end-points abroad could be an easy way to confirm if the apps are accessible or not. This may likely help circumvent IP geo-blocking. However, our aim was to first identify how exactly geo-blocking was implemented, but VPNs not only change the source IP addresses of apps' requests but also the edge servers to which they communicate (depending on the DNS resolvers the VPNs used). This makes it hard to discern how the requests are being filtered.

Thus, we devised heuristics involving changing a single factor at a time. Corresponding to these two factors, we examined four possible scenarios. For instance, one scenario is accessing apps by selecting foreign edge servers while still using an Indian IP address. Since the apps were using DNS-based CDNs, switching to DNS resolvers in uncensored countries could force the apps to communicate with foreign edge servers without changing the Indian source IP address. Alternately, another case would be to access apps with foreign source IP and connect to Indian edge servers. For this, our overseas contacts (whose phones bear foreign IPs) used Indian DNS resolvers to communicate with Indian edge servers. We now elucidate all four possible scenarios.

Case 1: Indian Source IP and Indian edge-server: The blocked apps were accessed directly from our Indian mobile phone, configured to use Indian resolvers. This is the typical situation where a regular user tries to use the app. Thus while 136 apps were trivially accessible after installation, the 24 apps we identified fell in this category and were inaccessible (ref. Table 1).

Case 2: Indian Source IP and Foreign edge-server: The apps were accessed from phones configured to use open resolver in non-censoring countries (Germany) that do not block apps based on government orders. This enabled the apps to connect to an edge server probably located in such countries. We verified this by inspecting the `traceroute` path from an Indian mobile phone to the resolved IPs of the edge servers. The last few IP addresses in the `traceroute` paths belonged to the same (uncensored) country as that of the DNS resolver.

Unfortunately, the 24 apps were still inaccessible, even when they communicated to foreign edge servers. While the DNS resolvers of the phones were changed, their IP addresses weren't. This indicated that the app publishers were filtering requests based on source IP through the edge servers, even when the latter were outside India.

Case 3: Foreign Source IP and Indian edge-server: To use a foreign source IP, we set up a VPS in an uncensored country and ran our own OpenVPN service on it. We configured our Indian mobile phone (with blocked apps installed) to use the said OpenVPN service. This ensured that even if we accessed apps from the mobile phone (in India), the requests would bear a foreign source IP address. Both the OpenVPN service and the VPS host were configured to use an open DNS resolver in India. This forced the apps to connect to edge-servers that cater to Indian users. We found that 15 among the 24 apps mentioned above were accessible; their traffic bore foreign source IPs and was destined to Indian edge servers. Thus based on the hitherto 3 cases, we observed that:

1. All the 24 apps were censored when their requests bore Indian source IPs and connected to Indian edge servers.
2. They were censored even when connected with foreign edge servers while using Indian source IPs.
3. However, 15 of them *were accessible* when connected to Indian edge servers but used foreign source IPs. *This confirmed IP geo-blocking for these apps.*

Case 4: Foreign Source IP and Foreign edge-server: Finally, we accessed the apps through a VPN with endpoints in foreign countries. This resulted in the requests bearing foreign source IPs and terminating at foreign edge servers. We expected all the 24 censored apps to be accessible. To our surprise, we were able to access only 16 out of 24 apps! These 16 apps included the previously accessible 15 apps.

Interestingly, the additional app *Chess Rush,* was both IP geo-blocked as well as unavailable at the Indian edge server. It was only accessible when using both foreign source IP addresses and foreign edge servers. These 16 apps with their censorship mechanisms are listed in Table 1 (rows 1–16). To understand the censorship mechanics of the remaining 8 apps, we ran additional experiments.

Investigating the Blocking of Remaining Eight Apps: As previously mentioned, we were unable to access these apps using VPNs. Other than IP geo-blocking and CDN edge-server restrictions, likely there were additional location revealing parameters sent by the apps to their server, which might have led to censorship. In general, mobile phones (both Android and iOS) present multiple interfaces that reveal the location *e.g.,* GPS, and time-zone information. Before conducting our experiments we ensured that all such user-configurable interfaces were turned off from revealing the location, *e.g.,* we turned off the GPS, changed the time-zone of the phone to a foreign country *etc.* But, we were still unable to access these apps whether we used VPNs or not.

To investigate further, we once again selected TikTok for the detailed analysis (as it was one of the remaining 8 apps). We relayed its traffic via our MITM proxy [9], so as to see if location identifying parameters were being relayed via the requests (ref. Sect. 4.1). Interestingly, the TikTok app was sending the country code "IN" as a part of the query string in multiple HTTP requests to the app server, even when all configurable location revealing attributes were turned off (*e.g.,* GPS). Thus, we changed *some* of the parameters (*e.g.,* op_region) in the requests to a different country (*e.g.,* "US"), on the fly using the MITM proxy. But still, we suffered censorship.

As a last resort, we reverse-engineered the TikTok app to identify the potential censorship logic (if any), embedded within the app's code. We used the `jadx` decompiler [4] for the same. We obtained a partly decompiled code of the app. Careful inspection of TikTok's code, revealed the use of functions like `getSimCountryISO()`. This function is a part of the Android `TelephonyManager` API and is used to access SIM information. This revealed that TikTok might be fetching country-related information from the SIM card.

Thereafter, we confirmed that only when an Indian SIM is installed in the mobile phone, TikTok sends a `carrier_region=IN` parameter in HTTP requests; otherwise, this parameter was absent. Using the MITM proxy, we changed this parameter's value from "IN" to "US" on-the-fly, and finally, we were able to bypass the censorship. Suppressing the parameter also worked, hence an alternative is to simply remove the installed SIM card. It must be noted that there are other parameters like `op_region=IN` that are also sent in different HTTP requests. But only changing the `carrier_region` parameter resulted in circumvention.

Simply accessing the app without the SIM (through a WiFi network), was sufficient to bypass censorship for each of the remaining 8 apps. This confirmed that these apps were identifying requests from India by probing the installed SIM card. To further confirm our deductions, we ran some additional tests. (1) When our overseas contacts (in an uncensored country, Germany) accessed these eight apps with Indian SIMs on their phones, their requests were also censored. However, with foreign SIMs, they were able to freely access the apps. (2) Indian mobile phones installed with foreign SIM cards had no problems accessing these apps.

Additionally, in dual SIM phones, the apps inspect location information only from the primary SIM. Thus using an Indian SIM in the secondary slot, while leaving the primary slot empty (or installing with a non-Indian SIM) allows uncensored access.

To conclude, the apps transmit country information to the servers by probing the primary SIM. The app servers use this to identify and censor Indian users, irrespective of their actual geographic location. These 8 apps with their censorship mechanisms are enlisted in Table 1 (rows 17–24).

Table 2. Censorship mechanisms employed by different blocked apps (after the permanent ban).

Sl No.	App Name	App Type	Censorship Technique Used		
			Client Source IP	CDN Edge server	Client SIM Card
1	TikTok	Social	✓	✗	✓
2	Likee	Video Players	✓	✗	✓
3	Kwai	Social	✓	✗	✓
4	UC Browser	Browser	✓	✗	✓
5	FaceU	Photography	✓	✗	✓
6	Hago	Social	✓	✗	✓
7	V-Fly	Tools	✓	✗	✓

Permanent Ban on the Apps: At the end of January 2021, the Indian government imposed a permanent ban on the said 220 apps. Interestingly, soon after the permanent ban was enforced, we observed changes in the censorship mechanisms of *only* the previously mentioned eight apps. Out of the eight blocked apps (based on the SIM card's location), we were able to access only one app (MICO Chat) after removing the SIM. The remaining seven apps were inaccessible, even when the Indian SIM card was not present on the phone.

This change in censorship mechanism could be attributed to two possibilities: (1) The app servers (for these seven apps) have now adopted geo-blocking (using IP addresses or disabling the content on edge servers serving Indian users), or (2) instead of fetching the country information from the SIMs, the apps might be accessing locale information via other parameters.

To check the possibility of geo-blocking, we removed the SIM card and repeated our previously mentioned four cases that involved changing the source IP address and the CDN edge servers. We confirmed that these 7 apps were now censored using IP geo-blocking.

Further, to check if the location information from the SIM card was still being used or not, we plugged the SIMs back into the phones before accessing the apps. Thereafter, we accessed the apps via VPNs, to ensure foreign source IPs and edge servers. To our surprise, the app servers were still filtering the apps' requests. Examination of the network traffic using MITM proxy revealed the presence of the earlier location parameter (`carrier_region=IN`). Like earlier, masking this parameter (either via the MITM proxy or by simply uninstalling the SIM) makes it difficult for the app servers to identify the country of origin.

We conclude that following the permanent ban, the app servers use both the source IP and the location revealing parameter (fetched by the app from the SIM card), to identify Indian users. We tabulate these 7 apps with their censorship techniques in Table 2.

Summary: *Tier 3* apps are not available in official app stores in India and can be accessed if their *apk* files can be downloaded from third-party sources like `apkmirror.com`. *Tier 2 apps*, even after installation, and restrict Indian users based on their source IP addresses; using VPNs can bypass the server-side filtering. Lastly, *tier 1 apps*, use both source IP and locale information extracted from SIM cards to block the Indian users. Thus, in addition to using VPNs, users need to remove their Indian SIM card and access the apps via WiFi to access the apps. Caution must be exercised by the users because VPNs can help bypass the filtering but may not safeguard them from surveillance as VPN providers have been required to collect and store user data in India [62].

5   Limitations and Future Work

In this work, we studied the blocking mechanisms of 220 officially banned apps in India. However, there can be more apps that are filtered in India but are not made public. In the future, we can use techniques such as those in [47,65] to identify more apps that are otherwise not known to be filtered. Moreover, our research reveals that if users remove their Indian SIM cards from their phones and use VPNs over WiFI, they can bypass app filtering in India. However, we did not conduct any user studies confirming whether these techniques can be easily adopted by ordinary users without much technical knowledge. Thus, we keep it as our future work. Moreover, Indian users often rely on mobile Internet for Internet connectivity. Thus, removing SIM cards may not be the best solution for bypassing the filtering, and in the future, efforts can be made to change country parameters from IN to some other country within the mobile phone. This would enable users to access the blocked apps without removing the SIM card (see Sect. 4.3 for more details).

6   Conclusion

Internet filtering has been used by many nation-states in the past. In this paper, we focused on India (a country with more than 880 million Internet subscribers), to analyze the recent app blocking therein. Our research reveals a novel form of "three-tiered" mobile app filtering, with every tier increasing the censorship sophistication. Notably, India does not use the traditional model of censorship for blocking apps—i.e., filtering performed by the ISPs. Rather, following the orders of the Indian government, app publishers are themselves filtering the Indian users on their servers. They achieve server-side censorship either by geo-blocking the clients based on source IP or by identifying Indian users using the country codes fetched from the SIM cards. This is a worrisome trend; other countries may coerce app publishers to adopt these techniques, and app filtering can be achieved simply by updating the app. This would not involve any upgradation in the censorship infrastructure or the involvement of the ISPs. This is particularly concerning for users who access the apps using mobile Internet, as removal of the SIM card would lead to loss of Internet connectivity.

A   Appendix

A.1   Identifying Type of CDNs

In Sect. 4.3, we investigated censorship mechanics used by app publishers. This required us to identify whether app publishers were using CDNs or not. Our approach to identify the use of CDNs and their types relies on how DNS and anycast CDNs work. We now describe the same. For each of the 24 apps:

1. We recorded the app's network traffic as a pcap file.
2. Using the pcap file we identified the unique domains, to which apps communicate.
3. We resolved the same set of domains from 5 different uncensored countries[6], and recorded the IP addresses obtained from each location.
4. Across each location, for each of the domains, we checked if the resolved IP addresses were the same or different.
   (a) If from each of the 5 locations we observed different IP addresses corresponding to the same domain, we classified the domain to be using DNS based CDN.
   (b) Else, if a domain is resolved to the same IP address at every location, then two possibilities exist:

---

[6] We used VPSes in these countries for the same.

i. The domain is unicasted (*i.e.*, it is hosted on a non-CDN infrastructure): To confirm the same, we ran `traceroute` from the five geographically diverse VPSs to the same IP addresses. If all the `traceroute` paths end in the same country, we classified it as unicasted. [We used the Maxmind geolocation database to map the IP addresses of the routers (in the traceroute path) to their respective country. We observed that at least the last two IP addresses in all the `traceroutes` (to unicasted domains) belong to the same country.]

ii. The domain is anycasted: If the `traceroute` paths end in separate countries (likely the ones where they originate), we classified the domain as anycasted.

We observed that, on average, each of the apps was communicating with 8 unique domains, and the majority of these (> 6) were using DNS-based CDNs. A few of them were anycasted (or unicasted).

A.2   Why App Publishers are Filtering Indian Users

Overall, it is natural to ask why app publishers are filtering Indian users when many of them do not operate from India anymore. There was anecdotal evidence that they were hoping that the ban would be temporary [57], and thus they obliged with it. Some companies were in communication with the Indian government and were awaiting their approval for relaunching the apps [14]. However, in January 2021, the government imposed a permanent ban on all the 220 apps (ref. Sect. 4.3). Even then, the app publishers not only continued the filtering but also imposed stricter censorship for Indian users, while the ISPs continued to have no role in this. Before the ban, 8 apps were using only SIM-based censorship, but after the ban, 7 of them adopted IP geo-blocking as well. The precise reason for app publishers (and not the ISPs) filtering Indian users remains unclear.

A.3   The Apps Unavailable in Official Play Stores in Non-censoring Countries

In Sect. 4, we mentioned that our overseas contacts (residing in uncensored countries) were also unable to find 60 apps that were blocked in India. Thus, we assumed that they were likely defunct, or else they would be available at least in uncensored countries.

However, it could be argued that some of these apps might be functional yet unavailable in uncensored countries. This is because some of these apps may have been launched specifically for Asia (or India). Thus, to confirm that this was not the case, and 60 apps were likely defunct, we searched them on third-party sources *e.g.*, `apkmirror.com`. Barring a few, the installation packages of most of these apps were unavailable on such sites as well. For the few that we found, they were last updated around four to five years ago. This indicated that they were no longer operational. Our overseas contacts installed them and confirmed that they were unable to access them. Thus, we ignored these 60 apps and focused on the remaining 160 apps.

References

1. Indian government bans 220 apps. https://bit.ly/31ECpeA
2. The Indian telecom services performance indicators report. https://www.trai.gov.in/sites/default/files/QPIR_0.pdf
3. Iran bans messaging apps. https://en.radiofarda.com/a/iran-lawmakers-aim-to-fully-ban-all-foreign-messaging-apps/30802448.html
4. Jadx decompiler. https://github.com/skylot/jadx
5. List of blocked apps. https://pib.gov.in/PressReleseDetailm.aspx?PRID=1635206
6. List of blocked apps. https://pib.gov.in/PressReleasePage.aspx?PRID=1650669
7. List of blocked apps. https://www.pib.gov.in/PressReleasePage.aspx?PRID=1675335
8. Missing links: A comparison of search censorship in China. https://citizenlab.ca/2023/04/a-comparison-of-search-censorship-in-china/
9. Mitm proxy. https://mitmproxy.org/
10. No access: Lgbtiq website censorship in six countries. https://citizenlab.ca/2021/08/no-access-lgbtiq-website-censorship-in-six-countries/
11. Not OK on VK an analysis of in-platform censorship on Russia's VKontakte. https://citizenlab.ca/2023/07/an-analysis-of-in-platform-censorship-on-russias-vkontakte/
12. Planet blue coat: Mapping global censorship and surveillance tools. https://citizenlab.ca/2013/01/planet-blue-coat-mapping-global-censorship-and-surveillance-tools/
13. Press Information Bureau (Government of India) officially confirms the ban of 59 Chinese apps. https://pib.gov.in/PressReleseDetailm.aspx?PRID=1635206
14. Pubg to be relaunched in India. https://bit.ly/39viUcu
15. Tiktok blocked in India. https://www.nytimes.com/2020/06/29/world/asia/tiktok-banned-india-china.html
16. Total downloads of Tiktok app. https://www.theverge.com/2020/4/29/21241788/tiktok-app-download-numbers-update-2-billion-users
17. Triple threat: NSO group's pegasus spyware returns in 2022 with a trio of iOS 15 and iOS 16 zero-click exploit chains. https://citizenlab.ca/2023/04/nso-groups-pegasus-spyware-returns-in-2022/
18. Website of Canadian bobsledder blocked in Russia due to collateral filtering. https://citizenlab.ca/2014/02/website-of-canadian-bobsledder-blocked-in-sochi/
19. what-do-ooni-probe-tests-do? https://ooni.org/support/faq/_what-do-ooni-probe-tests-do
20. What is citizen lab? https://citizenlab.ca/about/
21. You move, they follow: Uncovering Iran's mobile legal intercept system. https://citizenlab.ca/2023/01/uncovering-irans-mobile-legal-intercept-system/
22. Aceto, G., et al.: Internet censorship in Italy: an analysis of 3G/4G networks. In: IEEE International Conference on Communications (ICC), pp. 1–6. IEEE (2017)
23. Alharbi, F., et al.: Opening digital borders cautiously yet decisively: digital filtering in Saudi Arabia. In: 10th USENIX Workshop on Free and Open Communications on the Internet (2020)
24. Anonymous: Censored Commemoration Chinese Live Streaming Platform YY Focuses Censorship on June 4 Memorials and Activism in Hong Kong. https://citizenlab.ca/2019/06/censored-commemoration-chinese-live-streaming-platform-yy-focuses-censorship-june-4-memorials-activism-hong-kong/

25. Niaki, A.A., Hoang, N.P., Gill, P., Houmansadr, A.: Triplet censors: demystifying great firewall's DNS censorship behavior. In: USENIX workshop on Free and Open Communications on the Internet (FOCI). USENIX Association (2020)
26. Aryan, S., et al.: Internet censorship in Iran: a first look. In: USENIX workshop on Free and Open Communications on the Internet (FOCI) (2013)
27. BBC: China bans mobile apps. https://www.bbc.com/news/technology-55230654
28. Beauchamp, T.L.: The belmont report. In: The Oxford Textbook of Clinical Research Ethics, pp. 149–155 (2008)
29. Beznazwy, J., Houmansadr, A.: How China detects and blocks shadowsocks. In: Proceedings of the Internet Measurement Conference, pp. 111–124 (2020)
30. Bock, K., et al.: Detecting and evading {Censorship-in-Depth}: a case study of {Iran's} protocol whitelister. In: 10th USENIX Workshop on Free and Open Communications on the Internet (2020)
31. Calder, M., et al.: Mapping the expansion of Google's serving infrastructure. In: Proceedings Internet Measurement Conference, pp. 313–326. ACM (2013)
32. Calder, M., et al.: Analyzing the performance of an anycast CDN. In: Proceedings of Internet Measurement Conference, pp. 531–537. ACM (2015)
33. Chaabane, A., et al.: Censorship in the wild: analyzing internet filtering in Syria. In: Proceedings of Internet Measurement Conference, pp. 285–298. ACM (2014)
34. Chai, Z., et al.: On the importance of encrypted-SNI (ESNI) to censorship circumvention. In: USENIX Workshop on Free and Open Communications on the Internet (FOCI) (2019)
35. Cicalese, D., et al.: A first look at anycast CDN traffic. arXiv preprint arXiv: 1505.00946 (2015)
36. Deibert, R.: Citizel lab's list of publication. https://citizenlab.ca/publications//
37. Dittrich, D., et al.: The menlo report: ethical principles guiding information and communication technology research. Technical report, US Department of Homeland Security (2012)
38. Dunna, A., et al.: Analyzing China's blocking of unpublished tor bridges. In: USENIX Workshop on Free and Open Communications on the Internet (FOCI) (2018)
39. Ensafi, R., et al.: Examining how the great firewall discovers hidden circumvention servers. In: Proceedings of Internet Measurement Conference, pp. 445–458 (2015)
40. Filasto, A., Appelbaum, J.: OONI: open observatory of network interference. In: USENIX Workshop on Free and Open Communications on the Internet (FOCI) (2012)
41. Gosain, D., et al.: Mending wall: on the implementation of censorship in India. In: Lin, X., Ghorbani, A., Ren, K., Zhu, S., Zhang, A. (eds.) SecureComm 2017, pp. 418–437. Springer, Cham (2017). https://doi.org/10.1007/978-3-319-78813-5_21
42. Griffiths, J.: The Great Firewall of China: How to build and control an alternative version of the internet. Zed Books Ltd. (2019)
43. Jermyn, J., Weaver, N.: Autosonda: discovering rules and triggers of censorship devices. In: USENIX Workshop on Free and Open Communications on the Internet (FOCI) (2017)
44. Khattak, S., et al.: Towards illuminating a censorship monitor's model to facilitate evasion. In: USENIX Workshop on Free and Open Communications on the Internet (FOCI) (2013)
45. Knockel, J., Ruan, L.: Bada Bing, Bada Boom: Microsoft Bing's Chinese Political Censorship of Autosuggestions in North America. https://citizenlab.ca/2022/05/bada-bing-bada-boom-microsoft-bings-chinese-political-censorship-autosuggestions-north-america/

46. Knockel, J., et al.: Measuring decentralization of Chinese keyword censorship via mobile games. In: USENIX workshop on Free and Open Communications on the Internet (FOCI) (2017)
47. Kumar, R., et al.: A large-scale investigation into geodifferences in mobile apps. In: 31st USENIX Security Symposium (USENIX Security 2022), pp. 1203–1220 (2022)
48. Levis, P.: The collateral damage of internet censorship by DNS injection. ACM SIGCOMM CCR **42**(3) (2012)
49. Li, F., et al.: lib• erate,(n) a library for exposing (traffic-classification) rules and avoiding them efficiently. In: Proceedings of Internet Measurement Conference, pp. 128–141 (2017)
50. MacRae, P.: India-china border tension: app developers, tech sector win with chinese apps banned. https://www.scmp.com/week-asia/economics/article/3170368/india-china-border-tension-app-developers-tech-sector-win
51. Marczak, B., et al.: An analysis of China's great cannon. In: USENIX Workshop on Free and Open Communications on the Internet (FOCI) (2015)
52. Marczak, B., et al.: China's great cannon. Citizen Lab 10 (2015)
53. McDonald, A., et al.: 403 forbidden: a global view of CDN geoblocking. In: Proceedings of the Internet Measurement Conference 2018, pp. 218–230 (2018)
54. Nabi, Z.: The anatomy of web censorship in Pakistan. In: USENIX Workshop on Free and Open Communications on the Internet (FOCI) (2013)
55. Niaki, A.A., et al.: IClab: a global, longitudinal internet censorship measurement platform. In: IEEE Symposium on Security and Privacy (SP), pp. 135–151 (2020)
56. O'Driscoll, A.: Apps banned in Russia. https://www.comparitech.com/blog/vpn-privacy/websites-blocked-russia/
57. Punj, V.: App ban in India could be temporary. https://www.businesstoday.in/current/economy-politics/tiktok-denies-plans-for-legal-recourse-against-ban/story/408741.html
58. Ramesh, R., et al.: Decentralized control: a case study of Russia. In: Network and Distributed Systems Security (NDSS) Symposium (2020)
59. Rowley, J.: Certificate pinning. https://www.digicert.com/dc/blog/certificate-pinning-what-is-certificate-pinning/
60. Singh, K., et al.: How India censors the web. In: 12th ACM Conference on Web Science, pp. 21–28 (2020)
61. Sundara Raman, R., et al.: Censored planet: an internet-wide, longitudinal censorship observatory. In: Proceedings of the 2020 ACM SIGSAC Conference on Computer and Communications Security, pp. 49–66 (2020)
62. Bansal, V.: VPN Providers Flee India as a New Data Law Takes Hold. https://www.wired.co.uk/article/vpn-firms-flee-india-data-collection-law
63. Verkamp, J.P., Gupta, M.: Inferring mechanics of web censorship around the world. In: USENIX Workshop on Free and Open Communications on the Internet (FOCI) (2012)
64. Ververis, V., et al.: Understanding internet censorship in Europe: the case of Spain. In: 13th ACM Web Science Conference 2021, pp. 319–328 (2021)
65. Ververis, V., et al.: Shedding light on mobile app store censorship. In: Adjunct Publication of the 27th Conference on User Modeling, Adaptation and Personalization, pp. 193–198 (2019)
66. Ververis, V., et al.: Understanding internet censorship policy: the case of Greece. In: USENIX Workshop on Free and Open Communications on the Internet (2015)

67. Wang, Z., et al.: Your state is not mine: a closer look at evading stateful internet censorship. In: Proceedings of the Internet Measurement Conference, pp. 114–127 (2017)
68. Winter, P., Lindskog, S.: How the great firewall of china is blocking tor. In: USENIX Workshop on Free and Open Communications on the Internet (FOCI) (2012)
69. Wohlfart, F., et al.: Leveraging interconnections for performance: the serving infrastructure of a large CDN. In: Proceedings of the SIGCOMM 2018, pp. 206–220 (2018)
70. Xu, X., et al.: Internet censorship in China: where does the filtering occur? In: Spring, N., Riley, G.F. (eds.) PAM 2011. LNCS, vol. 6579, pp. 133–142. Springer, Heidelberg (2011). https://doi.org/10.1007/978-3-642-19260-9_14
71. Xue, D., et al.: TSPU: Russia's decentralized censorship system. In: Proceedings of the 22nd ACM Internet Measurement Conference, pp. 179–194 (2022)
72. Yadav, T.K., et al.: Where the light gets in: analyzing web censorship mechanisms in India. In: Proceedings of the Internet Measurement Conference 2018 (2018)

On the Dark Side of the Coin: Characterizing Bitcoin Use for Illicit Activities

Hampus Rosenquist[1], David Hasselquist[1(✉)], Martin Arlitt[2],
and Niklas Carlsson[1]

[1] Linköping University, Linköping, Sweden
david.hasselquist@liu.se
[2] University of Calgary, Calgary, Canada

Abstract. The decentralized nature of Bitcoin allows for pseudonymous money exchange beyond authorities' control, contributing to its popularity for diverse illegal activities such as scams, ransomware attacks, money laundering, and black markets. In this paper, we characterize this landscape, providing insights into similarities and differences in the use of Bitcoin for such activities. Our analysis and the derived insights contribute to the understanding of Bitcoin transactions associated with illegal activities through three main aspects. First, our study offers a comprehensive characterization of money flows to and from Bitcoin addresses linked to different abuse categories, revealing variations in flow patterns and success rates. Second, our temporal analysis captures long-term trends and weekly patterns across categories. Finally, our analysis of outflow from reported addresses uncovers differences in graph properties and flow patterns among illicit addresses and between abuse categories. These findings provide valuable insights into the distribution, temporal dynamics, and interconnections within various categories of Bitcoin transactions related to illicit activities. The increased understanding of this landscape and the insights gained from this study offer important empirical guidance for informed decision-making and policy development in the ongoing effort to address the challenges presented by illicit activities within the cryptocurrency space.

1 Introduction

Bitcoin, a decentralized digital currency, is attempting to revolutionize finance by facilitating pseudonymous exchanges outside the oversight of traditional authorities. Bitcoin's unique pseudonymous design, coupled with its lack of regulation, has propelled its widespread popularity. However, this has also made it a favored tool for illicit activities such as scams, ransomware attacks, money laundering, and black market transactions. As a result, Bitcoin poses significant challenges to law enforcement agencies globally, straining traditional legal frameworks.

Furthermore, as our paper demonstrates, Bitcoin use for illicit activities is widespread and turns over large sums of money. With many of the abuse types

P. Richter et al. (Eds.): PAM 2024, LNCS 14538, pp. 37–66, 2024.
https://doi.org/10.1007/978-3-031-56252-5_3

studied here preying on the weak, it is clear that these activities have increasingly negative societal effects. While the public often focuses on Bitcoin's energy consumption, much less attention has been placed on Bitcoin's role in various illicit activities affecting large numbers of victims. With the effect of Bitcoin abuse on humans being both *apparent* and *current*, we argue that it is important to shine a light on the Bitcoin patterns associated with different illicit activities.

Despite prior works having considered a wide range of criminal activities with relations to Bitcoin [10,22,27,28,41], most prior works either try to estimate the global cybercrime Bitcoin revenue [14,19,32] or focus only on a single category of illegal activities, including money laundering (using tumblers) [23], ransomware [9,13,17,20,29,35,37,42], sextortion [25,26], cryptojacking [38], darknet markets [7,8,18], and human trafficking [30]. In contrast to these works, we present a comprehensive characterization of the money-flow to and from a large set of addresses linked to *various categories of illegal activities,* and provide insights into both similarities and differences in the Bitcoin transactions and Bitcoin flows associated with the addresses of the different categories.

This paper uses the Bitcoin Abuse Database and Bitcoin's blockchain as its primary data sources for analysis. The Bitcoin Abuse Database [4] provides information on attacks and related Bitcoin addresses from reports submitted by victims and other individuals or organizations, detailing the attack type and often including additional information such as email examples. By identifying Bitcoin addresses used by attackers and extracting information about these addresses (and addresses they send money to) directly from the Bitcoin blockchain, we provide a comprehensive comparison of the quantity of funds directed to addresses associated with different types of attacks. Importantly, this methodology enables the observation of transactions involving a larger number of victims beyond those who reported an attack, acknowledging that many actual victims may not report their experiences and that some reports may come from individuals who did not transfer funds themselves. We next outline our main contributions.

First, we perform a high-level characterization of the transactions received by the Bitcoin addresses reported to the Bitcoin Abuse Database [4] from May 16, 2017 to April 25, 2022; both as an aggregate across all reported addresses (Sect. 3) and on a per-category basis (Sect. 4). Our characterization reveals a high skew in the distribution of funds attracted by different Bitcoin addresses involved in illicit activities. Our observations also highlight significant variations in the success of different abuse categories, with "Blackmail scams" and "Sextortion" receiving numerous reports but attracting smaller funds, while categories like "Ransomware" and "Darknet markets" receive fewer reports but attract substantial funds, indicating differences in effectiveness and financial impact. The category attracting the most transactions and funds, however, is the "Other" category. While only the fourth-most reported category, this category includes many of the top addresses attracting the most and the biggest transactions.

Second, we perform a temporal analysis (Sect. 5) that captures both long-term trends, differences in the weekly patterns associated with the different categories, and temporal correlations with when reports of an illicit address are first reported. While the number of reports in the Bitcoin Abuse Database remained relatively steady between 2019 and 2022, the daily number of bitcoins received by reported addresses increased by a factor of 100 over the same period, indicating a substantial rise in funds transferred to these addresses. Weekly variations were observed, with higher volumes and more funds transferred during weekdays compared to weekends, with notable patterns in "Ransomware", "Darknet markets", and the "Other" category. Although the reports typically were obtained around the time that the addresses saw peak activity and there were significant variations between abuse categories, most transactions occurred before the first report was filed, suggesting that victims may not report abusive addresses. This raises questions about the effectiveness of using reports to ban addresses.

Third, we analyze the outflow of bitcoins from the reported addresses associated with each abuse category (Sect. 6). This analysis reveals several additional interesting observations. For example, when considering the outgoing money from reported addresses, there is a concentration of funds towards specific addresses, while the majority of receiving addresses have a node degree of one, indicating a dispersion of funds after the first step. In our multi-step tracking of money flows, Bitcoin tumblers stand out with higher node degrees and concentration, suggesting relatively fewer actors are involved in this category or that many Bitcoin-using miscreants use tumblers. There are significant differences in graph structure and transaction patterns between categories, with Bitcoin tumblers having more connecting edges and loops, and the "Other" category receiving significantly more transactions going back to reported addresses. Finally, transactions between categories show increased inflow/outflow to/from Bitcoin tumblers, indicating interest in their money laundering services.

Summary of Contributions: We present a comprehensive characterization of money flows to and from a large set of Bitcoin addresses associated with different categories of illegal activities. Our analysis and the derived insights contribute significantly to the understanding of Bitcoin transactions associated with illegal activities through three main aspects. First, our aggregate and category-based characterizations reveal variations in flow patterns and success rates both within and across addresses associated with the different categories. Second, our temporal analysis captures long-term trends, weekly patterns, and the relative timing of when illicit addresses of each category are first reported. Finally, our analysis of the outflow from reported addresses uncovers differences in graph properties and flow patterns among illicit addresses and between abuse categories. Overall, the paper provides comprehensive insights into the money-flow characteristics in Bitcoin transactions linked to various illegal activities, revealing differences and similarities in distributions, temporal patterns, and interconnections among different categories.

Outline: After presenting our data collection methodology and dataset (Sect. 2), we first present a brief aggregate characterization (Sect. 3), followed by a category-based characterization (Sect. 4), a temporal analysis (Sect. 5), and an outflow analysis (Sect. 6). Finally, we present related work (Sect. 7) and conclusions (Sect. 8).

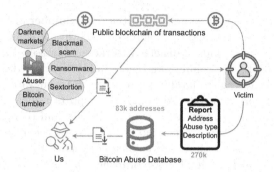

Fig. 1. Our data collection framework in the context of Bitcoin Abuse reports (filled by victims and other entities) and the public blockchains storing information about all transactions to/from the attacker operated addresses.

Ethics: Our research discusses the significant challenges presented by Bitcoin, including its pseudonymous transactions and lack of regulation, particularly in facilitating illicit activities. It emphasizes that Bitcoin's use for illegal purposes is widespread and has negative societal impacts, often harming vulnerable individuals. Our study respects privacy and confidentiality by using data from the Bitcoin Abuse Database while adhering to legal and ethical guidelines, and our insights can be used by law enforcement, regulatory bodies, and cryptocurrency service providers to develop strategies for safer and more secure financial practices. We discuss ethical concerns in more detail in Appendix A.

2   Data Collection Methodology

We rely on two primary data sources in this paper: the Bitcoin Abuse Database and Bitcoin's blockchain. Figure 1 presents an overview of our data collection framework in the context of these two information sources.

High-Level Overview: First, we use the "abuse reports" collected by the Bitcoin Abuse Database to obtain knowledge about attacks and the Bitcoin addresses that the attackers used in these attacks. These reports are typically submitted by victims and other persons/organizations and contain information about what type of attack was performed (e.g., blackmail scam, ransomware, sextortion, etc.) and typically some additional information about the attack (e.g., an email example) and the Bitcoin address(es) used in the attack.

Second, we use a series of tools to extract various information about the identified Bitcoin addresses that the attackers used directly from the Bitcoin blockchain itself. Using this information, we compare and contrast how successful attackers were in attracting funds from potential victims to the addresses associated with different types of attacks.

The above methodology allows us to observe transactions made by victims beyond those who report an attack and accounts for reports sometimes being

Table 1. Summary of primary dataset.

Time period of reports	2017-05-16 to 2022-04-25
Reports	267,708
Unique addresses	82,527
Transactions	5,092,489
Received bitcoins	31,346,586
Approximate value in USD	815,011,236,000

filled by people who did not fall victim themselves. This is important since many victims never report that they have been attacked.

Data Sharing: To ensure reproducibility and help others continue this line of research, the combined dataset will be shared with other researchers as per steps outlined here: https://www.ida.liu.se/~nikca89/papers/pam24a.html.

2.1   Bitcoin Abuse Database

The Bitcoin Abuse Database [4] contained reports dating back all the way to 2017-05-16; with new reports still being added in the summer of 2023. (The website bitcoinabuse.com is now merged/integrated with chainabuse.com.) For our main dataset, we obtained all records reported to this database between 2017-05-16 and 2022-04-25. The first two rows in Table 1 summarizes the number of reports (267,708) and unique Bitcoin addresses (82,527) in this dataset.

In addition to our main dataset, we also collected data and analyzed the records reported between 2022-12-20 and 2023-05-19. A brief discussion of these results are presented in Appendix B. The reason for the gap in the dataset were an API issue (appearing in 2022) that only allowed access to recent reports combined with a gap in our data collection.

Dataset Information: The Bitcoin Abuse dataset includes the following fields: id, address, abuse type id, abuse type other, abuser, description, from country, from country code, and created at. "id" is a unique number assigned to each report by the database. "Address" is the Bitcoin address that is reported for abuse. "Abuse type id" is a number representing the abuse type (category): Ransomware (1), Darknet markets (2), Bitcoin tumbler (3), Blackmail scam (4), Sextortion (5), and Other (99). "Abuse type other" is an optional free text column where the reporter may describe the abuse type whenever choosing "Other". A closer look at the free text classification of the top-1K accounts from the "Other" category (in terms of funds transferred) reveal that many reporters selected to list terms such as "scam", "investment scam", "ponzi", or use words such as terror, fraud/fake/phishing, hacker/attacker, or stolen/theft in their free text answers. "Abuser" is a free text field where the reporter may describe the abuser's identity. "Description" is a free text field where the reporter usually describes the abuse in more detail; many simply paste an email they have received from a perpetrator.

Here, we have observed high similarity between some reports (e.g., copied text), suggesting they may be submitted by the same person, but also quite specific descriptions that appears to be provided by first-hand victims. "From country" represents the reporter's (victim's) home country. "From country code" is the reporter's home country code. "Created at" is a date and time field representing the time the *report* was made.

Limitations: First, as noted above, an API issue and a gap in our data collection prevented us from obtaining data for the time period 2022-04-26 to 2022-12-19. Due to this gap, we decided to focus our analysis on our main dataset: 2017-05-16 to 2022-04-25. Second, bitcoinabuse.com has merged with chainabuse.com and is no longer making its full database freely available, making it difficult to fully extend the analysis into 2023 and beyond. While the new site provides an API, this API has a restrictive, rate-limited interface and uses a different categorization of the reported addresses. For these reasons, and after some exploration with the new API, we found the analysis presented here (of our complete main dataset) more comprehensive and insightful than we at this time can achieve with alternative or augmented datasets using data from the new API. Third, we only consider reported Bitcoin addresses. While other cryptocurrencies may also be used for their illicit activities, Bitcoin is still the dominating currency for such activities. For example, chainabuse.com has received close to nine times as many reports for Bitcoin as for the second-most reported cryptocurrency (Ethereum). Fourth, Bitcoin Abuse has a limited category selection, with the "Other" category being the fourth reported category. While it would be interesting to see a finer split of the "Other" category, we felt that the quality of the free-text answers were not sufficient to provide an accurate sub-classification here, and note that only two categories "Darknet markets" and "Bitcoin tumbler" saw fewer reports (cf. Fig. 4). Finally, we acknowledge that Bitcoin Abuse only collects reports in English, which potentially causes some biases in the reported addresses and note that it is difficult to know to what degree the full set of *reported* addresses accurately represent the addresses *most used* for illicit activities.

2.2   Blockchain Information

We tested several APIs to retrieve information about each observed address from the blockchain. For the analysis presented here, we used the Blockchain.com API [5]. The data for each address was saved to two files each. One includes the raw JSON form retrieved from the API and one contains a list of the address' transactions in CSV format with the headers: hash, timestamp, received/sent, address, and value. The list was created to summarize the data points of interest in an easy-to-process format for later analysis.

2.3   Pre-processing and Summary Files

To simplify our data analysis, we created two summary files: one with summary information about each reported address and one with information about each transaction associated with these addresses. Both these files contained summary information based on (1) all reports from the Bitcoin Abuse Database containing the address, (2) the raw JSON files from the blockchain API that were associated with the address, and (3) the list of transactions (and their properties).

Per-address Summary File: For each address, this file contains the following information (additional fields): received BTC, sent BTC, balance in BTC, # of received transactions, # sent transactions, # total transactions, average received BTC/transaction, average sent BTC/transaction, median received BTC/transaction, median sent BTC/transaction, date of last transaction, most common abuse type id, abuse type ids, abuse type freetext, # reports, date of the first report, country that the address was most commonly reported in, abuser identity, abuse description. Here, we note that the field "most common abuse type id" captures only the most common abuse type (i.e., the category selected by the reporter). To capture the full set of abuse types that an address has seen reports associated with, we included the field "abuse type ids", which contains a list of all different abuse types that the address has been labeled with. The same applies to the fields for in which country the abuse was reported in.

Per-transaction Summary File: This file contains all transactions that were made, with some additional information about the involved address (from the per-address summary file) about the abuse type (category) that the transaction's address belongs to and the date that the transaction's address was first reported. The complete list of headers for the transaction file were: the hash, timestamp, value, address1 (the reported address), received/sent, address2 (other sender/receiver), most common abuse type id, first reported.

2.4 Dataset Summary

Table 1 presents an overview of the dataset for our analysis (based on reports made May 16, 2017, to April 25, 2022). We also use an extra dataset (based on reports made the last five months) to confirm that we observe similar reporting rates (114 vs. 147 reports/day) and transactions per address (62.9 vs. 61.7 transactions/address) as seen in the past few years. The statistics for this dataset are provided in Appendix B.

Focusing on our main dataset, based on 268K reports, we identified 83K unique Bitcoin addresses that together have received 31M bitcoins across 5M transactions. Using the average price of a bitcoin (BTC) from 2023 (estimated at roughly $26K USD/BTC) [16], this amounts to a staggering $815 billion USD in total transaction value, and using the daily closing prices (given by Yahoo finance data) the day of each transaction, this amounts to $687 billion USD.

At this time it should also be noted that the value of the cumulative transferred funds should not be seen as a revenue estimate. As we show later in the paper, funds are often moved between several accounts (possibly owned by the same entity), complicating revenue estimates as well as the identification of the initial money transfers made by victims.

3   Aggregate High-Level Characterization

This section presents an aggregate analysis of how successful each address is (Sect. 3.1) and examines how to best model the amount of BTC obtained by the set of addresses (Sect. 3.2).

3.1   How Successful is Each Address?

In our Bitcoin Abuse dataset, 83K unique Bitcoin addresses were reported, and as one may expect, their success in (illicitly) attracting funds varied.

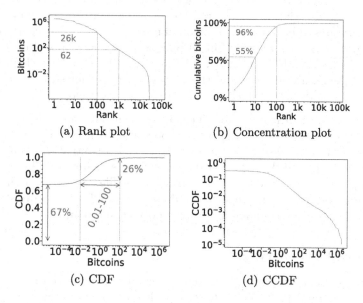

(a) Rank plot   (b) Concentration plot

(c) CDF   (d) CCDF

Fig. 2. Distribution statistics. Rank plots of (a) the received BTC per address and (b) the cumulative fraction of received BTC. The last two sub-plots show (c) the CDF and (d) CCDF of received BTC per address.

High Skew: We observed a significant skew in the distribution of funds, with a relatively small subset of addresses attracting the bulk of the attracted funds. This skew is characterized and quantified in Figs. 2(a) and 2(b). Figure 2(a) shows the total bitcoins received per address (reported to bitcoinabuse.com) as a function of the rank of each address. Figure 2(b) shows the cumulative fraction of the total observed bitcoins that the top-X addresses have attracted as a function of the cumulative rank X. The top-10 addresses each received more than 700K bitcoins; together these ten addresses were responsible for 55% of the total bitcoins received across all 83K addresses (i.e., 17M out of 31M bitcoins). Similarly, the top-100 all have each received more than 26K bitcoins, combining for more than 29M bitcoins or 96% of the total observed bitcoins in the dataset.

The top-1K have each received more than 62 bitcoins (together being responsible for 99.8% of the total bitcoins observed). While 62 bitcoins may seem small relative to the most successful addresses, we note that this still suggests that there are more than 1K abusive addresses that may have attracted over $1.6M USD (based on the $26K USD/BTC estimate of the average Bitcoin price during 2023) and that these 1K addresses together have attracted an estimated $814B USD. For a more granular estimation, using the daily transaction values, we refer to Sect. 4.1. Sorting the top-1K addresses based on the daily price of Bitcoins for transaction value estimation reveals that all of them have received transactions exceeding $2.8M USD.

Table 2. Overview of the top-10 highest receiving reported addresses.

Received [BTC]	Median [BTC]	Category	Description
3,048,040	40.0	Other	Trading investment scam.
2,845,086	18.0	Other	Forex trading scam, "investment in terror".
2,009,608	25.0	Other	"Investment in terror", begs for treatment money.
1,815,619	800	Other	"Investment in terror".
1,535,341	45.0	Other	"Investment in terror".
1,459,182	160	Ransomware	"Investment in terror".
1,378,975	800	Other	"Investment in terror".
1,259,824	0.50	Other	"Investment in terror".
1,030,376	505	Other	"Inhumane" bank account theft via remote desktop.
724,340	1,150	Other	"Investment in terror", begs for treatment money

Big Hitters: Table 2 provides an overview of the number of bitcoins that each of the top-10 accounts have received and the type of reports that have been filed against these accounts. Perhaps most noteworthy, the address that received the most bitcoins during our study received more than 3M bitcoins (worth $79B USD in 2023). While it is difficult to convert Bitcoin to usable funds (e.g., without impacting its value) and some of these funds are likely being double-counted (e.g., due to use of Tumblers), this staggering amount is of the same order of magnitude as the Gross Domestic Product (GDP) of entire US states such as Maine and North Dakota [39] or European countries such as Luxembourg [15]. The reports associated with this attack list it as being associated with trading investment scams and link it to services such as CapitalBullTrade [36]. The second-ranked address is reported to be associated with a foreign exchange trading scam (ROFX). The sixth-ranked address has primarily been associated with many ransomware attacks, and the ninth-ranked address is associated with "inhumane" bank account theft through remote desktop software. The remaining addresses on the top-10 list have been reported as organized Bitcoin scam groups that also make worldwide financial "investment in terror", especially in the US, Russia, and Eastern and Central Europe. One reporter of several of these reports claims to have worked for the organized criminals using these addresses for various illicit Bitcoin abuse (e.g., financial scams, begging scams, etc.) and for financial support of "terror".

The Most Common Cases: We next identify the most common cases and how much money these accounts attract. For this, refer to the cumulative distribution function (CDF) of the total received bitcoins per address shown in Fig. 2(c). 67% of the reported addresses did not receive any bitcoins at all (i.e., the CDF starts at 0.67), suggesting that many of the reported addresses were not successful in attracting funds. Furthermore, among the addresses that received some funds, most received between 0.01 and 100 bitcoins, with the frequency in this interval being s-shaped on log-scale, suggesting a log-normal-like distribution for this region. In total, these addresses make up 26% of all the reported addresses.

Table 3. Summary of distributions and their model fits with individual x_{min} and their goodness-of-fit (Kolmogorov-Smirnov distance) to the empirical data.

Distribution	$f(x)$	x_{min}	Shape parameter(s)	KS
Power law	$f(x) = Cx^{-\alpha}$	1	$\alpha = 1.35$	0.057
Power + Cutoff	$f(x) = Cx^{-\alpha}e^{-x/\beta}$	1	$\alpha = 1.36, \beta = 4.71 \cdot 10^{-7}$	0.099
Lognormal	$\frac{1}{x} \cdot e^{-\frac{(\ln x - \mu)^2}{2\sigma^2}}$	8,372	$\mu = 9.72, \sigma = 2.17$	0.035
Stretched Exponential	$\lambda\beta x^{\beta-1}e^{-\lambda x^\beta}$	9,444	$\beta = 0.30, \lambda = 1.01 \cdot 10^{-4}$	0.036

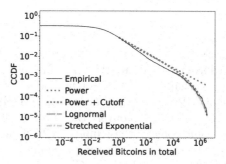

Fig. 3. Curve fitting comparison of the CCDF when computing x_{min} for each class.

Heavy-Tailed Distribution: As seen in Fig. 2(a) and 2(b), a smaller subset of addresses are responsible for the majority of the received bitcoins, suggesting that the distribution may be heavy-tailed. This is confirmed in Fig. 2(d), where we plot the CCDF of the amount of bitcoins received per address (with both axes on log-scale). While the distribution clearly is heavy-tailed (i.e., heavier than an exponential), the curvature towards the end suggests that the tail is not power law (as often seen in the wild). We next model this tail behavior and discuss potential implications.

3.2   Model of the Tail Distribution

To better understand the shape of the tail, we applied model fitting using the following probability distributions: (1) power law, (2) power law with exponential cutoff, (3) lognormal, and (4) stretched exponential. For each class, we determined both the x_{min} from which the distribution gave the best goodness-of-fit (using the Kolmogorov-Smirnov test [21]) and the best model parameters (using maximum likelihood estimation [24]). Table 3 summarizes the selected parameters and Fig. 3 shows the curves fitted from their respective x_{min} values. While lognormal and stretched exponential provide the best fits for the range they are fitted, we note that they only capture the very end of the tail (as they use x_{min} values of 8,372 and 9,444, respectively). In contrast, the power-law-based distributions capture a much bigger portion of the tail properly (both models using $x_{min} = 1$). Of these two distributions, we note that the power-law distribution with the exponential cutoff better captures the shape of the distribution visually, while the pure power-law function has a smaller Kolmogorov-Smirnov distance (as it better captures the convex-shaped portion of the body of the distribution, which due to the shape of the distribution is given more weight).

The presence of an exponential cutoff (as observed here) typically suggests the presence of a finite resource (e.g., funds from victims) or some form of constraints that limits extreme events (e.g., how much funds can be practically be obtained from victims). We also expect (conjecture) that some of the most successful actors may be responsible for several addresses, over which the funds may be distributed, both as a way to spread risks and as a means to make it more difficult to track funds). This is also suggested by several of the top addresses being reported by a person claiming to have worked for the fake companies

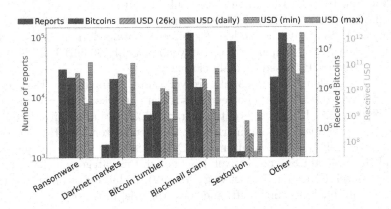

Fig. 4. Categories overview.

responsible for these addresses. One positive aspect here is that the presence of cutoffs can make predictions more reliable compared to systems with a power-law tail (often observed in nature, for example), as there appears to be some rough upper limit on how much funds these accounts have attracted.

4   Category-Based High-Level Characterization

This section examines the Bitcoin usage as seen across the different address categories reported. After a high-level comparison of the relative Bitcoin usage associated with the different categories (Sect. 4.1), we turn our attention to the transactions (Sect. 4.2) and reports (Sect. 4.3) themselves.

4.1   High-Level Comparisons

Consider first the number of reports received by Bitcoin Abuse regarding each abuse category and the number of bitcoins that each category of addresses received. Figure 4 summarizes these statistics for each of the abuse categories used by Bitcoin Abuse. To put the number of received bitcoins (shown in blue) in perspective we also show estimates and bounds of the corresponding transfer amounts in USD (shown in pink). Here, we include four estimates: (1) based on our 26k USD/BTC estimate of the average price during 2023, (2) based on daily closing value of BTC price at the day of each individual transaction, as estimated using Yahoo finance source, (3) based on the minimum value of BTC during our abuse report's collection period (2017-05-16 to 2022-04-25), and (4) based on the maximum value of this same time period. While the first two values are used as estimates, the latter two can seen as very rough lower and upper bounds of the price of Bitcoins over the period of interest ($1,734 and $67,567, respectively).

The two most reported abuse categories (i.e., "Blackmail scam" and "Sextortion") are among the three categories that attracted the least funds to the addresses associated with their reported attacks. While this may suggest that these attacks are not very successful, we note that the amount of money they attracted still are non-negligible. For example, while the addresses reported in the 120K reports about Blackmail scams "only" received a modest 1.1M bitcoins, this still corresponds to $29B USD (based on 26k/BTC) or $10B (based on daily closing price). Similarly, the modest 26k bitcoins obtained via addresses associated with Sextortion campaigns are still worth roughly $0.69B USD (based on 26k/BTC) or $0.22B (based on daily closing price).

Having said that, these amounts are very small compared to the amounts paid to the addresses of the reported Ransomware attacks (2.0M bitcoins worth $52B USD or $32B USD based on the average 2023 price and daily closing estimates, respectively) or Darknet markets (1.9M bitcoins worth $49B USD or $45B USD, respectively), not to mention the "Other" category (26M bitcoins worth $670B USD or $590 USD, respectively). As noted, this category includes the top addresses observed in our dataset (e.g., Table 2), including trading/investment scams, remote bank account theft, and "investment[s] in terror".

Also, the reported Bitcoin tumbler sees significant funds passing through them. Here we note that Bitcoin tumbler, also known as a mixing service, combines and shuffles bitcoins from different sources to obscure their original origin, making them an attractive service to be used by the organizations behind many of the illicit addresses. The propensity to employ Bitcoin tumblers for such purposes is evident, as detailed and explored further in Sect. 6, where we trace bitcoin flows within and across addresses linked to various illicit activities.

Fraction of Addresses Not Attracting any Funds: The relative success of the addresses associated with each abuse category becomes even clearer when looking at the distribution statistics. Figure 5 shows a CDF for each category. The leftmost point on each CDF indicates the fraction of accounts in that category that did not receive any bitcoins. Sextortion (93% of addresses), Blackmail scams (79%) and Ransomware (72%) had significantly more accounts that did not receive any funds (i.e., zero bitcoins) compared to the addresses associated with Bitcoin tumbler (12%), "Other" category (10%), and Darknet markets (6%).

Distribution Comparisons: While most addresses that received funds ranged between 0.01 and 100 bitcoins (seen by the s-shaped step in the CDFs for this region), we observe a noticeable shift in the distributions. For example, referring to the CDFs in Fig. 5, we observe a clear separation between where the different distributions approach one. This separation is more visible in the CCDFs shown in Fig. 6. Here, the labels of each class are ordered based on the number

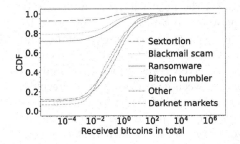
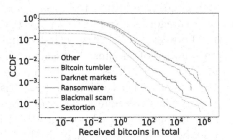

Fig. 5. CDF of received bitcoins.   **Fig. 6.** CCDF of received bitcoins.

Table 4. Power-law fitting of per-category CCDFs.

Category	Slope estimate		Confidence interval
	x_{min}	$\alpha\ (\sigma)$	95%
Sextortion	1	1.423 (0.041)	$\alpha \pm 0.000518$
Blackmail	1	1.419 (0.013)	$\alpha \pm 0.000161$
Ransomw.	1	1.388 (0.013)	$\alpha \pm 0.000234$
Darknet	1	1.309 (0.019)	$\alpha \pm 0.00101$
Tumbler	1	1.391 (0.016)	$\alpha \pm 0.000612$
Other	1	1.329 (0.005)	$\alpha \pm 0.0000851$

of accounts that received at least one bitcoin. We observe three distinct groups: (1) Sextortion addresses obtained the least funds, (2) Blackmail scams and Ransomware addresses in general received distinctly more but typically not as much as (3) the addresses associated with Darknet markets, Bitcoin tumbler, and the addresses those in the "Other" category.

Furthermore, when broken down on a per-category basis, the CCDFs become significantly more power-law-like (compared with the aggregate curve in Fig. 3), with clear straight-line behavior when plotted on log scale. This is further confirmed by the power-law fitting of each curve. Table 4 summarizes these fittings, with corresponding confidence intervals on the slope parameter. The slopes are relatively clustered around the range $1.31 \leq \alpha \leq 1.42$, each with a relatively tight confidence interval, and together encompassing the slope of the aggregate curve ($\alpha = 1.35$). Rather than the small slope variations, the most visible difference between the CCDFs is instead their relative shift to each other.

4.2 Transactions-Based Analysis

There are two primary contributors to the differences seen in the distributions of the number of bitcoins received per address when comparing the different abuse categories: the transaction sizes and number of transactions. First, as shown in Fig. 7, the size distributions of individual transactions differ substantially between the categories. Here, we note a clear shift in the size distributions; e.g., captured by noticeable differences when looking at the upper percentiles.

Second, in addition to bigger transactions, the most successful addresses in these categories also received more transactions. To capture the strong correlation between how successful individual addresses were at attracting funds and the number of victims, Fig. 8 shows per-category scatterplots of the received bitcoins (per address) and the number of received transactions (per address) for each category. To simplify comparisons between categories, the scatterplots (shown using red points) are overlaid on a heatmap of the overall per-address distribution (across all categories). Here, the color in the heatmap shows the probability density function (PDF) of addresses observed with that combination. While the distributions for the first four categories (i.e., Ransomware, Darknet markets, Bitcoin tumbler, and Blackmail scams) look relatively similar,

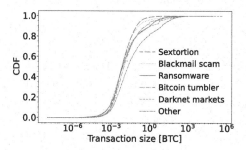

Fig. 7. CDF of received transaction sizes per category.

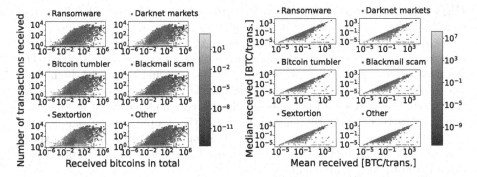

Fig. 8. Received bitcoins vs. the number of received transactions. Per-category scatterplots (red) overlayed on overall heatmaps (gradient color). (Color figure online)

Fig. 9. Mean vs. median number of received bitcoins per transaction. Per-category scatterplots (red) overlayed on overall heatmaps (gradient color). (Color figure online)

with a clear cluster receiving up-to 100 bitcoins spread over up-to 1K incoming transactions, Sextortion and the "Other" category stand out. Again, Sextortion addresses receive fewer bitcoins and fewer transactions compared to other categories. Notably, the "Other" category includes many of the highest receiving addresses (e.g., with 1K–2M received bitcoins) and some of the addresses with the highest transaction counts.

High Skew in Transaction Sizes Within Each Category: While we observe a high correlation between the number of transactions and the number of received bitcoins, especially when looking at individual categories, there are several noticeable exceptions. One reason for this is the high skew in the size distribution of transactions (CDFs in Fig. 7).

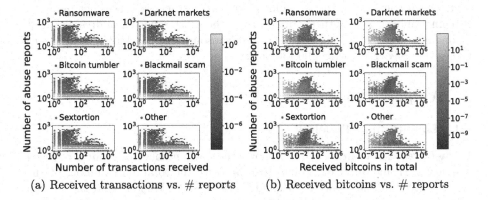

(a) Received transactions vs. # reports

(b) Received bitcoins vs. # reports

Fig. 10. Successfulness of addresses with different numbers of reports. Per-category scatterplots (red) overlayed on overall heatmaps (gradient color). (Color figure online)

High Skew in Transaction Sizes for Individual Addresses: We have also seen that the sizes can differ substantially for the transactions of individual addresses, best visualized in Fig. 9, where we plot the median vs. mean number of received bitcoins per transaction and address. Here, the addresses with relatively symmetric size distributions fall close to the diagonal and those with high skew fall below the diagonal. Perhaps most noticeable is a "line" of addresses at the bottom right of "Other". Those addresses have a very high mean but low median, due to a few very large incoming transactions driving up the mean significantly together with many smaller transactions dragging down the median. We expect that addresses with higher skew may be used for a more diverse set of abuses, targeting both "big" and "small" actors.

4.3   Report Frequencies

It is expected that (low-effort) attacks targeting many users will see many reports. It is therefore not surprising to see the much higher report frequencies of Blackmail scams and Sextortion abuse in Fig. 4. What is perhaps more interesting is that all categories, including these two categories, include a noticeable mix of low-effort attacks (e.g., spam campaigns) and high-effort, directed attacks. In addition to explaining the high skews observed in how successful different addresses within a category are at attracting funds (both in terms of bitcoins and incoming transactions), we note that these differences also can be observed in the relatively lower correlation between the number of transactions and reports (Fig. 10(a)), as well as between the number of received bitcoins and the number of observed reports (Fig. 10(b)).

Addresses Best at Attracting Funds are Not Highly Reported: Referring to Fig. 10(b), we note that the most successful addresses at attracting funds are only reported a few times (perhaps representing targeted efforts; e.g., of big companies that do not want the attack to be known) and that the number of reports per address are relatively independent of the quantity of received funds when considering the three most successful categories: Darknet markets, Bitcoin tumbler, and "Other". In contrast, the most reported addresses (most belonging to the other three categories: Ransomware, Blackmail, Sextortion) typically received less than 100 bitcoins.

5   Temporal Analysis

5.1   Longitudinal Timeline

High-Level Timeline: Figure 11 shows the daily number of reports between January 2017 and July 2022 (blue) together with the total daily number of bitcoins received by the reported set of addresses (green). We note that the Bitcoin Abuse Database was created in 2017 and gained popularity in late 2018 when it saw a steep rise in the number of reports (blue curve). The daily report count has remained relatively steady (at an order of 100's per day) since the beginning

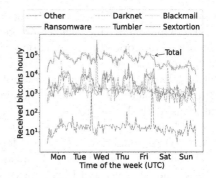

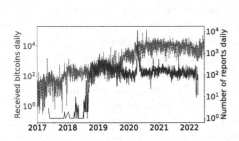

Fig. 11. Timeline of received bitcoins and number of reports between Jan 2017 and July 2022.

Fig. 12. Received bitcoins by time of the week. Weekday ticks show 12 pm UTC.

of 2019, with exceptions for some temporal peaks and dips. The timeline of the number of received bitcoins per day is more concerning, as there has been a substantial (rough $100x$) increase from $O(100)$ to $O(10,000)$ of bitcoins transferred to these addresses per day over the three-year period that reporting has been relatively stable (i.e., 2019–2022).

Noteworthy Spikes: There are several noteworthy spikes in the reporting. The biggest spike by far was observed on April 16th, 2020. On this day, 11K reports were filed, which is roughly 100 times more than the daily average (of 100) for the surrounding days. Our investigation revealed that many news articles around that time warned about a particular style of scam email reported by both the US [34] and Australian [2] governments. In these emails, the attacker (falsely) claims that they have recorded the victim visiting an adult website, while also showing the victim one of their passwords (likely from a leak) in the email.

Looking at the reports for this day, it is clear that a lot of the reports are talking about the same type of attack, matching the descriptions in the articles mentioned. We observed a mix of descriptions written by the victims themselves as well as copies of the emails they received. In many cases, the scammers asked for $1,000 or $2,000 to be paid in bitcoins and displayed one valid password belonging to the targeted victim as "proof" that they know the password.

5.2 Time of the Week

Figure 12 shows the time of the week that bitcoins were received for each category. This figure reveals both daily diurnal patterns (with much bigger volumes during daytime/evenings (UTC)) and more funds being transferred during weekdays than weekends. These observations are clearly seen by looking at total volume transferred per hour (grey line at the top marked with "Total") in Fig. 12 as well as the Ransomware, Darknet markets, and "Other" categories. With the victims of these categories more often paying during daytime and during the weekdays, suggests that these attacks may be more likely to hit victims on their work computers or that the scammers work during business hours. In contrast, the other categories (e.g., sextortion, tumbler) do not have a strong time of day or day of week pattern, with Bitcoin tumbler seeing the least pronounced patterns, possibly suggesting some level of automation. Here it should be noted that Bitcoin tumbler typically aim at pooling and redistributing the funds at random intervals, with the aim to enhance the anonymity of Bitcoin and achieve effective money laundering. In the case of sextortion, we also expect these scams to reach people on personal devices (or any device) and not just during work hours.

Finally, the biggest relative spikes can be seen for Sextortion, Blackmail scams, and Darknet markets. These spikes are due to large individual transactions affecting these typically smaller volume categories more. For example, the two by far largest transactions (1,000 BTC and 650 BTC, respectively) in the Sextortion category directly line up with the two biggest Sextortion spikes.

5.3   Initial Report Date Analysis

We next consider the timing of the payments to an address relative to the first time that the address was reported to Bitcoin Abuse. This is illustrated on a per-category basis in Fig. 13. This shows the CDFs of the relative time each transaction was made in relation to the *first* time the address was reported.

This figure provides several interesting insights. First, addresses are reported around the time that their incoming transaction count is high, indicating that the first report often is made around the time of the abuse's highest activity. This may be a reflection of a significant portion of the addresses only being used for specific attacks. However, significant category differences are observed, with Ransomware displaying the highest concentration around the time of the address first being reported, while Darknet markets exhibit the least concentration.

Second, for all categories except Darknet markets, most transactions take place before the first report is even filled. This may in part be a reflection of most victims not reporting addresses engaging in illicit behaviors.

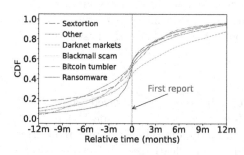 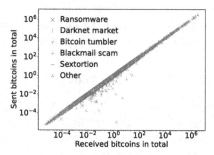

Fig. 13. CDFs of the relative timing of the transactions compared to the first reporting date of an address.

Fig. 14. Scatterplot of received and sent bitcoins.

While some might report the addresses somewhere other than Bitcoin Abuse, the large share of transactions before the first time an address is reported (to Bitcoin Abuse) also suggests that unless reporting behaviors change, there may be limited effectiveness to using such reports to "ban" addresses. As seen here, there is a need for a recognized central anti-fraud mechanism for cryptocurrencies. Without a centralized mechanism, malicious activity will exploit the gaps.

6   Following the Money

In this section, we analyze and share insights learned from following the outflow of bitcoins from the reported addresses.

Bitcoins Temporarily Passing Through Reported Addresses: This analysis is of particular interest since nearly all reported addresses have sent as many bitcoins as they received, leaving a balance of zero. This is illustrated in Fig. 14, where we show the total number of bitcoins sent vs. received (per address). This shows that the bitcoins only temporarily pass through the reported addresses, suggesting that these addresses typically are not the wallets that the perpetrators use to store their ill-obtained monetary gains. The following sections compare and share insights for different categories of reported addresses.

Scope of Analysis: The main goal of this analysis is to study and compare the potential concentration or dispersion of money for different abuse address categories. We defer to government agencies and law enforcement to identify individuals or organizations that extract or use the money.

6.1   Following the Money Methodology

The analysis thus far has not required us to keep track of who has transferred funds to whom. We simply counted the funds transferred. However, when following the money paid from one address to another (as done next), greater attention to detail is needed. We next describe the main challenge with this type of analysis and the decisions (and their limitations) we made to address this.

Basics: All Bitcoin transactions consists of one or more inputs (previous transactions) that are transferred to one or more outputs.

Trivial Cases: Since each input and output is labeled with how many bitcoins an address is contributing/receiving as the result of a transaction, for cases where there is a single input the transactions can easily be determined regardless if there are one or more outputs, since these can be split into several separate (virtual) transactions. By symmetry, the same approach works when there is a single output but one or more inputs that are part of the transaction.

Challenging Case and Our Solution: However, when there are multiple inputs *and* multiple outputs, the situation is like a melting pot and it is not obvious which bitcoins ended up where. In some cases, it is still possible to determine who transferred the funds to whom (with some accuracy) using heuristics based

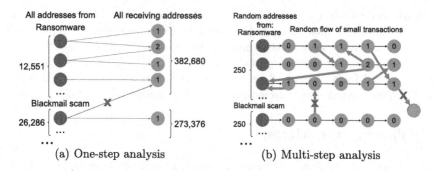

Fig. 15. Visualization of the follow the money analysis. Here, the node degrees are in the orange circles. For the multi-step analysis, we show both the basic chain of transactions (black) and "concentration" edges (blue arrows). (Color figure online)

on the input/output sizes. However, to avoid introducing potential inaccuracies, for the analysis presented here we opted to not use any transactions matching for the last case of our "follow the money" analysis (coming next) and instead only consider the transactions for which we are sure exactly who sent what bitcoins to whom. Fortunately, there are very many transactions that have limited inputs or outputs, allowing us to identify how funds flow between a series of Bitcoin addresses. (We again note that this limitation only is applied from here on and that it does not impact any of the analysis presented earlier in the paper.)

6.2 One-Step Concentration or Dispersion

Let's first follow the outgoing money from the reported addresses only *one* step. In particular, we consider the concentration of addresses that the reported addresses transfer funds directly to. Figure 15(a) illustrates how we did this analysis. First, for each category, we added a link from the reported addressees (red circles on the left) belonging to that category to any address that it directly transferred funds to (conclusively). Second, for each receiving first-hop address (orange circles) we count and report how many reporting addresses each such address has received at least some funds from. This corresponds to the in-degree of each (orange) address to the right in the graph. For example, if two reported addresses both send money to address x, then address x has a node degree of two. Please note that this metric does not consider how many transactions an address x receives, only how many unique senders (in this case from the set of reported addresses) that it receives some funds from.

Figure 16(a) and 16(b) show the CDFs and rank plots, respectively, of the per-category node degrees. First, we note a Zipf-like distribution (i.e., relatively straight-line behavior in the rank plots shown on log-log scale), capturing a high skew among the nodes that do receive money flows from multiple abuse addresses. For example, each category includes an address that received funds from 100 or more abuse addresses. Notably, an address in the "Other" category

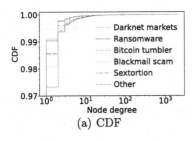
(a) CDF

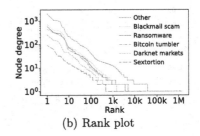
(b) Rank plot

Fig. 16. Node degrees distributions of receiving addresses being sent money from addresses in each category.

Table 5. Address expansion ratio comparison of categories when going one step deep.

Category	Abuse addr. (#)	Addr. one level deep (#)	Expansion ratio
Sextortion	24,218	32,982	1.36
Blackmail scam	26,286	273,376	10.40
Ransomware	12,551	382,680	30.49
Darknet markets	1,289	168,542	130.75
Bitcoin tumbler	2,507	334,160	133.29
Other	13,736	1,419,902	103.37

received funds from 2,000 abuse addresses, aligning with reports of organized crime using such addresses to pool funds from various attack vectors for global financial "investment in terror".

However, perhaps the main observation is the very long tail of addresses with node degree one. For example, looking at the CDF, 97–99% of the addresses associated with each category have a node degree of one (the minimum), meaning that nearly all receiving addresses are not visibly related when only tracing the money one step. This suggests that the money mostly is spread out across even more addresses after the first step, when going only one step deep from the reported addresses. This is confirmed when looking at the total addresses seen one level deep and the relative expansion ratio of each category, shown in Table 5. Notably, Bitcoin tumblers, Darknet markets, and "Other" categories exhibit significantly larger expansion ratios compared to the rest.

6.3 Multi-step Analysis

Having seen little concentration when following the transactions only one step, we next performed a multi-step analysis to track the money flow several steps deep. For this analysis, we again wanted to compare the categories fairly head-to-head and be able to answer questions such as whether some categories are more likely to shuffle around the money a couple of steps only to collect the money a few steps later.

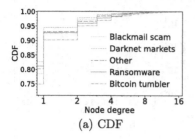
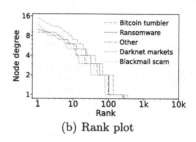

(a) CDF   (b) Rank plot

Fig. 17. CDF and rank plot of the node degrees of addresses in the chain, for respective category, when counting only blue "concentration" edges. (Color figure online)

For fair head-to-head comparison, we developed a "tracking the pennies" approach in which we tracked an equal amount of "penny flows" (flow of small transactions) as bitcoins were moved five steps deep. Figure 15(b) provides a visual overview of our sampling and tracking methodology. More specifically, for each category, we used a random (depth first) search to find 250 randomly selected reported addresses from which we were able to trace back at least one random chain of money five steps deep from that address. For each step in this search, a new random transaction was chosen from the last address in the chain. We typically gave preference to a small transaction (under 0.1 bitcoins), and if no such transaction existed, we used any random transaction as a fallback. Finally, if a chain of transactions reached a dead end (i.e., where there are no more outgoing transactions), the latest address was removed from the chain and a new random transaction (new path) was chosen.

The choice of picking 250 was made to ensure that we have a substantial number of random paths for each category (so that numerical properties can be compared with some statistical confidence). However, we note that this choice forces us to drop Sextortion from the analysis since we did not find 250 full five-step paths for this category. Therefore, the following analysis focuses only on the other five categories.

Furthermore, for the node degree analysis we did not count all types of address relationships that we identify (but report on these separately). For example, as illustrated with an × in Fig. 15(b), we did not count the basic chain (black arrows), cross-category links (e.g., vertical arrow in the figure) or links to addresses further away than five steps deep.

Fewer Addresses with In-degree One: While all categories still had nodes with an in-degree of one, compared to the one-step analysis, this fraction reduced noticeably (from 97–99% to 83–89%). Here, Bitcoin tumbler saw the biggest reduction (from 98.5% down to 83%).

Bitcoin Tumblers: In general, Bitcoin tumbler stands out in our multi-step analysis. For example, in addition to the above finding, it stands out with higher node degrees (e.g., see CDFs of "concentration" edges in Fig. 17(a)) and substantially higher concentration (e.g., see the rank plot in Fig. 17(b)) than the other

Table 6. Comparison of graph and transaction metrics calculated on each category's flow graph.

Category	Graph metrics		Transaction metrics		
	Connecting edges	Loops	To reported	To reported category	To reported 250
Ransomware	254	4	2,526	399	169
Darknet	209	17	2,240	269	263
Tumbler	354	25	2,524	585	97
Blackmail	267	16	2,239	307	154
Other	247	10	5,164	3,155	1,299

categories. These findings suggest that fewer actors are involved with this category, typically used for anonymity/money laundering. These differences can perhaps be explained by the increased effort associated with running such addresses. In particular, we note that tumbling bitcoins typically requires more effort and expertise than simply sending blackmail scam emails (which has the lowest node degree and concentration of the categories). Another potential explanation is that most Bitcoin-using miscreants use tumblers, and there are more users of tumblers than tumblers.

Money-Flow Comparisons: When looking closer at the structure of the graphs formed by the 1,250 edges (250 chains × 5 steps) we observed significant differences between the categories. The first two columns of Table 6 summarize some of these properties. Here, the "Connecting edges" represent the blue arrows in Fig. 15(b), which are transactions among the set of addresses in the graph, excluding the "penny flow" itself (the white arrows in Fig. 15(b)) and "Loops" measures the number of distinct cycles that exist in the graph structure for that category. Looking at these two metrics, Bitcoin tumbler again stands out with significantly higher "connecting edge" (354) and "loop" (25) counts than the other categories. This again matches the intuition that the addresses in this category are more likely to send money among a relatively smaller set of addresses. In contrast, Darknet markets have the fewest "connecting edges" (209) and Ransomware has by far fewest "loops" (4).

Transaction-Based Analysis on the Graph: Finally, we have found that some of the edges go back to the original reported addresses, and that these in some cases carry a non-negligible number of transactions. The remaining columns of Table 6 summarizes the metrics we used here, where "to reported" counts the number of transactions going back to any of the 267K reported addresses, "to reported category" counts transactions to any reported address in the category, and "to reported 250" only counts transactions back to the 250 randomly picked reported addresses of that category.

Here, we again observe some major differences between the categories. First, the "Other" category has much more transactions going back to reported addresses, especially to its own category (3,155 transactions compared to 585 for the second-ranked category) as well as back to the 250 random (reported)

Table 7. Transactions across categories.

From/to	Ransomware	Darknet	Tumbler	Blackmail	Other
Ransomware	-	982	2,658	1,566	1,228
Darknet	767	-	2,126	664	915
Tumbler	2,173	1,638	-	2,282	2,588
Blackmail	1,512	914	4,087	-	2,230
Other	1,086	1,825	3,015	1,903	-

addresses of its own category (1,299 compared to 263 for the second-ranked category). These findings suggest that a significant number of transactions are directed towards some of the reported addresses in the "Other" category.

Transactions Across Categories: To better understand how money flowed between addresses associated with the different categories, we next counted the transactions made between the subgraphs of each category (note that these were not included above, since we did not include that type of cross-category "connecting edges" in the original graph analysis (marked with × in Fig. 15(b)). Table 7 summarizes the total number of transactions over such cross-category edges. Here, Bitcoin tumbler again stands out with both a higher inflow and outflow of transactions to/from the category compared to to/from the other categories. Given the nature of Bitcoin tumbler (money laundering), it also makes sense that other categories are interested in their service, which may explain why all categories have more outgoing transactions to Bitcoin tumbler to any of the other categories; e.g., Ransomware (2,658 vs. 1,566 for 2nd ranked), Darknet markets (2,126 vs. 915 for 2nd ranked), Blackmail scams (4,087 vs. 2,230 for 2nd ranked), and "Other" (3,015 vs. 1,903 for 2nd ranked).

Finally, we note that the "Other" category receives the most transactions (2,588) from Tumbler addresses (of all categories) and send the most transactions (1,825) of any category outside Tumblers to Darknet addresses and the second-most transactions (3,015) after Blackmail (4,087) to Tumbler addresses. While it is difficult to label these accounts or pinpoint where their funds are directed based only on this analysis, it is clear that several of these accounts play a central role in the transfer of illicit funds (matching some reporters' claims that some of these addresses are associated with organized crime). Here, it should also be noted that our methodology did not track the amount of funds transferred between the address types, so the skew in transferred funds between the account types may be substantially bigger (and different) when accounting for the transactions of the "Other" category generally being bigger than for the rest (e.g., Fig. 7).

7   Related Work

Anonymity: Many works study anonymity aspects of Bitcoin and identify ways to deanonymize users. Reid and Harrigan [31] present an early study of the anonymity aspects of Bitcoin. Herrera-Joancomart [12] provides an exhaustive review of Bitcoin anonymity. Biryukov et al. [3] show that combining Bitcoin with the anonymizing service Tor creates a new attack vector, jeopardizing their privacy. Androulaki et al. [1] investigate user privacy in Bitcoin by simulating usage of Bitcoin in accordance with Bitcoin's recommended privacy measures, finding that almost 40% of the simulated participants could be accurately profiled using behavior-based clustering techniques. Meiklejohn et al. [22] discuss the challenges Bitcoin's public flow of transactions causes for larger-scale criminal and fraudulent activity. Harrigan et al. [11] explain how "unreasonably" effective address clustering is—i.e., heuristics that group addresses together.

Criminal Activities: As we are not the first to characterize the landscape of Bitcoin abuse, many previous works have studied criminal activities related to Bitcoin [10,14,19,27,28,32,41]. For example, Pastrana et al. [28] perform a large measurement of 4.5M crypto-mining malware samples, revealing campaigns with multi-million dollar earnings. Pastrana et al. [27] measure the practice of "eWhoring" (selling photos and videos with sexual content of another person). While most transactions involved PayPal and Amazon giftcards, Bitcoin was found to be a popular tool for offloading eWhoring profits.

Money Laundering and Tumbling: Möser et al. [23] present the first study on Bitcoin money laundering (tumblers) and conclude that applying a Know-Your-Customer principle to Bitcoin is likely not possible. Others have created protocols that facilitate the service of mixing (tumbling) transactions. Bonneau et al. [6] propose a protocol called MixCoin, later improved to BlindCoin by Valenta and Rowan [40]. Concurrently, Ruffing et al. [33] proposes a decentralized mixing system called CoinShuffle.

Ransomware: Bitcoin use with ransomware [9,13,17,20,29,35,37,42] is well studied. For example, Kharraz et al. [17] present a long-term study of observed ransomware attacks between 2006 and 2014. More recently, Wang et al. [42] present a large-scale empirical analysis based on data from 2012–2021. Huang et al. [13] study the landscape of ransomware and trace the money-flow from when the victim acquires Bitcoins to when the perpetrator converts it back to fiat. For a two-year period, they trace 19,750 victims' (likely) ransom payments of more than $16M. Conti et al. [9] conduct a large study of the economic impact of many different ransomwares from a perspective of Bitcoin transactions, including ransomwares like WannaCry, Jigsaw and many more. Liao et al. [20] focus on one particular family of ransomware called CryptoLocker, i.e., ransomware that simply encrypts files until the ransom is paid.

Sextortion: Paquet-Clouston et al. [26] study sextortion spam that requires a payment in Bitcoin using a dataset of 4M entries, concluding that one entity is likely behind the majority of them and has gained around $1.3M over an 11-month period. Oggier et al. [25] also analyze sextortions, but focus on those where the victim is blackmailed (scammed) *with* compromising sexual information, rather than being blackmailed *into* committing sexual actions.

Darknet Markets: Christin [8] perform a measurement analysis of the darknet market Silk Road over an 8-month period in 2012. Broséus et al. [7] study the structure and organization of darknet markets from a Canadian perspective. Lee et al. [18] study how criminals abuse cryptocurrencies on the dark web using over 27M dark webpages and 10M Bitcoin addresses, learning that more than 80% of the addresses on the dark web were used for malicious activity.

8   Conclusion

This paper presented a comprehensive analysis of money flows to and from Bitcoin addresses linked to different abuse categories. Our analysis revealed valuable insights for understanding Bitcoin transactions linked to illicit activities, guiding future efforts to combat cryptocurrency-related illicit activities, with significant implications for legitimate users and stakeholders.

First, our high-level characterization of money flows revealed substantial variations in flow patterns, report rates, and success rates within and across addresses associated with different abuse categories (e.g., high skew, heavy tails, and big differences between categories). This understanding aids law enforcement and regulators in identifying patterns and trends in illegal Bitcoin activities, and improve their strategies to detect, prevent, and mitigate illicit activities.

Second, our temporal analysis captured long-term trends, weekly patterns, and the relative timing of when illicit addresses of each category are reported or receive funds. The observed increase in the daily number of Bitcoins received by reported addresses over time (e.g., $\approx \times 100$ over three years) indicates a significant rise in funds transferred to these addresses. This calls for continuous vigilance and adaptive approaches to keep up with the evolving landscape of illegal transactions. Moreover, the weekly and daily variations in activity levels and transaction volumes highlight the importance of targeted enforcement efforts during periods of heightened activity. To counter dynamic illicit transactions and improve reporting, stakeholders should adopt agile, real-time monitoring, proactive intervention, and international cooperation for early warnings.

Third, our analysis of the outflow of bitcoins from reported addresses sheds light on significant differences in graph properties and flow patterns among illicit addresses and between abuse categories. For example, the concentration of funds toward specific addresses, the dispersion of funds after the initial step, and the presence of loops highlight the complexity of money laundering schemes and the need for enhanced measures to track and disrupt these networks. The significant differences in graph structure and transaction patterns between categories, particularly the prominence of Bitcoin tumblers, underscore the importance of addressing the role of specific services in facilitating illicit financial flows.

Finally, our results also highlight that authorities need a coordinated effort to monitor all Bitcoin activities, and cryptocurrency activities in general. While there is a lot of illicit activity on Bitcoin, only a fraction of it gets reported, and at least to Bitcoin Abuse many of the reports come in relatively late. Furthermore, while databases like Bitcoin Abuse are great data sources, we note that researchers (as we have found here) are limited to the availability and APIs provided by those data sources. When they are not accessible, transparency is hurt, emphasizing the need for transparent methods to monitor fraud on these networks. We advocate for global government collaboration on an official centralized abuse monitoring effort for all cryptocurrencies to capture money flows across diverse illicit activities and national borders. Our follow-the-money analysis avoids pointing to specific actors, yet highlights the potential use of sophisticated techniques to identify threat actors involved in multiple illicit activities.

Acknowledgments. This work was partially supported by the Wallenberg AI, Autonomous Systems and Software Program (WASP) funded by the Knut and Alice Wallenberg Foundation. We would also like to thank our shepherd Lucianna Kiffer and the anonymous reviewers, who provided valuable feedback as well as several students that have contributed to early results in this project, including Axel Flodmark, Markus Jakum, Vera Antonov, and Karl Söderbäck.

A Ethics

Our research highlights the significant challenges posed by Bitcoin's pseudonymous transactions and lack of regulation, particularly in relation to its use in illicit activities. In the paper, we provide a comprehensive analysis of Bitcoin transactions associated with different categories of illegal activities, conducted so as to ensure that ethical considerations were upheld.

Addresses an Important Societal Problem: As the paper demonstrates, Bitcoin use for illicit activities is clearly widespread and turns over very large sums of money. Many of the abuse types prey on the weak, and it is clear that these activities have increasingly negative societal effects. While the general public often focuses on Bitcoin's energy consumption, much less attention has been put on the numerous victims that fall prey to Bitcoin's role in various illicit activities. We note that while Bitcoin's energy consumption *might* have long-term effects on *humans*, the effect of Bitcoin abuse on humans is both *apparent* and *current*.

Respect Privacy and Confidentiality of Individuals: The data used for analysis is sourced from the Bitcoin Abuse Database, which collects information from reports submitted by victims and other individuals or organizations, and the public Bitcoin chain itself. While the database provides insights into attacks and associated Bitcoin addresses, care is taken to ensure the anonymity of victims and attackers. We recognize that not all victims report their experiences and that reports may come from individuals who did not fall victim themselves.

Adhere to Legal and Ethical Guidelines: The analysis focuses on publicly available blockchain data and information obtained from the Bitcoin Abuse Database. No attempts are made to compromise the security or integrity of the Bitcoin network or any other systems.

Table 8. Comparison of recent reporting rates and the volume of new addresses being reported in the past five months, and the transactions they receive.

	Primary dataset	Latest reports
Reports time frame	2017-05-16 – 2022-04-25	2022-12-20 – 2023-05-19
Reports	267,708	17,116
Unique addresses	82,527	2,249
Transactions	5,092,489	141,485
Received bitcoins	31,346,586	269,070
Received in USD	815,011,236,000	6,995,820,000

Promote Responsible and Ethical Use of the Findings: Law enforcement agencies, regulatory bodies, and cryptocurrency service providers can leverage our insights to enhance their strategies, policies, and compliance measures. Overall, the study aims to contribute to the development of effective strategies to mitigate the risks and vulnerabilities associated with Bitcoin's potential for misuse, promoting a safer and more secure financial landscape.

B   Additional Statistics

Table 8 provides a high-level overview of the recent reporting rates, the volume of new addresses having been reported in the past five months, and the transactions they receive. We note that reporting rates (114 reports/day on average) are similar to those observed in Fig. 11 and that the average transactions/address is almost the same (61.7 for primary vs. 62.9 for latest dataset). The main difference is a reduction in the average number of bitcoins received/address (380 for the primary dataset vs. 120 for the latest dataset) and the rate new unique addresses are observed. These later differences are easily explained by (1) these addresses being earlier in their lifecycle (e.g., Fig. 13) and/or (2) a bias towards many of the most successful addresses (in terms of attracting funds; e.g., the top-hitters in the "Other" category) already having been reported. Yet, the large amount of funds that these *newly reported* addresses obtain shows that there continually are many more (new) illicit addresses being reported that are attracting significant funds, including at the present moment.

References

1. Androulaki, E., Karame, G.O., Roeschlin, M., Scherer, T., Capkun, S.: Evaluating user privacy in bitcoin. In: Proceedings of Financial Cryptography and Data Security (FC) (2013)
2. Australian Cyber Security Centre: Sextortion email campaign impacting Australians (2020). https://www.cyber.gov.au/about-us/alerts/sextortion-email-campaign-impacting-australians. Accessed 17 May 2023

3. Biryukov, A., Pustogarov, I.: Bitcoin over tor isn't a good idea. In: Proceedings of IEEE Symposium on Security and Privacy (S&P) (2015)
4. BitcoinAbuse: Bitcoin Abuse Database (2023). https://www.bitcoinabuse.com. Accessed 08 May 2023
5. Blockchain: Blockchain Developer APIs (2023). https://www.blockchain.com/explorer/api. Accessed 25 May 2023
6. Bonneau, J., Narayanan, A., Miller, A., Clark, J., Kroll, J.A., Felten, E.W.: Mixcoin: anonymity for bitcoin with accountable mixes. In: Proceedings of Financial Cryptography and Data Security (FC) (2014)
7. Broséus, J., Rhumorbarbe, D., Mireault, C., Ouellette, V., Crispino, F., Décary-Hétu, D.: Studying illicit drug trafficking on darknet markets: structure and organisation from a Canadian perspective. Forensic Sci. Int. **264**, 7–14 (2016)
8. Christin, N.: Traveling the silk road: a measurement analysis of a large anonymous online marketplace. In: Proceedings of World Wide Web (WWW) (2013)
9. Conti, M., Gangwal, A., Ruj, S.: On the economic significance of ransomware campaigns: a bitcoin transactions perspective. Comput. Secur. **79**, 162–189 (2018)
10. Gomez, G., Moreno-Sanchez, P., Caballero, J.: Watch your back: identifying cybercrime financial relationships in bitcoin through back-and-forth exploration. In: Proceedings of ACM Computer and Communications Security (CCS) (2022)
11. Harrigan, M., Fretter, C.: The unreasonable effectiveness of address clustering. In: Proceedings of UIC/ATC/ScalCom/CBDCom/IoP/SmartWorld (2016)
12. Herrera-Joancomartí, J.: Research and challenges on bitcoin anonymity. In: Proceedings of Workshop on Data Privacy Management (DPM) (2015)
13. Huang, D.Y., et al.: Tracking ransomware end-to-end. In: Proceedings of IEEE Symposium on Security and Privacy (S&P) (2018)
14. Huang, D.Y., et al.: Botcoin: monetizing stolen cycles. In: Proceedings of Network and Distributed System Security Symposium (NDSS) (2014)
15. International Monetary Fund: IMF.org (2023). Accessed 15 Oct 2023
16. Investing.com: Bitcoin Historical Data (2023). https://www.investing.com/crypto/bitcoin/historical-data. Accessed 17 May 2023
17. Kharraz, A., Robertson, W., Balzarotti, D., Bilge, L., Kirda, E.: Cutting the gordian knot: a look under the hood of ransomware attacks. In: Proceedings of Detection of Intrusions and Malware, and Vulnerability Assessment (DIMVA) (2015)
18. Lee, S., et al.: Cybercriminal minds: an investigative study of cryptocurrency abuses in the dark web. In: Proceedings of Network and Distributed System Security Symposium (NDSS) (2019)
19. Li, X., Yepuri, A., Nikiforakis, N.: Double and nothing: understanding and detecting cryptocurrency giveaway scams. In: Proceedings of Network and Distributed System Security Symposium (NDSS) (2023)
20. Liao, K., Zhao, Z., Doupé, A., Ahn, G.J.: Behind closed doors: measurement and analysis of cryptolocker ransoms in bitcoin. In: Proceedings of Electronic Crime Research (eCrime) (2016)
21. Massey, F.J., Jr.: The Kolmogorov-Smirnov test for goodness of fit. J. Am. Stat. Assoc. **46**(253), 68–78 (1951)
22. Meiklejohn, S., et al.: A fistful of bitcoins: characterizing payments among men with no names. In: Proceedings of ACM Internet Measurement Conference (IMC) (2016)
23. Möser, M., Böhme, R., Breuker, D.: An inquiry into money laundering tools in the bitcoin ecosystem. In: Proceedings of APWG eCrime Researchers Summit (2013)
24. Myung, I.J.: Tutorial on maximum likelihood estimation. J. Math. Psychol. (2003)

25. Oggier, F., Datta, A., Phetsouvanh, S.: An ego network analysis of sextortionists. Soc. Netw. Anal. Mining **10**, 1–14 (2020)
26. Paquet-Clouston, M., Romiti, M., Haslhofer, B., Charvat, T.: Spams meet cryptocurrencies: Sextortion in the bitcoin ecosystem. In: Proceedings of ACM Advances in Financial Technologies (AFT) (2019)
27. Pastrana, S., Hutchings, A., Thomas, D., Tapiador, J.: Measuring ewhoring. In: Proceedings of ACM Internet Measurement Conference (IMC) (2019)
28. Pastrana, S., Suarez-Tangil, G.: A first look at the crypto-mining malware ecosystem: a decade of unrestricted wealth. In: Proceedings of ACM Internet Measurement Conference (IMC) (2019)
29. Pletinckx, S., Trap, C., Doerr, C.: Malware coordination using the blockchain: an analysis of the cerber ransomware. In: Proceedings of IEEE Communications and Network Security (CNS) (2018)
30. Portnoff, R.S., Huang, D.Y., Doerfler, P., Afroz, S., McCoy, D.: Backpage and bitcoin: uncovering human traffickers. In: Proceedings of Knowledge Discovery and Data Mining (KDD) (2017)
31. Reid, F., Harrigan, M.: An Analysis of Anonymity in the Bitcoin System. Springer, Heidelberg (2013)
32. Ron, D., Shamir, A.: How did dread pirate roberts acquire and protect his bitcoin wealth? In: Proceedings of Financial Cryptography and Data Security (FC) (2014)
33. Ruffing, T., Moreno-Sanchez, P., Kate, A.: Coinshuffle: practical decentralized coin mixing for bitcoin. In: Proceedings of ESORICS (2014)
34. Small, B.: Scam emails demand Bitcoin, threaten blackmail – consumer.ftc.gov (2020). https://consumer.ftc.gov/consumer-alerts/2020/04/scam-emails-demand-bitcoin-threaten-blackmail. Accessed 17 May 2023
35. Spagnuolo, M., Maggi, F., Zanero, S.: Bitiodine: extracting intelligence from the bitcoin network. In: Proceedings of Financial Cryptography and Data Security (FC) (2014)
36. Staugh, G.: Bull capital trading review 2022: 5 disturbing facts about bullcapitaltrading.com (2023). https://www.forexbrokerz.com/brokers/bull-capital-trading-review. Accessed 2 Nov 2023
37. Taniguchi, T., Griffioen, H., Doerr, C.: Analysis and takeover of the bitcoin-coordinated pony malware. In: Proceedings ACM Asia Computer and Communications Security (ASIACCS) (2021)
38. Tekiner, E., Acar, A., Uluagac, A.S., Kirda, E., Selcuk, A.A.: SoK: cryptojacking malware. In: Proceedings of IEEE European Symposium on Security and Privacy (EuroS&P) (2021)
39. U.S. Bureau of Economic Analysis (BEA): GDP by State (2023). https://www.bea.gov/data/gdp/gdp-state. Accessed 15 Oct 2023
40. Valenta, L., Rowan, B.: Blindcoin: blinded, accountable mixes for bitcoin. In: Proceedings of Financial Cryptography and Data Security (FC) (2015)
41. Vu, A.V., et al.: Turning up the dial: the evolution of a cybercrime market through set-up, stable, and covid-19 eras. In: Proceedings of ACM Internet Measurement Conference (IMC) (2020)
42. Wang, K., et al.: A large-scale empirical analysis of ransomware activities in bitcoin. ACM Trans. Web **16**(2), 1–29 (2021)

Routing

Insights into SAV Implementations
in the Internet

Haya Schulmann[1,2] and Shujie Zhao[2,3(✉)]

[1] Goethe-Universität Frankfurt, Frankfurt, Germany
[2] ATHENE, Darmstadt, Germany
zsjstart@gmail.com
[3] Fraunhofer SIT, Darmstadt, Germany

Abstract. Source Address Validation (SAV) is designed to block packets with spoofed IP addresses. Obtaining insights into the deployment
and implementation of SAV is essential for understanding the potential
impact of attacks that exploit spoofed IP addresses and also poses an
interesting research question.

No current approaches for identifying networks that enforce SAV can
infer information on the specific SAV techniques employed by the network operators. To address this gap, we present the first study of the
SAV implementation techniques: Access Control Lists (ACLs) and unicast Reverse Path Forwarding (uRPF). While uRPF is more effective
than ACLs, our large-scale Internet measurement reveals that network
operators underutilize uRPF. Our study highlights the need for increased
efforts to incentivize uRPF adoption and achieve broader network security benefits.

1 Introduction

Packet spoofing is a basic building block in many network attacks. As a Best
Current Practice (BCP) for Internet security, Source Address Validation (SAV)
[RFC2827, RFC3704, RFC8704] [5,33,34] operates at the network boundaries
and validates the source IP addresses in packets to identify and block packets with spoofed IP addresses. Understanding the deployment of SAV across
Autonomous Systems (ASes) on the Internet can assist security researchers in
assessing the potential attack surface.

Numerous efforts have been dedicated to measuring the SAV deployment
across ASes [6,11,17,19–22,24]. However, current studies are confined to identifying the absence of SAV at the edge of a target network. They fail to locate where
on the path SAV filtering is enforced. This is relevant when SAV is deployed by
any of the ASes along the path to the target AS. This limitation hinders gaining
valuable insights into the techniques employed by network operators for implementing SAV. Exploring the adoption of SAV techniques (e.g., its prevalence)
would be of broad interest to both research and operational communities. It has
the potential to assist in addressing the challenges and limitations associated
with the deployment of specific techniques, as well as in developing advanced
approaches for SAV implementation.

© The Author(s), under exclusive license to Springer Nature Switzerland AG 2024
P. Richter et al. (Eds.): PAM 2024, LNCS 14538, pp. 69–87, 2024.
https://doi.org/10.1007/978-3-031-56252-5_4

Access Control Lists (ACLs) and unicast Reverse Path Forwarding (uRPF) are two primary approaches applied to SAV, enabling Internet Service Providers (ISPs) and network operators to ensure that only legitimate traffic flows to and from their networks. ACLs work by blocking incoming traffic from unauthorized sources using pre-defined prefixes, while uRPF utilizes BGP path forwarding tables to verify that the interface on which the incoming packet is received could potentially be used for communication with the packet source. However, ACLs are prone to errors due to manual updates and are not ideal in dynamic routing environments. The uRPF method is regarded as more flexible and effective than ACLs, particularly for larger ISPs [5, 34], extending security coverage to a wider range of addresses. We detail these two techniques in Sect. 2.

We perform the first empirical analysis of SAV implementation strategies across ASes, with a specific focus on two techniques: ACLs and uRPF. First, we identify the presence of destination-side SAV at the ingress of the tested networks. Once the SAV presence is determined, we proceed to verify whether it is implemented through ACLs or uRPF. The differentiation between the two techniques relies on AS topologies and AS relationships. We conduct an extensive evaluation of our methods by collecting data from 485,462 IPv4 web servers that support globally incrementing IPID (IP identification [RFC791] [30]) counters. These servers are distributed across 8,280 ASes, including 1,516 stub, 2,833 multi-homed, 3,913 transit, and 18 tier-1 ASes, spanning 195 countries. We use these servers as vantage points for SAV inference. We analyze the study results and derive two key findings:

(1) We find that 95.6% of the tested ASes adopted ACLs, indicating that ACL is the primary method for implementing SAV. Only 6 multi-homed edge, 45 transit, and 2 tier-1 networks that employ uRPF for SAV. This suggests a potential reluctance among network operators to employ this technique.

(2) We discover 26 ASes in which some/24 networks employ ACLs while others use uRPF. This finding suggests that the implementation of SAV may vary across subnets within an AS, indicating a decentralized approach to SAV implementation.

Organization. We explain SAV and IPID, and discuss related work in Sect. 2. In Sect. 3 we present our methodologies. We measure SAV implementations on the Internet in Sect. 4. We discuss the limitations and the ethical aspects of our research in Sect. 5. We conclude our work in Sect. 6.

2   Overview of SAV and IPID

Source Address Validation (SAV), also referred to as BCP38 [RFC2827] [33], is the de facto practice to prevent IP spoofing-based attacks. Two primary methods to implement SAV are Access Control List (ACL) and unicast Reverse Path Forwarding (uRPF) [5, 34].

ACL. An ACL defines a list of prefixes or addresses that border routers are permitted to forward, typically located at the boundary between the provider and customer network [23]. For example, if a network provider assigns 203.0.113.0/24

to a customer, the ACLs at the customer network edge would prevent all packets with source addresses other than 203.0.113.0/24 from leaving the network
and would prevent ingress packets with source addresses 203.0.113.0/24 from
entering the network.

uRPF. uRPF validates the source address in a received packet against the BGP
routing table to prevent IP address spoofing. Three typical modes for uRPF are
strict uRPF, feasible-path uRPF, and loose uRPF [34]. Strict uRPF mandates
that a router only accepts an ingress packet if it arrives on the same interface that
is used to forward the reply packet back to the source. In cases of asymmetric
routing or multihoming, this approach can block legitimate traffic [5]. Feasible-
path uRPF provides greater flexibility regarding directionality. It requires the
acceptance of an ingress packet if it arrives via alternative routes in addition
to the best route (which is required by strict uRPF). This makes feasible-path
uRPF more effective in complex network architectures. Loose uRPF has limited
effectiveness in preventing IP spoofing since it can only filter packets with bogon
or unallocated IP addresses.

Measurements of SAV. Inferring the deployment of SAV is a non-trivial task
due to the unavailability of confidential network data, such as network architectures or network management policies. Nevertheless, researchers have made
numerous efforts to achieve this through non-intrusive and creative means. One
long-term effort that has been studying network spoofability across the Internet since 2005 is the Spoofer project [6,20,22]. It requires volunteers to run the
Spoofer agent software on their networks. The agent spoofs the source IP address
in the sent packet and measures if spoofed packets are filtered. However, requiring the installation of agents imposes limitations on its coverage and scalability.
Other studies like [17,19,21,24] relied on configuration errors on a tested network
to verify whether the network filters packets with fabricated source addresses.
For example, [17,19,24] exploit the misconfiguration of DNS resolvers to identify
networks that do not block spoofed packets. These measurements are limited in
scope to networks that have misconfigurations. Once misconfiguration is fixed,
the measurement becomes ineffective. Additionally, the works [12,16] send DNS
queries with fake source IP addresses to recursive DNS servers within destination
networks to verify whether the spoofed queries can reach the DNS server. If they
receive the corresponding DNS query at the authoritative DNS server they control,
it indicates that the destination network lacks SAV deployment. More recently, Dai
and Shulman [11] developed a tool called SMap for inferring SAV absence remotely
by utilizing globally incrementing IPID counters. SMap shares a basic concept with
the TCP idle scan [4]. SMap sends fake packets to a host with a globally incremental IPID counter within the target network to perturb its IPID values and identify
the absence of SAV by detecting the resulting increase in the IPID value. Unlike
existing studies, our work focuses on developing methodologies to infer specific
SAV implementation techniques by network operators.

Global IPID. The IP Identification (IPID) field in the IP header is used to iden-
tify fragments of the same IP packet for reassembly at the destination [7,30,35].
Each outbound IPv4 packet is assigned a unique 16-bit IPID value by the server.
Global IPID refers to a sequentially increasing counter (referred to as the global

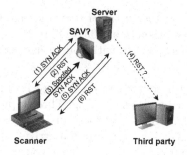

Fig. 1. SAV inference using IPID values. (1) The Scanner sends a SYN-ACK to an IPv4 server with a global IPID counter inside the target network. (2) The server responds with an RST containing the IPID value i in the IP header. (3) Scanner sends a SYN-ACK packet from an IP address of a third-party host to the server. (4) If SAV is not deployed, the spoofed packet reaches the server, and the server issues an RST packet to the third party, incrementing the counter. (5) Scanner sends another SYN-ACK. (6) The server responds with the current IPID value ($i + 2$ when the network lacks SAV).

counter) used for IPID allocation, which increments for all outgoing packets, without regard to their destinations [27]. Global counters are more efficient and easier to implement. They however also leak information on the volume of packets sent by the target server and hence can be used as a side-channel for indirect network measurements [11, 14, 26, 29, 36].

3   Methodologies

In this section, we develop methodologies to distinguish between networks that use different SAV implementation techniques. Since ACLs and uRPF are standardized techniques for implementing SAV as defined in RFCs, our main focus is on the identification of these two common techniques.

3.1   SAVscan

The widespread distribution of the global IPID side-channel, as demonstrated by [29], allows it to provide much better network coverage for measurements compared to techniques that rely on volunteers or agents, while also reducing the associated financial expenses. Similar to SMap, we also leverage global counters as vantage points for SAV inference. In this section, we introduce a tool called SAVscan, which relies on IPID increments to infer different SAV implementation techniques. It's worth noting that, while both our work and SMap employ IPID values for SAV inference, our work primarily focuses on distinguishing between SAV implementation techniques, setting it apart from SMap.

The fundamental process of SAV inference based on IPID increments is straightforward, as depicted in Fig. 1. The inference process involves sending SYN-ACK[1] packets with fake source IP addresses to the server with a global

---

[1] Inspired by the TCP idle scan, we utilize SYN-ACKs for probes.

Table 1. Experiment results of two classifiers in terms of the performance: macro-averaging precision, recall, F1-score, and accuracy on the holdout data.

	Precision	Recall	F1-score	HoldOut-Acc
DT	93.1%	92.9%	92.9%	92.2%
SVM	99.7%	99.7%	99.7%	98.6%

IPID counter inside a target network. If the network does not enforce SAV at the ingress, the spoofed packets will incur responses from the server, leading to an abnormal increase in IPID values.

Global Counter Identification. The initial step of SAVscan involves identifying global counters within target networks. To achieve this, SAVscan incorporates an IPID classifier, which is an improvement over the decision tree (DT)-based classifier proposed by Salutari et al. [31]. We integrate nine additional features extracted from the time and frequency domains of an IPID time series. Details about the features are provided in Appendix A.1. Following the previous work [31], we collect ground truth data for training a classifier and validating it. We begin by randomly selecting 5,000 web servers from Rapid7 [2], and we send 100 SYN-ACK packets to a random destination port[2] on these servers at a rate of one probe per second. We visually inspect captured IPID sequences over the measurement period and manually label them into five kinds of IPID time series: global, per-destination, random, constant, and odd. We exclude the IPID time series that contains missing values or any other types of noisy data, e.g., frequently changing global counters that appear like random IPIDs, resulting in a training data set including 788 global, 1048 per-destination, 815 random, 1000 constant, and 660 odd IPID time series. In addition, following the same procedure as the above, we collect 1000 new IPID time series respectively for each category as holdout data to test the performance of the classifier trained.

Assuming that various IPID time series are not linearly separable, we utilize the Support Vector Machine (SVM) model with an RBF kernel, which is commonly used for nonlinear classification, to validate our approaches. We train an SVM classifier on the features extracted from five types of IPIDs in the training dataset collected above. We normalize the features to the range of [0, 1] before training to prevent features with larger values from causing bias in the model. We apply grid search with 10 cross-validations for hyper-parameter optimization, and search for the regularization parameter C in the list of [0.01, 0.1, 1, 100, 1000, 10000], obtaining the optimal model when $C = 100$. We use the existing classifier proposed by Salutari et al. [31] as baselines for comparison with our classifier. The experimental results are presented in Table 1. Our classifier outperforms the previous one, achieving macro-averaging F1-score of approximately 99.7% on the training set and around 99% accuracy on the holdout data.

---

[2] We utilize random ports to avoid interference with commonly used services such as HTTP and DNS.

IPID Prediction. Based on an idealistic assumption that IPID values increase steadily, SMap utilizes a simple linear model to verify whether abnormal increases in IPID values have been caused by spoofed packets. However, this method is susceptible to network noise introduced by communication with other Internet sources, making it prone to errors in SAV inference. In contrast, SAVscan utilizes a machine learning model to learn the historical changing behavior of a global counter and predict future IPID values to assess the counter's predictability (i.e., the extent to which the IPID counter is predictable). The predictability assessment of SAVscan enables it to filter out noisy (less predictable) counters, ensuring reliable downstream SAV inference.

For a given IPv4 server with a sequentially incremental IPID counter, we collect IPID values by sending one probe per second. To enable learning of changes in historical IPID values, we utilize a sliding window with a size of 5, which allows for the prompt capture of new patterns in IPID changes while ensuring sufficient samples for learning. The sliding window is initialized by appending IPID values sampled until it reaches its maximum capacity. We employ a Gaussian Process (GP) model to fit historical IPID data within the window and forecast the IPID value for the next second. The GP model, being non-parametric, eliminates the need for extensive parameter tuning, making it suitable for fast forecasting. Before training a model, we fill in missing values in the IPID data by using existing IPID values (prior to missing data) to address the potential impact of packet loss on IPID prediction. Global IPID counters exhibit periodicity, i.e., resetting to zero when reaching the maximum value of $2^{16} - 1$, which can also affect the IPID prediction. We remove it using the following expression:

$$\Delta x_n = (x_{n+1} - x_n + 2^{16}) \bmod 2^{16}, \qquad n \in [0, 4]$$

with x representing raw IPID values. We direct readers to Appendix B for details about the GP model's training and prediction process. When a new IPID value arrives, we remove the first (oldest) value in the window and add the new value at the end for the next prediction. This enables continuous updating of the model with new data, ensuring accurate tracking and prediction of IPID values. To strike a balance between minimizing communication overhead and obtaining accurate IPID predictability, we conduct 30 predictions for each IP server. We use the mean absolute error (MAE) metric to assess prediction errors of the GP-based learning model. Lower MAE values indicate that the tested counter is more predictable, which is advantageous for accurate inference. In our measurements, we target servers with MAE values below ten[3], which ensures reliable SAV inference while maintaining a wide range of tested networks.

SAV Inference. Then, SAVscan utilizes the Gaussian distribution property of prediction errors to identify anomalous IPID increases caused by spoofed packets. This idea is inspired by previous studies, such as [9,10,15], which demonstrate effective anomaly detection in time series data. SAVscan models the errors generated by the GP model when making predictions as a Gaussian distribution

---

[3] Our experiments showed that around 70% of the tested counters exhibited an MAE value lower than 10.

function. For N (e.g., 30) IPID predictions, it computes the prediction errors $E = \{e_n\}$, $n \in [0, N-1]$, where $e_n = \hat{x}_n - x_n$. Since E follows a Gaussian distribution, the variable $Z = \frac{E-\mu}{\sigma}$ conforms to the standard normal distribution of $N(0,1)$, with μ and σ being the mean and the standard deviation of E. We formulate the null hypothesis for a Z-test as there is no significant prediction error at a given significance level α (e.g., 0.05).

Suppose we send a certain number of spoofed packets, denoted as n_s, between the $(N-1)_{th}$ and N_{th} seconds. When perturbations on the counter occur, it causes the value of e_N to decrease, namely $e_N = \hat{x}_N - (x_N + n_s) = \tilde{e}_N - n_s$, where $\hat{x}_N$ indicates the predicted value at the N_{th} second, and x_N represents the IPID value in the case of no spoofed packets sent. As a result, the e_N value would fall in the left tail of the distribution. Therefore, we use a left-tailed Z-test to detect anomalous IPID value increases caused by spoofed packets. We compute the p-value, i.e., $\Phi(\frac{e_N - \mu}{\sigma})$ and if the p-value is less than α, we reject the null hypothesis, indicating that an abnormal increase in the IPID value occurred, which in turn, suggesting a successful spoofing and an absence of SAV at the network ingress. Otherwise, it indicates that SAV on the path filtered the spoofed packets, resulting in a failed spoofing. We compute the number of spoofed packets sent (i.e., n_s) in Appendix C.

3.2 Locating SAV

As mentioned earlier, SMap can detect networks with a lack of SAV but cannot identify networks that deploy SAV. To investigate the techniques used for implementing SAV, SAVscan is designed to initially identify networks enforcing SAV by spoofing two different IP addresses: one from inside the target network (internal IP) and another from outside the network (external IP). As shown by (3) in Fig. 2, SAVscan, located in AS111, is measuring the target network using two spoofing tests, AS333, which has deployed SAV at its ingress. The first spoofing is aimed at verifying if SAV is present along the path from the measurement network (AS111) to the tested network (AS333), while the second is used to ascertain whether SAV is deployed at the ingress of AS333.

We begin by spoofing an internal IP from the address space of the tested network (203.0.113.0/24)[4]. Following SMap, we use the neighboring IP (203.0.113.2) of the target server (203.0.113.1) within the network as the first spoofed address. When the spoofed packets fail to reach the target server within AS333, it indicates that SAV is possibly applied on the path from AS111 to AS333. For instance, when the upstream network, AS222, employs uRPF at the ingress, the spoofed traffic would be filtered as they arrive from the wrong direction.

Then, we perform five consecutive traceroutes (e.g., using the MTR tool) to obtain a consistent AS path from the measurement network to the target, i.e., [AS111, AS222, AS333]. Measurement exits when the AS path changes. In the second spoofing, we choose an IP from the immediate upstream network (AS222) of AS333 as the return address. As depicted in the figure, we deceive the target

---

[4] We consider /24 networks as the smallest measurement unit.

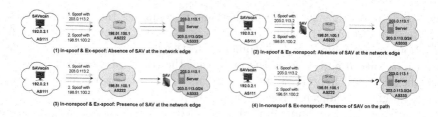

Fig. 2. Different spoofing states. "In" and "Ex" refer to spoofing the internal and the external IPs respectively. "In/Ex-spoof" and "In/Ex-nonspoof" mean the tested network is spoofable and non-spoofable when spoofing with the internal or external IP.

network with the IP address 198.51.100.2, which corresponds to the adjacent IP of the transit router (198.51.100.1) in AS222. In this case, if the upstream network, AS222, has deployed SAV (using uRPF or ACLs) at its network ingress, it would detect this forged IP and discard the bogus packets. Otherwise, the spoofed packets could potentially reach the target server. However, AS333's SAV is not effective in detecting the second spoofed IP as SAV could not handle such spoofed packets, regardless of whether it uses ACLs or uRPF: 198.51.100.2 is excluded from the AS333's ingress ACLs, and spoofed packets arrive via the same route as the return route, which also causes uRPF to fail to detect them.

We define four possible states in two spoofing tests, as illustrated in Fig. 2: (1) If both the internal and external IP addresses can be successfully spoofed, it indicates that SAV is not deployed at the target network ingress; (2) If only the internal IP can be spoofed, it suggests that SAV is absent at the network edge, but the immediate upstream AS (such as AS_{222}) has detected that the second spoofed IP address (i.e., the external IP) belongs to its own network and therefore discarded the spoofed packets; (3) If only the external IP can be spoofed, it implies that SAV is probably deployed at the target network ingress; (4) If neither address can be spoofed, it indicates that SAV is implemented on the path but is still unclear if SAV is present at the network ingress.

Note that the third state also suggests that other nodes along the path leading to the target network likely do not enforce SAV (e.g., AS222), or only enforce SAV (e.g., through ACLs) to secure their own addresses.

Our work exclusively focuses on the third state to extract networks with potential SAV deployment at the ingress for the subsequent inference of SAV implementation techniques. While in some cases, AS222 may perform SAV at its egress for AS333 (e.g., when AS333 is a customer network of AS222), we do not differentiate these cases. This is because the primary goal of the SAV deployment is to protect AS333, and thus, we still consider AS333 as deploying SAV at the network edge.

3.3   Identifying ACLs and uRPF

Subsequently, we differentiate SAV-enforcing networks that use distinct techniques: ACLs and uRPF. In cases of single-homed edge networks (i.e., stub

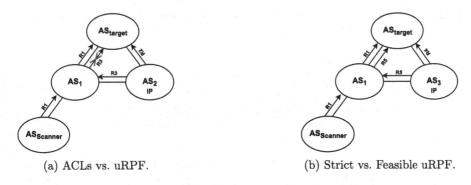

(a) ACLs vs. uRPF.   (b) Strict vs. Feasible uRPF.

Fig. 3. Identifying SAV implementation techniques.

ASes), uRPF operates in an equivalent manner to ACLs due to no directionality needed to be considered. Both of them discard incoming packets that appear to originate from inside the network. Thus, we exclude stub ASes from this analysis.

As shown in Fig. 3a, given a target network with the potential deployment of SAV (AS_{target}), we use SAVscan ($AS_{Scanner}$) to infer whether the SAV is implemented via ACLs or uRPF. "R1" is a BGP route sourced from $AS_{Scanner}$, while routes "R2" and "R3" are initiated by AS_2. Our approach is based on the premise that uRPF relies on traffic directionality, whereas ACLs do not. $AS_{Scanner}$ spoofs a source address ("IP" in the figure), and the spoofed packet travels along the "R1" path. Recall that, other nodes, apart from the target, in the path either do not use SAV or only secure their own addresses, which ensures that the spoofed packet is not dropped along the path. If ACLs exist at AS_{target}'s ingress, the spoofed packet passes through. To differentiate uRPF from ACLs, announcements for the spoofed IP address must not appear on the interface where "R1" route is received. This way, the spoofed packet would be filtered if AS_{target} uses uRPF.

As mentioned previously, we employ traceroutes to acquire the AS path ("R1") from the measurement network to the target network: [$AS_{Scanner}$, AS_1, AS_{target}]. We then select the spoofed IP address and AS_2 based on three criteria: 1) The spoofed IP is owned by a BGP neighbor of AS_{target}, such as AS_2; 2) AS_1 and AS_2 are BGP neighbors; 3) AS_1 does not announce routes learned from AS_2 to AS_{target} (see "R3").

Note that, in the second criterion, we require these two ASes to be BGP neighbors because ensuring no connectivity (direct and indirect) between them is more challenging. Neighbors in BGP typically include providers, customers, and peers. To determine whether two specific ASes are neighbors or not, we retrieve information about AS relationships (i.e., customer-provider, provider-customer, and peer-to-peer) from CAIDA [8]. BGP announcements should adhere to the valley-free routing policy, which means that an AS is not allowed to export announcements it learned from its peers or providers to other peers or providers. The third criterion cannot be met when AS_{target} is a customer of AS_1. Thus, measurement continues only when AS_{target} is a provider or peer of AS_1. AS_2

Table 2. Number of /24 networks and ASes identified across different spoofing states.

	In-spoof Ex-spoof	In-spoof Ex-nonspoof	In-nonspoof Ex-spoof	In-nonspoof Ex-nonspoof
/24 (#)	34,763	3,325	11,631	3,248
AS (#)	3,889	1,043	1,456	687

must be a provider or peer of AS_1. In this scenario, if we are unable to spoof the target network with such an IP, it indicates the use of uRPF at the network ingress. Otherwise, the network has ACLs installed.

3.4 Identifying Strict and Feasible-Path uRPF

Next, regarding networks identified as using uRPF, we conduct further spoofing tests to determine the specific type of uRPF implemented by the networks. As mentioned earlier, SAV based on loose uRPF only filters packets with unallocated IP addresses (e.g., bogon IPs). We exclude the identification of this uRPF type since this function can also be achieved through methods such as ACLs or strict/feasible-path uRPF.

In this spoofing test, we falsify the source IP address in packets with an IP from AS_3 (as shown in Fig. 3b). The selection of the fake IP and AS_3 must meet three requirements: 1) The falsified IP belongs to a BGP neighbor of the target network (AS_{target}), such as AS_3; 2) AS_1 and AS_3 are BGP neighbors; 3) AS_3 announces routes for its IP addresses to AS_{target} and AS_1 (see "R4" and "R5"), and AS_1 forwards announcements learned from AS_3 to AS_{target}.

For the third requirement, since AS_{target} is a provider or peer of AS_1 (as described in Sect. 3.3), AS_3 must be a customer of AS_1, in accordance with the valley-free BGP routing policy. In this scenario, if AS_{target} utilizes feasible-path uRPF, the spoofed packets transmitted via "R1" would be allowed to pass through since "R5", which shares the same interface as "R1", is a valid alternative route from AS_3 to the target network. However, if the strict uRPF is used, which prefers the best BGP route (i.e., "R4") when validating a packet against the forwarding routing table, the spoofed packets would be discarded.

Notably, we discuss technical limitations, including the reliance on AS relationships, in Sect. 5.

4   Measurements and Results

In this section, we collect global IPID counters used for measuring SAV deployment and implementation from the wild. To minimize potential load, we restrict our search for target servers to public infrastructure resources such as web servers associated with public domain names, avoiding the targeting of residential networks or hosts. We obtained a list of 100 million domain names from [1] and resolved their associated web servers, resulting in 6,782,310 unique IPv4 servers. We use SYN-ACK probes and send packets to a randomly selected destination port within the range [10000, 65535] to collect IPID values from the servers mentioned above and identify global counters using the SVM-based classifier. This yielded a dataset of 485,462 IPv4 servers with global counters, which are distributed across 8,280 ASes, including 1,516 stub networks, 2,833 multi-homed edge networks, 3,913 transit networks, and 18 tier-1 networks in 195 countries.

To minimize potential errors and biases in our measurements, we perform five rounds of tests on each server collected above. In each test, we send ten spoofed packets to avoid any inference with the tested network. We adopt IPv4/24 networks as the smallest unit for measuring SAV and conduct analysis at the AS level, consistent with existing research [16,18,22].

Networks Deploying SAV. We perform spoofing tests towards the 485,462 servers collected above to identify networks that deploy SAV at the ingress, and we exclude failed tests due to traceroute issues or non-compliance with the measurement conditions, obtaining a total of 515,934 results from 185,980 IPv4 servers residing on 53,563 /24 networks across 5,485 ASes. We filtered out 596 IPv4/24 networks with inconsistent results. The remaining results are presented in Table 2. Out of the tested networks, 3,579 ASes were identified as non-enforcing SAV at the network edge. 849 ASes had a partial deployment of SAV, in which some tested /24 networks can be spoofed while others can not. In addition, we discovered 1,456 ASes that have SAV deployed at the network ingress, covering 29,489 web servers with global IPID counters across 11,631 IPv4/24 networks.

Table 3. Distribution of SAV implementations across AS types.

	ACLs	Feasible	Strict	Hybrid
Multihomed (#)	125	3	1	2
Transit (#)	419	18	5	22
Tier-1 (#)	13	0	0	2

Networks Using ACLs, Strict and Feasible-Path uRPF. Subsequently, we performed IP spoofing tests on the identified SAV-deploying networks to distinguish between ACLs and uRPF. We exclude 181 stub ASes since ACLs and uRPF are not distinguishable in these cases. We conducted tests successfully on 8,258 IP addresses across 2,743 IPv4/24 networks in 610 ASes. The failed tests occurred because the test conditions were not met, such as the absence of an appropriate spoofed IP. We also excluded 25 IPv4/24 networks with inconsistent results and show the distribution of networks with implementation techniques for SAV in Table 3.

It can be seen that 583 (95.6%) ASes employed ACLs, indicating that ACLs-based SAV is the most commonly used technique for preventing IP spoofing.

Table 4. The AS number, the AS type, and the methods used for SAV in 18 replies.

ASN	Type	Method	ASN	Type	Method
2635	Edge	ACLs	8258	Transit	ACLs
24806	Edge	ACLs	559	Transit	ACLs
29081	Edge	ACLs	41075	Transit	ACLs
1205	Edge	ACLs	12637	Transit	ACLs+uRPF
29484	Edge	ACLs	12859	Transit	ACLs+uRPF
7034	Edge	ACLs	137	Transit	ACLs
224	Transit	ACLs+uRPF	1200	Transit	ACLs
8271	Transit	ACLs	39928	Transit	ACLs
39928	Transit	ACLs	15474	Transit	ACLs

Out of these networks, 26 use a hybrid technique of ACLs and uRPF ("Hybrid"). This finding suggests that SAV may vary across subnets within an AS, indicating that the SAV implementation could be decentralized. Our analysis also found that 27 ASes adopted uRPF, with the majority (21) using it in feasible-path mode. This is reasonable because feasible-path uRPF is a better option than strict uRPF, particularly for networks that often involve asymmetrical routing or multi-homing [34]. While uRPF is considered more effective in larger or more complex networks, our study indicates that this technique is underutilized, with only 6 multi-homed edge, 45 transit, and 2 tier-1 networks adopting uRPF. This finding aligns with our expectations because operators are often concerned about the loss of legitimate traffic when it arrives through an unexpected route.

Validation with Email Survey. To confirm our findings, we conducted an email survey of network operators. Given the potential concerns among network operators about disclosing their security weaknesses, especially among those with inadequate SAV deployment, their responses to our survey Email may be less likely. Therefore, the survey specifically targeted 610 ASes identified as having SAV deployed. We acquired email addresses through the *whois* tool. A total of 544 emails were sent, with the remainder being unobtainable. The emails inquired about the use of SAV and the associated techniques employed. We received 18 responses, which are listed in Table 4. All of them confirmed our SAVscan inference results.

It can be seen that, ACLs are the predominant method for preventing IP spoofing. This, in turn, indicates the reluctance of network operators toward using uRPF. Two ISPs, AS2635 and AS137, responded that they faced challenges in implementing uRPF. AS2635 stated that uRPF was not tenable for them due to their web services being hosted on their content delivery network (CDN), which was connected to multiple providers simultaneously, while AS137 reported that many of their clients lacked the technical skills required for uRPF adoption. The findings underscore the need to address concerns around uRPF, particularly the risk of discarding legitimate traffic in multi-homed networks. 3 ISPs used a combination of ACLs and uRPF techniques. For instance, AS12637 implemented ACLs or uRPF depending on available features on their routers. In contrast, AS224 used ACLs at the network edge, while their customers were required to implement uRPF on their individual local routers. These findings suggest that SAV can vary in how it's implemented within an AS.

The email survey findings align well with our measurement results, highlighting the widespread use of ACLs and the decentralized implementation of SAV within networks, which supports the effectiveness of our approaches.

5   Discussion

Limitations. Our methods rely on AS relationship data. Yet, accurately inferring this information is challenging without access to target networks. The dynamic nature of the Internet can lead to AS relationship instability. Future work will investigate robust techniques for AS relationship inference. We mainly focus on three SAV implementations: ACLs, strict uRPF, and feasible-path uRPF. The adoption of other complex SAV techniques (e.g., enhanced feasible path introduced in RFC8704 [34]) may impact our findings. We will focus future research on a wider range of SAV implementation techniques. Our approach employs rigorous criteria to select an appropriate IP for conducting spoofing tests, resulting in a smaller number of measurable networks. In cases where the AS relationship is unobtainable, it results in a lack of AS topology information, which also leads to unmeasurable networks. Future work will integrate new methods, including using BGP routing information to determine AS topologies, rather than relying solely on inferred AS relationships, to expand network coverage in measurements. In addition, our measurements were limited to paths between SAVscan and target networks. In cases where SAV exists in other paths, it remains unidentified. Future work will establish multiple measurement points to cover more AS paths to target networks. Inaccuracies in CAIDA's data, potential technical flaws in the MTR tool, and violations of the valley-free routing policy may lead to skewed findings in our research. Furthermore, obtaining ground truth data for SAV implementations is challenging due to data confidentiality maintained by network operators, posing challenges for our approach validation. We addressed this through an Email survey. While the survey findings closely align with our measurements, the limited number of respondents offers only partial validation support.

Ethical Considerations. In our study and data collection we follow the ethical guidelines for network measurements [13,28]. By following these ethical guidelines, we ensure that the equipment in the target networks is not affected and not overloaded. We also take precautions to minimize any negative impact on all parties involved in a test, such as inducing a one-second delay between consecutive probes, randomly selecting destination ports and limiting the number of spoofed packets sent to 10.

6 Conclusions and Future Works

We introduce methodologies to infer the implementations of SAV across IPv4 networks. Our evaluation yields two key insights: first, SAV implementation can be decentralized within a network, and second, uRPF has been underutilized by network operators. Our study provides the first empirical analysis of Internet SAV implementations and highlights the need to incentivize network operators to deploy SAV, particularly using uRPF, for wider security advantages.

This work is limited to utilizing SYN-ACK probes, which may restrict measurement coverage. Future work will include the use of other probes like ICMP and UDP. Our goal is to make the first step towards developing such a method and evaluating it on IPv4. The challenge of measuring uRPF on IPv6 is the size of the address space. Additionally, the IPID value in IPv6 is included in the fragment header appended to the packet when fragmentation occurs. To adapt the method to IPv6 would similarly require identifying servers that send fragments, which could result in increased measurement and communication overhead. The scan of the IPv6 is of independent interest which we leave for future work.

We make our SAVscan as well as the datasets public at https://github.com/zsjstart/SAV-Scanner.

Acknowledgements. This work has been co-funded by the German Federal Ministry of Education and Research and the Hessen State Ministry for Higher Education, Research and Arts within their joint support of the National Research Center for Applied Cybersecurity ATHENE and by the Deutsche Forschungsgemeinschaft (DFG, German Research Foundation) SFB 1119.

A SVM-Based IPID Classifier

The initial step of SAVscan is to identify global counters from target networks. To achieve this, SAVscan first incorporates an IPID classifier, which is an improvement upon the decision tree (DT) based classifier proposed by Salutari et al. [31]. The latter classifier relies on six features, including the entropy, expectation, and standard deviation of IPID sequences, to distinguish between five categories of IPID implementations. We implement an improved classifier with Support Vector Machine (SVM) model using nine additional features extracted from the time and frequency domains of an IPID time series.

Based on the various IPID assignments in [31], four primary types of IPID time series are outlined: global IPID time series from global counters, per-destination/per-host IPID time series from per-destination counters, random IPID time series from random number generators, constant IPID time series from unchanged IPID allocations. Figures 4 and 5 display four types of IPID time series in the time and frequency domains, respectively, demonstrating noticeable differences between them.

A.1   Features

We send N requests to a given IP server at a constant rate of one packet per second (1 pps or 1 Hz), alternately using two unique IP addresses (which can distinguish between global and per-destination counters), and extract IPID values x_n from responses, resulting in an IPID time series, denoted as $(x_n, t_n), n \in [0, N-1]$.

Let s be the N-length IPID time series, with a and b being the two subsequences collected by two unique addresses. We first extract six features $Nwrap(a)$, $\Delta_{max}(s)$, $\Delta_{max}(a)$, $\Delta_{max}(b)$, $\overline{\Delta}(s)$, $Autocorr(s)$ from the time domain, introduced below in detail:

$Nwrap(\cdot)$: This operator measures the frequency of IPID wraparound (which occurs when the IPID value wraps to zero after reaching $2^{16} - 1$) in a sequence. For global IPIDs, the feature value depends on the rate of counter increase and approaches zero in a stable network with little or no wraparound during the measurement period. In contrast, for random IPIDs, the feature value approximates 50%, with the extreme case being wraparounds occurring every two seconds.

$\Delta_{max}(\cdot)$ and $\overline{\Delta}(\cdot)$: We define Δx_n as the difference between two consecutive IPID values to remove the potential periodicity (i.e., the IPID value periodically changes from zero to $2^{16} - 1$) in IPID samples:

$$\Delta x_n = (x_{n+1} - x_n + 2^{16}) \bmod 2^{16}, \qquad n \in [0, N-2]$$

$\Delta_{max}(\cdot)$ refers to the maximum difference in a given sequence, while $\overline{\Delta}(\cdot)$ means the average difference in an N-length time series:

$$\overline{\Delta} = \frac{1}{N-1} \sum_{n=0}^{N-2} \Delta x_n$$

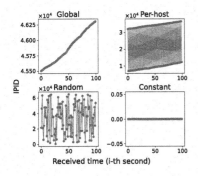

Fig. 4. IPID values of four categories changing over 100 s.

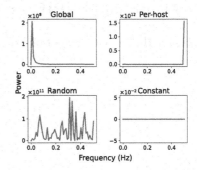

Fig. 5. DFT power spectra over a half frequency period (0, 0.5) Hz.

$\Delta_{max}(s)$ or $\overline{\Delta}(s)$ will be extremely large for per-destination or random IPIDs because the sequence contains many negative increments between two consecutive IPID values.

$Autocorr(\cdot)$: This operator measures the linear relationship between a given time series and itself using Pearson's correlation [25] at lag $= 1$. Global IPID sequences exhibit a strong positive relationship ($Autocorr(s) = +1$), whereas per-destination sequences show a negative relationship. We assign a zero value to this feature of constant IPIDs since no correlation is defined for this class. This has no impact on IPID identification, as all other features of this class are also zeros.

Next, we transform the N-sample IPID sequence into frequency components using Discrete Fourier Transform (DFT):

$$X_k = \sum_{n=0}^{N-1} x_n e^{-\frac{i2\pi}{N}kn}, \qquad f_k = k\frac{f_s}{N}, k \in [0, N-1]$$

where X_k is the k_{th} element of the DFT and f_k represents its corresponding frequency. We subtract the mean of IPID values in the time domain to eliminate the DC (zero frequency) component in the frequency domain to avoid the effect on the analysis of other frequencies. Three features are selected from the frequency domain:

f_d: it refers to the corresponding frequency at the peak of the power spectrum [32]. For per-destination IPIDs, we expect a peak at the frequency of 0.5 Hz (e.g., at a sampling rate of 1 Hz, the per-destination IPID has a period of 2 s).

B: it means the width of the frequency band in which 95% of the total power is located [3]. Ideally, random IPIDs have a broadband spectrum characteristic, while global IPIDs have a narrowband as they only contain low frequencies.

$f_{rolloff}$: it represents the frequency, under which 85% of the total power lies [3]. The $f_{rolloff}$ value of global IPIDs is relatively small due to their low frequency properties.

B   Algorithm for IPID Prediction

We display the pseudo-code of our IPID prediction approach in Algorithm 1.

Algorithm 1: Pseudo-code of IPID prediction

```
 1: for each ip ∈ ip_list do
 2:     Probe the IP server per second
 3:     Append the IPID value into the sliding window
 4:     if the sliding window is full (with the data: x₀, x₁, x₂, x₃, x₄) then
 5:         Fill in missing values if applicable
 6:         Remove IPID periodicity and obtain: Δx₀, Δx₁, Δx₂, Δx₃
 7:         Train a model with model inputs: [Δx₀ Δx₁; Δx₁ Δx₂] and model outputs: [Δx₂; Δx₃] (assum-
            ing the model with two inputs and one output)
 8:         Make a prediction with the input [Δx₂ Δx₃] and obtain the output [Δx̂₄]
 9:         Restore IPID periodicity and obtain a predicted value for the next second
            (e.g., the fifth second): (x₄ + Δx̂₄) mod 2¹⁶
10:        Remove the first value from the sliding window
11:    end if
12:    Repeat step 2 to step 11 until N (e.g., 30) IPID predictions
13: end for
```

C   Spoofed Packet Number

We then estimate how many packets need to be sent for the perturbation of the counter to work. Aforementioned, there will be $\Phi(\frac{e_N - \mu}{\sigma}) \leq \alpha$ in the case of successful IPID perturbation. Then we deduce the value of n_s as follows:

$$\frac{e_N - \mu}{\sigma} \leq \Phi^{-1}(\alpha)$$

$$\tilde{e}_N - n_s \leq \Phi^{-1}(\alpha) * \sigma + \mu$$

$$n_s \geq -\Phi^{-1}(\alpha) * \sigma - \mu + \tilde{e}_N$$

We use e_{max}, the maximum prediction error in E, as the estimated value of $\tilde{e}_N$ (which equals $\hat{x}_N - x_N$, with an ideal value of 0 when MAE is 0) to yield a relatively large n_s value, ensuring the triggering of the anomaly detection. We also ensure that we send at least one spoofed packet. Then, we define $n_s = 1 + \lceil -\Phi^{-1}(\alpha) * \sigma - \mu + e_{max} \rceil$. To mitigate potential harm to the tested network, we limit the number of spoofed packets sent to 10 during measurement.

References

1. Domains Monitor. https://domains-monitor.com/. Accessed 25 Jan 2023
2. Rapid7 labs. https://opendata.rapid7.com/. Accessed 11 Dec 2022
3. Fraunhofer AICOS: TSFEL documentation release 0.1.4 (2021). https://tsfel. readthedocs.io/_/downloads/en/development/pdf/. Accessed 2 Nov 2021
4. Antirez: http://seclists.org/bugtraq/1998/Dec/0079.html. Accessed 16 Jan 2022
5. Baker, F., Savola, P.: RFC 3704: ingress filtering for multihomed networks (2004)
6. Beverly, R., Bauer, S.: The Spoofer project: inferring the extent of source address filtering on the internet. In: USENIX SRUTI, vol. 5, pp. 53–59 (2005)

7. Braden, R.T.: Requirements for internet hosts - communication layers. RFC 1122, October 1989. https://doi.org/10.17487/RFC1122. https://rfc-editor.org/rfc/rfc1122.txt

8. CAIDA: https://publicdata.caida.org/datasets/as-relationships/serial-1/. Accessed 10 Oct 2023

9. Chandola, V., Vatsavai, R.R.: A Gaussian process based online change detection algorithm for monitoring periodic time series. In: Proceedings of the 2011 SIAM International Conference on Data Mining, pp. 95–106. SIAM (2011)

10. Chauhan, S., Vig, L.: Anomaly detection in ECG time signals via deep long short-term memory networks. In: 2015 IEEE International Conference on Data Science and Advanced Analytics (DSAA), pp. 1–7. IEEE (2015)

11. Dai, T., Shulman, H.: SMap: internet-wide scanning for spoofing. In: Annual Computer Security Applications Conference, pp. 1039–1050 (2021)

12. Deccio, C., Hilton, A., Briggs, M., Avery, T., Richardson, R.: Behind closed doors: a network tale of spoofing, intrusion, and false DNS security. In: Proceedings of the ACM Internet Measurement Conference, pp. 65–77 (2020)

13. Durumeric, Z., Wustrow, E., Halderman, J.A.: ZMap: fast internet-wide scanning and its security applications. In: USENIX Security Symposium, vol. 8, pp. 47–53 (2013)

14. Ensafi, R., Knockel, J., Alexander, G., Crandall, J.R.: Detecting intentional packet drops on the internet via TCP/IP side channels. In: Faloutsos, M., Kuzmanovic, A. (eds.) PAM 2014. LNCS, vol. 8362, pp. 109–118. Springer, Cham (2014). https://doi.org/10.1007/978-3-319-04918-2_11

15. Guo, T., Xu, Z., Yao, X., Chen, H., Aberer, K., Funaya, K.: Robust online time series prediction with recurrent neural networks. In: 2016 IEEE International Conference on Data Science and Advanced Analytics (DSAA), pp. 816–825. IEEE (2016)

16. Korczyński, M., Nosyk, Y., Lone, Q., Skwarek, M., Jonglez, B., Duda, A.: Don't forget to lock the front door! Inferring the deployment of source address validation of inbound traffic. In: Sperotto, A., Dainotti, A., Stiller, B. (eds.) PAM 2020. LNCS, vol. 12048, pp. 107–121. Springer, Cham (2020). https://doi.org/10.1007/978-3-030-44081-7_7

17. Kührer, M., Hupperich, T., Rossow, C., Holz, T.: Exit from hell? Reducing the impact of Amplification DDoS attacks. In: 23rd USENIX Security Symposium (USENIX Security 14), pp. 111–125 (2014)

18. Liu, B., Bi, J., Vasilakos, A.V.: Toward incentivizing anti-spoofing deployment. IEEE Trans. Inf. Forensics Secur. 9(3), 436–450 (2014)

19. Lone, Q., Frik, A., Luckie, M., Korczyński, M., van Eeten, M., Ganán, C.: Deployment of source address validation by network operators: a randomized control trial. In: Proceedings of the IEEE Security and Privacy (S&P) (2022)

20. Lone, Q., Luckie, M., Korczyński, M., Asghari, H., Javed, M., Van Eeten, M.: Using crowdsourcing marketplaces for network measurements: the case of Spoofer. In: 2018 Network Traffic Measurement and Analysis Conference (TMA), pp. 1–8. IEEE (2018)

21. Lone, Q., Luckie, M., Korczyński, M., van Eeten, M.: Using loops observed in traceroute to infer the ability to Spoof. In: Kaafar, M.A., Uhlig, S., Amann, J. (eds.) PAM 2017. LNCS, vol. 10176, pp. 229–241. Springer, Cham (2017). https://doi.org/10.1007/978-3-319-54328-4_17

22. Luckie, M., Beverly, R., Koga, R., Keys, K., Kroll, J.A., Claffy, K.: Network hygiene, incentives, and regulation: deployment of source address validation in the internet. In: Proceedings of the 2019 ACM SIGSAC Conference on Computer and Communications Security, pp. 465–480 (2019)
23. MANRS: Anti-Spoofing - Preventing traffic with spoofed source IP addresses. https://www.manrs.org/netops/guide/antispoofing/. Accessed 25 Jan 2023
24. Mauch, J.: Spoofing ASNs. https://seclists.org/nanog/2013/Aug/132. Accessed 25 Jan 2023
25. Mukaka, M.M.: A guide to appropriate use of correlation coefficient in medical research. Malawi Med. J. **24**(3), 69–71 (2012)
26. NMAP: TCP Idle Scan. https://nmap.org/book/idlescan.html. Accessed 10 Nov 2022
27. Orevi, L., Herzberg, A., Zlatokrilov, H.: DNS-DNS: DNS-based De-NAT scheme. In: Camenisch, J., Papadimitratos, P. (eds.) CANS 2018. LNCS, vol. 11124, pp. 69–88. Springer, Cham (2018). https://doi.org/10.1007/978-3-030-00434-7_4
28. Partridge, C., Allman, M.: Ethical considerations in network measurement papers. Commun. ACM **59**(10), 58–64 (2016)
29. Pearce, P., Ensafi, R., Li, F., Feamster, N., Paxson, V.: Augur: internet-wide detection of connectivity disruptions. In: 2017 IEEE Symposium on Security and Privacy (SP), pp. 427–443. IEEE (2017)
30. Postel, J.: Internet protocol. RFC 791, RFC Editor, September 1981. https://www.rfc-editor.org/info/rfc791
31. Salutari, F., Cicalese, D., Rossi, D.J.: A closer look at IP-ID behavior in the wild. In: Beverly, R., Smaragdakis, G., Feldmann, A. (eds.) PAM 2018. LNCS, vol. 10771, pp. 243–254. Springer, Cham (2018). https://doi.org/10.1007/978-3-319-76481-8_18
32. Semmlow, J.: The Fourier transform and power spectrum: implications and applications. In: Semmlow, J. (ed.) Signals and Systems for Bioengineers, 2nd edn., pp. 131–165. Biomedical Engineering, Academic Press, Boston (2012). https://doi.org/10.1016/B978-0-12-384982-3.00004-3. https://www.sciencedirect.com/science/article/pii/B9780123849823000043
33. Senie, D., Ferguson, P.: Network ingress filtering: defeating denial of service attacks which employ IP source address spoofing. RFC 2827, May 2000. https://doi.org/10.17487/RFC2827. https://www.rfc-editor.org/info/rfc2827
34. Sriram, K., Montgomery, D., Haas, J.: RFC 8704 enhanced feasible-path unicast reverse path forwarding (2020)
35. Touch, D.J.D.: Updated Specification of the IPv4 ID Field. RFC 6864, February 2013. https://doi.org/10.17487/RFC6864. https://rfc-editor.org/rfc/rfc6864.txt
36. Zhang, X., Knockel, J., Crandall, J.R.: ONIS: inferring TCP/IP-based trust relationships completely off-path. In: IEEE INFOCOM 2018-IEEE Conference on Computer Communications, pp. 2069–2077. IEEE (2018)

A Tale of Two Synergies: Uncovering RPKI Practices for RTBH at IXPs

Ioana Livadariu[1,5(✉)], Romain Fontugne[2,5], Amreesh Phokeer[3,5], Massimo Candela[4,5], and Massimiliano Stucchi[4,5]

[1] Simula Metropolitan, Oslo, Norway
ioana@simula.no
[2] IIJ Research Laboratory, Tokyo, Japan
romain@iij.ad.jp
[3] Internet Society, Reston, USA
phokeer@isoc.org
[4] NTT, Barneveld, The Netherlands
massimo@ntt.net, max@stucchi.ch
[5] AS58280, Brüttisellen, Switzerland

Abstract. Denial of Service (DoS) attacks and route hijacking have become the most predominant network attacks. To address these threats, network operators currently rely on mitigation services like Remotely Triggered Black Hole (RTBH) and Resource Public Key Infrastructure (RPKI). In this paper, we seek to understand how operators leverage both of these mechanisms. Using data collected at multiple IXPs we infer network operators that use RTBH services. We collect RPKI data for the same set of organizations and determine which of those rely on both RTBH and RPKI. One-third of the selected operators do not use any of these services, while most of the ASes that trigger blackholes also deploy RPKI. Some of these operators employ poor RPKI practices that make their prefixes vulnerable to attacks. However, most operators rely on an RTBH-agnostic approach indicating the need to devise an approach that effectively combines these two mechanisms.

1 Introduction

Distributed Denial of Service (DDoS) attacks are a pervasive threat to networking services and generally to the Internet Infrastructure itself. There have been different research studies to address the impact of DDoS attacks at scale [1–4], but in practice, they are difficult to tackle as they exploit the fault lines of the Internet, mainly due to the inherent lack of security at the protocol level.

Remotely Triggered Black Hole (RTBH) is a DDoS mitigation technique used to filter out undesirable traffic before it enters a protected network. BGP blackholing is signaled through BGP communities through "special" BGP announcements [5] that allow network operators to block unwanted traffic towards a specific destination. Network operators that rely on blackholing drop traffic towards these targets, thus making them unreachable. Hence, this mitigation approach

P. Richter et al. (Eds.): PAM 2024, LNCS 14538, pp. 88–103, 2024.
https://doi.org/10.1007/978-3-031-56252-5_5

is highly effective against high-volume attacks. Many Internet Exchange Points (IXPs) have implemented RTBH to help protect participants' networks against unwanted traffic. However, as for any BGP announcement, blackhole routes are vulnerable to BGP hijacks such as prefix mis-origination and AS-path manipulation attacks. A solution to mitigate prefix mis-origination is to use Resource Public Key Infrastructure (RPKI) [6]. Using RPKI, network operators "authorize" specific Autonomous Systems (ASes) to originate their prefixes. This information is saved in the Route Origin Authorizations (ROAs) object which includes the prefix, the origin ASN, and the maximum length for the prefix.

In this paper, we analyze the prevalence of RPKI as a means to protect RTBH announcements against prefix mis-origination attacks but also we seek to understand the "challenging synergy" between these two frameworks. On one hand, RTBH is designed for fast[1], sporadic, and very specific BGP announcements, while on the other hand, RPKI is designed to cover routes planned by operators, therefore avoiding overly specific prefixes (e.g., /32 for IPv4 and /128 for IPv6 address space). RTBH makes use of hyper-specific prefixes (greater than /24 in IPv4 and /48 in IPv6, or possibly even /32 in IPv4 and /128 in IPv6) and is very common at IXPs [8]. However, RFC 9319 recommends that operators SHOULD NOT create non-minimal ROAs (i.e., with max-length = /32 for IPv4 or /128 for IPv6) as it makes the announcement vulnerable to forged-origin sub-prefix hijacks and even discourages the use of RPKI to protect blackhole prefixes [9]. Currently, there are no mechanisms that combine the functionality of these two frameworks. Hence, network operators that use both systems have to find RPKI workarounds to ensure the RTBH effectiveness.

We seek to understand how operators use RPKI to protect RTBH announcements by collecting and analyzing BGP updates from 27 Internet Exchange Point (IXP) route servers [10]. We found that approximately 10% of the 2665 ASes that peer at the IXPs rely on the IXPs' blackholing service and most of the blackholed prefixes are /32 s for IPv4 and /128 s for IPv6. We also collected and analyzed RPKI data from the RIPE archive [11] to get a comprehensive view of the ROAs created by operators. Our results show that one-third of these operators do not deploy any of these two mechanisms, while most of the ASes that use RTBH also deploy RPKI.

Using these two datasets, we analyze how the RPKI management practices of the network operators impact the effectiveness of the RTBH announcements. Our analysis shows that few operators register very specific ROAs (/32 IPv4 and /128 IPv6) for IPs that are susceptible to DoS attacks. We also find that some operators create ROAs with a maximum value for the maxLength attribute. Networks that use this approach, however, can potentially have their IP address space hijacked [12]. However, most of the operators appear to rely on the IXPs' blackholing services which means that RTBH announcements from these members are going to be most likely rejected.

---

[1] A recent study by Fontugne et al. [7] showed that RPKI can add significant delays to the propagation of BGP announcements.

2 Background and Related Work

2.1 RTBH and RPKI

Remotely Triggered Black Hole (RTBH). BGP blackholing is a common technique used to mitigate DoS attacks. Network operators that detect such attacks on specific targets in their network can rely on BGP updates to blackhole the traffic towards these targets and thus making these destinations unreachable. Hence, this mitigation approach is highly effective when the attack volume is high. IXPs are interconnection points in the Internet infrastructure that facilitate traffic exchange among a significant number of networks. Thus, IXPs are the perfect locations to implement blackholing services. In fact, many IXPs provide RTBH services to protect their members from unwanted traffic. During such an attack, the victim announces the target IP prefix using a well-known *BGP blackholing community*. Route servers propagate the RTBH announcement to other IXP members. After accepting the BGP update, the traffic destined for the victim is forwarded to the blackhole.

Resource Public Key Infrastructure (RPKI). The Resource Public Key Infrastructure (RPKI) [6,13] is a public key infrastructure designed to protect operators against BGP hijacks. Network operators use RPKI to digitally sign Route Origin Authorization (ROA) objects, through which the IP address space owner states the *IP prefix(es)* and the *AS* number authorized to advertise the address block. ROAs also contain a *maxLength* attribute which allows the authorized AS to advertise multiple prefixes within the limits set by this attribute. Routers on the Internet use the information in RPKI (via a Relying Party) to validate incoming announcements through a process called Route Origin Validation (ROV). Based on the ROV outcome and on the router's local policy, ingress BGP announcements are either allowed or dropped.

ROV by IXP Route Servers. RTBH was not designed with RPKI in mind and vice-versa, hence an unplanned blackholing announcement is likely to be RPKI invalid and dropped by networks implementing ROV. Therefore, in order to make RTBH and RPKI work together IXP route servers have to implement exceptions to handle these special cases. From the considered IXPs, DE-CIX is the only IXP that documents a detailed approach to implementing ROV and RTBH [14]. Equinix also lists how it implements RPKI [15]. Specifically, the IXPs route servers employ a loose ROV process that disregards the ROA's maxLength attribute for matching BGP announcements marked with the blackholing community or next hop IP address. IXPs that rely on BIRD [16] can choose to implement the same approach as DE-CIX [17] for RTBH and ROV. Manually checking the IXP route servers in our study, we find that five route servers run BIRD [18–20]. Moreover, we devised and sent to IXPs a survey that aims to understand the current practices in RTBH and ROV. Note that we targeted the IXPs selected in this study. We received one reply that confirmed our assumption. This loose RPKI validation has the disadvantage of being vulnerable to maxLength attacks [9,12]. Furthermore, although the route servers allow IXP members to make these, strictly speaking, RPKI invalid announcements to propagate to other members, the members that implement ROV are likely to drop these announcements since the loose ROV process is deprecated for ASes.

2.2 Related Work

During the last few years blackholing has been the focus of several research studies [3, 21–25]. Streibelt *et al.* showed how the propagation of BGP communities can be exploited by third-party networks to trigger remote blackholing [25]. Focusing on the Internet-wide usage of blackholing, Giotsas *et al.* found an increase in the BGP blackholing activity [21]. The authors inferred RTBH services from a large number of transit providers and a few IXPs. In their work [3] Dietzel *et al.* analyze the usage of the blackholing service of one IXP over the span of three months and report heavy usage of this service. The same authors later proposed an advanced blackholing system [22]. Wichtlhuber *et al.* also proposed a machine learning-based system for detecting and filtering DDoS attacks at IXP that considers as input blackholing announcements [24].

The Internet Engineering Task Force (IETF) has placed significant efforts in developing the RPKI management system [6, 13]. Researchers and network operators have started studying different aspects of the RPKI deployment [7, 12, 26, 27]. In our work, we seek to evaluate how RPKI and RTBH can efficiently be utilized by network operators. A recent IETF draft [28] looked into this question and proposed an approach to combine both RPKI and RTBH. Thus, indicating the need to understand how these two systems can efficiently co-exist. To the best of our knowledge, no other measurement study has focused this problem.

3 Blackholing Activity at IXPs

3.1 BGP Data from RTBH-Enabled IXPs

We collect and analyze BGP data from Packet Clearing House (PCH) over the span of four months (from April to July 2022) to identify the prefixes blackholed by network operators. PCH maintains 217 route collectors hosted at different IXPs and located in 165 different cities across 95 countries [29]. In our study, we manually identify the PCH IXP route servers that publicly documented RTBH services. Thus, our collected BGP data comes from seven IXPs that are monitored by 27 PCH collectors located in Europe (16), United States (10) and Australia (1). Previous studies have extensively analyzed blackholing activity at IXPs [3, 22]. However, these studies focused only on one location, whereas our study includes a higher number of route servers. Moreover, our study does not solely focus on RTBH practices at the selected PCH route collectors but aims to understand the synergies between two network attack mitigation mechanisms.

The collected data includes BGP announcements originated by both the IXP members and their customers. In order to avoid wrong inferences due to BGP communities that are unintentionally propagating across multiple ASes [25] we filter out all BGP announcements originated by ASes that are not members of the IXP focusing in this study only on the IXP members. Consequently, our BGP dataset contains 239,345 IPv4 and 79,162 IPv6 prefixes advertised by 2665 ASes. These numbers are not uniformly distributed across the PCH route collectors, DE-CIX Frankfurt, Equinix New York, and France-IX Paris have the highest number of ASes originating prefixes.

3.2   Identifying Blackholed Prefixes

To identify when a blackhole is remotely triggered, we leverage the RTBH documentation provided by IXPs [30–34]. Members of the selected IXPs can blackhole traffic by crafting BGP announcements that either contain a specific BGP community and/or a specific next-hop IP address.

For most of the selected IXPs, this community is 65535:666, while the next-hop IP address varies from one IXP to another. We monitor these attributes in our BGP dataset and set the *start of a blackholing period* for a prefix when we first observe the blackholing community or next-hop IP address prefix BGP announcement information. The *end of the blackholing period* corresponds either to the blackholed prefix withdrawal or the prefix being re-announced without any blackholing signal (i.e., BGP community or next-hop IP address).

We identify 12,670 IPv4 and 32 IPv6 prefixes blackholed by 225 members across 24 (out of the 27) analyzed collectors. We compute the number of such prefixes at each monitor and plot in Fig. 1 these values. Our analysis also shows variability in the blackholing activity across the collectors. Significant part of prefixes are /32 s for IPv4 and /128 s for IPv6. For half of the collectors analyzed, we observe more than 400 IPv4 blackholed prefixes. We also found that some locations have more blackholing activities,

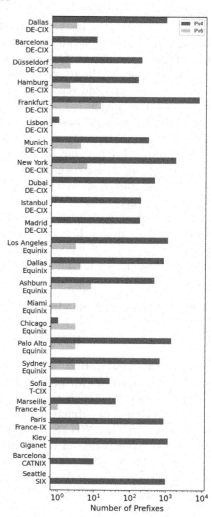

Fig. 1. Total number of unique blackholed prefixes at each of the 24 BGP collectors from April to July 2022.

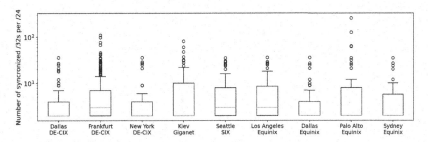

Fig. 2. Distribution of the number of synchronized /32s per /24 prefixes per collector. The figure shows only collectors with more than 150 blackholed IPv4 /32 prefixes.

for example, more than 10% of all prefixes observed at DE-CIX Frankfurt and Giganet Kiev are blackholed prefixes. We hypothesize that DE-CIX Frankfurt is a favored place for mitigating DDoS traffic because it is one of the largest IXPs, and the relatively high number of blackholed prefixes observed at Giganet Kiev is most likely due to the ongoing conflict in Ukraine [35–38].

Focusing on the ASes that trigger these blackholes, we observe an average of 57 IPv4 and 2 IPv6 prefixes per AS. Only one-quarter of the ASes blackhole more than 28 IPv4 prefixes. Thus, the overall number of blackholed prefixes is by a few members that appear to heavily rely on the RTBH service as the median value per ASN for IPv4 (IPv6) is 5 (1) blackholed prefixes. 75% of unique blackholing ASes seen across all collectors trigger blackhole prefixes at only one location. We observe that some ASes trigger blackholing at numerous locations. For instance, more than 10% of unique ASes were monitored across all collectors' blackhole prefixes at six different locations, usually including DE-CIX Frankfurt and Giganet Kiev. Our results confirm that in practice network operators rely on blackholing services for network mitigation attacks. Therefore, understanding the IXPs' practices for these services when coupled with RPKI is vital.

3.3 Synchronized Blackholed IP Prefixes

Having seen that network operators mostly blackhole very specific IPv4 address blocks (i.e., /32s), we further analyze whether these /32s share the same /24 prefix. One-third of the blackholed /32s are isolated as they solely map to different /24 address blocks. However, we find cases where the blackholed /32s cover most of their corresponding /24 prefix. Moreover, these blackholing activities are also synchronized in time meaning that the /32 prefixes belonging to the same /24 prefix have overlapping blackholing time periods. Half of all blackholed /32s are reported at the same time as related /32s (i.e. in the same /24). Figure 2 shows the number of blackholed /32s that are in the same /24 and reported at the same time. Note that we filtered out collectors with less than 150 blackholed /32s to improve the readability of the figure. Thus our plot shows only nine of the overall collectors. For almost all collectors the median value is equal to 2, meaning that we usually observe /32s blackholed by pair. Since the third quar-

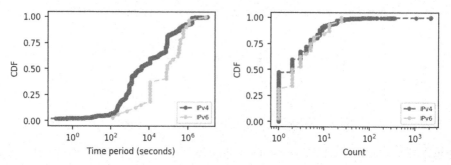

(a) Average blackholing periods per prefix   (b) Blackholing periods count per prefix

Fig. 3. Distribution of the (a) average blackholing periods and (b) number of periods per prefix.

tile is below 10 /32 s for most collectors, we usually observe a limited number of related /32 s reported at the same time but we found a few cases where more than 100 /32 s from the same /24 are blackholed at the same time (see outliers in Fig. 2). We further analyze the length of time during which pairs of prefixes are blackholed together and find that one-quarter of the pair prefixes are blackholed together for less than 17 min. At the same time, half of the prefix pairs are blackholed for at least 1007 min. Thus, our results show variability in the synchronized blackholed period.

3.4 Blackholing Time Periods

To better understand the temporal dynamics of blackholing activities we investigate the duration and recurrence of the identified blackholed prefixes. Figure 3 shows the distribution of the average period per prefix as well as how many times a prefix is blackholed. Most of the prefixes are blackholed at most ten times, with half of the IPv4 prefixes blackholed just once. A small number of IPv4 prefixes appear to be blackholed more than 100 times and two IPv6 prefixes are blackholed 17 times.

The overall blackholing period for each prefix is half of the prefixes approximately one hour. Still, we see a lot of diversity in the blackholing periods. One-quarter of the IPv4 prefix blackholed periods last at most 10 min, while 10% of the blackholed periods last more than 80 h.

4 RPKI Deployment

Using data from RIPE NCC's RPKI repository [11] we analyze the RPKI practices for blackholed prefixes. We thus fetch ROA records over the span of nine months, i.e., from January to September 2022. Our collected data comprises 336,338 IPv4 and 84,860 IPv6 RPKI ROA records registered for 34,212 ASes.

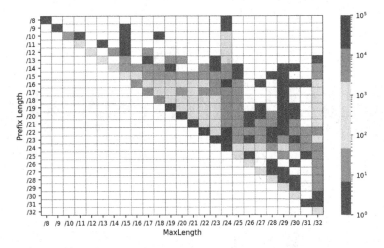

Fig. 4. Heatmap of the number of ROAs for IPv4 prefixes per prefix length and maxLength.

For approximately 42% of ASes that have registered ROAs, we find records for both IPv4 and IPv6 prefixes, while 52% and 6% of the ASes are registered only for IPv4 and IPv6 prefixes, respectively. We note that this result is consistent with the size of the IPv4 and IPv6 routing table.

Analyzing the ROAs across the five regions shows that 47%, 25% and 18% of these are registered within RIPE, APNIC and ARIN, respectively. ROAs registered with LACNIC and AFRINIC account for 8% and 1.5% of the ROAs. The observed ROA distribution is similar also for the ASes across the five registries. Through their policies, RIRs decide how long a ROA is valid and varies depending on the region. Specifically, ROAs for IPv4 prefixes registered in ARIN and AFRINIC are valid on average at least twice as long.

Breaking down the overall number of ROAs per prefix length shows that IPv4 /24 prefixes and IPv6 /48 prefixes represent approximately half of the IPv4 and IPv6 ROA records, respectively. Taking one step further we split these numbers per maxLength. Figure 4 shows the heatmap for the number of IPv4 ROAs per prefix length and maxLength. Our analysis shows that most ROAs maxLength follows the prefix length; 82.58% (277,766) of the ROAs for IPv4 prefixes satisfy this criterion. Our analysis of the IPv6 ROAs reveals similar results, i.e., for 86.75% (73,622) ROAs the maxLength is equal to the prefix length.

To ease their RPKI management organizations can register ROAs with the maximum maxLength, i.e., /32 and /128 for IPv4 and IPv6 prefixes, regardless of their prefix length. Hence a single ROA could authorize announcements for a prefix and its sub-prefixes. However, this practice is discouraged as attackers can hijack the registered resources by announcing the sub-prefixes [12]. In our dataset, we found numerous ROAs where the maximum *maxLength* is used (i.e. /32 for IPv4 and /128 for IPv6). Specifically, we find 4985 IPv4 and 592 IPv6 such ROAs which involve 942 ASes. Figure 5 plots the distribution of these ROAs

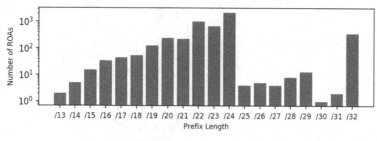

(a) ROAs for IPv4 prefixes

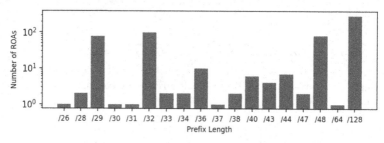

(b) ROAs for IPv6 prefixes

Fig. 5. Number of ROAs with *maxLength* is equal to (a) /32 and (b) /128.

per prefix length. We observe high variability among both the IPv4 and IPv6 prefixes and, although discouraged, the vast majority of these IPv4 ROAs are for prefixes that are not /32 s.

Focusing on our selected set of IXP members, we cross-check the advertised IP address space with the members' ROA information and filter the ROAs registered by the members. This step yields ROAs for 33,687 IPv4 and 4470 IPv6 prefixes registered for 1461 and 1031 ASNs. Among these ROAs, we also found cases where the IPv4 (IPv6) prefix length is also /32 (/128) and further focused our analysis on understanding if these ROAs are related to RTBH activities.

5   When RPKI Meets RTBH

5.1   Operators RPKI Management

RPKI object management can influence the effectiveness of RTBH announcements. For example, an operator can make sure that triggered /32 IPv4 or /128 IPv6 blackhole announcements are accepted by networks implementing ROV by registering the prefix in RPKI with the appropriate maxLength attribute beforehand. This is challenging in practice because of the fast response needed to mitigate DDoS attacks and the slow propagation of RPKI objects [7]. To further understand RPKI practice for blackholed prefixes, we devise three profiles that reflect how operators maintain their ROAs:

1. *RPKI-strict*: To comply entirely with the RPKI ecosystem operators may create very specific ROAs (/32 prefix) for IP addresses that are susceptible to DoS attacks. Thus, BGP announcements for RTBH will be RPKI valid and will be accepted by ROV-enabled networks. We believe that this approach comes with increased overhead as it requires a lot of planning that may not be possible for resources that may serve via arbitrary IP addresses.
2. *RPKI-loose*: An easier way to comply with RPKI is to create ROAs with a maxLength attribute set to /32 (/128) for IPv4 (IPv6) prefixes allowing BGP announcements for any prefix size. This practice is however strongly discouraged by the community, as it makes prefixes vulnerable to hijacks as shown by previous studies [12].
3. *RTBH-agnostic*: Operators may decide to manage their RPKI data as if they are not going to announce very specific prefixes for RTBH. IXPs' route servers implement mechanisms to handle these cases. If an RTBH announcement is made for a prefix covered by a ROA then the route server only validates the origin ASN disregarding the ROA's max length attribute. However, ROV-enabled networks will most likely drop these announcements.

Table 1. Number of IXP members per network operator profile that deploy RPKI.

Operator Profile	IPv4 ASes (Prefixes)	IPv6 ASes (Prefixes)
RPKI-strict	4 (4)	1 (1)
RPKI-loose	92 (553)	26 (44)
RTBH-agnostic	1438 (33177)	1021 (4731)
All Members utilizing RPKI	1461 (33687)	1031 (4770)

Using the members' ROAs from Sect. 4 we identify how these networks map to the three above profiles. Note that we deliberately chose different spanning periods for the routing and RPKI data, as we investigated whether implementing RPKI comes after a series of RTBH periods. Our initial results were however inconclusive. Out of all members for the selected IXPs, 98.42% of the members are RTBH-agnostic. We find that 4 (1) members have ROAs corresponding to the IPv4 (IPv6) RPKI-strict profile and 92 (26) members have IPv4 (IPv6) ROAs with maxLength set to /32 (/128). Tables 1 list the detailed number of ASes and prefixes for each profile. Analyzing whether operators rely only on one or multiple approaches to maintain their ROAs shows that in fact most of the operators map to one single profile. We list in Table 2 the number of members that map to just one single profile as well as multiple profiles. Most of the RTBH-agnostic operators choose only this approach for their ROA management. Some of these networks, however, also implement RPKI-loose or RPKI-strict practices for some of their IP addresses. Surprisingly, we find that a few operators rely only on the RPKI-loose approach.

Table 2. Number of IXP members per *unique* network operator profile that deploy RPKI.

Operator Profile	IPv4	IPv6
only RPKI-strict	0	0
only RPKI-loose	23	10
only RTBH-agnostic	1367	1004
RPKI-strict & RPKI-loose	0	0
RPKI-strict & RTBH-agnostic	2	1
RPKI-loose & RTBH-agnostic	67	16
All profiles	2	0

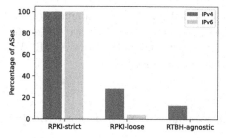

Fig. 6. Percentage of IXP members that blackhole IP addresses and deploy RPKI.

Table 3. Classification of IXP members per profile operator that *both* blackhole IP addresses and deploy RPKI.

Operator Profile	IPv4	IPv6
only RPKI-strict	2	1
only RPKI-loose	16	1
only RTBH-agnostic	172	6
RPKI-strict & RPKI-loose	1	0
RPKI-strict & RTBH-agnostic	1	0
RPKI-loose & RTBH-agnostic	9	0

5.2   IXP Member Classification

Our next step is to investigate the mapping of the devised profiles to IXP members which rely on blackholing services. To this end, for each AS we retrieve blackholed prefixes and their covering ROAs. One-third of the IXP members do not implement RPKI and are not using RTBH services. However, most of the AS that trigger blackholes also register ROAs in RPKI. Specifically, we find that 201 (8) of the 221 (15) AS that blackhole IPv4 (IPv6) prefixes also register ROAs. At the same time, our analysis reveals that few operators implement RPKI-strict and RPKI-loose practices. Table 3 provides the breakdown per profile. Unsurprisingly, we find that most of these are RTBH-agnostic. Recall that initially most of the network operators were mapped to this class. Still, our classification maps some of the operators to the other two profiles.

Figure 6 shows the percentage of ASes that trigger blackholing per operator profile. All the ASes that match the RPKI strict profile are using the RTBH services. The presence of ROA for /32 prefixes seems thus to be a good indicator of resources targeted by DDoS attacks. Unsurprisingly, blackholing ASes account for only 12.6% of all ASes that match the RTBH-agnostic profile. We find that a larger fraction (28.2%) of the RPKI-loose operators are using blackholing services for their IPv4 prefixes. Furthermore, we check whether the operators map to

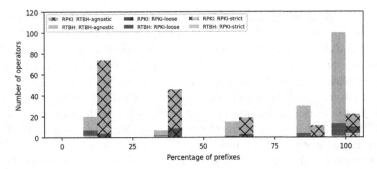

Fig. 7. Percentage of blackholed IPv4 prefixes (RTBH) and ROA prefixes (RPKI) that overlap per network per operator profile.

multiple profiles and find that 94% of the RTBH-agnostic operators are mapped only to this profile, while no operator is only RPKI-strict. Surprisingly, our results show that 16 operators are only RPKI-loose, which means that these operators have poor RPKI management for all their resources.

For the ASes that use both RPKI and RTBH, we investigate the overlap between the blackholed IP space and the IP space covered by ROAs. We find that for 172 of the 201 operators the registered ROAs overlap with the blackholed IPv4 addresses, and for IPv6 all eight members have overlapping ROA and RTBH spaces. Next, we group the overlapping percentage values into four intervals, 0%–25%, 25%–50%, 50%–75%, and 100%. Figure 7 shows the number of operators for each interval for the IPv4 address space. The pattern highlights the RPKI deployment. Our results show that 100 operators have registered ROAs for their entire blackholed IPv4 addresses. At the same time, we also find that 20 operators have only up to 25% of these IPs covered by ROAs. Our analysis of the members' RPKI deployment shows that for 74 of these organizations, the covering ROAs represent just up to 25% of their registered resources. For 22 members, the blackholed IPs match all their ROA records.

In addition, we analyze the time gap between the start of the blackholing period and the RPKI valid period. Most ASes triggering blackholes were already deploying RPKI for approximately one year on average. For only 120 blackholed IPv4 prefixes we find that the corresponding ROAs are registered after an average of 46 days. Our findings indicate that operators are more likely to blackhole their IP addresses whenever they suffer DDoS attacks. This in turn means that organizations place their trust in the IXPs.

6 Conclusion

RTBH and RPKI are frameworks currently used by a large number of network operators as mitigation techniques [14,39]. In this study, we seek to understand whether and how operators combine their functionalities. Currently, there is no standard that explains how to handle both RTBH and RPKI.

Using publicly available data we first characterize separately the RTBH usage by network operators at different IXPs. Then we rely on RPKI ROA data to devise three different operator profiles that characterize the operators' RPKI practices for RTBH announcements. RPKI-strict is impeding RTBH volatility since registering new ROAs takes significantly more time [7] compared to fast DoS response mechanisms. RPKI-loose is discouraged [12] although our results show that operators still implement this practice for both IPv4 and IPv6 prefixes. RTBH announcements from RTBH-agnostic operators are rejected by IXP members implementing ROV. Indeed ROV enabled networks disregard these RTBH announcements because they are RPKI invalid thus impeding the effectiveness of RTBH. Unless new mechanisms are designed to handle these cases, the effectiveness of RTBH is set to decrease as ROV gets more broadly deployed. Moreover, the RTBH-agnostic operators place their trust in the IXP blackholing services which implicitly increases the critical role played by IXP in Internet infrastructure.

Our study, however, comes with some limitations. Specifically, our initial set of IXP route collectors is relatively low since we study only IXPs that offer blackholing services. Also, our survey sent to the selected IXP regarding the RTBH and ROV practices only received one reply. The route collector selection process also impacts the geographic spread of the IXPs as most of the considered route collectors are based in Europe and US. Our analysis focuses only on the IXP members which represent a small fraction of the overall number of ASes.

Our results show that RTBH agnostic is the most common practice, so quantifying the current impact of ROV-enabled networks on RTBH is a good follow-up to this work. That is however out of scope for this paper as it requires significant research efforts in surveying which IXP members are implementing ROV and monitoring the way they handle RTBH announcements.

The considered three RPKI practices, however, do not offer a perfect solution in combining the two security frameworks. Thus, our current recommendation is that network operators follow current best practice of implementing a *RTBH-agnostic* RPKI approach, leaving to the IXP's the duty of checking the validity of RTBH requests. However, in the long term, operators and researchers should make an effort in devising and standardizing a technique that unambiguously describes the coexistence of RPKI and RTBH.

Acknowledgments. We thank the anonymous reviewers and our shepherd for their helpful comments. This research was supported in part by the MANRS Fellowship Program. Ioana Livadariu was partially funded by the SimulaMet's internal funding. We would like to thank the IXPs who responded to our survey.

A   Ethics

We are not aware of any ethical issue raised by this work. Our analysis relies on publicly available datasets.

References

1. Wagner, D., et al.: United we stand: collaborative detection and mitigation of amplification DDoS attacks at scale. In: Proceedings of the 2021 ACM SIGSAC Conference on Computer and Communications Security, pp. 970–987 (2021)
2. Czyz, J., Kallitsis, M., Gharaibeh, M., Papadopoulos, C., Bailey, M., Karir, M.: Taming the 800 pound gorilla: the rise and decline of NTP DDoS attacks. In: Proceedings of the 2014 Conference on Internet Measurement Conference, IMC 2014, pp. 435–448. Association for Computing Machinery, New York (2014)
3. Dietzel, C., Feldmann, A., King, T.: Blackholing at IXPs: on the effectiveness of DDoS mitigation in the wild. In: Karagiannis, T., Dimitropoulos, X. (eds.) PAM 2016. LNCS, vol. 9631, pp. 319–332. Springer, Cham (2016). https://doi.org/10.1007/978-3-319-30505-9_24
4. Kopp, D., Dietzel, C., Hohlfeld, O.: DDoS never dies? An IXP perspective on DDoS amplification attacks. In: Hohlfeld, O., Lutu, A., Levin, D. (eds.) PAM 2021. LNCS, vol. 12671, pp. 284–301. Springer, Cham (2021). https://doi.org/10.1007/978-3-030-72582-2_17
5. King, T., Dietzel, C., Snijders, J., Döring, G., Hankins, G.: BLACKHOLE Community. RFC 7999 (2016)
6. Lepinski, M., Kent, S.: An Infrastructure to Support Secure Internet Routing (2012). https://datatracker.ietf.org/doc/html/rfc6480
7. Fontugne, R., Phokeer, A., Pelsser, C., Vermeulen, K., Bush, R.: RPKI time-of-flight: tracking delays in the management, control, and data planes. In: Brunstrom, A., Flores, M., Fiore, M. (eds.) PAM 2023. LNCS, vol. 13882, pp. 429–457. Springer, Cham (2023). https://doi.org/10.1007/978-3-031-28486-1_18
8. Sediqi, K.Z., Prehn, L., Gasser, O.: Hyper-specific prefixes: gotta enjoy the little things in interdomain routing. ACM SIGCOMM Comput. Commun. Rev. **52**(2), 20–34 (2022)
9. Gilad, Y., Goldberg, S., Sriram, K., Snijders, J., Maddison, B.: RFC 9319 the use of maxlength in the resource public key infrastructure (RPKI) (2022)
10. Packet Clearing House. Internet Exchange Directory (2023). https://www.pch.net/ixp/dir
11. RIPE NCC. RPKI repository archive (2023). https://ftp.ripe.net/rpki/
12. Gilad, Y., Sagga, O., Goldberg, S.: Maxlength considered harmful to the RPKI. In: CoNEXT 2017. Association for Computing Machinery, New York (2017)
13. Lynn, C., Kent, S., Seo, K.: X.509 Extensions for IP Addresses and AS Identifiers (2004). https://www.rfc-editor.org/rfc/rfc3779
14. DE-CIX. RPKI at the DE-CIX route servers (2023). https://www.de-cix.net/en/resources/service-information/route-server-guides/rpki
15. Equinix. Resource Public Key Infrastructure (RPKI) (2023). https://docs.equinix.com/en-us/Content/Interconnection/IX/IX-rpki.htm
16. The BIRD Internet Routing Daemon. https://bird.network.cz/
17. Luciani, F.: Checking prefix filtering in IXPs with BIRD and OpenBGPD (2023). https://blog.apnic.net/2021/11/15/checking-prefix-filtering-in-ixps-with-bird-and-openbgpd/
18. FranceIX, RAPPORT TECHNIQUE Q1 2020 (2020). https://blog.franceix.net/rapport-technique-q1-2020/

19. PeeringDB: T-CIX Route Servers. https://www.peeringdb.com/net/8295
20. Diego Neto (NL-ix). BIRD route-server configuration: click, done! (2017). https://indico.uknof.org.uk/event/39/
21. Giotsas, V., Smaragdakis, G., Dietzel, C., Richter, P., Feldmann, A., Berger, A.: Inferring BGP blackholing activity in the internet. In: Proceedings of the 2017 Internet Measurement Conference, IMC 2017, pp. 1–14. Association for Computing Machinery, New York (2017)
22. Dietzel, C., Wichtlhuber, M., Smaragdakis, G., Feldmann, A.: Stellar: network attack mitigation using advanced blackholing. In: Proceedings of the 14th International Conference on Emerging Networking EXperiments and Technologies, CoNEXT 2018, pp. 152–164. Association for Computing Machinery, New York (2018)
23. Miller, L., Pelsser, C.: A taxonomy of attacks using BGP blackholing. In: Sako, K., Schneider, S., Ryan, P. (eds.) ESORICS 2019. LNCS, vol. 11735, pp. 107–127. Springer, Cham (2019). https://doi.org/10.1007/978-3-030-29959-0_6
24. Wichtlhuber, M., et al.: IXP scrubber: learning from blackholing traffic for ml-driven DDoS detection at scale. In: Proceedings of the ACM SIGCOMM 2022 Conference, SIGCOMM 2022, pp. 707–722. Association for Computing Machinery, New York (2022)
25. Streibelt, F., et al.: BGP communities: even more worms in the routing can. In: Proceedings of ACM IMC 2018, Boston, MA (2018)
26. Reuter, A., Bush, R., Cunha, I., Katz-Bassett, E., Schmidt, T.C., Wählisch, M.: Towards a rigorous methodology for measuring adoption of RPKI route validation and filtering. ACM SIGCOMM Comput. Commun. Rev. 48(1), 19–27 (2018)
27. Chung, T., et al.: RPKI is coming of age: a longitudinal study of RPKI deployment and invalid route origins. In: Proceedings of the Internet Measurement Conference, IMC 2019, pp. 406–419. Association for Computing Machinery, New York (2019)
28. Snijders, J., Abrahamsson, M., Maddison, B.: Resource public key infrastructure (RPKI) object profile for discard origin authorizations (DOA). Internet-Draft draft-spaghetti-sidrops-rpki-doa-00, Internet Engineering Task Force (2022, work in progress)
29. Packet Clearing House. PCH raw routing data. https://www.pch.net/resources/Raw_Routing_Data/. Accessed 25 May 2023
30. DE-CIX. Blackholing guide (2023). https://www.de-cix.net/en/resources/service-information/blackholing-guide
31. Equinix. Remotely Triggered Black Hole (2023). https://docs.equinix.com/en-us/Content/Interconnection/IX/IX-rtbh-guide.htm
32. Giganet. Blackhole (BGP) (2023). https://giganet.ua/en/service/blackhole
33. FranceIX. Blackholing (2023). https://www.franceix.net/fr/services/infrastructure/blackholing
34. SeattleIX. Blackholing (2023). https://www.seattleix.net/blackholing
35. Techtarget Security. Major DDoS attacks increasing after invasion of Ukraine (2022). https://www.techtarget.com/searchsecurity/news/252521150/Major-DDoS-attacks-increasing-after-invasion-of-Ukraine. Accessed 25 May 2023
36. The Record. DDoS attacks surge in popularity in Ukraine - but are they more than a cheap thrill? (2022). https://therecord.media/ddos-attacks-surge-in-popularity-in-ukraine-but-are-they-more-than-a-cheap-thrill. Accessed 25 May 2023
37. Computer Weekly. Ukraine war drives DDoS attack volumes ever higher (2022). https://www.computerweekly.com/news/252523959/Ukraine-war-drives-DDoS-attack-volumes-ever-higher. Accessed 25 May 2023

38. National Cyber Security Center. UK government assess Russian involvement in DDoS attacks on Ukraine (2022). https://www.ncsc.gov.uk/news/russia-ddos-involvement-in-ukraine. Accessed 25 May 2023
39. National Institute of Standards and Technology (NIST). RPKI-ROV History of Unique Prefix-Origin Pairs (IPv4) (2024). https://rpki-monitor.antd.nist.gov/ROV

Anycast Polarization in the Wild

A. S. M. Rizvi[1,2(✉)], Tingshan Huang[2], Rasit Esrefoglu[2],
and John Heidemann[1]

[1] University of Southern California/Information Sciences Institute,
Marina del Rey, USA
asmrizvi@usc.edu
[2] Akamai Technologies, Cambridge, USA

Abstract. IP anycast is a commonly used method to associate users
with services provided across multiple sites, and if properly used, it can
provide efficient access with low latency. However, prior work has shown
that *polarization* can occur in global anycast services, where some users
of that service are routed to an anycast site on another continent, adding
100 ms or more latency compared to a nearby site. This paper describes
the causes of polarization in real-world anycast and shows how to observe
polarization in third-party anycast services. We use these methods to
look for polarization and its causes in 7986 known anycast prefixes. We
find that polarization occurs in more than a quarter of anycast prefixes,
and identify incomplete connectivity to Tier-1 transit providers and route
leakage by regional ISPs as common problems. Finally, working with a
commercial CDN, we show how small routing changes can often address
polarization, improving latency for 40% of clients, by up to 54%.

Keywords: Anycast · Polarization · BGP

1 Introduction

Anycast is a routing approach where *anycast sites* in multiple locations announce
the same service on the same IP prefix. First defined in 1993 [26], today anycast is used by many DNS services and Content-Delivery Networks (CDNs) to
reduce latency and to increase capacity [8,11,12,34]. With sites at many Points-
of-Presence (PoPs), clients can often find one physically nearby, providing low
latency [17,30]. With a large capacity of servers that are distributed across
many locations, anycast helps handle Distributed-Denial-of-Service (DDoS)
attacks [23,28].

With an anycast service, each client is associated with one of the anycast sites.
For IP anycast, neither clients nor the service explicitly choose this association.
Instead, each anycast site announces the same IP prefix and BGP Internet rout-
ing selects which site each client reaches, defining that site's anycast *catchment*.
While BGP has flexible policies [3], these do not always optimize for latency or
consider server performance [19,29].

P. Richter et al. (Eds.): PAM 2024, LNCS 14538, pp. 104–131, 2024.
https://doi.org/10.1007/978-3-031-56252-5_6

Polarization is a pathology that can occur in anycast where all traffic from an ISP ignores nearby, low-latency anycast sites and prefers a distant, high-latency site [2,17,19,24]. Polarization can add 100 ms or more to the round-trip time if traffic goes to a different continent. Polarization may send traffic to a specific anycast site which may result in an imbalanced load distribution and make that specific site more vulnerable to DDoS attack.

Polarization may happen for different reasons—incomplete transit connections, preference for a specific neighbor, and for unexpected route propagation. A prior study showed peering from the hypergiant picked one global exit from their corporate WAN, and it did not use the many local anycast sites for their .nl TLD [24]. This prior study showed the existence of polarization in two anycast services and explored some root causes, but it did not explore all known *root causes* of polarization, nor does it evaluate these causes over *many services* to understand how widespread this problem is. In this paper, we close this gap by providing a longitudinal analysis of polarization in the anycast services.

This paper makes three contributions. First, we describe two key reasons for polarization in known anycast prefixes and show how they can be observed remotely in real-world anycast prefixes (Sect. 3 and Sect. 4).

Second, we look for polarization in 7986 known anycast prefixes, finding it in at least 2273 (28.5%) showing that polarization is a common problem (Sect. 5.1). We show incomplete connectivity of Tier-1 providers (Sect. 5.4) and unwanted route leakage by regional ASes (Sect. 5.5) are the key reasons behind polarization. Our measurements show that polarization can have a large latency cost, often adding 100 ms latency for many users (Sect. 5). Our analysis only uses known IPv4 anycast prefixes. Our methods of classifying polarization problems apply to IPv6 as well, and IPv6 is an important area of future study because of its growth [9,16] and the potential different routing policies.

Finally, we show how a commercial CDN provider uses traffic engineering techniques to address polarization (Sect. 6) for their DNS service. We show small routing changes may significantly improve the overall anycast performance, and that community strings are an essential tool when other routing changes do not work. We demonstrate that simple routing changes can produce a 54% improvement in the mean latency, improving performance for 40% of all clients (Sect. 6.3).

Anonymization and Terminology: We anonymize all the names of the anycast service providers to emphasize technical issues rather than provider identity. In this paper, an anycast *service* is an application (such as DNS or web hosting) provided by an anycast *provider* using one or more anycast *prefixes*. A provider may operate multiple services (perhaps DNS for different companies, or optimized to different regions), and each service may be provided by one or more anycast prefixes. Each anycast prefix is typically announced by several sites.

2   Related Work

Extensive prior work has studied, with focuses on anycast topology, efficient routing, performance improvement, and DDoS mitigation.

Anycast Topology: Different organizations design their anycast services in different ways. Anycast services have topological differences in number of anycast sites [33], number of providers [21], and regional or global deployment [35]. These topological differences affect the performance of anycast services. In this paper, we show how topological differences with Tier-1 and regional ASes have impacts on anycast polarization. We show how the same topology with different routing configurations can mitigate polarization problems.

Anycast Latency: Providing low latency is one of the goals of anycast services, multiple studies focus on anycast performance [6,19,33]. Prior studies described the importance of number of sites [30], upstream transit providers [21], selection of paths [19], stability in path selection [33], the impacts of polarization [24], and path inflation [17] over anycast latency. Polarization can increase latency for many clients [2,24], a problem sometimes described as path inflation [19]; the cost of poor site selection can be large [1,6,19]. Although a prior study shows the cost of polarization [24] in two services, to our knowledge we are the first to examine polarization across thousands of anycast prefixes.

Anycast Performance Improvement: Prior studies showed different possible ways to improve the performance of an anycast service. Li et al. proposed to use BGP hints to select the best possible routing path [19]. Removing peering relationship [24] and selective announcement [21] also helped others with performance improvement. In our study, we use multiple traffic engineering techniques to improve the performance of anycast services.

Traffic engineering is used in other previous studies for other purposes like load balancing [3,14,27], traffic shifting [5,7,32], DDoS mitigation [18,28], and for blackhole routing in IXPs and ISPs [10,15]. In our study, we show multiple traffic engineering techniques are required and BGP community strings are essential to improve performance in cases when other traffic engineering methods do not work.

3   Defining Anycast Polarization and Its Root Causes

Recent work defined polarization [24], long a bane of anycast services (for example, [2]). We next give our definition of polarization, and add to prior work with a characterization of the two primary root causes of polarization. These steps pave the way for our measurement of polarization (Sect. 4) and evaluation of its consequences in the wild (Sect. 5).

3.1   Defining Polarization

Polarization is when an anycast client is served by a distant site for some specific prefix, even though there is a nearby site that could provide lower latency. We focus on polarization continent-by-continent. By a distant site, we mean an anycast site that is typically in a different continent, compared to a nearby site on the same continent.

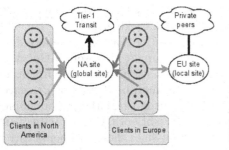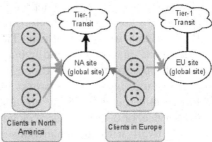

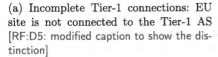

(a) Incomplete Tier-1 connections: EU site is not connected to the Tier-1 AS [RF:D5: modified caption to show the distinction]

(b) Routing to a distant site: EU site is connected to a Tier-1 AS but routing sends a client to a distant site [RF:D5: modified caption to show the distinction]

Fig. 1. Two scenarios of multi-pop backbone problems (each face represents a client in a different ASN)

We choose two thresholds to define distant and nearby sites. The thresholds are chosen to show the approximate delay between continents, with T_{lo} at 50 ms defining a nearby site, and and T_{hi} of 100 ms to define a distant site.

Lower than T_{lo} latency guarantees that at least some VPs have access to a nearby anycast site, while the high thresholds, T_{hi} shows that other VPs miss this site and reach a distant site. This combination of VPs with lower than T_{lo} and higher than T_{hi} latency indicates polarization. Latency that is between T_{lo} and T_{hi} may or may not represent a distant site on another continent, and thus we do not consider them for polarization. We also ignore high latency on continents when the anycast prefix has no sites there.

Many anycast sites are *global*, willing to serve any client. However, some larger anycast services have sites that are *local*, where routing is configured to provide service only for users in their host ISP (and sometimes its customers). We ignore classification of sites as local since prefixes that have both local and global sites typically are large enough to have multiple global sites on each continent. We focus on continent-level latency increases of T_{hi} or more, so this simplification has minimal change to our results. (Other work considers "optimal" latency, but we consider differences of a few milliseconds to be operationally unimportant.) In addition, it is often difficult to correctly identify local sites from only third-party observation. Next, we show two different types of polarization problems.

3.2 The Multi-PoP Backbone Problem

The *multi-PoP backbone problem* happens when a backbone network exists, and has points-of-presence (PoPs) in many places around the world, but that backbone forwards all traffic to a limited number of anycast sites that are not geographically distributed. We consider this case as polarization when some clients at least on some parts of the backbone could get lower latency while some other clients have to go to a distant site through the same backbone.

By backbone, we mean both the Tier-1 providers (for example, as reported in customer-cone analysis [4]), and hypergiants (for example, Microsoft or Google), since both operate global backbone networks and have many PoPs. Organizations with large backbone networks often peer in multiple Points of Presence (PoPs) around the globe. They often have many customers, either by providing transit service, or operating large cloud data centers, or both. Connectivity of an anycast network with these backbones is important since these backbones carry a significant amount of user traffic.

Polarization with multi-PoP backbones can occur for two reasons. First, although both the anycast prefix and backbone have many PoPs, if they share or peer in only a few physical locations, traffic may be forced to travel long distances, creating high latency.

Second, even when backbones and the anycast prefix peer widely, the backbone may choose to route traffic to a single site. This scenario was described when both the Google and Microsoft backgrounds connected to .nl DNS prefixes, with global Google traffic going to Amsterdam and ignoring anycast sites in North America [24].

Figure 1 shows two examples of multi-PoP backbone problems. Often *local anycast sites* are deployed in certain ASes for the benefit of that ISP's customers. Such sites may serve a few customers of the host AS, or a few of its customers, but if they are not connected to an IXP or a transit provider, they have limited scope. Given no-valley routing policies [13], these sites are not widely visible. These sites will not be the preferred sites, even by the clients on the same continent. Many anycast providers design these sites to serve local clients. Figure 1a shows a multi-PoP backbone problem, where the site in Europe is a local anycast site, meaning it has only a few private peers, is not connected to a popular IXP, and does not have any transit connections. On the other hand, the site in North America is a global site connected to a Tier-1 provider. Since the Tier-1 AS has a missing connectivity in Europe, we call this problem as *incomplete Tier-1 connection*. Due to incomplete Tier-1 connection, some clients from Europe will go to North America (marked by two sad faces), where the Tier-1 AS is connected, resulting in two different latency levels inside Europe.

Multi-PoP backbone polarization due to backbone routing choices is shown in Fig. 1b. In this scenario, a Tier-1 provider or hypergiant connects multiple sites in Europe and North America. However, due to routing preference, we can see a client from Europe is going to North American site (marked by a sad face).

3.3   The Leaking Regional Routes Problem

Our second class of polarization problems is *leaking regional routes*. In this scenario, the anycast operator peers with a regional AS at some location, but that peering attracts global traffic and so incurs unnecessarily high latency. By regional ASes, we mean non-Tier-1 ASes that purchase transit from another provider.

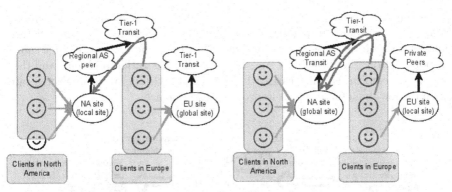

(a) Regional AS connected as private peer

(b) Regional AS connected as transit

Fig. 2. Regional leakage problem

This scenario causes polarization because of the *prefer-customer* routing policy common in many ASes. Because the regional AS purchases transit, presumably from a Tier-1 AS, that transit provider will prefer to route to the regional network and its customer, *over* any other anycast sites. Often this preference will influence all customers of the Tier-1, and most Tier-1 ASes have many customers. In addition, by definition, a regional AS has a limited geographic footprint, so its connectivity does not offset the shift of the Tier-1's customer cone. Thus when anycast prefixes peer with a regional network can have global effects.

Regional ASes may be connected to the anycast prefix as a private peer or as a transit provider. As a private peer, the regional ASes are not expected to propagate the anycast prefix to their Tier-1 upstream. However, sometimes a regional AS with private peering may violate this assumption and propagate the anycast prefixes to its Tier-1 transit provider. We can see a route leakage event in Fig. 2a where a regional AS peer propagates routes to its Tier-1 transit and brings traffic from Europe (as shown by the sad client in Europe).

The regional ASes may also serve as the anycast service's transit provider at this site. As a transit provider, these regional ASes rely on their upstream Tier-1 ASes to propagate their customer prefixes. We can see such polarization in Fig. 2b, where a regional AS is connected as a transit in North America and propagates anycast prefix to its upstream Tier-1 provider. The upstream Tier-1 transit is globally well-connected, and attracts traffic from Europe (illustrated by two sad faces in Europe).

4 Detecting and Classing Polarization in the Wild

To meet our goal to study polarization in the wild, we must take third-party observations that can detect polarization and its root causes.

Our measurement approach has three steps: First, we use prior work that identified anycast prefixes [31] to get a list of /24 anycast prefixes to study.

Second, we test each /24 anycast prefix for polarization by measuring latency from many locations with RIPE Atlas. Finally, for prefixes that demonstrate polarization, we take traceroutes and use what they find to identify root causes for polarization. Figure 3 shows the steps to find polarization problems and their causes; we confirm specific cases when we can reach operators in Sect. 5, and examine how one operator can improve cases in Sect. 6.

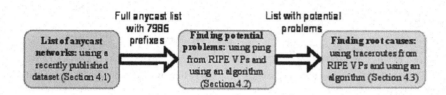

Fig. 3. Steps to find polarization problems and root causes

4.1 Discovering Anycast Prefixes

We first need to find anycast prefixes to search. Fortunately, prior work has developed effective methods to discover anycast prefixes [31]. We directly use the results of their work and begin with their list of 7986 anycast prefixes with 3 to 60 anycast sites distributed around the world.

We evaluate each of these known anycast prefixes in our study. However, we expect that the chance of polarization is low for prefixes with many anycast sites (more than 25); with many sites, there is often one nearby. For prefixes with few sites (less than 5), the sites are sparsely distributed and many clients will observe high latency, even without polarization (Sect. 5.3).

4.2 Finding Potential Polarization

To find anycast polarization, we ping from the RIPE Atlas Vantage Points (VPs) to the known anycast prefixes in September 2023 and look for latency variability within the VPs of a continent. We use 100 RIPE Atlas VPs—72 worldwide VPs, and to ensure global coverage, we pick 7 VPs from each Asia, South America, Africa, and Oceania continents to analyze the latency from the RIPE Atlas VPs to the anycast destinations. We selected the country from each continent, and the VPs were assigned randomly. Our selection results in a diverse list of VPs from approximately 50 countries and 85 different ASNs. We create a separate measurement for each anycast prefix with worldwide VPs, which results in 7,986 different PING measurements with different numbers of source countries, and AS numbers.

Using 100 RIPE Atlas VPs, we list potential polarization problems. By using a bigger list of RIPE Atlas VPs, one may observe even more polarization problems (we may miss identifying local sites with a small number of probes, and thus a potential polarization). However, these 100 RIPE Atlas VPs covering all the continents are sufficient for our analysis to determine the causes of polarization.

Based on the ping latency measurements, as we mentioned in Sect. 3.1, we detect polarization as when some VPs get good latency ($T_{lo} < 50$ ms) and other nearby VPs see bad latency ($T_{hi} > 100$ ms).

Filtering to Reduce False Positives: Next, we show how we reduce the number of false positives for more accurate results. We may identify false polarizations because of the regional anycast prefixes—covering only one or two continents like Edgio [35]. Also, the initial anycast prefix list may not be 100% accurate because of the reassignment of addresses or falsely identified anycast prefixes. To ensure global coverage, we pick VPs from all the continents to verify the prefix is a meaningful anycast prefix to find polarization. We evaluate the anycast prefixes where some VPs from at least three continents get a low latency ($< T_{lo}$). Low latency from at least three continents ensures global coverage of the anycast sites.

We acknowledge that some prefixes may occasionally experience large latency due to either polarization or other network situations. However, prior studies showed anycast catchment normally remains stable [28]. Also, we took ping and traceroutes measurements on different days.

4.3 Finding Root Causes

Next, we describe the measurement methods that indicate each of the root causes for polarization that we identified in Sect. 3. We take traceroutes to each anycast prefixes with potential polarization and examine the penultimate AS hop as seen from different VPs.

Finding Penultimate AS Hop and Its Type: At first, we find out the penultimate AS hop in the AS path to the destination. We observe the whole AS path, and pick the AS that is present just before the anycast prefix's AS. Multiple routers before the final destination may represent the same penultimate AS hop.

After getting the penultimate AS hop, we determine the type of the penultimate AS hop. We consider CAIDA top 10 ASes as the Tier-1 ASes (AS3356: Lumen/Level-3, AS1299: Arelion/Telia, AS174: Cogent, AS6762: Telecom Italia, AS2914: NTT America, AS6939: Hurricane Electric, AS6461: Zayo Bandwidth, AS6453: TATA Communications, AS3257: GTT Communications, and AS3491: PCCW Global) [4], and the others are regional ASes. Hypergiants have heavy outbound traffic. We consider AS15169: Google, AS8075: Microsoft, AS40027: Netflix, AS16509: Amazon or AS32934: Facebook [25] as hypergiants. We classify them by their AS numbers.

Finding Multi-pop Backbone Problems: Multi-pop backbone problems happen when Tier-1 providers or hypergiants are either partially connected or route traffic to a distant site. We identify the partial connectivity when we find VPs with Tier-1 AS or hypergiant in the penultimate AS hop in their paths to a distant site, and when no other VPs from the same continent go to a nearby site using the same penultimate AS. To find routing problems to a distant site, we check for VPs from the same continent that get both good and poor latency with the same Tier-1 AS or hypergiants in the AS path. We use our latency thresholds (Sect. 4.2) to understand whether VPs are going to a nearby site or a distant cross-continent site. This method cannot find poor routing instances when all the VPs are going to a distant site even though they have nearby sites. These nearby sites cannot be identified by the traceroutes since their routing sends all the VPs to the distant site. We must talk to the operators to learn such poor routing cases.

Finding Leaking Regional Problem: We identify a leaking regional problem when a regional AS with a smaller customer cone attracts a lot of traffic to a specific anycast location.

The regional AS can be connected as a transit or as a private peer that is leaking routes to its upstreams. To identify private peer leaking routes, we search for other Tier-1 ASes that are present in the penultimate hops and connected in multiple locations. The existence of other penultimate Tier-1 ASes indicates the possible real transit providers. When there is another Tier-1 transit, the regional AS should emphasize on the regional propagation of the announcements. To find regional ASes that are connected as transits, we check for other Tier-1 ASes in multiple locations. If we find other Tier-1 ASes, then the regional AS is possibly connected as a private peer but leaking routes to its upstream.

This approach can predict *possible* regional route leaking, but it may also happen that these regional ASes are connected as transit providers. Knowing the exact peering relationship is only possible when we can talk to the operators as the inferred peering relationships from the public databases are not always accurate, and corner cases like route leakage may infer wrong peering relationships [20]. Hence, to validate actual route leakage we must talk to the operators.

4.4   Finding Impacts

After getting the polarization problems and their root causes, we want to see the impacts of polarization. We find out the penultimate AS hop that is common in the paths to the distant site. We measure the median and 95th percentile latency from a continent. Polarization results in inter-continental traffic, and its impact is expected to show in high 95th percentile latency. Using the difference between the median and 95th percentile latency, we show the impact of polarization.

Next, we show that polarization problems are common and they have a significant impact over anycast performance.

5   Measurement Results and Impacts of Polarization

We next show how common polarization is in known anycast prefixes, and how polarization affects service performance.

We validate results for all prefixes with operators we could reach.

5.1 Detecting Polarization in Anycast Prefixes

Our first goal is to understand how common polarization is. Following our methodology in Sect. 4, we first examine all known anycast prefixes for polarization. We see that of the 7986 examined prefixes, about 28% show potential polarization (Table 1).

In this paper, we focus on the 626 anycast prefixes that show polarization problems for clients in Europe and North America. We focus on these anycast prefixes to detect root causes because these continents have mature Internet service and multiple IXPs, so they are locations where polarization can occur and we believe we have cases where actions can be taken to resolve the issue. We leave the study of polarization on other continents as future work, since polarization that occurs due to incomplete in-country peering will be addressed as the domestic Internet market matures and interconnects. (An anycast prefix that peers with one AS cannot avoid polarization with other ISPs in the same country if there is incomplete domestic peering.)

Since we only focus on the EU and NA continents to find the root causes behind polarization using traceroutes (Sect. 4.3), we select 46 European VPs and 20 North American VPs. We choose 2–3 VPs each from 20 different European countries to make 46 European VPs, and we select 15 VPs from the USA and 5 VPs from Canada to make 20 North American VPs. These probes are chosen randomly from a specific country (we select the country and probes are chosen randomly), and they cover approximately 55 different ASes from these countries. We take traceroute measurements from these VPs to each of 626 anycast prefixes. To find the catchment, we use the penultimate routing hop's geo-location reported by RIPE or a CDN's internal tool for IP to geo translation. This location may not be the true catchment, but this location is sufficient to find out the cross-continent traffic to the destination. We confirm the catchments of 18 anycast prefixes where we had the chance to contact the operators.

5.2 Detecting Root Causes

Given potential polarization in known anycast prefixes, we then apply root cause detection (Sect. 3) to these prefixes.

We find multi-pop backbone problems in 376 anycast /24 prefixes out of 626 prefixes (Table 1). We observe a Tier-1 AS in the penultimate AS hop for these 376 anycast prefixes. Among these multi-pop backbone problems, our methodology finds 218 instances where a Tier-1 provider is incompletely connected. We suspect this behavior when nearly all VPs from a continent have catchment in a distant site through the same Tier-1 AS. We also find 158 cases when VPs route to a distant site. We suspect this event when some VPs from a continent experience good latency (<50 ms) while others observe poor latency (>100 ms), and when these VPs utilize the same Tier-1 AS in the penultimate AS hop.

Our methodology shows 233 cases where a regional AS leaks routes. Among these, in 177 cases we find other Tier-1 ASes in the penultimate AS hop. As there are other Tier-1 ASes in the path, we suspect these Tier-1 ASes are the real transits, and the regional ASes are possibly leaking routes. In 56 other instances, we find no other Tier-1 ASes in the path. We suspect a regional AS is connected as a transit in these 56 cases.

We contacted the operators of 18 of these 626 cases. The operators confirmed all these polarization events.

An anycast service provider may have multiple /24 prefixes, and because of their topological similarity we find polarization problems in many of their /24 prefixes. Table 2 shows top providers who have polarization problems in many of their /24 anycast prefixes. We can see some providers have polarization in almost all of their anycast /24 prefixes.

Table 1. Detected polarization and inferred root causes.

Category	Count	%	Confirmed
Known anycast prefixes	7986	*100*	
No observed potential polarization	5713	*72*	
Potential polarization	2273	*28*	
In continents outside EU and NA	1647	*20*	
In EU and NA	626	*8*	18
No class found (a)	161	*2*	
Only multi-pop backbone problem (b)	232	*3*	
Only regional leakage (c)	89	*1*	
Both classes (d)	144	*2*	
Multi-pop backbone problem (b+d)	376	*5*	9
Incomplete Tier-1 connections	218	*3*	9
Routing to a distant site	158	*2*	0
Leaking regional problem (c+d)	233	*3*	9
Leakage by regional	177	*2*	6
Leakage by regional transits	56	*1*	3

Table 2. Top anycast prefixes with potential polarization problems

Provider	Potential problems	Total anycast
Anon-DNS-2	214	216
Anon-DNS-3	94	159
Anon-CDN-1	20	47
Anon-DNS-4	12	75
Anon-DNS-5	9	9

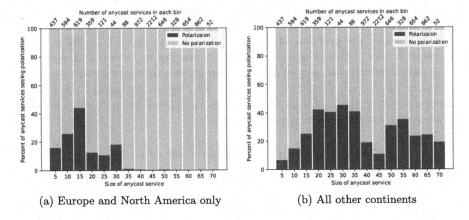

(a) Europe and North America only   (b) All other continents

Fig. 4. Percent of anycast prefixes that see polarization, grouped in bins by number of anycast sites per anycast prefix.

5.3 Impacts of the Number of Sites on Polarization

Does polarization correlate with the total number of anycast sites? Prior work [30] suggested that 12 sites can provide good geographic latency, but those results assume good in-continent routing. Does that assumption hold in practice?

To answer this question, we explore the relationship between the number of anycast sites and the degree of polarization. To get the number of anycast sites, we utilize the count reported by the recent study [31] that we used to get the anycast prefixes.

Figure 4 shows how much polarization occurs relative to the number of any-cast sites. We group anycast prefixes by number of sites into bins of 5 (so the first bin is 5 sites or less, the next is 6 to 10, etc.). The number of sites in each part of the graph varies and is shown on the top of each bin, but is always at least 52 prefixes, and often hundreds. For each bin, we show the percentage of prefixes that appear polarized.

We see some polarization in prefixes of many different number of sites. But for Europe and North America, polarization is most common in prefixes with 30 or fewer sites (the left part of Fig. 4a). For other continents, some polarization occurs regardless of how many sites the prefix has. In Fig. 4b, we can see polarization even for prefixes with 30 to 70 sites.

We conclude that prefixes with many sites generally get good routing in continents with mature Internet markets. However, routing is more challenging, as shown by greater polarization, for prefixes with only a few sites, and when operating globally. In mature Internet markets, high rates of AS interconnectivity decrease risks of polarization. However, outside EU and NA, anycast is more difficult to deploy well, likely because of poor local inter-AS connectivity means some local customers cannot use a local anycast site.

Next, we show examples of such connectivity issues that cause polarization and their impacts on latency.

5.4   Impacts of Multi-pop Backbone Problems

We next look at the problem of multi-PoP backbones (Sect. 3.2). We examine several examples of this in real-world anycast prefixes in Table 3 and show how it can result in extra latency of 100 ms or more due to inter-continental traffic (shown in Fig. 5). We show the number of /24 prefixes for each of the anycast services, however, the problems that we show in Table 3 demonstrate a problem for a specific /24 prefix of that anycast service.

Table 3. Polarization in real-world anycast prefixes

Provider	No. of /24 prefixes	Reason of the problem	Common AS to the distant site	Source cont	Med	95th	Example
Anon-CDN-2	14	Incomplete Tier-1	AS1299	EU NA	12 25	173 88	Poland to USA
Anon-Cloud-1	1	Incomplete Tier-1	AS3356, AS6939	EU NA	51 55	158 162	Canada to Germany
Anon-CDN-6	67	Incomplete Tier-1 (peers as transits)	AS6762	EU NA	16 39	122 141	Greece to USA
Anon-CDN-3	9	Exceptional incomplete Tier-1	AS6453	EU NA	32 25	113 39	Germany to USA
Anon-CDN-1	67	Leaking regional transit	AS1273	EU NA	21 88	53 150	USA to UK
Anon-DNS-1	18	Leaking regional peer	AS4826	EU NA	174 37	314 214	USA to Australia
Anon-CDN-5	67	Leaking regional peer	AS7473	EU NA	39 24	248 252	USA to Singapore
Anon-CDN-7	67	Leaking regional peer (merging org)	AS209	EU NA	29 26	84 65	Finland to USA
Anon-DNS-2	216	Leaking regional Incomplete Tier-1	AS4637 AS1299	EU NA	165 81	301 254	Canada to Tokyo

5.4.1   An Incomplete Tier-1 Connection in Anon-CDN-2 We find an any-cast prefix of Anon-CDN-2 where a fraction of traffic from Europe was going to the US. We believe this event is an example of polarization for incomplete Tier-1 connections. We find 40 out of 46 VPs (87%) of the European VPs remain within the continent, and 6 out of 46 VPs (13%) of the other VPs end up in San Jose, USA using a fixed Tier-1 AS.

We find European sites are globally well connected. We observe a Tier-1 AS (AS3356 - Level-3) connected to a European site. We believe the European site is a global site attracting VPs from many locations. As proof, we find that African VPs have catchments in Europe. European sites also increase their connectivity by having many private peers connecting most small ASes within the continent. Even with this well-connectivity, 13% of the European VPs have catchment in the US. As a result, we believe this is an example of polarization.

The VPs that are going to North America have AS1299 (Arelion Sweden AB) in common within their paths. We believe AS1299 is working as a transit although we do not know the contract type between Anon-CDN-2 and AS1299 for that anycast site. Based on the other traceroutes, we did not find any path that remains within Europe through AS1299. That means AS1299 has a missing

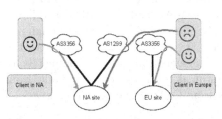

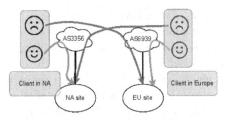

(b) **Anon-Cloud-1**: incomplete connection of AS3356 and AS6939 in two different continents [RF:A6, E2: added figure]

(a) **Anon-CDN-2**: incomplete connection with AS1299 [RF:A6, E2: added figure]

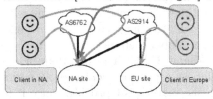

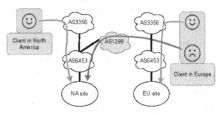

(c) **Anon-CDN-6**: incomplete connection of AS6762, which was assumed a private peer [RF:A6, E2: added figure]

(d) **Anon-CDN-3**: incomplete inter-AS connection[RF:D10]

Fig. 5. Real-world multi-pop backbone problems

connection in Europe. Figure 5a shows NA site is incompletely connected to AS1299 and causes polarization for European clients.

Impacts: The impact of this cross-continent traffic has a significant impact over latency. As an example, we find a VP from Poland goes to San Jose, USA. The cross-continent traffic results in a high 95th percentile latency. While the median is only 12 ms, we get the 95th percentile latency is 173 ms (Table 3).

5.4.2 Multiple Incomplete Tier-1 in Anon-Cloud-1

Next, we show an example from **Anon-Cloud-1** where an anycast prefix uses two different Tier-1 ASes in two different continents.

We find two global sites in Europe and North America connected through two Tier-1 ASes as shown in Fig. 5b. We observe traffic going to Dallas, USA using AS3356 (Level-3), and to Frankfurt, Germany through AS6939 (Hurricane Electric). Both these ASes are Tier-1 ASes and have a wide range of connectivity. We are unsure about their contract type with **Anon-Cloud-1**. They can be incomplete transit connections, or one of these Tier-1 ASes has a private peering relationship with **Anon-Cloud-1**, but works like a transit.

The traceroutes exhibit the preferred route to reach an anycast site. Of course, a client may have multiple paths to reach European and North American sites via two Tier-1 ASes. However, going to a distant site through a specific Tier-1 AS means that the client has a preference for that particular AS, and that AS may not have any connectivity within the client's continent.

Impacts: When we have two big Tier-1 ASes have incomplete transit connections in two continents, we observe a significant fraction of cross-continent traffic. We observe 40% VPs from Europe and North America end up in a different continent. The cross-continent traffic using AS3356, and AS6939 add over 100 ms of latency. The cross-continent traffic makes $3\times$ 95th percentile latency compared to the median latency (Table 3). This example shows how bad the impact can be when we have two Tier-1 providers connected incompletely in two continents. As an example of cross-continent traffic, we observe traffic from Denmark goes to Dallas, USA, and traffic from Canada goes to Germany.

5.4.3 Incomplete Tier-1: Peers Working as Transits in Anon-CDN-6

We find another case where a Tier-1 AS has incomplete connections with Anon-CDN-6. We contacted the operators, and they confirmed their peering relationship with this Tier-1 AS. But that Tier-1 AS has a huge customer cone, and their policy is to propagate the routes to their global customer cone.

In this event, Anon-CDN-6 has a site in Miami, USA where the Miami location is connected to AS6762 (Telecom Italia) as a private peer. The operators confirmed that AS2914 (NTT America) is the real transit provider since it is connected to three continents—Asia, Europe, and North America. AS6762 is only connected in one location. The anycast operators did not expect the prefix to be propagated out of the continent by AS6762 since it is connected as a private peer. But in reality, it was propagated to other ASes connected in other continents. From Fig. 5c, we can see that a client from Europe has catchment in North America via AS6762.

Impacts: AS6762 propagates the anycast prefix out of the continent. As a result, we found 5 out of 46 VPs (10%) from Europe have catchment in Miami, USA, and experienced over 100 ms of extra latency.

5.4.4 Exceptional Incomplete Tier-1: Incomplete Inter-AS Connections

We find a case when we observe a polarization incident even with complete Tier-1 connections. We find this case using manual observation of the traceroutes when we could not find a proper classification of the polarization problem.

Traceroutes to Anon-CDN-3 show that AS6453 (Tata Communications) as a penultimate AS hop in many different paths to Europe and North America. This behavior proves AS6453 is working as a transit connected in both Europe and North America with Anon-CDN-3 (Fig. 5d). So, we define this connectivity as a complete transit connection. Even with this complete connection, we observe some European VPs have catchments in North America, which results in polarization and high latency.

Many traceroutes show Tier-1 ASes like AS3356 and AS1299 just before the penultimate hop AS6453, as we can see from Fig. 5d. The presence of these Tier-1s two hops back from the anycast site suggests that this anycast prefix mostly relies on the Tier-1 ASes to get into AS6453 and then to Anon-CDN-3. We find the VPs from Europe with AS1299 in the paths end up in North America through AS6453. We suspect AS1299 is connected to AS6453 only in North America, or for Anon-CDN-3, AS1299 has a preference for the North American connection. On the contrary, we observe the opposite for AS3356. AS3356 has connectivity with AS6453 in both continents and as a result, we are not observing any performance issues.

Impacts: We find 8 out of 46 VPs (18%) of the European VPs choose a path through AS1299 to go to North America to connect to AS6453 and Anon-CDN-3. While the median and 95th percentile latency have a small difference for the North American VPs; because of this polarization, European VPs observe over 3×95th percentile latency (Table 3).

5.5   Impacts of Leaking Regional Problems

We next turn to leaking regional (Sect. 3.3), our second class of polarization problems. We find several cases where regional ASes (non-Tier-1 ASes) send a great deal of traffic to a distant site. These regional ASes purchase transit from a Tier-1, and so polarization results when their transit-providing Tier-1 adopts a prefer-client routing policy. Alternatively, these regional ASes are private peers but make unwanted route propagation to their upstream. Figure 6 shows the leaking regional problems.

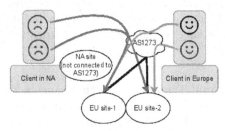

(a) **Anon-CDN-1**: incomplete connection of AS1273 in Europe [RF:A6, E2: added figure]

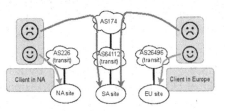

(b) **Anon-DNS-6**: leakage by AS64112 to a Tier-1 provider in South America [RF:A6, E2: added figure.]

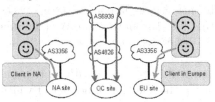

(c) **Anon-DNS-1**: possible leakage by AS4826 in Oceania [RF:A6, E2, E19: added figure]

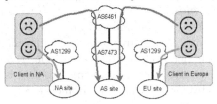

(d) **Anon-CDN-5**: possible leakage by AS7473 in Asia [RF:D10, E19: newly added]

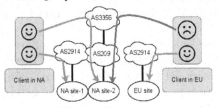

(e) **Anon-CDN-7**: merging of AS209 and AS3356 makes a North American site busy[RF:A6, E2: added figure, E19: new]

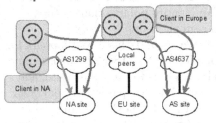

(f) **Anon-DNS-2**: leakage by AS4637 in Asia [RF:D10]

Fig. 6. Real-world leaking regional problems

5.5.1 Anon-CDN-1: Leaking by Regional Transits with Multiple Connectivity We find a polarization instance because of the leaking of an anycast prefix by a regional AS in one of Anon-CDN-1 anycast prefixes. We confirmed this event with the anycast operators. The operators informed us that the regional AS is connected as a transit provider.

In this polarization problem, we find a significant portion of traffic from North America ends up in Europe using AS1273 (Vodafone). Contacting Anon-CDN-1 operators about this issue, we confirmed that AS1273 is indeed connected as a transit for their anycast prefix. We did not find any VPs having AS1273 in the path that stays within North America (Fig. 6a). We believe AS1273 is only connected in Europe, not in North America, resulting in incomplete regional transit connections and polarization. We also confirmed this finding with Anon-CDN-1, and they informed us that AS1273 is connected to multiple countries in Europe.

Impacts: Since AS1273 is only connected in Europe as a transit, we find around 13 out 20 VPs (64%) of the North American VPs end up in Europe. Only 36% VPs stay within North America. As an example of cross-continent traffic, we find a VP from the USA that goes to London, UK. As a result, we find both median and 95th percentile latency are high for this polarization (Table 3).

5.5.2 Anon-DNS-6: Leaking by a Regional Transit in South America A global DNS provider (Anon-DNS-6) peers in several locations. A South American site peers with a regional network (AS64112, PIT-Chile) who purchases transit from a Tier-1 provider (AS174, Cogent). Because of AS174's prefer-customer routing policy, peering with the regional network causes all customers of the Tier-1 provider in North America and Europe to go to South America (Fig. 6b).

Impact: Cross-continent routing adds 100 ms or more latency, so Anon-DNS-6 instead prevents route announcements to this Tier-1 from this site. With limited routing, this anycast site is unavailable to other regional networks in South America that can be reached via transit.

Better solutions to this problem is for Anon-DNS-6 to peer with all regional networks, or that they influence routing inside the Tier-1 AS, neither of which is easy.

5.5.3 Anon-DNS-1: Possible Route Leakage by Regional as in Oceania We identify polarization in Anon-DNS-1 anycast prefix due to route leakage by a regional peer.

We suspect this anycast prefix has route leakage because many VPs have a non-Tier-1 AS (AS4826: Vocus Connect, Australia) as the penultimate AS hop in all the paths to the distant site, and some other VPs have a Tier-1 AS (AS3356) in multiple AS paths (Fig. 6c). Our assumption is that AS3356 is the actual transit, and AS4826 is connected as a peer but it does not work as a peer, rather it leaks Anon-DNS-1 routes to its peers and transits. We find AS4826 propagates its routes to many different peers including a Tier-1 AS (AS6939). Since AS6939 is well-connected to the rest of the world, it brings a large fraction of VPs to AS4826.

We must talk to the operators to know whether AS4826 is really a private peer or a transit provider. However, having a transit connection with a smaller AS is highly unlikely since this anycast network (/24 prefix) has connectivity with another Tier-1 AS with a large geographic presence.

Impacts: We observe severe polarization due to this route leakage by AS4826, where AS4826 is only connected in Australia (as shown in Fig. 6c). Since AS4826 is propagating its routes to AS6939, and since AS6939 is a well-connected Tier-1 AS, traffic from all over the world ends up in Australia. We find a case where traffic from the Ashburn, USA connects to AS6939 in Los Angeles, USA, then travels to AS4826 in San Jose, USA, and then ends up in Sydney, Australia, resulting in over 200 ms of latency. From Europe, we find a case when a VP from Switzerland travels to Ashburn, USA, Los Angeles, USA, San Jose, USA, and then Sydney, Australia, which takes over 300 ms latency.

5.5.4 Anon-CDN-5: Route Leakage by a Regional as in Asia

We have already shown how a possible route leakage brings traffic to South America and Oceania. Next, we show a similar case in Asia with a different autonomous system.

We find another polarization event due to route leakage by AS7473 (Singapore Telecom). We confirm this event with Anon-CDN-5 that AS7473 is connected with Anon-CDN-5 as a private peer but it propagates Anon-CDN-5 prefix to a big Tier-1 AS (AS6461 - Zayo Bandwidth) as shown in Fig. 6d. Since AS6461 is connected heavily with the rest of the world, we find many VPs from Europe and North America end up in Singapore. From the traceroutes, we find a Tier-1 AS (AS1299) is the real transit connected to different locations worldwide.

Impacts: We find 7% VPs from Europe and 6% VPs from North America end up in Singapore, even if this anycast network has multiple presence in those continents. While VPs that stay within the continent observe low latency, due to this long path to Singapore, we observe over 200 ms difference between the median and 95th percentile latency (Table 3).

5.5.5 Regional Route Leakage: A Special Case When Organizations Merge

We find a polarization problem in one of CDN prefixes (Anon-CDN-7) due to the merging of two organizations.

We find this case by looking over the traceroutes from the VPs to a distant site for a specific prefix of Anon-CDN-7. We find "AS3356 AS209" in many of the paths that show bad latency to a distant site (Fig. 6e). In that particular anycast prefix, AS209 (Century Link) is connected only in one location. Since AS209 propagates its routes to AS3356 (Level-3), and since AS3356 is a big

Tier-1 AS with global connectivity, we observe a significant fraction of cross-continent traffic to the distant site where AS209 is connected. Contacting the CDN, we learn that AS209 is connected as a private peer, and so it should not propagate the CDN prefix to a big Tier-1 provider. We *suspect* that this issue occurs because of the merging of AS209 and AS3356 [22]. We confirmed this incident with the operators of `Anon-CDN-7`.

Impacts: `Anon-CDN-7` network (announced by a /24 prefix) peers with AS209 in Sterling, USA location. Since AS209 propagates its route to AS3356, we find VPs from Europe and even from Asia have catchment in the USA (Fig. 6e), resulting in over 200 ms of latency.

5.6   Combination of Problems

We find several `Anon-DNS-2` prefixes where we believe multiple connectivity problems exist that cause severe polarization.

`Anon-DNS-2` has multiple anycast prefixes that are announced from different locations connected to different transits and peers. We are certain that `Anon-DNS-2` has anycast sites at least in North America, Europe, and Asia since some of the VPs from these continents experienced good latency. However, the big Tier-1 ASes like AS1299 or AS174 is only connected in North America. Based on our traceroutes, we also find European and Asian sites have peers that are not big Tier-1 ASes. With a connectivity like this, we expect most North American VPs will stay within North America because of the Tier-1 AS, and some European and Asian VPs will go to North America because of the incomplete transit connectivity.

In reality, we observe cross-continent traffic in different directions. We find the peers (AS4637 Telstra Global) in Asia leaks routes (or working as a transit) to its Tier-1 providers. Since that Tier-1 provider is well-connected, we find North American traffic goes to Asia (left side unhappy user goes to Asia in Fig. 6f). We also find Asian VPs going to North America since North American sites are connected to Tier-1 ASes. We find only a few European VPs stay within the continent because of their local peers, but a significant portion moves to North America and Asia (shown in Fig. 6f by two unhappy European users). This cross-continent traffic results in increased latency, in some cases they add more than 200 ms of latency.

6   Improvement by Routing Nudges

We already show polarization exists in many different anycast prefixes and that it can have a significant impact on performance. However, often small changes in routing can address polarization, even without adding new peering relationships with other ASes. We find many potential polarization problems as mentioned in Table 1. In this section, we show two examples of how `Anon-CDN-4` improves anycast performance in two anycast systems. While we would love to have improvements for more anycast systems, we could only obtain before-and-after results for changes by the operators of this CDN.

6.1 Anycast Configuration

Anon-CDN-4 uses anycast for their DNS services. To ensure reliability, Anon-CDN-4 uses multiple anycast /24 prefixes for DNS. These anycast prefixes are announced from around 268 sites located in 93 cities distributed around the world. Each site has multiple machines to serve the client load. Each site has different upstream connectivity, with different numbers of peers, network access points, and transit providers. Anon-CDN-4 uses multiple Tier-1 ASes as the transits for their anycast prefixes (/24 s). These transits differ in each anycast prefix.

We show improvements in two anycast prefixes after making routing changes by Anon-CDN-4. The first anycast prefix has a presence in 15 cities covering 9 countries. AS2914 (NTT America) provides transit connectivity and is connected in multiple geographic locations covering Asia, Europe, and North America. There are other peers and network access points connected the anycast sites. The second anycast prefix covers 17 cities in 11 countries. AS1299 (Arelion Sweden) provides transit for this anycast prefix covering Europe and North America continents.

6.2 Routing Problems

The two anycast prefixes mentioned in Sect. 6.1 have different routing problems. In the first anycast prefix, Anon-CDN-4 encounters two different problems: multi-pop backbone problems (Sect. 3.2), and leaking regional problems (Sect. 3.3). The second anycast prefix only has a leaking regional problem (Sect. 3.3).

First Anycast Prefix Has Both Multi-pop Backbone and Leaking Regional Problems: The first anycast prefix has multi-pop backbone problems with multiple Tier-1 ASes. Anon-CDN-4 connects to AS1299 (Arelion Sweden) and AS3356 (Level-3) as private peers in Dallas, USA. We also find AS6762 (Telecom Italia) as a private peer connected in Virginia, USA, and Milan, Italy. Anon-CDN-4 operators expected these peers to confine their announcements within a smaller customer cone. But we find that these peers propagate Anon-CDN-4 routes to the rest of the world. We suspect these peers treat Anon-CDN-4 as their customers since they are also connected as a transit for other anycast prefixes of the same anycast service.

In the second problem of the first anycast prefix, Anon-CDN-4 connects to AS209 (Lumen) as a private peer in Virginia, USA location, and propagates routes to AS3356. Since AS3356 is well-connected to the rest of the world, Anon-CDN-4 observes cross-continent traffic to Virginia, USA.

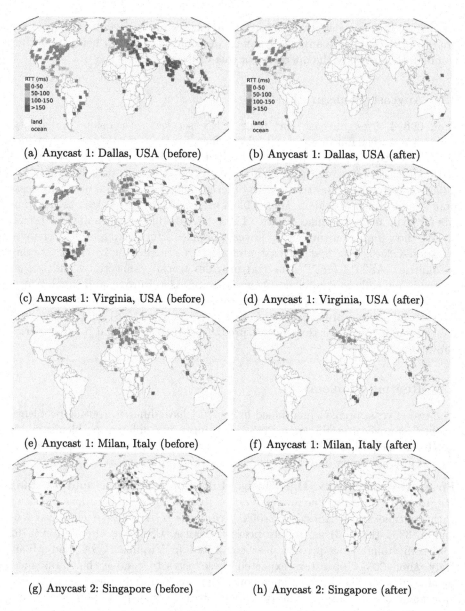

(a) Anycast 1: Dallas, USA (before)   (b) Anycast 1: Dallas, USA (after)

(c) Anycast 1: Virginia, USA (before)   (d) Anycast 1: Virginia, USA (after)

(e) Anycast 1: Milan, Italy (before)   (f) Anycast 1: Milan, Italy (after)

(g) Anycast 2: Singapore (before)   (h) Anycast 2: Singapore (after)

Fig. 7. Changes in Anycast catchment for a anycast site due to a routing change

Second Anycast Prefix Has a Leaking Regional Problem: In the second problem, Anon-CDN-4 has a regional private peer (AS7473) connected in Singapore, leaks their routes to other upstream Tier-1 ASes. As a result, Anon-CDN-4 observes cross-continent traffic from other continents to Singapore.

6.3 Solving Problems

`Anon-CDN-4` solves these performance issues by changing their routing configuration.

Solving Two Problems in the First Anycast Prefix: To solve the two problems in the first anycast prefix, `Anon-CDN-4` stops announcing to the peers that were causing the polarization problem. `Anon-CDN-4` blocks announcements to each of the Tier-1 private peers (AS1299, AS3356, and AS6762), and to AS209 to prevent the propagation of routes to AS3356.

Solving Leaking Regional Problem in the Second Anycast Prefix: For the second anycast prefix, `Anon-CDN-4` tries two things. Since many local VPs were taking advantage by using AS7473, `Anon-CDN-4` realized that blocking AS7473 may result in even worse performance overall. That is why, instead of blocking the announcement to AS7473, `Anon-CDN-4` takes a more cautious action. In one change, they prepend twice from Singapore location so that fewer VPs end up in Singapore. In another change, they use community strings to tell AS7473 to keep the `Anon-CDN-4` prefix within Asia and Oceania regions. Only the second change results in better performance overall which we will describe next. This example shows the importance of having multiple routing configurations for traffic engineering, and using the one that results in best performance.

Measuring Performance, Before and After: We use `Anon-CDN-4`'s internal measurement system, observing latency from about 2300 global VPs. These vantage points have a global coverage with 74 African, 839 Asian, 772 European, 315 North American, 90 Oceanian, and 171 South American VPs. We do not use RIPE Atlas VPs from this point onwards.

6.3.1 Changes in the Catchments
After making the routing changes, `Anon-CDN-4` observes significant changes in the catchment distribution. We show the catchment distribution based on the `Anon-CDN-4`'s internal measurement of the catchments. We examine the VPs going to an anycast site before and after the routing change. In Fig. 7, we visualize the geolocations of the VPs to an anycast site, along with the measured latency. Each point on the map represents a VP and the colors represent the latency level from that VP to the anycast site.

Catchment Changes in the First Anycast Prefix: For the first one, `Anon-CDN-4` blocks their private peering with AS1299 and AS3356 from Dallas.

The topmost left graph (Fig. 7a) shows the catchment before making the change. As we can see many VPs from Europe and Asia (shown by red dots) end up in Dallas, USA. As a result, these VPs experience bad latency (over 100 ms). Traceroutes confirm cross-continent VPs using AS1299 and AS3356 to reach Dallas, USA. After blocking the announcement to AS1299 and AS3356, we

Table 4. Continent-wise improvement in latency by routing changes

Anycast prefix	Routing changes	Improvement(%)					
		Africa	Asia	Europe	North America	Oceania	South America
Prefix-1	Blocking AS1299 and AS3356 from Dallas, USA, AS209 and AS6762 from Sterling, USA, and AS6762 from Milan, Italy	5.4	23.4	54.6	23.0	2.2	−0.15
Prefix-2	Announcement to AS7473 only within Asia Pacific and block others (using community strings)	10.5	12.3	34.8	19.7	2.3	1.9
Prefix-2	Announcement to AS7473 with two prepending	3.8	−9.6	6.5	6.4	6.3	3.8

observe no cross-continent VPs from Europe and Asia (Fig. 7b). We can only see VPs from the US have catchment in Dallas, USA, and experience better latency (less than 50 ms).

Anon-CDN-4 also blocks private peers AS209 and AS6762 from Virginia, USA. With these two ASes, Virginia, USA was receiving traffic from different continents (Fig. 7c). After blocking the announcement, Virginia, USA site receives traffic mostly from North and South America (Fig. 7d). We also observe a less number of cross-continent VPs when we block AS6762 from Milan, Italy (Fig. 7e and Fig. 7f).

Catchment Changes in the Second Anycast Prefix: In the second anycast prefix, the Singapore site was receiving traffic from other continents (Fig. 7g). Anon-CDN-4 uses community strings to keep the announcement propagation within the Asia and Oceania continents. As a result, we can see less number of VPs to Singapore from other continents (Fig. 7h).

6.3.2   Impacts over Performance We have shown above the catchment changes after deploying the new routing configurations. Next, we show how the performance changes.

Improvement in the First Anycast Prefix: After the changes in the first anycast prefix, we find most improvement in the Europe, Asia, and North America continents (Table 4). We find 54.6%, 23.4%, and 23.0% improvement in mean latency in these continents, respectively. Many European and Asian VPs were going to Dallas, USA, and Virginia, USA. After the new announcement, we do not see this cross-continent traffic. Even if we block announcement from the North American sites, we observe 23.0% improvement among the North American VPs. This is because many North American VPs from the West Coast had catchments to the Dallas and Virginia sites. After the routing change, the traffic

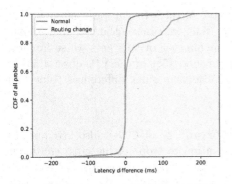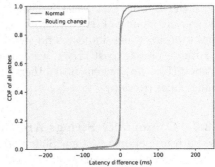

(a) Prefix-1: blocking in Dallas, USA, Virginia, USA, and Milan, Italy

(b) Prefix-2: changes in Singapore - announcing only within Asia Pacific

Fig. 8. CDF of all the VPs wrt latency difference (ms)

starts going to their nearby locations. The performance in the other continents remains mostly stable.

Improvement in the Second Anycast Prefix: After the change in the second anycast prefix using community strings, we find the most improvement in the European and North American VPs. From Table 4, we can see that European VPs observe 34.8% improvement, and North American VPs observe 19.7% improvement. This is because several European and North American VPs had catchments in Singapore. After the new announcement, we do not observe this type of cross-continent traffic. We observe improvement in other continents as well.

New Latency Distribution in Both Anycast Prefixes: Since Anon-CDN-4 blocks routing announcements to different peers in different geo-locations, some VPs may observe worse performance who are dependent on the peers that Anon-CDN-4 blocks. However, if there are nearby sites, then the VPs may be redirected to the nearby sites after the routing changes, and still observe good latency. To know how many VPs are getting worse latency after the routing change, we show a CDF graph with respect to latency difference in Fig. 8. We measure the latency decrease for each VP after the routing change. A positive difference indicates an improved performance (light green region in Fig. 8), and a negative difference indicates a degraded performance (light red region in Fig. 8). Since latency may vary slightly between two measurements, the graphs show a normal difference line (blue lines) to show the regular latency variance without any routing changes. The orange lines show the latency decrease after the routing changes.

In the first anycast prefix, we can see 40% of the VPs get lower latency after the routing change (Fig. 8a). On the other side, we can see the blue and orange lines overlap, which indicates no significant number of VPs gets worse latency. For the second anycast prefix, we can see around 15% of the VPs observe lower latency (Fig. 8b), when most other VPs observe regular differences (blue and orange lines overlap).

6.3.3   Community Strings Are Important Anon-CDN-4 also attempts to use path prepending at their Singapore location to stop getting cross-continent traffic to Singapore. (Since many local VPs are dependent on AS7473 to reach Singapore site, Anon-CDN-4 did not want to fully block the announcement through AS7473 fully.) Table 4 shows the outcome after they use path prepending for two times. Even after twice prepending from Singapore, they could only reduce 6.5% mean latency in Europe, and 6.4% mean latency in North America. At the same time, the mean latency becomes 9.6% worse in Asia. Path prepending is an available tool for traffic engineering—anycast operators can make path prepending without requiring support from their upstream providers. However, as we can see from this result that path prepending may not always be useful.

On the other hand, when we restrict the announcements only within Asia and Oceania continents using community string, we observe significant performance improvement for all the continents (Table 4). We recommend the anycast operators to have transits with providers that support community strings.

Anon-DNS-6 has also explored the use of community strings to adjust their routing. However, while community-strings are supported at most commercial sites, support at non-commercial (research and education) sites is less uniform. Without pre-deployed community strings, routing changes typically require custom tickets. Standardization of community strings across all sites would avoid this cost.

7   Conclusion

This paper proposes a way to discover and resolve the polarization problems in anycast services. We evaluate nearly 7,986 anycast prefixes, and show that the polarization problem is common in the wild Internet. We present our method to classify the polarization problems. We demonstrate two different classes of polarization problems. Our evaluation shows that the causes for both are common in known anycast prefixes. Polarization can take the clients to a distant site, often in a different continent, when the clients have a nearby anycast site. Because of the cross-continent routes, clients can observe over 100 ms of extra latency. We show some polarization problems can be solved using traffic engineering techniques. Small changes in the routing policy can improve the latency for many VPs. We also show network operators should have multiple traffic engineering techniques, including BGP community strings, to improve the performance of their anycast service.

Acknowledgments. ASM Rizvi and John Heidemann's work was partially supported by DARPA under Contract No. HR001120C0157. Any opinions, findings and conclusions or recommendations expressed in this material are those of the author(s) and do not necessarily reflect the views of DARPA. John Heidemann's work was also partially supported by the NFS projects CNS-2319409, CRI-8115780, and CNS-1925737. ASM Rizvi's work was begun while on an internship at Akamai. We thank the anonymous shepherd and reviewers for their input.

References

1. Ballani, H., Francis, P., Ratnasamy, S.: A measurement-based deployment proposal for IP anycast. In: Proceedings of the 6th ACM SIGCOMM Conference on Internet Measurement, pp. 231–244 (2006)
2. Bellis, R.: Researching F-root anycast placement using RIPE Atlas. RIPE Blog, October 2015. https://labs.ripe.net/Members/ray_bellis/researching-f-root-anycast-placement-using-ripe-atlas
3. Caesar, M., Rexford, J.: BGP routing policies in ISP networks. IEEE Network Mag. **19**(6), 5–11 (2005). https://doi.org/10.1109/MNET.2005.1541715
4. CAIDA: AS rank (2020). https://asrank.caida.org/. Accessed 12 Oct 2021
5. CAIDA: CAIDA UCSD BGP community dictionary (2020). https://www.caida.org/data/bgp-communities/. Accessed 12 Oct 2021
6. Calder, M., Flavel, A., Katz-Bassett, E., Mahajan, R., Padhye, J.: Analyzing the performance of an anycast CDN. In: Proceedings of the 2015 Internet Measurement Conference, pp. 531–537 (2015)
7. Chandra, R., Traina, P., Li, T.: BGP communities attribute. Technical report, 1997, RFC Editor (1996). https://www.rfc-editor.org/rfc/rfc1997.txt
8. Cicalese, D., Augé, J., Joumblatt, D., Friedman, T., Rossi, D.: Characterizing IPv4 anycast adoption and deployment. In: Proceedings of the 11th ACM Conference on Emerging Networking Experiments and Technologies, pp. 1–13 (2015)
9. Cloudflare: IPv6 adoption (2024). https://radar.cloudflare.com/reports/ipv6/
10. Dietzel, C., Feldmann, A., King, T.: Blackholing at IXPs: on the effectiveness of DDoS mitigation in the wild. In: Karagiannis, T., Dimitropoulos, X. (eds.) PAM 2016. LNCS, vol. 9631, pp. 319–332. Springer, Cham (2016). https://doi.org/10.1007/978-3-319-30505-9_24
11. Fan, X., Heidemann, J., Govindan, R.: Evaluating anycast in the domain name system. In: 2013 Proceedings IEEE INFOCOM, pp. 1681–1689. IEEE (2013)
12. Flavel, A., et al.: FastRoute: a scalable load-aware anycast routing architecture for modern CDNs. In: 12th USENIX Symposium on Networked Systems Design and Implementation (NSDI 2015), pp. 381–394 (2015)
13. Gao, L.: On inferring autonomous system relationships in the Internet. ACM/IEEE Trans. Network. **9**(6), 733–745 (2001)
14. Gao, R., Dovrolis, C., Zegura, E.W.: Interdomain ingress traffic engineering through optimized AS-path prepending. In: Boutaba, R., Almeroth, K., Puigjaner, R., Shen, S., Black, J.P. (eds.) NETWORKING 2005. LNCS, vol. 3462, pp. 647–658. Springer, Heidelberg (2005). https://doi.org/10.1007/11422778_52
15. Giotsas, V., Smaragdakis, G., Dietzel, C., Richter, P., Feldmann, A., Berger, A.: Inferring BGP blackholing activity in the internet. In: Proceedings of the Internet Measurement Conference, pp. 1–14. ACM (2017)

16. Google: Google IPv6 statistics (2024). https://www.google.com/intl/en/ipv6/statistics.html/
17. Koch, T., Li, K., Ardi, C., Katz-Bassett, E., Calder, M., Heidemann, J.: Anycast in context: a tale of two systems. In: Proceedings of the ACM SIGCOMM Conference. ACM, Virtual, August 2021. https://doi.org/10.1145/3452296.3472891
18. Kuipers, J.H.: Anycast for DDoS (2017). https://essay.utwente.nl/73795/1/Kuipers_MA_EWI.pdf. Accessed 12 Oct 2021
19. Li, Z., Levin, D., Spring, N., Bhattacharjee, B.: Internet anycast: performance, problems, and potential, Budapest, Hungary, pp. 59–73, August 2018. https://doi.org/10.1145/3230543.3230547. https://www.cs.umd.edu/projects/droot/anycast_sigcomm18.pdf
20. Luckie, M., Huffaker, B., Dhamdhere, A., Giotsas, V., Claffy, K.: As relationships, customer cones, and validation. In: Proceedings of the 2013 Conference on Internet Measurement Conference, pp. 243–256 (2013)
21. McQuistin, S., Uppu, S.P., Flores, M.: Taming anycast in the wild Internet. In: Proceedings of the Internet Measurement Conference, pp. 165–178 (2019)
22. Monroe, L.: CenturyLink completes acquisition of level 3 (2017). https://news.lumen.com/2017-11-01-CenturyLink-completes-acquisition-of-Level-3
23. Moura, G.C.M., et al.: Anycast vs DDoS: evaluating the November 2015 root DNS event. In: Proceedings of the ACM Internet Measurement Conference, November 2016. https://doi.org/10.1145/2987443.2987446
24. Moura, G.C.M., et al.: Old but gold: prospecting TCP to engineer and live monitor DNS anycast. In: Hohlfeld, O., Moura, G., Pelsser, C. (eds.) PAM 2022. LNCS, vol. 13210, pp. 264–292. Springer, Cham (2022). https://doi.org/10.1007/978-3-030-98785-5_12
25. Munteanu, C., Gasser, O., Poese, I., Smaragdakis, G., Feldmann, A.: Enabling multi-hop ISP-hypergiant collaboration. In: Proceedings of the Applied Networking Research Workshop, pp. 54–59 (2023)
26. Partridge, C., Mendez, T., Milliken, W.: Host anycasting service. Technical report, 1546, RFC Editor (1993). https://www.rfc-editor.org/rfc/rfc1546.txt
27. Quoitin, B., Pelsser, C., Swinnen, L., Bonaventure, O., Uhlig, S.: Interdomain traffic engineering with BGP. IEEE Commun. Mag. 41(5), 122–128 (2003)
28. Rizvi, A., Bertholdo, L., Ceron, J., Heidemann, J.: Anycast agility: network playbooks to fight DDoS. In: 31st USENIX Security Symposium (USENIX Security 2022), pp. 4201–4218 (2022)
29. Schlinker, B., et al.: Engineering egress with edge fabric: steering oceans of content to the world. In: Proceedings of the Conference of the ACM Special Interest Group on Data Communication, pp. 418–431 (2017)
30. Schmidt, R.D.O., Heidemann, J., Kuipers, J.H.: Anycast latency: how many sites are enough? In: International Conference on Passive and Active Network Measurement, Sydney, Australia, pp. 188–200, March 2017. https://www.isi.edu/%7ejohnh/PAPERS/Schmidt17a.html
31. Sommese, R., et al.: MAnycast2: using anycast to measure anycast. In: Proceedings of the ACM Internet Measurement Conference, IMC 2020, pp. 456–463. Association for Computing Machinery, New York, NY, USA (2020). https://doi.org/10.1145/3419394.3423646
32. One Step: BGP community guides. https://onestep.net/communities/. Accessed 12 Oct 2021

33. Wei, L., Heidemann, J.: Does anycast hang up on you? In: 2017 Network Traffic Measurement and Analysis Conference (TMA), pp. 1–9. IEEE, Dublin, Ireland, July 2017. https://doi.org/10.23919/TMA.2017.8002905
34. Weiden, F., Frost, P.: Anycast as a load balancing feature. In: Proceedings of the 24th International Conference on Large Installation System Administration, pp. 1–6. USENIX Association (2010)
35. Zhou, M., et al.: Regional IP anycast: deployments, performance, and potentials. In: Proceedings of the ACM SIGCOMM 2023 Conference, pp. 917–931 (2023)

Ebb and Flow: Implications of ISP Address Dynamics

Guillermo Baltra[1,2(✉)], Xiao Song[1,2], and John Heidemann[1,2]

[1] University of Southern California, Los Angeles, CA 90089, USA
[2] Information Sciences Institute, Marina del Rey, CA 90292, USA
{songxiao,johnh,baltra}@isi.edu

Abstract. *Address dynamics* are changes in IP address occupation as users come and go, ISPs renumber them for privacy or for routing maintenance. Address dynamics affect address reputation services, IP geolocation, network measurement, and outage detection, with implications of Internet governance, e-commerce, and science. While prior work has identified diurnal trends in address use, we show the effectiveness of Multi-Seasonal-Trend using Loess (MSTL) decomposition to identify both daily and weekly trends. We use ISP-wide dynamics to develop IAS, a new algorithm that is the first to automatically detect ISP maintenance events that move users in the address space. We show that 20% of such events result in /24 IPv4 address blocks that become unused for days or more, and correcting nearly 41k false outages per quarter. Our analysis provides a new understanding about ISP address use: while only about 2.8% of ASes (1,730) are diurnal, some diurnal ASes show more than 20% changes each day. It also shows greater fragmentation in IPv4 address use compared to IPv6.

1 Introduction

Millions of devices connect to the Internet everyday, but some come and go. Many ISPs *dynamically assign* devices to public IP addresses. While some users have IP addresses that are stable for weeks, ISPs often reassign users for many reasons: to promote privacy, to prevent servers on "home" networks, and to shift users away from routers scheduled for maintenance. IP policies vary: some renumber users every day [17,20,23,28,33], some show large diurnal changes [26].

Understanding ISP address dynamics is important in Internet policy, network measurement, and security. In Internet policy, ISPs need to make business-critical decisions that include purchasing carrier-grade NAT equipment versus acquiring more address space, or evaluating the costs of carefully reusing limited IPv4 space versus transitioning to IPv6. Regulators like national or Regional Internet Registries (RIRs) must consider address dynamics when crafting policies about transferring limited IPv4 address space and tracking IPv4 and IPv6 routing table sizes. For network measurement and security, dynamics affect services like IP address reputation [7,24], IP geolocation [15], and generating IPv4 [8] and IPv6 hitlists [5,9–11,18,34]. Stable addresses also simplify attack targeting, traffic fingerprinting, and have implications for privacy and anonymity.

The topic of address dynamics has been explored previously. Some have shown the stagnation of the total number of active IPv4 addresses and identified address block activity patterns [28]. Others have tracked address changes for a subset of addresses and analyzed lease durations [20,21], studied diurnal patterns where blocks stay active during the day, but remain inactive during the night [26], and built a statistical model from few ISPs to provide address churn estimation [17]. While important, all prior work focuses on behavior inside specific address blocks, not ISP-wide.

Address dynamics also affect the accuracy of outage detection. Diurnal changes can misinterpret nighttime quiet as outages [26] and must be considered in passive data [12]. CDN-based outage detection showed that ISP-level user movement, often correlated with scheduled router maintenance, can produce false outages [27]. Although CDN-measurements were more robust to ISP-level events than prior work, they did not quantify how often maintenance events happen, nor suggest how to address this problem in other systems. Finally, recent work showed that tracking changes in address use can detect changes in human behavior, such as shifts to working from home [31]. The goal of this paper is to explore how these related outcomes—diurnal effects, maintenance detection, and tracking overall user changes—all benefit from an improved understanding of address dynamics. We then use this understanding to build more accurate models of address activity, improving these existing services.

The primary contribution of this paper is to develop ISP Availability Sensing (IAS, Sect. 3.4), a new algorithm that identifies maintenance events in the ISP, allowing us to recognize that apparent outages are actually users being reassigned. This algorithm uses ISP Diurnal Detrending (IDD, §sec:diurnaldesign), to separate daily and weekly patterns from underlying trends and residual, both of which are important in detection algorithms. Our second contribution is to validate IAS using data from ISPs with known maintenance patterns and data from RIPE Atlas (Sect. 4.1). Although such events have been previously identified, IAS and this validation are the first to automate their detection. Our final contribution is to use IAS and IDD for three new observations: we quantify how many ISPs are diurnal (Sect. 5.4), how many maintenance events occur (Sect. 5.1), and how IPv6 shows more consistent address usage than IPv4 (Sect. 5.2).

All of the data used and created in this paper is available at no cost [32]. While our primary datasets date from 2017 to 2020, when data from 6 Trinocular sites was available, we confirm key results hold in 2022 (Sect. 5.4). Evidence of diurnal behavior in networks has been shown over nearly a decade of observations (from [26] to [31]), so we expect our algorithms and our qualitative observations to apply today. Our work poses no ethical concerns (Sect. A): although we use data on individual IP addresses, we have no way of associating them with individuals. Our work was IRB reviewed and identified as non-human subjects research (USC IRB IIR00001648).

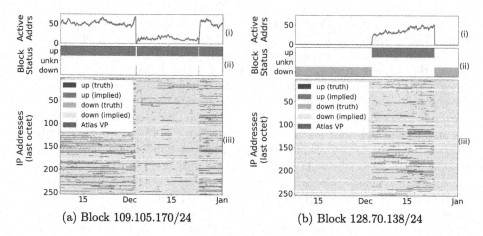

(a) Block 109.105.170/24   (b) Block 128.70.138/24

Fig. 1. Sample Atlas VP (Id 1001049) shifting between different /24 blocks during maintenance events, 2020q4. Datasets: Trinocular A42N, Atlas MsmId 1010.

2   Implications of Address Dynamics

This paper examines two challenges in how addresses are managed: maintenance events and diurnal networks. Both cause problems to outage detection systems because they cause individual /24 blocks to become vacant and so appear unreachable, resulting in a *false outage*. An outage is incorrect because users are receiving service elsewhere (due to maintenance or other address reassignment), or are sleeping (diurnal changes). We focus on blocks going fully vacant, since outage detection already accommodates blocks that partially reduce use [26].

Our premise is that a *whole-ISP* viewpoint is necessary to address these challenges. In fact, initially we hoped we could fix algorithms that examined only individual /24 s. However, because ISPs can shift addresses from one to many /24 s, we believe that a combination of block-level and ISP-level examination is necessary to provide outcomes robust to now known challenges.

ISP Maintenance Events: Fig. 1 shows two /24 address blocks, with green dots showing ping responses (the bottom area marked (iii)), block status (area (ii) shown up, unknown, or down), and a count of number of active addresses (the line graph in area (i)). We have a RIPE Atlas VP [30] that moved from the left block to the right during three weeks in December—a maintenance event that left the left block mostly idle. This event is difficult for an external outage detection system to handle: gaps on December 3 and 24 are outages in the left block, and the much lower utilization for the period is hard to track. Yet someone watching the *whole* Autonomous System (AS) would realize users shifted addresses temporarily. In Sect. 3.1 we show how we build an AS-level view, and in Sect. 3.4 how we can avoid false outages from these type of events, while in Sect. 5.3 we show how often these events occur.

Diurnal ASes: Other ASes have large changes in user populations over the course of a day. In these *diurnal ASes*, dynamic users (possibly on mobile devices,

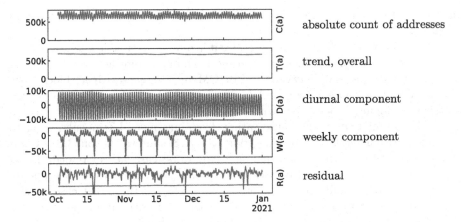

Fig. 2. MSTL decomposition of AS9829 during 2020q4. Dataset: A42.

or connecting during the workday) disconnect at night, leaving their addresses unused. Although many users in North America and Europe have always-on home routers with device changes hidden behind NAT, many users in Asia, South America, and Africa disconnect at night [26]

The top graph in Fig. 2 shows the number of active IP addresses in AS9829 (Bharat Sanchar Nigam Limited) over three months, based on measurements updated every 11 min (Sect. 3.1). With an average of 600k active addresses (the second graph), this major national Indian ISP has *many* active users. But the timeseries in the top shows daily changes in the number of active addresses of ±20%, more than 100k users! In addition, close examination shows activity drops for two days after every five—evidence of weekends. These trends show that this AS has *strong diurnal and weekly trends*.

Such large shifts cause problems for outage detection systems, because losing 100k users every night vacates some /24 blocks. (Sect. B shows a specific block with daily outages.) Tracking outages across ASes with this much daily change motivates diurnal AS detection (Sect. 3.2) and detrending (Sect. 3.3). We show the importance of detrending and tracking ISP-wide behavior in Sect. 4.2.

3 Methodology

We next describe how we track AS-wide address usage, identify diurnal ASes and trends, and detect maintenance events.

3.1 AS-Wide Address Accumulation

Since ASes move users around in their address space, we find that *the number of active addresses across the AS* helps characterize the current population. The first step in our AS-wide algorithms is to track active addresses. Determining active addresses in an AS is difficult because some ASes have millions of addresses, too many to monitor instantly—we reanalyze existing data to get an approximate snapshot of global state.

Our input is from Trinocular [32], since it is publicly available and it has years of address-specific ping responses covering much of the Internet (4M to 5M /24 blocks). Trinocular sends between 1 and 16 ICMP echo-requests to each block every 11 min, each to a different address. Addresses rotate in a fixed order unique to each block, so a single Trinocular site will scan all planned addresses in 48 h or less.

We accumulate individual observations from incremental Trinocular scans to approximate current state following prior work [1,31] and validation [3,31]. Combining results from all six Trinocular sites cuts worst-case latency to eight hours (each site scans independently with different and varying phases). We update estimates incrementally each 11-minute round, so even this worst case usually tracks diurnal changes. We apply 1-loss repair to recover from measurement loss [25]. For efficiency, we aggregate results by the hour.

We add AS information from Routeviews [16] and combine reports for all addresses in each AS. The result is $C_i(a)$, a timeseries *counting addresses* for each AS a at time i.

We currently treat each AS as independent. Although most large ISPs employ multiple ASes (for example, one each for Asian, American, and European operations), in Sect. 5.2 we show that renumbering usually occurs within the same AS, so this simplification does not change our primary results.

3.2 Diurnal ISP Detection

Given $C(a)$, address counts for an AS (Sect. 3.1), our next step is to identify ASes with a strong diurnal component. Following prior block-level diurnal analysis [26], we take the Fast-Fourier Transform (FFT) of this timeseries, giving a set of coefficients showing the strength and phase at all frequencies. We then label that AS as diurnal if the energy in the frequency corresponding to a 24-hour period is the largest of all other (non-zero frequency) components.

3.3 ISP Diurnal Detrending (IDD)

Since we know some ASes are strongly diurnal, we next *decompose* $C(a)$ to extract long-term trends, cyclic components, and any residual changes. Each component is useful to identify usual events.

We apply MSTL [4] to extract *four* components, one for diurnal (daily) behavior, one for weekly patterns, along with trend and residual components. We find some networks have both diurnal and weekly patterns, while others are only diurnal. We decompose $C(a)$ in four components: trend (T), diurnal (D), weekly (W), and residual (R) components.

Figure 2 shows trend decomposition of AS9829 during 2020q4 (three months). The top graph shows the AS-wide timeseries $C(a)$, ranging from 500k to 800k active addresses. The next graph down $T(a)$ shows the long-term trend. We can see that this AS has a static user population over this quarter.

The third and fourth graphs show $D(a)$ and $W(a)$, how much regular change there is each day and week. The strong diurnal pattern that we first identified at the 24 h frequency in the FFT (Sect. 3.2) shows up in $D(a)$ with swings that range across 30% of responsive addresses (±100k). The weekly component ($W(a)$) show a weekend drop of about 50k addresses. Diurnal and weekly trends are both visible in $C(a)$, but easier to quantify after decomposition.

The residual in the final row, $R(a)$, isolates any remaining changes. We use this residual when detecting address dynamics in Sect. 5.1.

3.4   ISP Availability Sensing (IAS)

The ISP Availability Sensing algorithm (IAS) recognizes maintenance events by comparing a global count of active users at AS-level against local changes in portions of the network. Our insight is that the AS-wide count of active users *remains stable* during maintenance, even though specific parts of the network *lose* and *add* users. This stability distinguishes user movement from outages.

Detecting AS-Wide Address Stability. We first show that the AS' active addresses are roughly stable.

We define Δ_i as the relative fraction of change of active addresses across an AS at time interval i, using the residual and trend decomposition from Sect. 3.3: $\Delta_i = R_i(a)/T_i(a)$.

When $\Delta_i = 0$ there is no change in number of active users. Of course we expect some accident changes ($\Delta_i \neq 0$) as individual hosts come and go in real networks, or due to loss of probing packets or replies. These small changes appear in the residual, $R(a)$, in Figure 2. Finally, we identify large changes ($\Delta_i \geq 0.05$) as outages, while smaller changes ($0 < \Delta_i < 0.05$) are more typical jitter. We select a threshold large enough to avoid noise, but not so large as to miss outages. As future work we hope to optimize this value by training against external observations.

IAS assumes complete knowledge of each AS' address space. However, ASes bring new address space on-line to serve new customers, such space may not immediately appear in $C(a)$. We evaluate how frequently we miss users due to unmonitored address space in Sect. 4.3.

Detecting Network Changes IAS' second requirement is the presence of some blocks changing. We enforce this requirement by identifying the number of blocks that change state (become or cease being reachable) from outage detection. We currently require $\delta = 4$ blocks to change state, and study this choice in Sect. 4.2. Larger values reduce the number of events (Fig. 3). We select $\delta = 5$ because it is just past the knee of the curve, in a plateau $5 \leq \delta \leq 9$ (Table 1). Exploration of an adaptive threshold to account for larger ASes is future work.

4   Validation

We validate IAS against external sources, and then examine design choices.

4.1   IAS Detecting Known ISP Maintenance?

We next evaluate IAS' ability to detect maintenance events using ground truth from an ISP. Our first source of ground truth are ISPs that have public maintenance windows; we use this case study to validate. Lumen Technologies (AS209, at the time called CenturyLink) announces that midnight to 6 a.m. local time [14] is a public maintenance window, and they report specific events [6]. We identify Lumen address blocks from 18 peers in Routeviews [16].

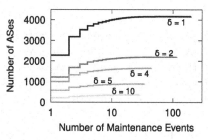

Fig. 3. Cumulative number of ASes with x or fewer maintenance events (2020q4).

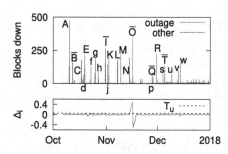

Fig. 4. Down events (top) from six observers (top) and Δ_i (bottom) from Los Angeles. Lumen AS209. Dataset: A30, 2017q4.

Figure 4 shows data for 2017q4. The top graph counts the number of blocks that are down over time, from all Trinocular data, but without IAS.

IAS finds 23 events in this merged data, each involving 35 or more blocks. Of the 23 events, more than half (13, indicated with capital letters) are in Lumen's published maintenance window, suggesting they are maintenance events. Five of these (with lines over the letters) are documented events and datacenters from the service log on their website. (We do not examine regional aspects of maintenance, since our work focused on ISP-wide dynamics.) IAS identifies *all* these events as maintenance, except for event ($\overline{O}$). The best-available ground truth (service logs and maintenance window), suggests that these events are true positives.

We believe event $\overline{O}$ on 2017-11-16 is a true outage. We show Δ_i, the changes in the number of active addresses from one observer, in the bottom graph. The 40% drop in active addresses, followed by the recovery indicates an outage. IAS classifies event $\overline{O}$ as an outage, not a maintenance event. This event is unusual, in that it affected Los Angeles VP mostly (20,211 blocks and 8.5 h, not shown in graph) than from other sites (where it was 348 blocks and 2 h). 2024-01-23 It shows that the IAS will correctly pass through large outages (a true negative).

4.2   Validating IAS and IDD from RIPE Atlas

RIPE Atlas VPs live in edge networks and report their current IP address, providing ground truth for ISP maintenance.

Atlas as Ground Truth. We take Atlas VPs built-in measurement 1010 [29] as our known addresses. We aggregate VP address changes using 4-min timebins, since new address reports are provided every 4 min. We omit address changes where Atlas VP failed to reach a root DNS server to rule out address changes due to outages [20]. Finally, to rule out individual VP changes, we require four VPs in the same AS to move at about the same time to declare a maintenance event. During 2020q4, we count 164 events by this criteria.

Table 1. Atlas VP address change events (≥ 4 VPs) compared against IAS detection thresholds, 2020q4.

			blocks that change state (δ_i)												
			0	1	2	3	(1–3)	4	5	6	7	8	9	≥ 10	(≥ 4)	all
Addr. drop	without IDD	$\Delta_i \leq 5\%$	42	15	9	4	(28)	11	4	7	8	6	5	42	(83)	153
		$\Delta_i > 5\%$	1	0	0	0	(0)	0	0	0	0	0	0	10	(10)	11
	with IDD	$\Delta_i \leq 5\%$	43	15	9	4	(28)	11	4	7	8	6	5	52	(93)	164
		$\Delta_i > 5\%$	0	0	0	0	(0)	0	0	0	0	0	0	0	(0)	0

Validating IAS. We first validate IAS with IDD, considering its two requirements: stable AS-level addresses ($\Delta_i \leq 5\%$) and four or more blocks that move ($\delta_i \geq 4$). We show our results in Table 1.

We first look at the bottom two rows of Table 1, labeled "with IDD". The fourth row shows no blocks change when $\Delta_i > 5\%$ because of the large threshold. The third row shows 164 blocks where VPs move, of which 93 are found in IAS and occur as part of a large movement (right, in green), while 43 move by themselves (left, gray), and 28 move with 1 to 3 others (center, yellow). We consider the 93 to be IAS successes. All will be found and recognized as maintenance events.

The 43 in gray represent independent movements that are not large maintenance events, but may be routers at home rebooting to a new address. These are not found by IAS, but are not necessarily maintenance events, so we count them neither as true nor false positives.

Finally, the 28 marked yellow are likely maintenance events that IAS misses as being too small. These are false negatives.

Not having all negative cases prevents us from computing recall and precision, but we can show a True Positive rate of 0.77 ($93/(28 + 93)$). We conclude that IAS works reasonably well, although there is room for improvement.

Validating IDD. To validate the importance of IDD, we turn it off and compare the results in the first two rows of Table 1 with the bottom two rows. IDD helps filter out diurnal changes, making large shifts more common: compare the 10 cases with $\Delta_i > 5\%$ without IDD to zero cases with it. We also see that it helps

IAS: the TPR is 0.75 without IDD (83/(28 + 83)) compared to 0.77 with IDD. We conclude that accounting for diurnal changes helps.

4.3 Does Unmonitored Space Harm IAS?

Measurement systems do not track the complete address space, discarding some segments due to low response rate, or lack of any historic responses [2]. Users reassigned to unmonitored space implies that IAS may erroneously infer outages due to drops in the total active address count, IAS false negatives.

For 2020q4, we find that the majority of reassignments (51%) occur within monitored addresses, and that most addresses (84%) stay in the same category. IAS is not impeded by incomplete measurement (see Sect. C).

Table 2. Active RIPE Atlas Vantage Points during 2020q4

	IPv4		IPv6	
Total VPs	12,855	100.0%	6,319	100.0%
Do not change IP	8,501	66.1%	4,730	74.9%
Change IP	4,354	33.9%	1,589	25.1%
Do not change routable prefix	973	7.6%	1,182	18.7%
Change routable prefix	3,381	26.3%	407	6.4%
Do not change AS	2,411	18.8%	75	1.1%
Change AS	970	7.5%	332	5.3%

4.4 Choice of Spatial Granularity

We next consider what spatial granularity to use when tracking address dynamics. Our goal is that IAS can identify when users move. To do so, we must assess how "far" a user moves: do they stay in the same routable prefix, or within the same AS, or move between ASes. We compare address movement (a baseline) against how often a device moves within a routable prefix or an AS.

Table 2 shows how often 12,855 RIPE Atlas VPs change their address, routable prefix, or AS in 2020q4, for both IPv4 and IPv6. We see that the majority of devices are stable, with 66.1% (v4) and 74.9% (v6) never changing address and 7.6% and 18.7% staying in the same routable prefix. Of the remaining that move, some change only once, but many change frequently, perhaps because they are in ISPs that renumber their users regularly. We conclude that most devices are very stable, but a few move frequently,

Surprisingly, we find about 7.5% (970 v4) and 5.3% (332 v6) change AS. As changes are very rare, with a few (2%) changing once, perhaps because a user changed their home ISP. The remaining 3% change frequently, perhaps because they are mobile and regularly move between home and work.

We conclude that AS granularity is almost always suitable to capture most movement and so IAS' use of ASes is correct.

5   Evaluation

We now study ISP address dynamics across the Internet with IDD and IAS. We evaluate the addressing efficiency, improvements to outage detection, quantify diurnalness, and compare IPv4 and IPv6 management practices.

5.1   Quantifying ISP Address Dynamics

Several groups have looked at different aspects of address dynamics [17, 20, 21, 26–28, 31]. While prior work identified ISP maintenance as a type of network disruption [28], they did not quantify how often such events occur. We examine maintenance and diurnal events over a quarter using IAS.

We use IAS to identify maintenance events across all 63k ASes active in 2020q4. Figure 3 shows the cumulative distribution of number of maintenance events for 6.5% of ASes with at least one event in this period. We compare results for different detection thresholds, that is, the number of Trinocular blocks going up or down during the same timebin, with an AS-level responsive address count remaining stable (less than 5% drops).

With a threshold of one changed block (the minimum), IAS detects at least one event in 2k ASes. The number of ASes decreases to only 210 ASes with our strictest threshold ($\delta = 10$).

We also see that some ASes regularly move users around, seeing 100 maintenance events in these 90 days. One example of these frequent-maintenance ISPs are ISPs that renumber users every 24 h.

The area under each curve corresponds to the number of maintenance events and diurnal events that occurred during this quarter. For our default preferred threshold of four blocks, we see 2.5k events in 2020q4. At a block level, these events cause 41k false outages.

5.2   Address Space Refactoring

Address management is a business-critical decision for ISPs. Limited IPv4 addresses require careful management and reuse, while IPv6 transition requires updating current practices. Each of these choices incurs costs. To provide ground truth for the kind of AS-level changes observed by our IDD and IAS algorithms, we next examine address churn in both IPv4 and IPv6 inferred from RIPE Atlas.

We take Atlas VP IPv4 and IPv6 address changes during 2020q4, and perform longest prefix match for these addresses using Routeviews RIB archives to obtain routable prefixes and ASes for the quarter. We count the number of times each VP changes address, routable prefix and AS, and the times unique addresses are assigned. Figure 5 and Fig. 6 show IPv4 and IPv6 aggregates as heatmaps. This analysis of RIPE Atlas data provides new ground truth about the number of maintenance events we aim to detect with IAS.

For IPv4 *address* changes (Fig. 5, bottom) we observe that most VPs do not change address during the quarter, but those that do change, often are assigned a new address, as the dark heatmap diagonal shows. Prefixes (middle) are mostly

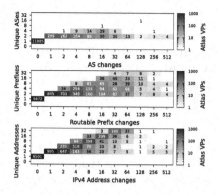

Fig. 5. IPv4 changes by AS (top), routable prefix (center), and address (bottom), for Atlas VPs with at least one change, 2020q4.

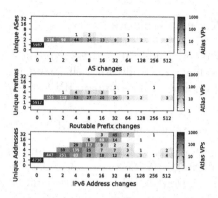

Fig. 6. IPv6 changes by AS (top), routable prefix (center), and address (bottom), for Atlas VP with at least one change, 2020q4.

reused, although many address changes involve a routable prefix change, too. Finally, addresses almost always stay in the same AS (top).

On the other hand, in IPv6 we observe that address changes generally occur within the same prefix. Our data confirms that IPv4 exhaustion and fragmentation make address management more challenging, while IPv6 uses fewer prefixes more efficiently because addressing aligns better with routing. While prior work has mentioned these trends [20,21], we look at both protocols together. Quantifing behavior at granularities other than routable prefixes is future work.

5.3 How Often Does IAS Repair False Outages?

Analysis of CDN traffic [27] showed that incorrect block-level outages are often due to users being assigned to different IP addresses. Measurements from end-user devices show users changing addresses, but external outage detection systems cannot distinguish the now-vacant old address block from a network problem. After users are reassigned, their old address blocks remain empty for minutes or months, and external outage detection systems (like Trinocular or Thunderping) incorrectly interpret this absence as an outage.

Figure 7 shows the distribution of durations of the time a block stays unresponsive before or after the 41k address reassignments that are detected by IAS during 2020q4 (Sect. 5.1). All of these events are false outages that IAS repairs. To understand root causes we identify three regions of unresponsive duration.

Durations less than 11 min (the bottom 2% on the left, about 800 unshaded events) are less than the scanning frequency of our data source (Trinocular). Such short outages occur in blocks with large numbers of scanned addresses where only a few are in use (blocks with large $|A(b)|$ and small A, with terms from [25]). These false outages of shorter-than-probing-interval events is natural

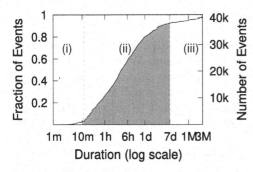

Fig. 7. CDF of unresponsive duration of blocks before or after an IAS-detected maintenance event, 2020q4.

Table 3. Number of diurnal networks at different granularities. 2022q4.

	IPv4	
ASes	62,310	100.0%
Diurnal	1,730	2.8%
Non-diurnal	60,580	97.2%
Routable prefixes	606,187	100.0%
Diurnal	30,029	5.0%
Non-diurnal	576,158	95.0%
/24 blocks	5,124,967	100.0%
Diurnal	111,908	2.2%
Non-diurnal	5,013,059	97.8%

due to the nature of active probing at regular intervals; IAS suggests these are measurement "noise".

The majority of events (the center, shaded region, 88% or about 36k events) are blocks that are inactive between 11 min and one day. These false outages are typically due to diurnal address assignment, when customers are regularly reassigned, and part of the assigned blocks sometimes appear to have no activity. IAS detects and corrects these false outages because it knows the AS-wide activity is constant.

Finally, about 10% or 4k blocks are empty for more than a week. Trinocular already classified these blocks as "gone dark", inferring that a long period of no responses cannot be a transient outage, but must be ISP renumbering. Our AS-wide analysis with IAS confirms that this policy is correct.

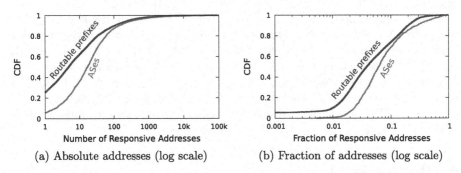

(a) Absolute addresses (log scale)   (b) Fraction of addresses (log scale)

Fig. 8. CDFs of diurnalness of all ASes (red) and routable prefixes (blue); 2020q4. (Color figure online)

5.4   How Many ASes Are Diurnal?

Diurnal networks are important to assess allocation policies in Internet governance and to avoid false outages in outage detection. While diurnal behavior has previously studied at the /24 block granularity [26,31], we next examine diurnalness in the larger groupings of routable prefixes and ASes.

Here we use address accumulation data for 2022q4 from Trinocular, following Sect. 3.1, grouped by prefixes and ASes from Routeviews [19] on 2022-10-01. We assess diurnalness as described in Sect. 3.2.

In Table 3 we show how many diurnal networks are detected at different granularities. While only 2.8% of ASes are diurnal (1,730), 112k blocks are diurnal. Recent work has used these blocks to help understand human activity [31].

5.5   How Much of a Diurnal as Is Diurnal?

Although we can identify networks as diurnal as we described in Sect. 3.2, in many ISPs, only *part* of the AS is diurnal, while part is more static.

Here we examine what fraction of an AS' address space is diurnal. Prior work has examined individual blocks, but our decomposition allows us to examine "diurnalness" for the AS as a whole. We judge AS-level diurnalness by the size of the daily change in addresses. From our MSTL decomposition (Sect. 3.3), that is $(P_{95}(D(a)) - P_5(D(a)))/P_{95}(C(a))$, where P_n is the n-percentile of the given timeseries over the quarter.

Figure 8 shows how diurnal ASes (red) and routable prefixes (blue) are by numbers (Fig. 8a) and fraction (Fig. 8b) of responsive addresses.

First, we see that *most networks are not very diurnal*: activity in 85% of ASes change by 100 addresses or fewer each day, accounting for only 20% of their address space. This stability is typical of ISPs with customers using always-on home gateways. Stable address usage is why IAS can detect maintenance events.

When comparing routable prefixes to ASes, we see that routable prefixes are more often mostly diurnal (comparing the two lines in Fig. 8b). Although most prefixes are fairly stable (69% change by only 10% of their active addresses), some (about 20%) have a very large daily swing (15% of addresses or more). Finally, because routable prefixes are necessarily smaller than ASes, they see a smaller absolute size of diurnal change (compare the lines in Fig. 8a).

This trend suggests that routable prefixes are a useful size to study diurnalness, and it supports suggestion for its study in Sect. 5.4.

6   Related Work

Other work has considered maintenance events in relation to outages. Richter et al. used internal information from clients to demonstrate that address reassignment cause false outages, defining *disruptions* to include both true and false outages [27]. Guillot et al. proposed Chocolatine to detect outages at AS level and geographical areas using Internet background radiation [12]. These works do not show how to differentiate true outages from maintenance events, nor perform a quantitative analysis of maintenance events. Recently Padmanabhan et al. showed that some events span parts of multiple blocks [22], a result consistent with our goal of studying whole ISPs.

Other groups have studied address changes and usage. Some have examined the duration hosts keep the same address [13,20,21], estimated Internet-wide address churn [17], and address utilization [28]. However, these techniques either do not scale to the entire address space, are estimations, or require CDN access, while we do Internet-wide, third-party detection and identify ISP renumbering.

Address counting was first used in outage detection with CDN data [27], then darknet analysis [12]. We previously described address accumulation with Trinocular [1,31]. We use this signal to detect ISP maintenance.

Previous work has considered seasonal patterns. Quan et al. detected diurnal patterns using FFT at block level [26]; Chocolatine used SARIMA in ISP-wide detection to factor out seasonal trends [12]. Unlike prior work, we show the importance of multi-seasonal trends to account for both daily and weekend effects, and show that we can distinguish maintenance events from outages at the /24-granularity.

7   Conclusions

AS-wide diurnal changes and maintenance are part of our Internet ecosystem, yet they challenge outage detection systems. Our new IAS algorithms, with IDD, can often recover from such dynamics. We showed that IAS is effective and can correct 41k false outages per quarter.

Acknowledgments. The work is supported in part by the National Science Foundation, CISE Directorate, award CNS-2007106 and NSF-2028279. The U.S. Government is authorized to reproduce and distribute reprints for Governmental purposes notwithstanding any copyright notation thereon.

A   Research Ethics

Our work poses no ethical concerns for several reasons.

First, we collect no additional data, but instead reanalyze data from existing sources. Our work therefore poses no additional risk in data collection.

Our analysis poses no risk to individuals because our subject is network topology and connectivity. There is a slight risk to individuals in that we examine responsiveness of individual IP addresses. With external information, IP addresses can sometimes be traced to individuals, particularly when combined with external data sources like DHCP logs. We avoid this risk in three ways. First, we do not have DHCP logs for any networks (and in fact, most are unavailable outside of specific ISPs). Second, we commit, as research policy, to not combine IP addresses with external data sources that might de-anonymize them to individuals. Finally, except for analysis of specific cases as part of validation, all of our analysis is done in bulk over the whole dataset.

We do observe data about organizations such as ISPs, and about the geolocation of blocks of IP addresses. Because we do not map IP addresses to individuals, this analysis poses no individual privacy risk.

Finally, we suggest that while our work poses minimal privacy risks to individuals, to also provides substantial benefit to the community and to individuals. For reasons given in the introduction it is important to improve network reliability and understand how networks fail. Our work contributes to that goal.

Our work was reviewed by the Institutional Review Board at our university and because it poses no risk to individual privacy, it was identified as non-human subjects research (USC IRB IIR00001648).

B   A Sample Block with Diurnal Behavior

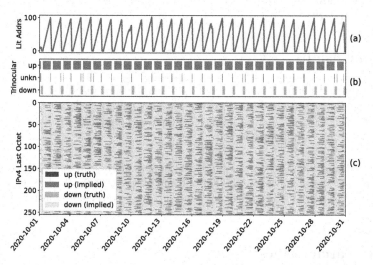

Fig. 9. Diurnal blocks in AS9829 observed from Trinocular, Los Angeles, October 2020. Dataset A42.

The block in Fig. 9 from AS9829 shows how one /24 occupancy varies over the course of a day. Green dots show active addresses, and gray non-response. This address block is 50% full every day at its peak, but empty every night. This trend can be seen in the count of active address (the top graph). It causes daily outage events in Trinocular, as shown in the middle graph, showing *up* most of the day but *down* every night. Blocks that look like this are common in this AS, and they show the need for our IDD algorithm (Sect. 3.3).

C   Does Unmonitored Space Harm IAS?

Measurement systems do not track the complete address space, as some segments are discarded due to low response rate, as well as addresses that historically have not responded [2]. Users reassigned to unmonitored space implies that IAS may erroneously infer outages due to drops in the total active address count, IAS false negatives. To evaluate if unmonitored space interferes with IAS, we count the number of times known VPs move to and from our underlying measurement system's unmonitored address space. We expect most of VPs to move within monitored addresses, as unmonitored space has been historically unresponsive implying low usage.

Trinocular strives to probe as much as it can (the *active* addresses), Trinocular excludes addresses for two reasons, *inactive* addresses used to reply to pings but have not in two years, and *non-trackable* blocks have less than three responsive addresses.

Table 4. Atlas VP address changes in Trinocular (un)monitored address space.

FROM / TO	active		non-trackable		inactive	
active	66,892	51%	3,487	3%	5,086	4%
non-trackable	3,392	3%	30,101	22%	1,251	1%
inactive	4,915	4%	1,303	1%	14,602	11%

As with Sect. 4.2, we use RIPE Atlas VPs as ground truth, since they track their current IP addresses. Table 4 counts how many addresses Atlas VPs have in each of the three Trinocular categories (active, inactive, non-trackable).

As expected, the majority of reassignments (51%) occur within monitored addresses (the top, left, green cell). In addition, most addresses (84%) stay in the same category (the diagonal).

A few addresses (7% in the yellow, left column) become active as they move in to measurable space, and about an equal number move out (the 7% in the red, top row). Finally, a surprisingly large 35% are never tracked (the gray region). Since the IAS goal is identify steady or changing addresses, never tracked blocks do not matter. The number that becomes and cease to be active is small (7% each) and about equal in size, so they should not skew IAS. We therefore conclude IAS is not impeded by incomplete measurement.

References

1. Baltra, G., Heidemann, J.: Improving the optics of active outage detection (extended). Technical Report ISI-TR-733. USC/Information Sciences Institute (2019)

2. Baltra, G., Heidemann, J.: Improving coverage of internet outage detection in sparse blocks. In: Sperotto, A., Dainotti, A., Stiller, B. (eds.) PAM 2020. LNCS, vol. 12048, pp. 19–36. Springer, Cham (2020). https://doi.org/10.1007/978-3-030-44081-7_2

3. Baltra, G.P.: Improving network reliability using a formal definition of the Internet core. Ph.D. Dissertation (2023)

4. Bandara, K., Hyndman, R.J., Bergmeir, C.: MSTL: a seasonal-trend decomposition algorithm for time series with multiple seasonal patterns (2021). https://doi.org/10.48550/ARXIV.2107.13462

5. Beverly, R., Durairajan, R., Plonka, D., Rohrer, J.P.: In the IP of the beholder: strategies for active IPv6 topology discovery. In: Proceedings of the ACM Internet Measurement Conference. ACM, Boston, Massachusetts, USA, pp. 308–321 (2018). https://doi.org/10.1145/3278532.3278559

6. CenturyLink. Event History (2019). https://status.ctl.io/history

7. Fail2ban (2023). https://github.com/fail2ban/fail2ban

8. Fan, X., Heidemann, J.: Selecting representative IP addresses for internet topology studies. In: Proceedings of the ACM Internet Measurement Conference. ACM, Melbourne, Australia, pp. 411–423 (2010). https://doi.org/10.1145/1879141.1879195

9. Foremski, P., Plonka, D., Berger, A.: Entropy/IP: uncovering structure in IPv6 addresses. In: Proceedings of the ACM Internet Measurement Conference. ACM, Santa Monica, CA, USA, pp. 167–181 (2016). https://doi.org/10.1145/2987443.2987445

10. Gasser, O., et al.: Clusters in the expanse: understanding and unbiasing IPv6 hitlists. In: Proceedings of the ACM Internet Measurement Conference, ACM, Boston, Mass., USA (2018). https://doi.org/10.1145/3278532.3278564

11. Gasser, O., Scheitle, Q., Gebhard, S., Carle, G.: Scanning the IPv6 internet: towards a comprehensive hitlist. In: Proceedings of the IFIP International Workshop on Traffic Monitoring and Analysis. IFIP, Louvain La Neuve, Belgium (2016). http://tma.ifip.org/2016/papers/tma2016-final51.pdf

12. Guillot, A., Fontugne, R., Winter, P., Merindol, P., King, A., Dainotti, A., Pelsser, C.: Chocolatine: outage detection for internet background radiation. In: 2019 Network Traffic Measurement and Analysis Conference (TMA), pp. 1–8. IEEE (2019)

13. Heidemann, J., Pradkin, Y., Govindan, R., Papadopoulos, C., Bartlett, G., Bannister, J.: Census and survey of the visible internet. In: Proceedings of the ACM Internet Measurement Conference. ACM, Vouliagmeni, Greece, pp. 169–182 (2008). https://doi.org/10.1145/1452520.1452542

14. Lumen technologies. Lumen master service agreement (2023). https://www.lumen.com/en-us/about/legal/business-customer-terms-conditions.html

15. MaxMind. GeoIP geolocation products (2017). http://www.maxmind.com/en/city

16. Meyer, D.: University of Oregon Route views (2018). http://www.routeviews.org

17. Moura, G.C., Ganán, C., Lone, Q., Poursaied, P., Asghari, H.. van Eeten, M.: How dynamic is the isps address space? towards internet-wide DHCP churn estimation. In: 2015 IFIP Networking Conference (IFIP Networking), pp. 1–9. IEEE (2015)

18. Murdock, A., Li, F., Bramsen, P., Durumeric, Z., Paxson, V.: Target Generation for Internet-wide IPv6 Scanning. In: Proceedings of the ACM Internet Measurement Conference, ACM, San Diego, CA, USA, pp. 242–253 (2017). https://doi.org/10.1145/3131365.3131405

19. University of Oregon. Route Views Archive Project (2020). http://archive.routeviews.org/bgpdata/2020.10/RIBS/rib.20201001.0000.bz2

20. Padmanabhan, R., Dhamdhere, A., Aben, E., Claffy, K.C., Spring, N.: Reasons dynamic addresses change. In: Proceedings of the ACM Internet Measurement Conference. ACM, Santa Monica, CA, USA, pp. 183–198 (2016). https://doi.org/ 10.1145/2987443.2987461
21. Padmanabhan, R., Rula, J.P., Richter, P., Strowes, S.D., Dainotti, A.: DynamIPs: analyzing address assignment practices in IPv4 and IPv6. In: Proceedings of the ACM Conference on Emerging Networking Experiments and Technologies, ACM, Barcelona, Spain, pp. 55–70 (2020). https://doi.org/10.1145/3386367.3431314
22. Padmanabhan, R., Schulman, A., Dainotti, A., Levin, D., Spring, N.: How to find correlated internet failures. In: Choffnes, D., Barcellos, M. (eds.) PAM 2019. LNCS, vol. 11419, pp. 210–227. Springer, Cham (2019). https://doi.org/10.1007/978-3-030-15986-3_14
23. Plonka, D., Berger, A.: Temporal and spatial classification of active IPv6 addresses. In: Proceedings of the ACM Internet Measurement Conference, Tokyo, Japan, pp. 509–522. ACM (2015). https://doi.org/10.1145/2815675.2815678
24. The Spamhaus project (2023). https://www.spamhaus.org
25. Quan, L., Heidemann, J., Pradkin, Y.: Trinocular: understanding internet reliability through adaptive probing. In: Proceedings of the ACM SIGCOMM Conference, Hong Kong, China, pp. 255–266. ACM (2013). https://doi.org/10.1145/2486001.2486017
26. Quan, L., Heidemann, J., Pradkin, Y.: When the internet sleeps: correlating diurnal networks with external factors. In Proceedings of the ACM Internet Measurement Conference, Vancouver, BC, Canada, pp. 87–100. ACM (2014). https://doi.org/ 10.1145/2663716.2663721
27. Richter, P., Padmanabhan, R., Spring, N., Berger, A., Clark, D.: Advancing the art of internet edge outage detection. In: Proceedings of the ACM Internet Measurement Conference, Boston, Massachusetts, USA, pp. 350–363. ACM (2018). https:// doi.org/10.1145/3278532.3278563
28. Richter, P., Smaragdakis, G., Plonka, D., Berger, A.: Beyond counting: new perspectives on the active IPv4 address space. In: Proceedings of the 2016 Internet Measurement Conference, pp. 135–149 (2016)
29. RIPE Atlas. IPv4 B-root ping (2023). https://atlas.ripe.net/measurements/1010/
30. RIPE Ncc Staff. RIPE Atlas: a global internet measurement network. Internet Protocol J. 18(3), 2–26 (2015). http://ipj.dreamhosters.com/wp-content/uploads/ 2015/10/ipj18.3.pdf
31. Song, X., Baltra, G., Heidemann, J.: Inferring changes in daily human activity from internet response. In: Proceedings of the ACM Internet Measurement Conference, ACM, Montreal, QC, Canada (2023). https://doi.org/10.1145/3618257.3624796
32. USC/ISI ANT project (2017). https://ant.isi.edu/datasets/all.html. (Updated quarterly)
33. Xie, Y., Yu, F., Achan, K., Gillum, E., Goldszmidt, M., Wobber, T.: How dynamic are IP Addresses?. In: Proceedings of the ACM SIGCOMM Conference, Kyoto, Japan, pp. 301–312. ACM (2007). https://doi.org/10.1145/1282380.1282415
34. Zirngibl, J., Steger, L., Sattler, P., Gasser, O., Carle, G.: Rusty clusters?: dusting an IPv6 research foundation. In: Proceedings of the 22nd ACM Internet Measurement Conference, France, pp. 395–409. ACM (2022). https://doi.org/10.1145/3517745.3561440

Satellite Networks

Watching Stars in Pixels: The Interplay of Traffic Shaping and YouTube Streaming QoE over GEO Satellite Networks

Jiamo Liu[1]($\boxtimes$), David Lerner[2], Jae Chung[2], Udit Paul[3], Arpit Gupta[1], and Elizabeth Belding[1]

[1] University of California, Santa Barbara, USA
{jiamoliu,arpitgupta,ebelding}@ucsb.edu
[2] Viasat, Carlsbad, USA
{david.lerner,jaewon.chung}@viasat.edu
[3] Ookla, Seattle, USA
udit.paul@ookla.com

Abstract. Geosynchronous satellite (GEO) networks are an important Internet access option for users beyond terrestrial connectivity. However, unlike terrestrial networks, GEO networks exhibit high latency and deploy TCP proxies and traffic shapers. The deployment of proxies effectively mitigates the impact of high network latency in GEO networks, while traffic shapers help realize customer-controlled data-saver options that optimize data usage. However, it is unclear how the interplay between GEO networks' high latency, TCP proxies, and traffic-shaping policies affects the quality of experience for commonly used video applications. To address this gap, we analyze the quality of over 2 k YouTube video sessions streamed across a production GEO network with a 900 Kbps shaping rate. Given the average bit rates of the videos, we expected streaming to be seamless at resolutions of 360p, and nearly seamless at resolutions approaching 480p. However, our analysis reveals that this is not the case: 30% of both TCP and QUIC sessions experience rebuffering, while the median average resolution is only 404p for TCP and 360p for QUIC. Our analysis identifies two key factors that contribute to sub-optimal performance: (i) unlike TCP, QUIC only utilizes 70% of the network capacity; and (ii) YouTube's chunk request pipelining neglects network latency, resulting in idle periods that disproportionately harm the throughput of smaller chunks. As a result of our study, Viasat discontinued support for the low-bandwidth data-saving option in U.S. business and residential markets to avoid potential degradation of video quality—highlighting the practical significance of our findings.

Keywords: Video streaming · Geosynchronous satellite network · Quality of experience · Quality of service

---

Udit Paul was a PhD student at the University of California, Santa Barbara when the work was performed.

© The Author(s), under exclusive license to Springer Nature Switzerland AG 2024
P. Richter et al. (Eds.): PAM 2024, LNCS 14538, pp. 153–169, 2024.
https://doi.org/10.1007/978-3-031-56252-5_8

1   Introduction

Geosynchronous satellite (GEO) networks, through providers such as Viasat and HughesNet, are a key last-mile Internet access technology in challenging environments such as rural and other hard-to-reach communities, aircraft, sea ships, and others. While recently low Earth orbit (LEO) satellite networks have grown in availability, the high cost of deploying and maintaining LEO networks can hinder access for under-served communities [28], making GEO networks an attractive alternative. GEO satellites orbit 22 k miles above the earth and move at the same speed as the earth, ensuring that their location remains fixed relative to the ground stations over time. While convenient for routing simplification, the geosynchronicity comes at the cost of high latency; round trip times through GEO satellites are typically 500-600 ms. To mitigate the effects of this latency, GEO ISPs often employ a variety of techniques. These usually include TCP Performance Enhanced Proxies (PEP) with geo-optimized configurations. Additionally, many wireless plans, both terrestrial and satellite, provide customers with a fixed high-speed data quota (gigabytes) per month. After a customer consumes this data, their traffic is deprioritized, which can result in slow speeds for the user when the network is congested. To avoid data deprioritization, customers are typically provided with an option to reduce general data consumption by shaping their video traffic, thereby enabling high-speed data to last longer.

As the dominant Internet application, accounting for approximately 53% [6] of total Internet traffic, video streaming is a critical application to support in all network types. Particularly in remote areas, video streaming can be critical for activities such as online education and work. Prior studies of video streaming QoE have typically been conducted either in emulated or production terrestrial networks characterized by low delay and high bandwidth (e.g. [12,32]). Amongst the results, these studies show that QoE degradation events are rare in terrestrial networks. Prior studies have also analyzed the impact of the transport layer in video performance, in particular comparing TCP and QUIC, the latter of which has gained wide adoption by applications such as YouTube [4,7,29,31]. Some studies have shown that TCP and QUIC have similar performance for video streaming tasks in terrestrial networks [4,20,31], while in [14] Google claims that QUIC improves YouTube QoE key performance indicators (KPIs). However, because of their inherent differences, it is not clear whether these results hold in GEO networks, particularly when traffic shaping is employed.

We address this understanding gap through an extensive study of video streaming performance over an operational GEO satellite network. We focus our study on YouTube because of its widespread popularity; current data places YouTube video consumption as outpacing that of Netflix worldwide.[1] We stream 2,080 180-190 second videos, using either the TCP or QUIC protocol, and analyze the resulting QoE KPIs to characterize the video performance. Given the video bit rates to support 360p and 480p resolution, we expect consistent seamless streaming at an average resolution exceeding 360p. Critically and surprisingly,

---

[1] For instance, one study states that, in 2022, YouTube represented 15% of traffic on consumer broadband networks, while Netflix represented 9% [6].

our first key discovery is that neither TCP nor QUIC achieves consistent seamless streaming at an average resolution of more than 360p when traffic is shaped at 900 Kbps, the rate offered to customers in our production network. Specifically, we observe that 30% of each of TCP and QUIC sessions experience rebuffering events, while the median average resolution is 404p for TCP and 360p for QUIC.

To understand this observation, we analyze the video traffic and determine that TCP utilizes all available link capacity during transmission, while QUIC is only able to utilize 70% of the capacity. Our results suggest that the performance of QUIC, specifically in conjunction with the BBR congestion control algorithm, is suboptimal when used in GEO networks. Furthermore, both TCP and QUIC suffer from imperfect chunk request scheduling, resulting in idle time that further reduces the overall throughput for TCP by 36% and QUIC by 26%.

As a result of our study, Viasat discontinued support for the low-bandwidth data-saving shaping option in its U.S. business and residential network to avoid potential degradation of video quality. We encourage YouTube and other content providers to more fully consider the operational environment of GEO networks and optimize players to deliver high quality video despite the presence of high latency links and other GEO network features. Additionally, optimization is needed for the QUIC + BBR [14] stack to achieve performance comparable to PEP-enabled TCP + BBR in GEO satellite networks.

2   Background and Motivation

In this section, we provide background on the three key concepts in this paper. First, we describe video streaming, and in particular the use of adaptive bit rate algorithms and the KPIs that are used to measure video QoE. The characteristics of GEO satellite networks are then discussed, along with optimizations incorporated to provide customers with improved performance. Finally, we describe key features of the QUIC protocol, including a discussion of why QUIC is not necessarily the better protocol for GEO satellite networks despite its apparent suitability for video streaming.

2.1   Video Streaming Applications (VSAs)

Internet video streaming services typically divide a video into smaller segments called chunks. These chunks are often of different playback durations; hence the chunks can be of variable size [22]. The video quality is determined by the number of pixels in each frame (i.e., resolution) and the (average) number of bits per second of playback (i.e., bit rate). Most streaming service providers use variable bit rates (VBR) to encode the video into a sequence of frames. The number of bits needed to encode a specific chunk depends on the video type and its quality [17]. In general, high-action/high-resolution chunks require more bits to encode than motionless and/or lower-resolution chunks.

Adaptive bit Rate Algorithms. To optimize the viewing experience, each client maintains a buffer where it stores received chunks. With this repository, the likelihood of continuous playback during a video session is greatly increased. At the video session start, the client waits to fill this buffer to a predefined level before video playback begins. The client begins by sending an HTTPS request to retrieve a specific segment at a pre-selected quality (e.g., 360p). On receiving this request, the server sends the requested segment to the client.

Each client uses an application-layer *adaptive bit rate (ABR)* algorithm to determine the quality of the request in the next segment. The ABR algorithms employed by most video streaming services are proprietary, but previous work has shown that these algorithms typically use parameters such as estimated bandwidth and current buffer size to determine the quality of the next requested segment [18,38].

Quality of Experience for VSAs. Video stream QoE is determined by several KPIs. These include initial buffering time, resolution, and the number of rebuffering events. During a rebuffering event, video playback is paused while the received video is placed into the playback buffer. For optimal QoE, rebuffering events, resolution switches, and initial buffering time should be minimized [30]. A higher resolution is preferred as long as there is sufficient network bandwidth to deliver the video chunks before the playout deadline [11].

The goal of the ABR algorithm is to select the appropriate resolution for each chunk to maximize viewing resolution while also minimizing events that lower QoE. Most video streaming applications work very well in high-bandwidth (more than 10–15 Mbps), low-latency (few tens of ms) networks [26]. However, it is far less clear how well they perform in high-latency networks and shaped bandwidth, which are typical of GEO networks. Further, it is not well-understood how well these applications are able to interact with additional network components, such as TCP proxies and traffic-shaping algorithms, that are common in GEO networks. Hence, it is in these environments that our work focuses.

2.2 Geosynchronous Satellite Networks

Geosynchronous satellite networks use wireless links between ground stations and space satellites to connect subscribers to the Internet. Transparent TCP proxies, which speed up TCP slow-start and congestion recovery, are often employed to mitigate the effects of the long round-trip propagation delays of GEO links. Two TCP proxies are typically used: upstream and downstream. The upstream proxy runs at the ground station, while the downstream proxy runs at the satellite modems closer to the end-users. As a result of these proxies, each video streaming session entails three independent TCP connections: server-to-upstream-proxy (C1), upstream-to-downstream-proxy (C2), and downstream-proxy-to-client (C3), as shown in Fig. 1. The upstream proxy acknowledges packets coming from the video server aggressively and therefore increases the congestion window quickly. On the client side, packets are acknowledged immediately as well.

In addition to TCP proxies, many satellite and mobile wireless network operators provide data-saver options that use traffic shapers to constrain the bandwidth allocated to different applications [15]. This enables users to view more hours of video or engage in other network activities while reducing the likelihood they exceed their monthly data limit.

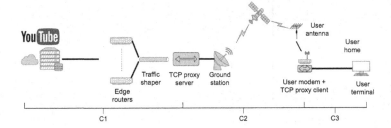

Fig. 1. Testbed configuration.

QUIC in GEO Satellite Networks: QUIC is rapidly becoming the default transport layer protocol for many online services [14,19]. YouTube, for example, is predominantly transmitted over QUIC. QUIC runs in user space, uses UDP for data transmission, and is designed for applications that use multiple HTTPS multiplexed connections. Compared to TCP, it expedites the connection setup by reducing the number of round trips required to establish a connection between the two end hosts. During packet losses, QUIC avoids head-of-line blocking by servicing unaffected streams while recovering lost packets. TCP proxies cannot be leveraged by QUIC-based connections because QUIC connections are cryptographically signed end-to-end. Hence the feedback loop of QUIC is delayed in GEO networks. As a result of these key differences, it is unclear how QUIC will perform over GEO links and how video QoE will be impacted when used with other components such as the PEP and traffic shaper. This observation serves as the driving force behind our investigation.

3   Methodology and Dataset

In this section, we describe the configuration of our testbed and the methodology used to stream YouTube videos while collecting HTTP logs and QoE KPIs. Additionally, we provide a summary of the dataset and experiment metrics collected.

Testbed. Figure 1 illustrates the primary components of our testbed network architecture, including the YouTube server, traffic shaper, server-side TCP proxy, satellite link, client-side proxy, and client laptop. Note that because this is a production network, the client laptop is the only component over which we have direct control. To improve TCP performance over the long latency satellite link, TCP traffic is split into three separate connections (C1, C2, and C3), as shown in the figure. On the other hand, QUIC traffic is not split into separate connections due to its use of end-to-end encryption; the proxies simply forward the traffic. The client laptop is used to collect HTTP logs. The satellite provider uses a token bucket traffic shaper to limit the throughput of video traffic on the low-latency link between the YouTube server and the upstream proxy, with an average bandwidth shaping rate of 0.9 Mbps and bursts up to

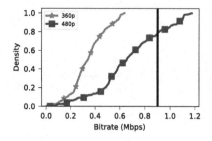

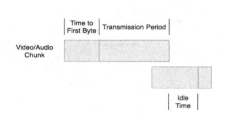

Fig. 2. Average video bit rates for each resolution. Vertical line is 900 Kbps, the shaped rate.

Fig. 3. Chunk request model.

0.99 Mbps. The authors of [15] found that multiple GEO satellite network ISPs utilize this shaping rate.[2] Importantly, we note that the playback resolution under either constant or variable bandwidth shaping will differ depending on the operation of the ABR and VBR algorithms. The client side congestion control algorithm is CUBIC (Ubuntu Default); however, we are more interested in the server side congestion control (CC) algorithm because it determines how quickly video/audio data is sent to the client. The server side congestion control algorithm is BBRv3 [1]. Finally, the congestion control algorithm used between the client and server proxies is a proprietary version of ECN-enabled CUBIC with modifications such as a large initial congestion window. Upon detecting congestion, the window size is reduced by 1/3. The congestion window then increases slowly at first, and eventually grows exponentially, similar to TCP CUBIC. The technical details of the testbed are summarized in Table 1.

Table 1. Technical details of the testbed.

Operating System	Ubuntu 22.04
Browser	Google Chrome
Client Congestion Control	CUBIC with hystart
Server Congestion Control	BBRv3

YouTube Experiments. We analyzed an open video catalog of approximately 8 million entries released by YouTube [2] to collect representative data from a variety of video types. We randomly selected 13 videos from each of the 16 distinct video categories[3] to form a total pool of 208 videos. We streamed each

---

[2] Note that traffic shaping is a subscriber opt-in feature for the ISP in the study.

[3] Categories collected are: Sports, Education, Science & Technology, Shows, Pets & Animals, Nonprofits & Activism, News & Politics, Gaming, Music, Comedy, People & Blogs, Autos & Vehicles, Film & Animation, Entertainment, Howto & Style,

video with YouTube's production ABR ten times: five with QUIC enabled and five with QUIC disabled, for a total of 2,080 sessions; TCP was utilized in the QUIC-disabled sessions. We restarted the browser before each session to avoid caching. Each video is between 180-190 seconds in length to improve the scalability of the experiments while simultaneously being long enough to allow the congestion window to saturate at its maximum capacity [13]. The average bit rate of each of the 208 videos at 360p and 480p is represented as a CDF in Fig. 2. The figure demonstrates that the videos selected are close to a uniform distribution; we verify this result for the other video resolutions but omit those results from the graph for clarity. The data collection process took place in October 2023.

Collection Methodology. We assess the QoE of each video stream by gathering multiple well-defined QoE KPIs [30] for every YouTube session. Each experiment starts by randomly selecting a video and streaming it twice, once with QUIC enabled (we confirm that QUIC is used via HTTP logs) and once with it disabled (TCP enabled). The order of the QUIC/TCP protocols is reversed for each randomly chosen video to minimize bias introduced by CDN caching [3]. The resolution is set to automatic and a Chrome extension is utilized to capture player events at 250 ms intervals. The player events are then transmitted to a local server for storage, while a Python script driving Selenium is used to capture HTTP logs. This process is repeated until every video in the dataset is streamed five times with each transport protocol. We identify advertisement videos by timestamp and their different Video ID in "stats for nerds" and remove them from QoE and chunk analysis. The collected QoE KPIs are as follows:

- **Average session resolution**: given n available resolutions $R = \{R_1, R_2, \ldots R_n\}$ in a session, the fraction of time each resolution is viewed within the session is $P = \{P_1, P_2 \ldots P_n\}$; the average session resolution is given by $\sum_{i=1}^{n} P_i R_i$.
- **Initial buffering time**: the time from the instant when the video player connects to a server to the time when the first video frame is rendered and played. For this metric only, we exclude video sessions with pre-roll advertisements, and analyze 509 TCP and 509 QUIC sessions.
- **Resolution changes**: the number of resolution switches per video. Frequent switches usually lead to unsatisfactory user experience [30].
- **Rebuffering events**: the number of times the playback pauses due to insufficient buffered video. Few or no rebuffering events are desired for better QoE.

Video/Audio Chunks. Video and audio chunks are the fundamental operational unit of ABR algorithms; therefore, our analysis focuses on network performance at the chunk granularity. To obtain the performance of these chunks, we first filter out all HTTP `Network.requestWillBeSent` events reported by Chrome. Then we ensure these requests contain `?videoplayback` in their URL as

---

Travel & Events. Categories such as Sports are usually of higher bit rate compared to Education.

well as `video` or `audio` as their MIME type. We keep track of the `request_id` of these events and obtain all `Network.dataReceived` events of the corresponding `request_id`. Finally, we group `Network.dataReceived` events by `request_id` to compute the size and performance metrics of each video/audio chunk.

Although such methods can only be applied if we have direct control over the client Chrome browser, previous work [9] has proposed methods to heuristically infer video/audio chunks based on the amount of data received between two HTTP requests. However, based on our HTTP logs, we found that the heuristic approach may no longer be viable because 40% of video and audio chunks are smaller than the previously defined threshold of 80 KB; these chunks could be as small as 4 KB. Additionally, contrary to previous literature [9], new chunks can be requested before the completion of the previous chunk's transmission in GEO satellite networks. This requires us to model the chunk-downloading mechanism slightly differently as shown in Fig. 3.

Chunk-level Metrics. In a GEO network, video and audio chunks are primarily requested sequentially, but there are instances where a new request for additional chunks may be initiated before the previously requested chunks are fully received. To analyze the streaming behavior of the chunks, we utilize the following chunk-level metrics:

- **Chunk time to first byte (TTFB)**: the interval between the time a request is initiated and the first byte of data for the chunk is received. [25] find that this metric has an impact on chunk throughput; however, this should be differentiated from the idle time since TTFB does not consider previous chunks.
- **Idle time**: the interval between the end of the previous chunk's transmission and the beginning of the following chunk's transmission. Due to a large accumulated playback buffer, YouTube may occasionally decide to pause chunk requests for an extended period of time (tens of seconds). This causes the chunk throughput to be low irrespective of network conditions. Therefore, we only consider chunks that are requested within one second of the completion of the previous chunk. We also group chunks with negative idle time into larger chunks during our throughput analysis. This approach allows us to account for the overlapping download periods of these chunks.
- **Chunk download time**: the interval between when the first and final bytes of a chunk are received.
- **Chunk size**: the amount of data received in the requested chunk.
- **Throughput with idle time** (T_{idle}): the chunk throughput when idle time is taken into account. This metric demonstrates how imperfect request pipelining affects the throughput of chunks. Under shaped bandwidth, where buffer health remains relatively low, video chunk requests are made continuously and in a sequential manner. When these requests are perfectly pipelined, there should not be any idle time. The metric is given by:

$$T_{idle} = \frac{Chunk\_Size}{Idle\_Time + Chunk\_Download\_Time}$$

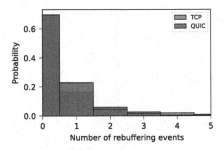

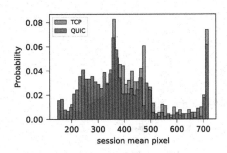

Fig. 4. Number of rebuffering events.

Fig. 5. Session average vertical pixel height.

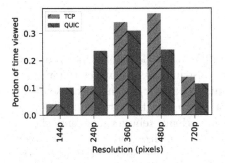

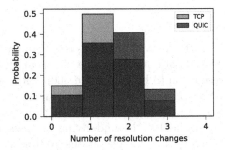

Fig. 6. Percent of time viewed at each resolution.

Fig. 7. Number of resolution changes.

- **Throughput without idle time** ($T_{network}$): the chunk throughput when idle time is not taken into consideration. This demonstrates how effectively the chunk download is using the underlying network resource and is given by:
$T_{network} = \frac{Chunk\_Size}{Chunk\_Download\_Time}$

4 Video Stream Performance

A key goal of our study is to understand the YouTube QoE received by users when they enable video bandwidth shaping to reduce data usage. As part of this analysis, we quantify any performance differences based on the use of QUIC or TCP + PEP at a bandwidth shaping rate and a burst rate of 0.9 Mbps and 0.99 Mbps, respectively, which is the bandwidth shaping option commonly supported by GEO network providers, including in our Viasat production network [15].

We begin by analyzing the QoE KPIs. In Fig. 2, we observed that the maximum average bit rate of 360p videos is only 0.63 Mbps, which is approximately

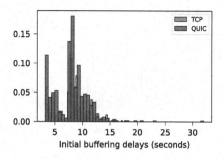
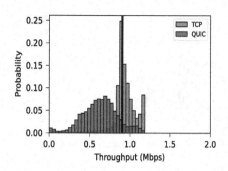

Fig. 8. Initial buffering time.

Fig. 9. Throughput without considering idle time. Vertical line is 900 Kbps.

70% of the traffic shaping rate. Similarly, 0.9 Mbps is also more than the average bit rate of 70% of the videos at 480p. Consequently, we expect the average resolution to be more than 360p with minimal rebuffering events because of the ABR behavior. The ABR should stream at 480p and then switch to 360p or lower only when the buffer health becomes low. Hence rebuffering events should be minimal if the underlying network resource is utilized efficiently. However, contrary to our expectations, we find that only 70% each of the TCP and QUIC sessions do not experience rebuffering, as shown in Fig. 4. Notably, the resolution achieved by QUIC sessions is significantly lower than that of TCP sessions, as shown in Fig. 5. The median average session resolution for TCP is 404p, whereas for QUIC the median average session resolution is only 360p. Specifically, Fig. 6 shows that 14% of the TCP streaming time is at a resolution less than 360p, while 33% of the QUIC streaming time is less than 360p. Surprisingly, these metrics indicate that neither the QUIC nor TCP sessions consistently meet our QoE expectations, with QUIC, in particular, struggling to stream at higher resolution consistently.

We next examine the initial buffering delay and number of resolution changes. Figure 7 shows that the number of resolution changes for TCP and QUIC are similar, with mean values of 1.28 and 1.57 per session, respectively. The mean initial buffering delay of TCP is 8.25 seconds while QUIC is 7.95 seconds, shown in Fig. 8.

In summary, the results show that QUIC and TCP have similar numbers of rebuffering events, resolution changes and initial buffering delay. Further, neither QUIC nor TCP is able to stream seamlessly at an average resolution of more than 360p when bandwidth shaping is utilized. We hypothesize that there are suboptimal transport and/or application layer operations that manifest in unexpectedly poor performance in long-latency networks, preventing both TCP and QUIC, in particular, from fully utilizing available network resources and achieving better performance. In the following section, we explore chunk-level QoS to uncover potential reasons for lower-than-expected QoE.

5 Diagnosis of Sub-optimal QoE

Sect. 4 showed that both TCP and QUIC fail to deliver expected QoE KPIs, with QUIC, in particular, struggling to provide higher resolution. In this section, we dig deeper into these results to understand this performance anomaly.

5.1 Insufficient Network Resource Utilization

Figs. 2 and 6 demonstrated that sufficient bandwidth was available to stream at 360p, yet 33% of the time, QUIC streamed at a lower resolution. Our goal is to understand why QUIC is unable to utilize available network resources efficiently. We begin with the throughput of individual chunks when the idle time is not considered, depicted in Fig. 9. The figure shows that TCP clearly forms a peak around 900 Kbps, the shaped bandwidth, whereas QUIC's throughput widely varies well below 900 Kbps. The mean and median of TCP $T_{network}$ are 0.92 Mbps and 0.91 Mbps, respectively, while the mean and median of QUIC $T_{network}$ are 0.63 and 0.64 Mbps.

Both TCP and QUIC use BBR as their server-side congestion control algorithm. BBR continuously probes for the bottleneck bandwidth and propagation delay to determine the sending rate; however, we have seen that QUIC does not send at a rate that saturates the capacity of the link. Therefore, we hypothesize that the BBR algorithm performs differently with QUIC compared to TCP in GEO networks, likely as a result of PEP in the network architecture. Specifically, QUIC BBR experiences the full 600 ms of latency across the satellite link, whereas TCP BBR experiences only the low-latency link (typically less than 100 ms round trip time) between the YouTube server and PEP server proxy. The difference in this propagation delay may cause the YouTube server to incorrectly estimate the available bandwidth and send data at a rate that never fully saturates the link when QUIC is used. Prior work, such as [35] and [5], has also observed that the combination of TCP+PEP+BBR achieves higher throughput than QUIC+BBR. Relatedly, [35] showed that the slow-start phase of QUIC+BBR is the cause of the lower throughput; QUIC+BBR requires up to 10 seconds to reach maximum throughput, whereas TCP takes less than one second. In our analysis, we observe that $T_{network}$ of QUIC is still variable well below 900 Kbps even for video chunks requested 30 seconds or more after the session start (this result is included in the Appendix). As a result, the start-up phase is not the only factor that affects the performance of QUIC+BBR in our test network.

5.2 YouTube Scheduling Inefficiencies

Prior work has shown that many YouTube videos are not watched to completion [24]. As a result, YouTube tries to reduce unnecessary bandwidth consumption by limiting the number of chunks downloaded in advance. Our analysis has

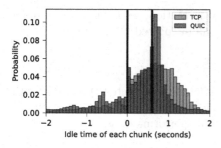
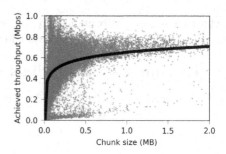

Fig. 10. Idle time. Vertical lines are 0 ms and 600 ms idle time.

Fig. 11. Chunk size vs throughput for QUIC.

shown that it is possible for the currently requested chunk to start transmission before the completion of the previous chunk. Ideally, the YouTube ABR should learn the RTT of the network and request the next chunk slightly before the completion of the current chunk (the TTFB of each chunk is shown in the Appendix). This would minimize the amount of time spent idling by the network and therefore increase network utilization. However, as shown in Fig. 10, we observe that more than 78% of the chunks experience idle time with both TCP and QUIC. Interestingly, we can also observe that a peak occurs around 600 ms. This suggests that the high propagation delay of the GEO network is not considered when making chunk requests. Note that we ignore chunks with long idle time caused by abundant playback buffers in our analysis. This allows us to focus on periods when high network utilization is critical.

To assess the impact of this idle time on smaller chunks whose throughput is dominated by idle time, we analyze the relationship between the size of the chunk downloaded and the throughput achieved for both TCP and QUIC. Figure 11 shows a logarithmic relationship between the two variables. Therefore, we calculate the Pearson correlation of achieved throughput and log(chunk size) to characterize the relationship. QUIC shows a positive Pearson correlation of 0.59 ($\ll$ 0.05 p-value), whereas these two variables are also correlated for TCP with a Pearson statistic of 0.62 ($\ll$ 0.05 p-value). Similar trends are observed in [16] for 4G and WiFi networks. This leads us to infer that these pipelining inefficiencies significantly reduce the throughput of smaller chunks. In addition, shaped traffic on GEO networks is disproportionately impacted due to their lower bandwidth and higher latency. According to [22], YouTube tends to request smaller chunks when bandwidth is lower. We observe that more than 53% of all chunks in our sessions are less than 0.1 MB; this, in turn, further exacerbates the problem. It is worth noting that the chunk-requesting inefficiency observed in our study may be specific to low-bandwidth high-latency scenarios.

To investigate this hypothesis, we compare the impact of idle time in the GEO network with that on our campus network, which is both high bandwidth and low latency. We stream the same 2,080 videos to a desktop in our campus research lab and find that the median idle time for both TCP and QUIC is short, approximately 15 ms (supporting the assumption of almost ideal sequential chunk requesting). Moreover, given the abundance of campus network capacity, the idle time has no practical impact on QoE in this setting, with achieved throughput T_{idle} exceeding 60 Mbps. In contrast, in the shaped GEO network, the median achieved throughput T_{idle} for TCP and QUIC is approximately 0.58 Mbps (0.64 $T_{network}$) and 0.47 Mbps (0.73 $T_{network}$), respectively. This suggests a correlation between idle time and the round trip propagation delay of the network, providing further evidence that the existing pipelining mechanism is sub-optimal in GEO networks. In summary, TCP experiences a 36% throughput reduction due to idle time, even with the link being saturated during transmission, while QUIC suffers a 27% reduction in throughput due to idle time, and then an additional 30% reduction because QUIC is unable to fully utilize the link capacity during transmission.

6   Related Work

Prior literature has studied the QoE of ABR streaming and YouTube [10,21,23, 36]. However, far fewer studies have investigated video streaming QoE in operational GEO networks. In [8], a framework that facilitates live 4k video streaming over a 5G core network via a GEO satellite backhaul is proposed. However, the focus of this work is live video streaming, as opposed to non-real-time video streaming in our study. [34] proposes a caching framework that improves video streaming QoE within GEO satellite networks. The limitations of this study include the utilization of an academic DASH player and the investigation of only a single video. Distorted versions of videos are generated in [37] by adjusting QoS parameters such as packet loss. The distorted videos are replayed to volunteers, and the corresponding Mean Opinion Score is recorded. This work uses an emulated satellite link, and the impact of ABR is not considered. A recent study [27] benchmarked multiple satellite ISPs across various tasks, including video streaming. The results are complementary to those of our study. Netflix's recent paper [33] demonstrates that server-side pacing effectively reduces congestion from bursty on-demand video transmission, maintaining QoE. This approach can also eliminate the need for ISPs to deploy traffic shaping. Extensive prior work has analyzed transport protocol performance [4,20,31]; however, these studies utilize a low-latency link. For instance, [31] uses a network emulator to shape home and mobile networks to 1 Mbps to study YouTube streaming QoE. In this environment, the authors conclude there is no meaningful difference between TCP and QUIC performance. Through the use of an academic DASH player in a terrestrial network and only one video, [4] concludes that the QUIC protocol does not improve QoE. Finally, the page load time difference between TCP and QUIC is studied in [20].

7 Conclusion

Our study characterizes the QoE KPIs of YouTube in a production GEO satellite network with 900 Kbps traffic shaping. We find that, despite the average bit rate of all the 360p resolution videos, and a majority of the 480p resolution videos, being less than the shaped bandwidth, the performance of these video streams is sub-optimal. Our work highlights the challenge of employing traffic shaping as an effective means to control video resolution, and therefore data-usage, on high latency networks, and the importance of accounting for network delay in chunk size and request timing for high quality video streaming. Many of the populations that stand to gain Internet access over the coming years will do so through non-traditional network architectures, including GEO networks. Application designers and content providers must consider a wide variety of network types and characteristics in their product, protocol design and content provisioning strategies to avoid unanticipated performance anomalies.

A   Appendix

A.1   Ethical Considerations

Although our work involves HTTP log analysis on an operational GEO satellite network, our work is not human subjects research. At no point is any data collected from the customers of the network. We collect and analyze only our own experimentally generated traffic.

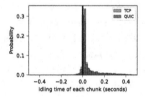 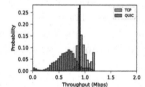 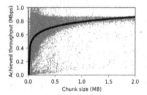

Fig. 12. Idle time of campus network.

Fig. 13. Post 30 s throughput without considering idle time. Vertical line is 900 Kbps.

Fig. 14. Chunk size vs throughput over TCP.

A.2   Supplementary Results

In this section we include some additional, supplementary graphs that were briefly described in the main body of the paper. The median idle time for both TCP and QUIC was short in our campus network experiment, around 15 ms, as shown in Fig. 12. This result suggests that the pipelining inefficiency is magnified by the high round trip time of the GEO satellite network. Figure 13 shows the $T_{network}$ after 30 seconds of playback, in order to eliminate any effect due to

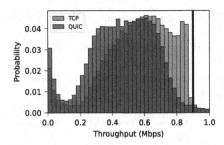

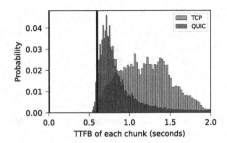

Fig. 15. Achieved throughput. Vertical line is 900 Kbps.

Fig. 16. Time to first byte of each chunk. Vertical line is 600 ms.

slow start. The figure indicates that QUIC throughput still varies well below the shaped bandwidth 900 kbps. This indicates that congestion control, and specifically the initial slow start, are not the source of the low throughput. Figure 16 shows the TTFB of each chunk. We can observe that almost all chunks have a TTFB larger than 600 ms; QUIC in particular forms a cluster close to 600 ms. The correlation between achieved throughput (T_{idle}) and chunk size for TCP is illustrated in Fig. 14. The Pearson statistic for correlation of achieved throughput and log(chunk size) is 0.62. Finally, Fig. 15 shows that the T_{idle} of TCP outperforms that of QUIC in GEO networks; the median TCP throughput is 0.58 Mbps, while QUIC's median throughput is 0.47 Mbps. Importantly, however, neither reach the shaped bandwidth rate. Figure 16 shows the TTFB of each chunk. The median chunk TTFB for TCP is 1.21 s, while it is 0.78 s for QUIC.

References

1. BBR development group. https://groups.google.com/g/bbr-dev, Accessed 13 Jan 2024
2. Abu-El-Haija, S., Kothari, N., Lee, J., Natsev, P., Toderici, G., Varadarajan, B., Vijayanarasimhan, S.: Youtube-8M: a large-scale video classification benchmark. arXiv preprint arXiv:1609.08675 (2016)
3. Adhikari, V.K., Jain, S., Chen, Y., Zhang, Z.L.: Vivisecting YouTube: an active measurement study. In: IEEE INFOCOM 2012 (2012)
4. Bhat, D., Rizk, A., Zink, M.: Not so QUIC: a performance study of DASH over QUIC, NOSSDAV 2017, pp. 13–18 (2017)
5. Border, J., Shah, B., Su, C.J., Torres, R.: Evaluating QUIC's performance against performance enhancing proxy over satellite link. In: IFIP Networking Conference, pp. 755–760 (2020)
6. Cantor, L.: The Global Internet Phenomena Report. Technical Report, Sandvine, Waterloo, ON, Canada (2022)
7. Flach, T., et al.: An internet-wide analysis of traffic policing, SIGCOMM 2016, pp. 468–482. ACM (2016)

8. Ge, C., et al.: QoE-assured live streaming via satellite backhaul in 5G networks. IEEE Trans. Broadcast. **65**, 381–391 (2019)

9. Gutterman, C., et al.: Requet: Real-Time QoE detection for encrypted YouTube traffic, MMSys 2019, pp. 48–59. ACM (2019)

10. Hoßfeld, T., Seufert, M., Hirth, M., Zinner, T., Tran-Gia, P., Schatz, R.: Quantification of YouTube QoE via Crowdsourcing. In: IEEE International Symposium on Multimedia, pp. 494–499 (2011)

11. Huang, T.Y., Ekanadham, C., Berglund, A.J., Li, Z.: Hindsight: evaluate video bitrate adaptation at scale, ACM MMSys 2019, pp. 86–97 (2019)

12. Khokhar, M.J., Ehlinger, T., Barakat, C.: From network traffic measurements to QoE for internet video. In: IFIP Networking Conference (2019)

13. Kuhn, N., Michel, F., Thomas, L., Dubois, E., Lochin, E.: QUIC: opportunities and threats in SATCOM. In: ASMS/SPSC (2020)

14. Langley, A., et al.: The QUIC transport protocol: design and internet-scale deployment, ACM SIGCOMM 2017, pp. 183–196 (2017)

15. Li, F., Niaki, A.A., Choffnes, D., Gill, P., Mislove, A.: A large-scale analysis of deployed traffic differentiation practices, ACM SIGCOMM 2019, pp. 130–144 (2019)

16. Lv, G., Wu, Q., Wang, W., Li, Z., Xie, G.: Lumos: towards better video streaming QOE through accurate throughput prediction. In: IEEE INFOCOM 2022, pp. 650–659 (2022)

17. Mansy, A., Ammar, M., Chandrashekar, J., Sheth, A.: Characterizing client behavior of commercial mobile video streaming services. In: ACM MoViD 2014 (2018)

18. Mao, H., Netravali, R., Alizadeh, M.: Neural adaptive video streaming with pensieve, SIGCOMM 2017, pp. 197–210. ACM (2017)

19. Joras, M., Chi, Y.: How Facebook is bringing QUIC to billions. https://engineering.fb.com/2020/10/21/networking-traffic/how-facebook-is-bringing-quic-to-billions

20. Megyesi, P., Krämer, Z., Molnár, S.: How quick is QUIC? In: 2016 IEEE ICC (2016)

21. Mok, R.K., Chan, E.W., Luo, X., Chang, R.K.: Inferring the QoE of HTTP Video streaming from user-viewing activities, W-MUST 2011, pp. 31–36. ACM (2011)

22. Mondal, A., et al.: Candid with YouTube: adaptive streaming behavior and implications on data consumption, NOSSDAV 2017, pp. 19–24. ACM (2017)

23. Nam, H., Kim, K.H., Calin, D., Schulzrinne, H.: YouSlow: a performance analysis tool for adaptive bitrate video streaming. SIGCOMM Comput. Commun. Rev. **44**, 111–112 (2014)

24. Nam, H., Kim, K.H., Schulzrinne, H.: QoE matters more than QoS: why people stop watching cat videos. In: INFOCOM 2016, IEEE (2016)

25. Nam, Y.S., et al.: Xatu: richer neural network based prediction for video streaming. Meas. Anal. Comput. Syst. **5**(3), 1–26 (2021)

26. Ramachandran, S., Gryta, T., Dapena, K., Thomas, P.: The truth about faster internet: It's not worth it. Wall Street J. (2019). https://www.wsj.com/graphics/faster-internet-not-worth-it/

27. Raman, A., Varvello, M., Chang, H., Sastry, N., Zaki, Y.: Dissecting the performance of satellite network operators. In: CoNEXT 2023, ACM (2023)

28. Reznik, S., Reut, D., Shustilova, M.: Comparison of geostationary and low-orbit "round dance" satellite communication systems. In: IOP Conference Series: Materials Science and Engineering, vol. 971 (2020)

29. Rüth, J., Wolsing, K., Wehrle, K., Hohlfeld, O.: Perceiving QUIC: do users notice or even care?, CoNEXT 2019, pp. 144–150. ACM (2019)

30. Seufert, M., Egger, S., Slanina, M., Zinner, T., Hoßfeld, T., Tran-Gia, P.: A survey on quality of experience of HTTP adaptive streaming. IEEE Commun. Surv. Tutorials **17**, 469–492 (2015)
31. Seufert, M., Schatz, R., Wehner, N., Casas, P.: QUICker or not? an empirical analysis of QUIC vs TCP for video streaming QoE provisioning. In: 2019 ICIN, pp. 7–12 (2019)
32. Seufert, M., Schatz, R., Wehner, N., Gardlo, B., Casas, P.: Is QUIC becoming the new TCP? On the potential impact of a new protocol on networked multimedia QoE. In: 2019 Eleventh International Conference on Quality of Multimedia Experience (QoMEX) (2019)
33. Spang, B., et al.: Sammy: Smoothing video traffic to be a friendly internet neighbor, SIGCOMM 2023, pp. 754–768. ACM (2023)
34. Thibaud, A., Fasson, J., Arnal, F., Pradas, D., Dubois, E., Chaput, E.: QoE enhancements on satellite networks through the use of caches. Int. J. Satell. Commun. Network. **36**, 553–565 (2018)
35. Thomas, L., Dubois, E., Kuhn, N., Lochin, E.: Google QUIC performance over a public SATCOM access. Int. J. Satell. Commun. Network. **37**, 601–611 (2019)
36. Wamser, F., Seufert, M., Casas, P., Irmer, R., Tran-Gia, P., Schatz, R.: YoMoApp: a tool for analyzing QoE of YouTube HTTP adaptive streaming in mobile networks. In: EuCNC 2015, pp. 239–243 (2015)
37. Xu, S., Wang, X., Huang, M.: Modular and deep QoE/QoS mapping for multimedia services over satellite networks. Int. J. Commun. Syst. **31**, e3793 (2018)
38. Yin, X., Jindal, A., Sekar, V., Sinopoli, B.: A control-theoretic approach for dynamic adaptive video streaming over HTTP. In: SIGCOMM Computer Communication Review, pp. 325–338 (2015)

Can LEO Satellites Enhance the Resilience of Internet to Multi-hazard Risks?

Aleksandr Stevens, Blaise Iradukunda, Brad Bailey,
and Ramakrishnan Durairajan[✉]

University of Oregon, Eugene, USA
ram@cs.uoregon.edu

Abstract. Climate change-induced and naturally-occurring multi-hazard risks (e.g., Cascadia megathrust earthquake followed by tsunamis in the U.S. Pacific Northwest or PNW) threaten humanity and society, in general, and critical Internet infrastructures, in particular. While mitigating the impacts of these hazards, in isolation, on terrestrial infrastructures has been the focus of prior efforts, we lack an in-depth understanding of infrastructure hardening efforts using *non-terrestrial deployments* such as low earth orbit or LEO satellites in the face of multi-hazard risks.

The main goal of this work is to evaluate whether LEO satellites can bolster the resilience of Internet infrastructure in the Pacific Northwest (PNW) against multi-hazard risks (Although we use the PNW as a demonstrative case in this work, we note that the solution can be applied to various geographic regions, at different granularities (e.g., city vs. state), and for a range of single- or multi-hazard risk scenarios.). To this end, we have developed a first-of-its-kind simulator called MAZE to understand the impacts that multi-hazard risks, each of which combined or in isolation, pose to wired and wireless infrastructures in the PNW. Using MAZE, we address two key challenges faced by first responders today: (1) navigating the cost vs. performance trade-offs in the hybrid routing of traffic between terrestrial and non-terrestrial networks during disasters, and (2) comparing the efficacy of using LEO satellites against a terrestrial risk-aware routing strategy (ShakeNet) and a global satellite network (BGAN) for emergency communication during multi-hazard risks. Our assessments show that LEO satellites offer two orders of magnitude latency improvement and 100s of thousands of dollars in saving, all while maintaining network connectivity in the face of multi-hazard risks. To demonstrate the practicality and versatility of MAZE, we perform two case studies including testing a traffic prioritization scheme for LEO satellites and assessing the impacts of cascading risk on network infrastructures along the U.S. west coast.

1 Introduction

The Internet plays a central role in our daily lives. However, since its inception, the Internet has grown increasingly exposed to small- and large-scale climate

P. Richter et al. (Eds.): PAM 2024, LNCS 14538, pp. 170–195, 2024.
https://doi.org/10.1007/978-3-031-56252-5_9

change [13,16] and naturally occurring risks [11,15,17,29,35,45]. Such risks can have significant consequences including economic loss and loss of connectivity for large sections of users/businesses for extended periods.

To illustrate, consider a multi-hazard risk such as a Cascadia megathrust (M9) earthquake followed by a tsunami in the Pacific Northwest (PNW). Since PNW is the Internet hub for several national and international networks, and hyperscale cloud providers, it is estimated that the state of Oregon alone, for example, could see an economic loss of several billion dollars due to damages to its Internet infrastructure [6,35]. Importantly, several critical monitoring and alerting systems (e.g., ShakeAlert [24] and ALERTWildfire [47]) depend on a resilient Internet to both detect events and disseminate alerts to first responders and the public. Hence, multi-hazard risks can severely impact our ability to use the Internet infrastructure to continuously monitor and alert on those events.

State-of-the-art from industry and academia alike that seek to mitigate the impacts of such risks are found wanting. For one, prior efforts focus only on isolated natural hazards on terrestrial network infrastructures [11,15–17,35,45]; none of them have investigated multi-hazard risks to the best of our knowledge. Second, emergency first-responder networks (e.g., AT&T's FirstNet [21] and Verizon's Frontline [51]) rely on terrestrial infrastructures such as cell towers for disaster mitigation. However, as shown recently in [11,16,35], terrestrial infrastructures are susceptible to major failures in the face of natural hazards. Third, risk-aware mitigation strategies (e.g., ShakeNet [35] and RiskRoute [17]) seek to harden network infrastructures by establishing geographically longer terrestrial backup routes that are less susceptible to risks. The success of such strategies relies critically on two assumptions: (1) backup routes do not suffer any damage during disasters, and (2) traffic can be routed *around* major damaged areas using those backup routes. However, in the face of multi-hazard risks, these assumptions are unlikely to hold. For example, what if primary routes are affected by an earthquake and backup routes are affected by landslides? Finally, as we show in our evaluation, existing hardening efforts that leverage non-terrestrial satellite deployments such as Broadband Global Access Network (BGAN) [20] are costly and offer sub-optimal performance during hazards.

Assessing the impacts of multi-hazard risks to Internet infrastructure is fraught with two key challenges. First is the cascading nature of the problem. For example, a Cascadia megathrust earthquake can result in several geographically-distant follow-up events such as tsunamis on the coast of Japan, landslides throughout the U.S. west coast, etc. Second is the lack of a simulation capability to quantify the benefits of hardening efforts that seek to mitigate the impacts of multi-hazard risks using non-terrestrial or hybrid deployments. For example, based on our interactions with first responders, it is unclear how to navigate the cost vs. performance trade-offs in the hybrid routing of traffic between terrestrial and non-terrestrial networks during disasters.

To address these challenges, the main goal of this work is to evaluate whether LEO satellites can bolster the resilience of Internet infrastructure in the Pacific Northwest (PNW) against multi-hazard risks. To this end, we have developed a first-of-its-kind simulator called MAZE to understand the impacts that multi-hazards, each of which combined or in isolation, pose to wired and wireless infrastructures in a geographic region of interest. MAZE can be used by first responders and federal agencies to compare and contrast the benefits of various emergency communication and disaster mitigation strategies in a practical and repeatable manner.

At the core of MAZE are the following novel aspects. First, MAZE allows simulations of cost-effective data transfer between different points in a network using a wide variety of backup network routing strategies (e.g., LEO, ShakeNet, shortest-path, etc.). This enables the navigation of performance (e.g., latency) vs. cost trade-offs in using terrestrial and/or non-terrestrial routing strategies. Second, MAZE also enables the simulation of hybrid routes where certain network hops are done via terrestrial fiber and other network hops are performed via LEO constellations. This enables the simulation of complex, hybrid routing scenarios where a subset of terrestrial infrastructure is still functional for routing but the backup paths for damaged infrastructure could be established with LEO satellites. Finally, MAZE is built to be easily extensible to allow the simulation of new backup routing strategies. This allows easy evaluation of other futuristic multi-hazard risk scenarios and novel emergency communication strategies to mitigate them.

Using MAZE, we compare the efficacy of LEO satellites for infrastructure hardening against two baselines: a terrestrial risk-aware routing strategy (i.e., ShakeNet) and a global satellite network (i.e., BGAN). Our assessments show that LEO satellite-based hardening strategies offer two orders of magnitude latency improvement and 100s of thousands of dollars in saving, all while maintaining network connectivity in the face of multi-hazard risks. In addition, we analyze the percentage of emergency responders that can be serviced based on different budgetary restrictions. We find that with only 0.006% of current budget for OR and 0.018% of current budget for WA, these states can benefit from LEO-based backup communication to provide 100% service to first responders. To showcase both the practicality and extensibility of MAZE, we apply it to two case studies. The first case study seeks to test the feasibility/practicality of a traffic prioritization scheme for LEO satellites, whereas the second one aims to assess the impacts of a cascading risk on network infrastructures across three states in the U.S. west coast.

Contributions and Roadmap. This work makes the following key contributions.

- A first-of-its-kind empirical illustration of multi-hazard risks to Internet infrastructures in PNW (Sect. 2).
- A novel yet practical discrete-event simulator called MAZE to compare and contrast the benefits of various emergency communication and disaster mitigation strategies in a repeatable manner (Sect. 3) (Source code of the MAZE simulator: https://gitlab.com/onrg/maze).
- Evaluation of MAZE with realistic isolated and multi-hazard risk scenarios (Sect. 4).
- Two case studies that demonstrate how MAZE can be used to transition a research prototype on traffic prioritization using LEO satellite into practice (Sect. 5.1), and enrich the resiliency analysis of researchers with

practical issues faced by first responders during multi-hazard disaster scenarios (Sect. 5.2).

2   Background, Motivation and Related Work

2.1   Motivation

Multi-hazard Risks are on the Rise and are Increasingly Affecting Terrestrial Critical Network Infrastructures. In recent years, there has been a steady increase in climate change-induced as well as naturally occurring risks in the U.S. that have affected substantial regions, such as the rise in wildfires in the west [7] and tornadoes in the south [23]. One concerning risk for the Pacific Northwest (PNW) is the possibility of a megathrust earthquake. PNW lies in the Cascadia Subduction Zone [6], a region where a megathrust earthquake that will cause major infrastructure damage is expected to hit in the near future. Areas in PNW that experience very strong shaking on the Modified Mercalli Intensity (MMI) scale during the megathrust earthquake are likely to see significant damage to cell towers, IXPs, fiber lines, and other essential communication infrastructure [35]. A megathrust earthquake is also expected to cause a series of cascading disasters, including a tsunami and landslides down coastal Oregon [10]. In addition to the threat of a future earthquake, wildfires, a yearly occurrence in the PNW, have been shown to damage essential communication infrastructure such as cell towers [11].

Extent of Infrastructure Damage in the PNW. To empirically illustrate the problem, we quantify the likely extent of infrastructure damage[1] in Oregon (OR) and Washington (WA) due to multi-hazard risk—Cascadia M9 earthquake followed by a tsunami in the U.S. West Coast. To this end, we use the USGS national seismic hazard maps from 2014 that are integrated into ShakeNet [35] and tsunami flooding models developed by the Washington Geological Survey (WGS) along with the National Oceanic and Atmospheric Administration (NOAA) [41] to predict how much infrastructure is susceptible to a multi-hazard disaster. We perform this by loading the damage models into ArcGIS [1] and performing a layer *merge*, creating a compound output layer which contains the total combined area containing susceptible infrastructure. We then performed an *Intersect* with the ShakeNet infrastructure layers which gave us a count of different types of affected infrastructure in the multi-hazard damage zone. For context, the seismic hazard resulting from earthquakes is commonly measured by indicating the expected frequency of shaking, expressed either as "return periods" corresponding to specific timeframes (e.g., every 50 years) or as the probability of surpassing a certain threshold (e.g., 2% or 10% probability of exceedance) within a defined interval [35].

Total counts of affected node infrastructures and surrounding fiber infrastructure (in km) is shown in Table 1. We note that the damage counts for infrastructure in major metropolitan areas such as Points-of-Presence (PoPs), Data

---

[1] In this context, the "impact" of infrastructure damage is characterized by complete failures resulting in the absence of any service.

Table 1. Count of infrastructure that are prone to damage during a Multi-Hazard Cascadia Earthquake+Tsunami scenario for expected PGAs with 10% probability of exceedance in the next 50 years [35].

Fiber (km)	Cell Towers	PoPs	Data Centers	Colos
32,057	204,585	422	32	59

Centers, and Colocation Facilities largely stayed the same between an isolated earthquake incident and a multi-hazard disaster scenario. This follows as most of this infrastructure is inland where tsunami damage is unlikely to reach (i.e., Portland), or in areas that are near the water but were already assumed to have major earthquake damage due to violent shaking (i.e., Seattle). Counts for cell towers and length of fiber effected for the multi-hazard scenario increased compared to the standalone earthquake scenario as fiber and cell towers on coastal Oregon, along with submarine fiber, would be additionally affected given the added tsunami and flooding.

Population Affected by Infrastructure Damage in the PNW. In addition to estimates of susceptible infrastructure, we also estimated the total population that may be affected by damage to communication infrastructure. By using the United States Census Bureaus 2021 population census by county [9] and seeing which counties overlapped with areas with expected infrastructure damage, we were able to get an estimate of the total population that will be impacted by damage to communication infrastructure. These estimates are shown in Table 2. In Washington, 89.2% of the state population is expected to be impacted by infrastructure damage during a multi-hazard earthquake scenario. Similarly, in Oregon, 91.4% of the population is expected to fall within zones experiencing high chance of infrastructure damage.

Table 2. Count of people in areas prone to damage during a Multi-Hazard Cascadia Earthquake+Tsunami scenario split into total population and emergency responders.

	Total Population	Emergency Responders
OR	3,879,430	6,681
WA	6,901,149	18,189

We also applied these population percentages to data from the Bureau of Labor Management [38–40] regarding total number of emergency responders employed by state to get the number of emergency responders whose communication channels are likely to be impacted by infrastructure damage. This quantification regarding the amount of infrastructure damage and expected effected population makes it clear that alternative communication strategies need to evaluated in the event of a multi-hazard disaster scenario in the PNW. This evaluation of communication strategies is especially prudent with regards to emergency responders as they will need reliable communication in the event of a natural disaster in order to service the community and save lives.

2.2   State-of-the-Art and Their Limitations

Existing Emergency Responder Networks Cannot Function in the Face of Multi-hazard Risks. The majority of past work on emergency communications has to do with establishing dedicated communication networks to avoid network congestion and to ensure that first responders can communicate with each other in the face of natural disasters. For example, there are several fully-functional emergency communication networks in the U.S. including AT&T's FirstNet [21] and Verizon's Frontline [51]. However, these emergency responder networks, e.g., use the Long-Term Evolution (LTE) standard and, rely on terrestrial cell towers. These cell towers, however, are likely to be nonfunctional following major natural disasters such as a megathrust earthquake [35] and wildfires [11], let alone multi-hazard risks.

Risk-Mitigation Strategies Consider Only Isolated Risks and Cannot Effectively Address Multi-hazard Risks. Risk-aware terrestrial routing and mitigation strategies such as ShakeNet [35] and RiskRoute [17] seek to harden network infrastructures against natural disasters by establishing geographically longer terrestrial backup routes that are less susceptible to risks. However, such strategies rely heavily on the assumption that certain areas, with backup routes, suffer little-to-no damage for routes to remain functional. However, this assumption is unlikely to hold during multi-hazard risks e.g., megathrust earthquakes in PNW followed by tsunamis or landslides in the U.S. west coast. Consequently, these strategies only account for routing *around* major damaged areas and fail to account for how communication *within* damaged areas can be established.

Existing GEO Satellite-Based Efforts are Either Costly or Offer Suboptimal Performance. Some of the aforementioned emergency communication networks extend beyond LTE and offer satellite communications using GEO satellites. For example, FirstNet currently offers satellite-based communication called Broadband Global Area Network (BGAN) [20] with upload speeds of up to 492Kbps for thousands of dollars [18]. Interest has also been expressed by FirstNet into possibly integrating LEO satellites into their network for emergency communications as a newer alternative to BGAN [28]. However, FirstNet has yet to formally announce plans to make use of LEO satellite constellations as the technology is still very new and evaluations of how these networks would fair in disaster scenarios compared to current systems such as BGAN is an open problem.

Recent work uses satellite constellations for post-disaster communications [34]. However, this work focuses primarily on mixing LEO satellites with the BeiDou Navigation Satellite (BDS) system [25]. BDS system, which is independently developed by China, is composed of GEO and MEO (Medium Earth Orbit) satellite constellations. Nevertheless, deployment of proprietary systems like BDS motivates our work on how current commercial LEO satellite options (e.g., Starlink [49], Kuiper [46], and Telesat Lightspeed [50]) would fair in the face of multi-hazard risks in the U.S.

Research has also been done by NASA into Delay/Disruption Tolerant Networking (DTN), which focuses on running space packet protocols that are resilient to the specific high latency and high fault communication channels between terrestrial (e.g., ground stations) and non-terrestrial (e.g., GEO satellite) communication infrastructures [12]. While this might apply to disaster scenarios, to the best of our knowledge, their current focus is limited to space missions. Furthermore, as we show in Sect. 4, with the use of LEO satellites, latency stays low enough to allow continued use of conventional routing protocols through the satellite constellations, rendering DTN unnecessary in this case.

2.3 Opportunity

Low-Cost Low Earth Orbit (LEO) Satellite-Based Communication Can Harden Network Infrastructures Against Terrestrial Multi-hazard Risks. Because of the rise in multi-hazard risks that threaten terrestrial communication infrastructure, making them non-functional, and the aforementioned shortcomings of prior efforts, it is important to evaluate alternative means of communication. One such alternative is LEO satellite-based communication which is attractive for disaster communications due to three key reasons. First, except for satellite ground stations, LEO satellites stay beyond the reach of terrestrial multi-hazard risks.[2] Second, an industry push in the deployment of commercial LEO satellite networks has resulted in relatively cheap hardware for connecting users to these satellite constellations. For example, a typical Starlink Satellite Kit is only USD 599 [48]. This means that scaling out to fit the bandwidth and network quality needs for a variety of disaster scenarios can be done cost-effectively. Third, because LEO satellites are much closer to earth than the older geosynchronous equatorial orbit (GEO) satellites that are currently in use by first responders, latency is significantly reduced during emergency communication scenarios.

2.4 The Key Challenge

Need: A Capability to Understand the Practicality of LEO Satellites for Multi-hazard Risk Mitigation. While the above benefits are compelling, we lack a capability to assess and evaluate the practicality of how LEO satellites-based disaster communications compare and contrast against other mitigation efforts both in terms of network performance and cost. In light of this challenge, we have four options. (1) *Analytic modeling* can be used to examine idealized behaviors of the disasters and mitigation strategies but it lacks realism. For example, it is unclear how to mathematically capture disaster scenarios and their impacts in practical deployment settings. (2) *Testbed-based evaluation* can be used to test details (e.g., implementation of mitigation strategies) but has scalability issues. Practically speaking, it is also unclear how to create disaster

---

[2] Similar to other terrestrial infrastructures (e.g., fiber-optic cables), ground stations are susceptible to availability and resiliency issues resulting from multi-hazard risks.

scenarios in testbeds. (3) *In-situ evaluation*, can be used to test more complete implementations of mitigation strategies with high practicality but it lacks repeatability. (4) *Simulations* offer a promising path to test mitigation strategies and disaster scenarios in a practical and repeatable manner. Due to this reason, we take the fourth option and build a simulator to test and assess the LEO satellite-based disaster communications for multi-hazard risks.

3   Design and Implementation of MAZE Simulator

3.1   Overview of MAZE Simulator

Motivated by the above need, we design MAZE: a first-of-its-kind simulator to understand the impacts that multi-hazard risks, each of which combined or in isolation, pose to wired and wireless infrastructures in a geographic area of interest. MAZE seeks to empower first responders and federal agencies with a *practical* tool to compare and contrast the benefits of various emergency communication and disaster mitigation strategies in a *repeatable* manner.

Novelty of MAZE. MAZE is designed with three novel aspects in mind. First, to empower first responders and disaster response agencies, MAZE allows simulations of cost-effective data transfer between different points in a network using a wide variety of backup routing and mitigation strategies (e.g., LEO, ShakeNet, shortest-path, etc.). This enables the navigation of performance (e.g., latency) vs. cost trade-offs in using terrestrial and/or non-terrestrial routing strategies. Second, MAZE also enables the simulation of hybrid routes where certain network hops are done via terrestrial fiber and other network hops are performed via LEO constellations. This enables the simulation of complex, hybrid routing scenarios where a subset of terrestrial infrastructure is still functional for routing but the backup paths for damaged infrastructure could be established with LEO satellites. Third, MAZE is built to be easily extensible to allow simulation of new backup routing strategies. This allows easy evaluation of other futuristic multi-hazard risk scenarios and novel emergency communication strategies to mitigate them.

Implementation of MAZE. MAZE consists of capabilities to (1) create multi-hazard risk scenarios (Sect. 3.2), (2) identify all terrestrial and non-terrestrial network routes (henceforth, *hybrid routes*) (Sect. 3.3), and (3) compare and contrast cost vs. performance trade-offs to provide decision support for first responders e.g., to pick the most optimal hybrid route (Sect. 3.4). At its core, MAZE builds on top of a geographic information system called ArcGIS [1]. ArcGIS provides robust visualization and geo-analytic capabilities atop an object-relational database. The database is purposefully built for datasets with geo-anchored features (e.g., network infrastructure node with <latitude, longitude> point features, census blocks as polygon features, etc.).

Scope of this Work. We limit the geographic scope of MAZE to the U.S. Pacific Northwest (PNW) and west coast, and three disaster scenarios (i.e., earthquake, wildfire, and earthquake followed by a tsunami; the former two are isolated disasters whereas the latter is a multi-hazard risk). We also consider a cascading risk scenario: an event that starts as an isolated risk but ends up as a multi-hazard risk These scenarios are not prescriptive but are representative of first responders' critical needs in PNW. Without loss of generality, MAZE can be used for different multi-hazard risks, geographic locations of interest, and at different granularities (e.g., city vs. state).

3.2   Creating Multi-hazard Risk Scenarios

MAZE offers an interface to either create realistic disaster scenarios manually or plug in existing risk models from the Earth Sciences and Hazards communities. In this work, we consider models for three disaster scenarios, each of which are in formats (e.g., KML) supported by ArcGIS.

First is a wildfire scenario, which we obtain from the Northwest Interagency Coordination Center's historical wildfire map [37]. The goal is to demonstrate how MAZE can be used to assess the efficacy of different emergency communication strategies in the context of past wildfires in the PNW. As a possible candidate model, we chose 2020 Lionshead and Beachie Creek wildfires due to their sheer size, as well as their proximity to the Salem and Portland areas, both of which are highly populated. These wildfire scenarios are shown in Fig. 1. Another reason for choosing this scenario is the fact that wildfires have been shown to damage cell tower infrastructure [11]. This means that primary emergency communication networks like FirstNet [21] are susceptible to failures and calls for alternative strategies.

Fig. 1. PNW Beachie Creek and Lionshead Wildfires Disaster Scenario constructed using Northwest Interagency Coordination Center's historical wildfire map [37].

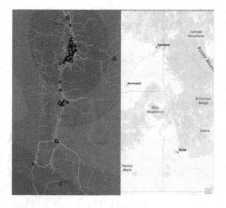

Fig. 2. PNW Megathrust Earthquake Disaster Scenario constructed using ShakeNet [35].

To create a model for an earthquake disaster scenario and estimate where the majority of infrastructure damage will occur, we use earthquake shaking models from the ShakeNet [35] framework and integrate them into MAZE. Note that this does *not* mean MAZE will identify the same backup routes for affected areas, similar to Mayer et al. [35]. This simply means that any area expected to experience very strong shaking is likely to suffer significant infrastructure damage and is therefore a viable area to evaluate alternate communication strategies within. For example, the inner ring engulfing Seattle in Fig. 2 represents the area expected to experience very strong shaking in the PNW. This inner ring is the damaged area we use in our simulations for the earthquake disaster scenario.

Third, from our conversation with hazards scientists and first responders, we create a multi-hazard risk scenario by augmenting the geographical areas from two different models. First are the areas from Mayer et al. [35] that are prone to very strong shaking due to the Cascadia M9 earthquake. Second are the areas susceptible to tsunamis and landslides along the Oregon coast following the megathrust earthquake [10].

3.3 Identifying Backup Routes

Given a risk model (such as the ones described above) and the resulting geographic locations of damage, the next component in MAZE seeks to identify all possible backup routes between a source-destination pair for emergency disaster response. To illustrate, consider the scenario in Fig. 3 where first responders from Salem (indicated as point A) are trying to coordinate with a disaster response agency in Harney Basin (indicated as point B). For this scenario, the first responders are interested in identifying all types of infrastructures to establish backup communication paths between the two points. Here, an infrastructure type can be terrestrial (e.g., routes that use fiber-optic cable), non-terrestrial (e.g., routes that use LEO satellites), or hybrid (e.g., routes that use a combination of terrestrial and non-terrestrial infrastructures).

MAZE performs this identification in three steps. Step 1 is to *fuse* terrestrial (e.g., fiber routes, cell towers, etc.) and non-terrestrial (e.g., satellite ground stations, locations of LEO satellites, etc.) network infrastructures from ShakeNet framework [35] atop the risk models described above to obtain functioning vs. non-functioning infrastructures. We use the *overlap* tool in ArcGIS to fuse infrastructure datasets with the models. Here, we define functioning infrastructures as those that are intact and are not impacted by the disaster considered in the risk model. By doing so, we implicitly consider "reliability" as a key design metric in MAZE. We encode infrastructure information as a path graph $P_{A,B}$ between two points A and B. $P_{A,B}$ is represented by a series of network segments $(x_1, x_2), (x_2, x_3), \ldots, (x_{n-1}, x_n)$. Each vertex x has two parameters: (1) a "type" parameter that stores hybrid, terrestrial, or non-terrestrial and describes the type of vertex; and (2) the geographic location of the vertex as latitude and longitude pairs. Note that x_1's location is the same as point A's location and x_n's location is the same as point B's.

Step 2 is to *enumerate* all possible backup paths that could be established atop the functioning infrastructures that could potentially be used to route traffic between any two points (e.g., A and B). These enumerated paths are also

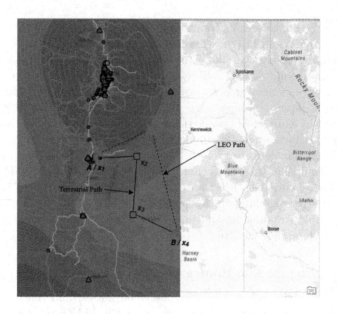

Fig. 3. PNW hybrid route example.

annotated with performance metrics[3] (e.g., latency values) from different sources (e.g., speed-of-light based round-trip times or RTT for fiber-optic paths between terrestrial points, estimates of ground station-to-LEO satellite and inter-satellite links from Chaudhry et al. [14]). Concretely, a network segment (x_1, x_2) will be annotated differently depending on the type of the vertices. For example, if x_1 and x_2 are of different types (i.e., ground station to terrestrial, or terrestrial to ground station), or they are both of terrestrial type, then they will be annotated speed-of-light RTT estimates. Otherwise, if x_1 and x_2 are both ground stations, the latency estimates will be calculated as if it was routed through the LEO satellite constellation using [14]. An example for both these annotations can be seen in Fig. 3 where the path can be established through a LEO constellation between two ground stations (x_1, x_4) or through terrestrial infrastructure segments $(x_1, x_2), (x_2, x_3), (x_3, x_4)$ sequentially. Nevertheless, the latency of a specific network segment (x_1, x_2) performed at time t will be notated as $RTT_t(x_1, x_2)$ and will be in milliseconds. The final RTT of the whole path at time t, $RTT_t(P_{A,B})$, will be defined as the sum of the RTTs of the individual network segments, or

$$RTT_t(P_{A,B}) = RTT_t(x_1, x_2) + RTT_t(x_2, x_3) + \ldots + RTT_t(x_{n-1}, x_n)$$

To make the performance values amenable for the simulations, we generate $T/\Delta t$ RTT values where T is the total time of a simulation in milliseconds and

---

[3] In this work, we consider latency as the key performance metric because it translates directly to response times of first responders during a disaster. In future work, we plan to consider other metrics such as path congestion, throughput, among others.

Δt is the time increment in milliseconds. So, a simulation would produce the following list:

$$RTT_0(P_{A,B}),\ RTT_{1*\Delta t}(P_{A,B}),$$
$$RTT_{2*\Delta t}(P_{A,B}),\ \ldots,\ RTT_T(P_{A,B})$$

Note that, as shown by Lai et al. [33] and subsequently confirmed by Izhike-vich et al. [27], the final RTTs obtained using the equation above are an *under-estimate* of the real-world RTTs. We note that the difference arises due to both system-level overheads (e.g., packet processing) and operational factors (e.g., congestion arising from an increased demand surge following a disaster). This difference is discussed further in Sect. 6.2.

Step 3 is to *delegate* the simulation of routing to appropriate sub-simulators based on the type of infrastructure segments in backup paths. For non-terrestrial segments, we use Hypatia framework [31]. In essence, Hypatia works by gener-ating the position of the satellites in the LEO constellation over time T at time increments Δt. We also provide Hypatia with parameters such as satellite alti-tude, number of orbits, etc., which correspond to specific commercial LEO con-stellation configurations such as Starlink [49], Kuiper [46], and Lightspeed [50]; see source code here [4] for all configurable parameters, including satellites per orbit, ISL link capacity, among others. Similarly, for simulating routing atop the terrestrial segments, we use the *route planner* capability in ShakeNet frame-work [35]. At the end of the simulation, all functional backup non-terrestrial and terrestrial paths will be produced by Hypatia and ShakeNet respectively.

3.4   Navigating Cost vs. Performance Trade-Offs

Network performance is important, however, the cost is arguably an equally important factor as it defines whether or not a solution is likely to be imple-mented by different government departments that are on a strict budget. In light of this, one of the key challenges faced by first responders today is the lack of decision support to identify the most performant yet cost-effective backup path during a disaster scenario. Another challenge is to compare and contrast the cost vs. performance trade-offs of different emergency communication strategies (e.g., Starlink vs. FirstNet vs. ShakeNet) for the backup paths.

To tackle these challenges, we (1) frame the issues as linear path optimization formulations (e.g., minimize latency, minimize cost), which are omitted due to space reasons, (2) input all backup paths with annotated performance values as well as the cost of operation, and (3) offer decision support to first responders e.g., to choose *the* most performant and cost-effective backup path. To calcu-late cost of operations in (2), for each strategy, we first calculate the cost for establishing a backup path i as follows:

$$Cost_{path}(i) = t + \left\lceil \frac{a}{b} \right\rceil \times p$$

where a is the average amount of upload bandwidth each user needs, b is the max. upload bandwidth supported, t is the capital equipment cost, and p is the cost of a network plan. We then calculate the total cost of operation using the individual backup paths. Concrete, for a specific disaster scenario (s), we use the total number of users u that need to be supported on each one of the backup paths on the network as follows.

$$Cost_{network}(s) = u \times t + \left\lceil \frac{u \times a}{b} \right\rceil \times p$$

We then limit the possible network paths to only utilize this subset of hardware and bandwidth allocated, allowing us to estimate the total cost of operation based on these maximum hardware and available bandwidth restrictions. Note that we chose to use upload bandwidth over download bandwidth as our variable because upload bandwidth is conventionally lower than download bandwidth. For bi-directional communication, available upload bandwidth would therefore be the limiting factor.

4   Evaluation of MAZE

For each disaster scenario (in Sect. 3.2), we seek to evaluate the efficacy of LEO constellation's performance and cost against two baselines: (1) risk-aware terrestrial routing strategy using ShakeNet [35], and (2) GEO satellite-based emergency communication strategy i.e., BGAN [20]. This first baseline will shed light on how well LEO satellites fare in comparison with geographically longer yet risk-aware terrestrial-only routing strategy. The second baseline will tell us how much better, if at all, LEO satellites are compared to the current standard satellite networks used by emergency responders today. We also employ MAZE to analyze the percentage of emergency responders that can be serviced based on different budgetary restrictions imposed by a particular state.

4.1   Performance Comparison of Emergency Communication Strategies

Using MAZE, we simulated the three disaster scenarios for 100 s in the Pacific Northwest. The network paths for the three scenarios tested were between points in the damaged areas with the largest geographic separation and population (i.e., Seattle and Portland). We obtained latencies for the MAZE-selected backup path. We used Hypatia (for Starlink LEO satellite-based backup path) and ShakeNet (for terrestrial backup path) to obtain latencies for the other baselines. We also compared these against the BGAN latencies reported by Inmarsat [3].

Each of the strategies along with the simulated performance is shown in Fig. 4. For wildfires, average RTTs increased by 2.153 milliseconds when routing through the Starlink constellation instead of the terrestrial ShakeNet path. This is due to ShakeNet's selection of a geographically closer yet more efficient backup route via Yakima instead of the direct route between Portland and Seattle. However, for earthquake and multi-hazard disasters, Starlink outperforms the terrestrial ShakeNet solution, offering a latency decrease of 2.7x and 3.3x

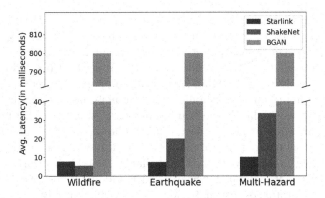

Fig. 4. Average latency comparison between Starlink, ShakeNet Fiber, and BGAN networks for Wildfire, Earthquake, and Multi-Hazard disasters in PNW.

respectively. This shows that as damage area increases, LEO satellites provide a more consistent latency when compared against risk-aware terrestrial routing solutions like ShakeNet. This is likely because as the damaged area increases, which is typical of multi-hazard risks, solutions like ShakeNet require very long terrestrial routes to be used to compensate for routing around large damage areas, dramatically increasing latency.

Of the three strategies, BGAN, which is the current standard in satellite network communication for emergency responders in disaster scenarios, is 104x slower than Starlink and 144x slower than ShakeNet's risk-aware terrestrial routing in the wildfire disaster experiment performed. Similarly, for the megathrust earthquake disaster scenario, BGAN is 108x slower than Starlink and 40x slower than ShakeNet. For the multi-hazard scenario, BGAN is 79x slower than Starlink and 24x slower than ShakeNet.

4.2   Total Cost of Emergency Communication Strategies

Using MAZE, we next compare the cost of establishing backup paths using Starlink and BGAN networks for the wildfire, earthquake, and multi-hazard disaster scenarios. Specifically, we use the formula to calculate total costs (for scenarios) from Sect. 3.4, and calculate the cost for supporting concurrent VoIP users on the Starlink and BGAN satellite networks:

$$Cost_{Starlink}(s) = u \times 599 + \left\lceil \frac{u \times 80}{9330} \right\rceil \times 110$$

and

$$Cost_{BGAN}(s) = u \times 4995 + \left\lceil \frac{u \times 80}{492} \right\rceil \times 2840$$

Based on our conversations with first responders, our calculations assume that the equipment is not shared by groups of users. Furthermore, the equations above assume users (e.g., first responders) are using the G.722 codec for VoIP which requires about 80 Kbps of upload bandwidth per caller [32]. We chose VoIP using G.722 as we could ensure that this was a communication method usable on both the Starlink and BGAN satellite networks. However, it is important to note that due to Starlink's much higher bandwidth support per user equipment and lower latency, more bandwidth-hungry and latency-sensitive services (e.g., HD video streaming) are viable on the Starlink network. We used the list price of $599 for Starlink user equipment with the network plan being $110/month [48]. The corresponding user equipment and plan prices for the BGAN network were $4,995 and $2,840/month respectively [2]. The available upload bandwidth per terminal and plan used was 9.33 Mbps for Starlink [19] and 492 Kbps for BGAN [18].

Table 3 shows total cost estimates for using Starlink- and BGAN-based emergency communication strategies in the modeled wildfire, earthquake, and multi-hazard disaster scenarios. We split costs into two parts in Table 3. First is the capital costs which represented by the $u \times t$ (i.e., Hardware) portion of the equation for user equipment. Second is the operational costs which is represented by $\left\lceil \frac{u \times a}{b} \right\rceil \times p$ (i.e., Network Plan column). For the wildfire scenario, we estimated up to 650 firefighters may have responded to the Lionshead and Beachie Creek wildfires [44]. Supporting 650 concurrent VoIP users on Starlink was 9x less expensive than supporting the same number of users on BGAN.

Table 3. Cost comparison between BGAN and Starlink for emergency responder use in Wildfire, Earthquake, and Multi-Hazard disaster scenarios.

	Hardware	Network Plan	Total Cost
Starlink Wildfire	$389,350	$660	$390,010
BGAN Wildfire	$3,246,750	$301,040	$3,547,790
Starlink Earthquake	$2,755,400	$4,400	$2,759,800
BGAN Earthquake	$22,977,000	$2,124,320	$25,101,320
Starlink Multi-Hazard	$6,235,590	$9,900	$6,245,490
BGAN Multi-Hazard	$51,997,950	$4,808,120	$56,806,070

In the case of the megathrust earthquake disaster scenario, it is estimated that ~4,600 emergency responders will be concurrently using an emergency communication network [26]. To support these first responders, using Starlink is cost-effective i.e., also a 9x reduction in cost compared to BGAN. For the multi-hazard scenario where with an estimation of ~10,410 emergency responders [8], Starlink is again cost-effective: 9x reduction in cost compared to BGAN.

4.3 Percentage of Serviceable Emergency Responders in PNW

The total number of emergency responders estimated to be within a zone that may experience any damage in a multi-hazard disaster scenario was estimated to be 18, 189 for Washington and 6, 681 for Oregon in Sect. 2. Given our equation for cost of using the Starlink constellation as a function of total concurrent users, we can calculate what percentage of emergency responders can be serviced based on different budgetary restrictions. These results can be seen in Table 4 separated by increments of 20%. The cost of serving the emergency responder population in Oregon (OR) ranges from $801,584 for 20% coverage to $4,008,299 for full coverage (100%). Similarly, in Washington (WA), the cost ranges from $2,182,083 for 20% coverage to $10,912,371 for complete coverage (100%).

Table 4. Cost of serving impacted emergency responder population by percentage in Oregon and Washington.

	20%	40%	60%	80%	100%
OR	$801,584	$1,603,058	$2,404,642	$3,206,116	$4,008,299
WA	$2,182,083	$4,364,655	$6,547,227	$8,729,799	$10,912,371

According to the National Association of State Budget Officers [42], the Oregon government spent a total of $66.8 billion in the 2021 fiscal year with Washington State spending a total of $60.5 billion. With these budget numbers in mind and the cost of servicing emergency responders in Table 4, we can deduce that to ensure 100% of emergency responders have reliable communication via Starlink in the event of a natural disaster, Oregon state would only have to allocate 0.006% of their yearly total expenditures and Washington State would only have to allocate 0.018% of their yearly total expenditures.

5 Case Studies

In this section, we present two case studies. These case studies demonstrate how extensible MAZE is (as mentioned in Sect. 3.1), and how MAZE can be used to (1) transition a research prototype into practice (Sect. 5.1), and (2) enrich the multi-hazard resiliency analysis of researchers with practical issues faced by first responders (Sect. 5.2).

5.1 How to Prioritize Traffic Classes During Multi-hazard Risks?

The first case study is obtained from *first responders* who were eager to assess the practicality of a traffic prioritization scheme proposed by Zhou et al. [52] in LEO satellites, and examine its performance under chaotic/varying network loads (which is very typical during multi-hazard risks) vs. a risk-aware routing strategy such as ShakeNet [35]. At its core, the scheme prioritizes various traffic classes (e.g., government vs. normal) in LEO satellite-based systems using a dynamic channel reservation algorithm [52]. In addition, the algorithm depends on three parameters—specifically, handover failures, new call blocking, and QoS decline—which are standard in essentially all LEO-based traffic prioritization schemes. We note that the first responders were interested in this particular scheme because of its focus on a small number of user classes (i.e., "normal", "senior", and "government"). The primary challenge stems from the common hurdle faced during the "transition to practice": the lack of capabilities to effectively implement an idea from a research paper into practical application.

We implemented the algorithm described in [52] in Python and plugged into MAZE. Similar to Zhou et al., we modeled the rate of new call arrivals to the network as a Poisson distribution. Consequently, the term "network load" is just the Poisson parameter λ for that distribution. Additionally, we acknowledge that the three parameters employed in our simulations (below) are random and we were not able to determine how the parameters from Zhou et al. [52] are applicable in the context of natural disasters. Nevertheless, we note that these parameters can be adjusted by first responders in relevant risk scenarios.

We conducted a test of the scheme using the MAZE. The test involved a simple path in the PNW region, utilizing the Starlink constellation. The path spanned from "Seattle -> Portland GS -> San Francisco GS -> Los Angeles." In the path, GS refers to a ground station, and the connection between GS nodes was established through a LEO satellite from Starlink. The purpose of the test was to simulate a multi-hazard risk scenario (specifically, an earthquake followed by a tsunami in the PNW), as discussed in Sect. 2. The simulation was run for ten seconds, and the highest priority was assigned to the government traffic class, prioritizing it over other classes.

During each simulation cycle, a list of RTT values (in milliseconds) was generated for each path segment, considering a specific network load value (λ). This process was repeated for various λ values and for each user class. The resulting lists of RTTs were then averaged over the entire duration of the simulation.

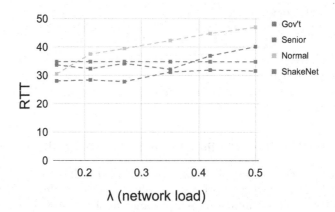

Fig. 5. Latencies experienced by different traffic classes under varying network loads.

Figure 5 illustrates the average latencies experienced by each traffic class under different network load conditions. Two key observations can be made from this figure. Firstly, as per our configuration, the scheme proposed by Zhou et al. effectively prioritized government traffic over other classes. This can be deduced from the lower RTT values observed for government traffic compared to other classes. Secondly, and unsurprisingly, the risk-aware routing strategy exhibited overall stability, as indicated by consistent RTT values despite varying network loads. This is due to longer risk-aware routing chosen by ShakeNet. Overall, these results demonstrates how MAZE can serve as a decision-support tool for first responders, enabling them to assess different backup strategies and identify an appropriate approach that would perform well under diverse network load conditions.

5.2   What Are the Impacts of a Cascading Risk to Network Infrastructures?

The second case study is more *academic* in nature and seeks to evaluate the consequences of cascading risks on network infrastructures along the U.S. West Coast, namely California (CA), Oregon (OR), and Washington (WA). Here, a cascading risk refers to an incident that initiates as a singular or isolated hazard (e.g., an earthquake like San Andreas or Cascadia) and has the potential to evolve into a multi-hazard situation (e.g., an earthquake followed by a tsunami).

In order to evaluate the effects of cascading risk on multiple states, we analyze the potential magnitude of infrastructure destruction by utilizing network assets such as long-haul fiber-optic cables, Starlink's satellite ground stations, and cell towers provided by ShakeNet. Figure 6 displays these infrastructure assets.

We also use the USGS national seismic hazard maps from ShakeNet, and tsunami flooding models developed by the Washington Geological Survey (WGS) along with the National Oceanic and Atmospheric Administration (NOAA) [41] to understand both the area of coverage of those disasters as well as how much infrastructure is susceptible to a cascading disaster. Seismic hazard includes both San Andreas earthquake as well as Cascadia earthquake. Figures 7 and 8 show areas in the U.S. west coast that are susceptible to damage from the two earthquakes with different magnitudes with 2% and 10% probability of exceedance, respectively, followed by tsunamis. Seismic hazard is commonly expressed by indicating the anticipated occurrence rate of shaking, either in terms of "return periods" relevant to specific timeframes (e.g., every 50 years) or as the probability of surpassing a certain threshold (e.g., 2% probabilty of exceedance or 10% probability of exceedance) within a defined interval [35].

Next, we load all these damage models along with infrastructure assets into MAZE and performing a layer *merge*, creating a compound output layer which contains the total combined area containing susceptible infrastructure. We then performed an *Intersect* with the infrastructure layers which gave us the extent of infrastructure damages due to a cascading risk.

We make several observations based on the data presented in Tables 5 and 6. Firstly, the magnitude of infrastructure damage escalates as the perceived intensity of shaking experienced by an observer increases (e.g., violent, severe, very

(a) Long-haul fiber optic cables and Starlink ground stations deployments.

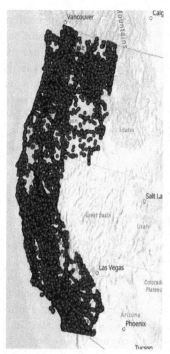

(b) Cell towers deployments.

Fig. 6. Network infrastructures spanning across three states in the U.S. west coast.

Table 5. Network infrastructures affected by earthquakes only scenario for expected PGAs with 10% and 2% probability of exceedances in the next 50 years [35].

	Cell towers		Fiber miles (km)		Ground stations	
Perceived shaking	10%	2%	10%	2%	10%	2%
Violent	516,474	237,294	11,285	11,024	5	6
Severe	462,040	597,941	9,106	15,171	1	4
Very strong	1,702	404,759	1,593	9,262	0	1

strong). Secondly, within each table, the extent of damage to each type of infrastructure asset resulting from earthquake shaking with a 10% probability of exceedance is generally lower than that with a 2% probability of exceedance. The only exception is violent shaking, where the damage from a 2% probability of exceedance is lower than that from a 10% probability of exceedance. Third, when comparing the two tables, we observe a significant increase in the extent of damage to infrastructure assets due to cascading risks.

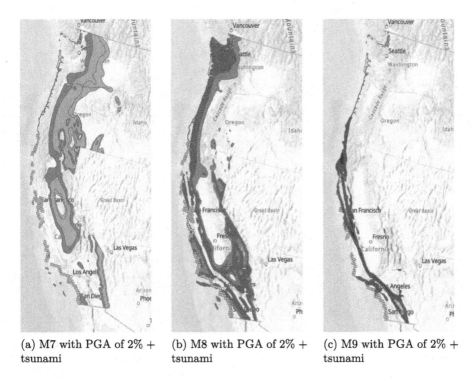

(a) M7 with PGA of 2% + tsunami

(b) M8 with PGA of 2% + tsunami

(c) M9 with PGA of 2% + tsunami

Fig. 7. Areas in the U.S. west coast that are susceptible to damage from earthquakes with different magnitudes that are expected with PGA of 2% followed by tsunamis.

Table 6. Network infrastructures affected by earthquakes + tsunami scenario for expected PGAs with 10% and 2% probability of exceedances in the next 50 years [35].

	Cell towers		Fiber miles (km)		Ground stations	
Perceived shaking	10%	2%	10%	2%	10%	2%
Violent	689,316	531,974	21,306	20,675	4	6
Severe	598,491	737,067	14,017	25,198	1	4
Very strong	302,656	573,983	7,905	14,258	0	1

In summary, this case study demonstrates the versatility of MAZE in assessing various risks across different regions of interest. It encompasses scenarios ranging from single-hazard to multi-hazard to cascading risks, highlighting the broad applicability of the tool.

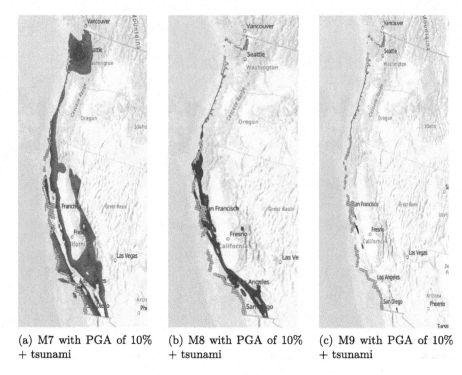

(a) M7 with PGA of 10%   (b) M8 with PGA of 10%   (c) M9 with PGA of 10%
+ tsunami   + tsunami   + tsunami

Fig. 8. Areas in the U.S. west coast that are susceptible to damage from earthquakes with different magnitudes that are expected with PGA of 10% followed by tsunamis.

6   Limitations and Discussion

6.1   Geographic Scope of MAZE and Its Applicability

While the paper focuses on the U.S. PNW as a canonical example, we note that MAZE is a general-purpose tool. Concretely, MAZE (1) can be used to assess the efficacy of a wide-variety of backup routing and hazard mitigating strategies, and (2) is not limited to any particular geographic area. For (1), while one might contend that the LEO-based strategies used in this paper is hypothetical, we emphasize that our framework has the capability to incorporate actual performance measurements from Starlink or any LEO-based satellites between the selected sources and destination. In addition, evolving satellite connectivity landscape (e.g., StarLink mobility plans for first responders [5]) and how they fare during natural disasters could be studied using MAZE. For (2), without loss of generality, MAZE can be applied to any single- or multi-hazard risks, each occurring at different granularities (e.g., city vs. state vs. multiple states). We plan to study different combinations of (1) and (2) as part of future work.

6.2   Factors Affecting the Performance of Backup Paths

The need for reconfiguring backup paths over time as subsequent disasters arise is a key factor that will affect the performance on backup paths. Note that this work only considers the evaluation of backup paths for a one-off damage scenario. This is a rich area for future research. For example, MAZE can be extended as follows to evaluate disaster-aware dynamic reconfiguration of backup paths. First, add a new reliability metric to MAZE that keeps track of network load, packet drops, available paths, etc., over time as certain hops in backup paths degrade due to cascading disasters. Next, determine the operational threshold for the reliability metric, e.g., the extent of infrastructure damage that a path can withstand before dropping packets. Finally, apply the threshold on the metric to trigger subsequent re-routing via communication strategy of interest (e.g., LEO-based backup paths) during cascading disasters.

Another factor influencing the performance of backup paths is the gap between simulations and real-world operational constraints in LEO networks. This is especially important when evaluating the behavior of latency in LEO-based backup paths both before and after the disaster to account for factors such as simultaneous traffic congestion, infrastructure damage, and more. Furthermore, as pointed in Sect. 3.3, the issue of RTT underestimates [27,33] resulting from system-level and operational overheads aggravates this issue further. Addressing this issue in MAZE requires significant domain expertise in disaster modeling and consideration of real-world measurement data [27]. This is another ripe area for future research, given the recent uptick in measurement efforts that collect real-world RTTs of LEO networks [22,27,30,36].

6.3   Non-terrestrial Risks to LEO Satellites

While LEO satellites could be used as "backup" communications infrastructure by first responders during terrestrial multi-hazard risks, as shown by Jyothi et al. [29], they are susceptible to another class of risk that is non-terrestrial in nature: Coronal Mass Ejections (CMEs). Potential impacts include disruption of communication due to damages resulting from radiation (e.g., charged particles from CMEs can disrupt communication), risk of Single Event Upsets (SEUs) (e.g., high-energy particles might flip one or more bits, impacting the sensitive electronics in LEO satellites), and power instabilities. Considering the limited knowledge we currently possess regarding the impact of these risks on LEO satellites as a whole, coupled with uncertainties surrounding the effectiveness of protective measures implemented by satellite operators, such as shielding sensitive components, we argue that LEO satellites should exclusively be utilized as backup communications infrastructure for terrestrial risks.

6.4   Lack of Community-Wide Datasets

Due to an increase in the frequency and severity of natural disasters, it is crucial to have comprehensive dataset on the impact of such disasters on network infrastructures. Community-wide datasets (1) serve as a central repository of valuable data, including historical records, real-time monitoring, and predictive models; and (2) facilitate informed decision-making, effective planning, and the implementation of appropriate mitigation strategies.

As discussed in Sect. 2, previous efforts have examined the impacts of various risks on network infrastructure on a case-by-case basis (e.g., isolated events). However, as a measurement community, we currently lack comprehensive datasets that capture the patterns, trends, and risks posed by climate change and natural disasters to network infrastructures. The notable exception to this is the diligent work conducted by the Thunderping team [43,45]. We believe that the availability of such datasets would enhance the realism and effectiveness of tools like MAZE.

The absence of datasets is not only a concern when it comes to understanding the impacts of natural hazards on network infrastructures but also extends to satellite providers and their associated costs. For instance, in addition to Inmarsat considered in MAZE, we know that there are several well-known satellite providers including HughesNet, ViaSat, among others. However, their pricing and service data are challenging to obtain, as they primarily provide consumer services with limited transparency regarding costs. This lack of pricing information hampers the assessment of the *long-term expenses* associated with using BGANs for communication during natural hazards. Additionally, the absence of data on the current hardware used by federal agencies for BGANs and the lifespan of these products makes it difficult to determine whether they offer any advantages over LEO-based services in the long run.

7   Summary and Future Work

Climate change-induced and naturally occurring multi-hazard risks are among the most significant threats to humanity and critical infrastructures alike. In this work, we seek to harden critical Internet infrastructures against multi-hazard risks. To this end, we develop a simple yet effective simulator called MAZE. Using MAZE, first responders and federal agencies can compare and contrast the benefits of various emergency communication, and can get better decision support on effective disaster mitigation strategies in a repeatable manner. We demonstrate the efficacy of MAZE by comparing LEO satellite-based emergency communication strategy against two baselines (i.e., ShakeNet and BGAN) in the face of different disaster scenarios. Our simulations show that LEO satellite-based hardening strategies offer two orders of magnitude latency improvement and 100 s of thousands of dollars in saving, all while maintaining network connectivity during multi-hazard risks.

While one of the case studies demonstrates how MAZE can be used to transition a research prototype to the real world, three key challenges (listed below) remain in using LEO-based satellites for multi-hazard risk scenarios. We believe MAZE could be used to tackle each one of these challenges, which we plan to focus on as part of future work.

- First, MAZE could be extended to study the issue of scalability and network capacity of LEO satellite-based communication systems in the face of increasing demands during multi-hazard events.
- Second, MAZE could be used for assessing and validating the practicality and effectiveness of risk-aware routing protocols or mitigation strategies for LEO satellite-based communication during multi-hazard risks. This, of course, requires partnerships with industry, academic, and government stakeholders alike.
- Third, MAZE could be used to explore the policy and regulatory considerations associated with using LEO satellite networks for emergency communication. Potential opportunities include investigating spectrum allocation, licensing requirements, and coordination with government agencies to ensure compliance and seamless integration of LEO satellite systems for emergency communications.

Acknowledgements. We thank the anonymous reviewers and our shepherd, Nitinder Mohan, for their insightful feedback. This work is supported by the Internet Society (ISOC) Foundation. The views and conclusions contained herein are those of the authors and should not be interpreted as necessarily representing the official policies or endorsements, either expressed or implied, of ISOC.

References

1. ArcGIS. https://www.arcgis.com
2. Inmarsat BGAN Data Plans. https://satellitephonestore.com/bgan-service
3. Inmarsat BGAN M2M. https://www.inmarsat.com/en/solutions-services/enterprise/services/bgan-m2m.html
4. Satellite Configurations Used in MAZE. https://gitlab.com/onrg/maze/-/raw/main/rtt_simulator/constellation_config.py
5. StarLink for Land Mobility. https://www.starlink.com/business/mobility
6. The Oregon Resilience Plan - Cascadia: Oregon's Greatest Natural Threat. https://www.oregon.gov/oem/Documents/01_ORP_Cascadia.pdf
7. Fourth National Climate Assessment: Volume II, Impacts, risks, and adaptation in the United States. Report-in-brief. U.S. Global Change Research Program, Washington, DC (2018)
8. State Occupational Employment and Wage Estimates Oregon, May 2021. https://www.bls.gov/oes/current/oes_or.htm
9. United states census bureau, county population: 2020–2021 (2021). https://www.census.gov/data/tables/time-series/demo/popest/2020s-counties-total.html
10. Allan, J., Zhang, J., O'brien, F., Gabel, L.: Columbia river tsunami modeling: toward improved maritime planning response, December 2018
11. Anderson, S., Barford, C., Barford, P.: Five alarms: assessing the vulnerability of us cellular communication infrastructure to wildfires. In: Proceedings of the ACM Internet Measurement Conference, IMC 2020, New York, NY, USA, pp. 162–175. Association for Computing Machinery (2020)
12. Burleigh, S., Scott, K.: Interplanetary Overlay Network, June 2020. https://www.inmarsatgov.com/firstnet/wp-content/uploads/2020/03/SATCOM-overview-firstnet.pdf

13. https://climate.nasa.gov/news/2926/can-climate-affect-earthquakes-or-are-the-connections-shaky/
14. Chaudhry, A.U., Yanikomeroglu, H.: Optical wireless satellite networks versus optical fiber terrestrial networks: the latency perspective. In: Nguyen, H., Le, L., Yahampath, P., Mohamed, E.B. (eds.) 30th Biennial Symposium on Communications 2021. Signals and Communication Technology, pp. 225–234. Springer, Cham (2022). https://doi.org/10.1007/978-3-031-06947-5_17
15. Cho, K., Pelsser, C., Bush, R., Won, Y.: The Japan earthquake: the impact on traffic and routing observed by a local ISP. In: Proceedings of the Special Workshop on Internet and Disasters, pp. 1–8 (2011)
16. Durairajan, R., Barford, C., Barford, P.: Lights out: climate change risk to internet infrastructure. In: Proceedings of Applied Networking Research Workshop (2018)
17. Eriksson, B., Durairajan, R., Barford, P.: Riskroute: a framework for mitigating network outage threats. In: Proceedings of the Ninth ACM Conference on Emerging Networking Experiments and Technologies, pp. 405–416 (2013)
18. FirstNet: Satellite Solutions for FirstNet, March 2020. https://www.inmarsatgov.com/firstnet/wp-content/uploads/2020/03/SATCOM-overview-firstnet.pdf
19. Fomon, J.: Here's How Fast Starlink Has Gotten Over the Past Year, June 2022. https://www.ookla.com/articles/starlink-hughesnet-viasat-performance-q1-2022
20. Franchi, A., Howell, A., Sengupta, J.: Broadband mobile via satellite: inmarsat BGAN. In: IEE Seminar on Broadband Satellite: The Critical Success Factors - Technology, Services and Markets (Ref. No. 2000/067), pp. 23/1–23/7 (2000)
21. Gallagher, J.C.: The first responder network (firstnet) and next-generation communications for public safety: issues for congress (2018)
22. Garcia, J., Sundberg, S., Caso, G., Brunstrom, A.: Multi-timescale evaluation of starlink throughput. In: Proceedings of the 1st ACM Workshop on LEO Networking and Communication, pp. 31–36 (2023)
23. Gensini, V.A., Brooks, H.E.: Spatial trends in united states tornado frequency. NPJ Clim. Atmos. Sci. 1(1) (2018)
24. Given, D.D., et al.: Revised technical implementation plan for the shakealert system-an earthquake early warning system for the west coast of the united states. Technical report, US Geological Survey (2018)
25. Han, C.: The BeiDou navigation satellite system. In: 2014 XXXIth URSI General Assembly and Scientific Symposium (URSI GASS), pp. 1–3 (2014)
26. King County Public Health: Division of emergency medical services 2021 annual report, September 2021. https://kingcounty.gov/depts/health/emergency-medical-services/~/media/depts/health/emergency-medical-services/documents/reports/2021-Annual-Report.ashx
27. Izhikevich, L., Tran, M., Izhikevich, K., Akiwate, G., Durumeric, Z.: Democratizing LEO Satellite Network Measurement. arXiv preprint arXiv:2306.07469 (2023)
28. Jackson, D.: FirstNet Authority seeks input on potential solutions to off-network challenges. Urgent Communications (2021)
29. Jyothi, S.A.: Solar superstorms: planning for an internet apocalypse. In: Proceedings of the 2021 ACM SIGCOMM 2021 Conference, pp. 692–704 (2021)
30. Kassem, M.M., Raman, A., Perino, D., Sastry, N.: A browser-side view of starlink connectivity. In: Proceedings of the 22nd ACM Internet Measurement Conference, pp. 151–158 (2022)
31. Kassing, S., Bhattacherjee, D., Águas, A.B., Saethre, J.E., Singla, A.: Exploring the "internet from space" with hypatia. In: Proceedings of the ACM Internet Measurement Conference, IMC 2020, New York, NY, USA, pp. 214–229. Association for Computing Machinery (2020)

32. Kimball, C.: How much bandwidth is needed for VoIP. https://www.avoxi.com/blog/how-much-bandwidth-is-needed-for-voip/
33. Lai, Z., et al.: {StarryNet}: empowering researchers to evaluate futuristic integrated space and terrestrial networks. In: 20th USENIX Symposium on Networked Systems Design and Implementation (NSDI 2023), pp. 1309–1324 (2023)
34. Li, B., et al.: A system of power emergency communication system based BDS and LEO satellite. In: 2021 Computing, Communications and IoT Applications (ComComAp), pp. 286–291 (2021)
35. Mayer, J., Sahakian, V., Hooft, E., Toomey, D., Durairajan, R.: On the resilience of internet infrastructures in pacific northwest to earthquakes (2021)
36. Michel, F., Trevisan, M., Giordano, D., Bonaventure, O.: A first look at starlink performance. In: Proceedings of the 22nd ACM Internet Measurement Conference, pp. 130–136 (2022)
37. Northwest Interagency Coordination Center: Northwest fire locations. https://gacc.nifc.gov/nwcc/information/firemap.aspx
38. Bureau of Labor Management: Occupational Employment and Wage Statistics of EMTs (2021)
39. Bureau of Labor Management: Occupational Employment and Wage Statistics of Firefighters (2021)
40. Bureau of Labor Management: Occupational Employment and Wage Statistics of Paramedics (2021)
41. Washington State Department of Natural Resources: Tsunami hazard maps (2022)
42. National Association of State Budget Officers: State Expenditure Report (2021). https://www.nasbo.org/reports-data/state-expenditure-report
43. Padmanabhan, R., Schulman, A., Levin, D., Spring, N.: Residential links under the weather. In: Proceedings of the ACM Special Interest Group on Data Communication, pp. 145–158 (2019)
44. Portland Fire & Rescue: FAQs (2021). https://www.portlandoregon.gov/fire/article/378460
45. Schulman, A., Spring, N.: Pingin' in the rain. In: ACM IMC, November 2011
46. SkyBrokers: Amazon Kuiper Systems, LLC (2022). https://sky-brokers.com/supplier/amazon-kuiper-systems-llc/
47. Smith, K., et al.: Integrated multi-hazard regional networks: earthquake warning/response, wildfire detection/response, and extreme weather tracking. Appl. Geol. Calif. Assoc. Environ. Eng. Geol. (AEG) Spec. Publ. (26), 599–612 (2016)
48. Starlink: Starlink kit. https://www.starlink.com
49. Starlink: World's most advanced broadband internet system (2021). https://www.starlink.com/satellites
50. Telesat: Telesat Lightspeed LEO Network, November 2021. https://www.telesat.com/leo-satellites/
51. Verizon: First responder benefits program (2020). https://www.verizon.com/business/solutions/public-sector/public-safety/programs/first-responder-benefits/
52. Zhou, J., Ye, X., Pan, Y., Xiao, F., Sun, L.: Dynamic channel reservation scheme based on priorities in LEO satellite systems. J. Syst. Eng. Electron. **26**(1), 1–9 (2015)

Topology

Following the Data Trail: An Analysis of IXP Dependencies

Malte Tashiro[1,2](✉) [iD], Romain Fontugne[2] [iD], and Kensuke Fukuda[1,3] [iD]

[1] SOKENDAI, Tokyo, Japan
[2] IIJ Research Laboratory, Tokyo, Japan
{malte,romain}@iij.ad.jp
[3] NII, Tokyo, Japan
kensuke@nii.ac.jp

Abstract. Internet exchange points (IXPs) play a vital role in the modern Internet. Envisioned as a means to connect physically close networks, they have grown into large hubs connecting networks from all over the world, either directly or via remote peering. It is therefore important to understand the real footprint of an IXP to quantify the extent to which problems (e.g., outages) at an IXP can impact the surrounding Internet topology. An IXP footprint computed only from its list of members as given by PeeringDB, or the IXP's website, is usually depicting an incomplete view of the IXP as it misses downstream networks whose traffic may transit via an IXP although they are not directly peering there. In this paper we propose a robust approach that uncovers this dependency using traceroute data from two large measurement platforms. Our approach converts traceroutes to paths that include both autonomous systems (ASes) and IXPs and computes AS Hegemony to infer their inter-dependencies. This technique discovers thousands of dependent networks not directly connected to IXPs and emphasizes the role of IXPs in the Internet topology. We also look at the geolocation of members and dependents and find that only 3% of IXPs with dependents are entirely local: all members and dependents are in the same country as the IXP. Another 52% connect international members, but only have domestic dependents.

1 Introduction

The Internet is continuously growing and its topology is getting increasingly more complex. Originally a clear hierarchy, the structure of the Internet transforms into a flat mesh [31]. This transformation is facilitated by the advance of internet exchange points (IXPs), that establish peering facilities where networks can connect directly. Enticed by the promise of cost reduction and potential latency improvements [16], the number of both IXPs and IXP members has seen consistent growth over the past years [24]. While the original idea of IXPs was to promote connectivity between physically close networks, reduce unnecessary routing detours, and "keep local traffic local" [27], their use has grown beyond

© The Author(s), under exclusive license to Springer Nature Switzerland AG 2024
P. Richter et al. (Eds.): PAM 2024, LNCS 14538, pp. 199–227, 2024.
https://doi.org/10.1007/978-3-031-56252-5_10

that. IXPs can now provide impressive reach [49], they have become important infrastructure for content delivery networks (CDNs) [25], and are used for DDoS mitigation [54,55].

This evolution makes it paramount to understand the footprint of IXPs in the Internet topology. Like any part of the Internet they are subject to failures and congestion [15,35]. The goal of this paper is to quantify the importance of IXPs beyond their members. A better understanding of how networks, maybe inadvertently, depend on IXPs, can help system engineers, peering coordinators, and policy makers in their decision process. For example, to increase resilience a network operator might want to avoid using two transit providers that both depend on the same IXP.

The Internet topology has been studied in the past by measuring dependency between autonomous systems (ASes). These studies mostly analyzed AS paths in BGP data [36,38,46], occasionally complementing it with traceroute data [19]. Our proposed method quantifies not only AS-level dependencies, but expands the analysis to IXPs. The study of IXP dependencies allows us to contextualize the role of IXPs for the Internet. Unfortunately, IXPs are generally not visible in AS paths, hence BGP data is unsuitable for our study (Sect. 3). Instead, we aim to infer dependency only from traceroute data as IXP peering LANs are easily identifiable there. We use IPv4 traceroute data from two large measurement platforms in combination with PeeringDB [9] and looking glass information to detect IXPs and how they are traversed. By transforming traceroutes to n-paths, AS paths enhanced with IXP identifiers, we can adapt the AS Hegemony [36] metric to reveal the inter-dependencies between ASes and IXPs (Sect. 4). We validate this new approach against results obtained from BGP data and find that both methods produce comparable numbers of AS dependencies (Sect. 5).

Based on the computed dependency values we highlight some of the differences and similarities between transit ASes and IXPs (Sect. 6). Then we investigate the *topological* footprint of IXPs by comparing the relationship between the number of members and dependent ASes, showing that they are not strictly correlated (Sect. 7). We also look at the *geographic* footprint of IXPs revealing that some IXPs have dependents in countries not covered by their members. In addition, we infer the *Regionality* of IXPs, i.e., if their members and dependents are from the same country, and show a comparison between all monitored IXPs. Finally, we dissect the dependents of two large IXPs, DE-CIX Frankfurt and IX.br São Paulo, highlighting the different roles played by these IXPs in the Internet topology; DE-CIX Frankfurt is acting mostly as an international hub for dependents from multiple countries, whereas IX.br São Paulo dependents are almost entirely from Brazil (Sect. 8).

In summary, our main contributions are:

- A method to infer IXP and AS dependencies from traceroute data.
- A high-level study of the role of IXPs in the Internet topology compared to ASes by analyzing the number and magnitude of dependencies.

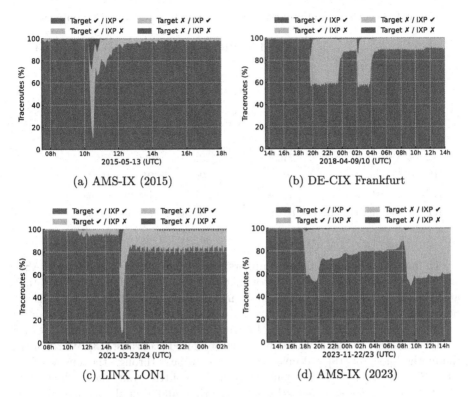

Fig. 1. Impact of partial outages at three IXPs on connectivity. Traceroutes are grouped into four categories, depending on if the target was reached (`Target ✓`) and if the IXP was on the path (`IXP ✓`).

- The analysis of the topological and geographical footprint of IXPs based on the location of dependent networks, as well as insights into the locality of connected networks.
- A case study highlighting the usefulness of dependencies by comparison of two large IXPs, `DE-CIX Frankfurt` and `IX.br São Paulo`, showing disparate topological footprints.
- The publication and periodic update of IXP dependency information [53].

2   Motivation

IXPs play an increasingly vital role in the global Internet topology. However, as any complex system they are not safe from failures caused by human error, power outages, or other sources. Understanding the potential impact of these failures is hindered by the fact that IXPs operate mostly at Layer 2, and thus, they are disregarded by large scale Internet topology studies which are usually based on BGP data [32,34,36,40].

Table 1. Composition of probe-target pairs used to investigate IXP outages.

	AMS-IX (2015)	DE-CIX	LINX	AMS-IX (2023)
Probe-target pairs	11,655	25,945	25,876	46,377
Atlas probes	3116	4437	4300	6595
Probe ASes	1186	1933	1631	2428
Probes/AS (median)	2	4	3	3
Target IPs	441	561	799	1241
Target ASes	240	358	500	719
IPs/AS (median)	10	20	21	16
RTT via IXP (avg.)	55 ms	87 ms	126 ms	81 ms
RTT bypassing IXP (avg.)	84 ms	93 ms	131 ms	84 ms

To motivate the importance of understanding the relationship between ASes and IXPs we take a look at four historical outages at large IXPs: A partial outage at AMS-IX in 2015 due to a configuration error during maintenance work [12], a power outage at a DE-CIX Frankfurt datacenter in 2018 [41], an outage caused by undisclosed technical reasons at LINX LON1 in 2021 [7], and finally another outage at AMS-IX in 2023 caused by a misconfigured access list [13]. We replicate the methodology of [15] and investigate these outages through the lens of RIPE Atlas [50]. We analyze the incidents with the help of traceroute data, which gives us a fine-grained view of the paths before, during, and after the outage. To infer the impact of these outages on connectivity, we want to inspect traceroutes from probes that consistently traverse the IXP in the absence of failures. We then monitor if these traceroutes continue to reach their targets during the outage, and if the IXP is still traversed.

To select a reliable set of probes and targets, we start with all traceroutes run by Atlas probes during the day before the outage. The traceroutes are grouped by probe-target pairs, and we keep only pairs for which (1) the IXP's peering LAN is visible in *all* traceroutes, (2) the target host responds to the traceroutes, and (3) we see at least 24 traceroutes within the inspected interval (i.e., on average one per hour). This filtering results in a diverse set of pairs as shown in Table 1.

Next, we inspect the behavior of traceroutes between these probes and targets around the time of the outage. Each traceroute is categorized based on the reachability of the target and if the peering LAN of the IXP is present on the path. Figure 1 shows the category distribution over time. The traceroute results are grouped into five-minute bins. In all cases, the time of the outage (two incidents in the case of DE-CIX and AMS-IX 2023) is clearly visible. The dark blue area represents the normal state in which the traceroute traverses the IXP and the target responds. However, at the time of the outage, a large share of traceroutes does not pass through the IXP anymore. Although the majority still reaches the target through rerouting (light blue), a significant amount loses

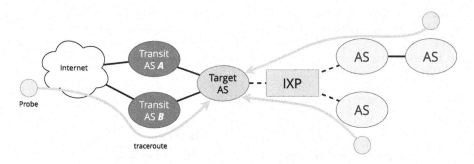

Fig. 2. Typical Internet topology: An AS connects to the Internet via transit providers and might also peer with other ASes via an IXP. Inference of the topology via traceroute may miss ASes that are not traversed (e.g., Transit AS *A*), but detects IXPs.

connectivity to the target temporarily (red). This impact is most visible in the AMS-IX 2015 and LINX LON1 outages, where up to 71% and 83% of traceroutes avoided the IXP and up to 30% and 37% failed to reach their target at the peak of the outage.

Although rerouting around the IXP allows some probes to reach the target (light blue), it does come with a price: Comparing the average RTT of a probe-target pair reaching the destination via the IXP to the same target but routing around the IXP we see an increase by 52% in the case of AMS-IX 2015 (from 55 ms to 84 ms, cf. Table 1). Even though the effect was smaller for DE-CIX (+7%), LINX (+5%), and AMS-IX 2023 (+4%) it is still clear that routing around the IXPs has a negative performance impact. In addition, these transitions between IXP and transit networks may incur additional financial costs for the operators.

This analysis demonstrates that an outage at the IXP does have consequences for networks that use it for connectivity. It is therefore imperative to understand which networks use IXPs, either directly or via transit ASes, and to what degree. The goal of this paper is to analyze the relationship between IXPs and networks and quantify how networks utilize IXPs for connectivity. We call this relationship a *dependency* between an AS and an IXP if we detect that the AS consistently uses the IXP for its global connectivity. A precise definition is given in Sect. 4.3.

3   Design Decisions

In this section we explain the differences between BGP data and traceroutes for dependency calculations (summarized in Table 2) and emphasize that traceroutes are required to detect dependencies on IXPs.

We identified three key differences that are relevant when inferring dependencies: The scope of the visible topology, the ability to identify IXPs, and the temporal granularity with which dependencies can be calculated. We illustrate these differences based on Fig. 2, which shows a simplified topology around a

Table 2. Property comparison of BGP and traceroute to infer the Internet topology and dependencies. BGP data is available in real time, gives a global view of the topology visible to the peers, but does not contain IXPs. Traceroutes reveal only the parts of the topology they traverse and thus need to be aggregated over a time window, but reveal the locations of IXPs.

Type	Topological granularity		Temporal granularity
	Scope	IXP visibility	
BGP	Global	No	Real time
traceroute	Per path	Yes	Time window

target AS for which we want to infer dependencies. The first difference is the topological scope of both datasets: BGP peers usually share their full routing tables with route collectors, and combining these tables reveals a large part of the Internet topology including all globally reachable ASes. Traceroutes only reveal ASes that are on the path the packets traverse, hence the number of discovered ASes is mainly governed by the number of collected traceroutes. However, because both BGP and traceroute data are obtained from a limited number of vantage points, both do not provide a complete view on AS links. The second difference is the ability to identify IXPs in the discovered topology. We can infer the presence of IXPs on the path with traceroute by detecting hops that are within the peering LAN of IXP as shown in Fig. 2. In contrast, IXPs are not visible in BGP data because they are not explicitly involved in the inter-domain routing process. The third difference is the temporal granularity with which the data can be retrieved. BGP data is available as snapshots in form of routing information databases (RIBs) complemented by update files, which enable seamless reconstruction of the visible topology at any time. As mentioned above, traceroutes discover ASes by actively traversing them. Since traceroutes obtained from measurement platforms run periodically—and to random targets—it is necessary to aggregate data over a long period of time to obtain a reasonable view of the topology (further discussed in Sect. 4.1). Therefore, traceroute data is unsuitable for the study of transient changes and should only be used to build a long-term view of the topology.

In summary, while there are differences when inferring dependencies from BGP and traceroute data (see Table 2), our study of IXPs makes the use of traceroutes mandatory. This requires the design of a new data processing pipeline to infer dependencies, which is described in the following section. Further limitations of traceroute are also explained in Sect. 9.

4   Methodology

Figure 3 illustrates the different parts of the proposed processing pipeline. Our analysis is based on large traceroute datasets retrieved from measurement platforms like RIPE Atlas and CAIDA's Ark. Each traceroute is transformed to a n-path, an AS path enhanced with IXP identifiers. Finally, the n-paths are fed to the AS Hegemony algorithm, resulting in Hegemony scores from which we infer dependencies.

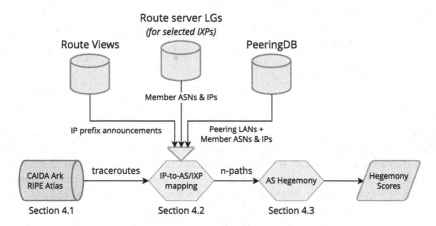

Fig. 3. The processing pipeline: First, traceroutes from CAIDA Ark or RIPE Atlas are converted to n-paths. The conversion uses a combination of Route Views, PeeringDB, and IXP looking glass information to map traceroute hops to ASes or IXPs. Finally, the n-paths are fed to the AS Hegemony algorithm to compute Hegemony scores.

4.1 Dataset

We consider two traceroute datasets: the topology measurements [14] from RIPE Atlas [50] and the IPv4 Routed /24 Topology Dataset from CAIDA's Ark platform [4]. The Atlas topology measurements[1] employ all Atlas probes but these are not evenly distributed and are known to have location bias [20,21,29,51]. Therefore, we select a sample of 1000 probes based on the approach in [18] that prioritizes AS-path diversity, i.e., the probes are selected in a way that increases the AS-path length between them, thus providing a set of probes that are widespread over the Internet topology. The probe set covers 115 countries and 1000 ASes. CAIDA's dataset consists of 90 probes (a.k.a. monitors) located in 36 countries covering 74 ASes. We select all of them.

Both datasets are attempts to reveal the Internet topology by conducting traceroute measurements from the probes to a very large number of target IP addresses. CAIDA computes its list of target IPs by selecting one random IP from each routed /24 prefix and distributes this list between all probes. It guarantees that the target list is entirely processed before the next round of measurements starts. The Atlas target IP list consists of the first address of each globally routed prefix seen in BGP, which includes large prefixes and is therefore coarser.

---

[1] Measurement IDs for IPv4: 5051 and 5151.

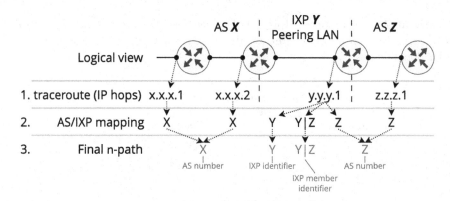

Fig. 4. Transformation of a traceroute to an n-path: Individual traceroute hops are mapped to their respective AS (2.). If a hop lies within an IXP peering LAN, it is mapped to an IXP identifier. If there is additional information available that assigns the precise IP to an IXP member, the hop is also mapped to an IXP member identifier and the AS of the member. Finally, duplicate AS numbers are removed (3.).

In addition, the list is reset daily and there is no guarantee that the target IPs have all been processed. Atlas probe scheduling makes the probe assignment less deterministic and probes are capped to one traceroute every 15 min. As a consequence, a preliminary comparison between the two datasets revealed challenges with the Atlas dataset.

We analyzed data for one week in September (2022-09-12–2022-09-19), which contained $\approx$ 1.8 million traceroutes for Atlas and $\approx$ 136 million traceroutes for Ark. When computing Hegemony scores for each dataset we found that 67% of target ASes are probed by RIPE Atlas probes from less than 10 ASes and are ignored as providing unreliable results (as explained in Sect. 4.3), whereas only 9% of targets are ignored with the Ark dataset. To increase the reliability of results we increased the size of the data window for Atlas to four weeks (2022-09-05–2022-10-03; $\approx$ 7.4 million traceroutes), which reduced the amount of ignored targets to 24%. When comparing the results with the previous and following weeks we found that they were similar. Thus, for ease of discussion we present only results based on one week of data for Ark and four weeks for Atlas.

4.2 Translating Traceroute Data to n-paths

The next step of the pipeline is to transform the traceroute results to n-paths. A n-path looks like an AS path, but contains additional hops that represent IXPs and IXP members. As shown in Fig. 3 we combine different data sources to build a comprehensive IP-to-AS/IXP mapping. Similar to existing approaches [26,43,47] we rely on IXP data from the PeeringDB [9] database and BGP data from Route Views [11] to detect IXPs and ASes in traceroutes. We identify IXPs in traceroute using IXP peering LANs from PeeringDB. Well maintained PeeringDB entries also contain interface information for individual

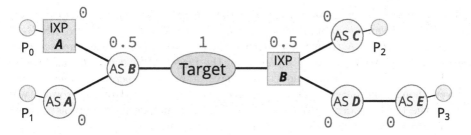

Fig. 5. A simplified view of AS Hegemony applied to n-paths: Hegemony scores are assigned to both ASes and IXPs. Nodes close to the vantage points are ignored to prevent biased scores caused by an uneven probe distribution.

IXP members, which enables us to also include the member AS in our paths. PeeringDB was validated in [44], where the authors show that PeeringDB membership is reasonably representative of the Internet's transit, content, and access providers in terms of business types and geography of participants, and data is generally up-to-date. For IXPs that use the Alice-LG [1] looking glass (e.g., DE-CIX, IX.br, LINX), we retrieve additional information to enhance membership data. BGP data from Route Views [11] is used to map other hops to ASes.

Figure 4 highlights the transformation process in more detail. In the first step, each hop of the traceroute is mapped to an AS number, an IXP identifier, or both. If detailed information about an IP is available, an IXP member identifier is added as well. If an IP address can not be mapped, the hop is ignored, which is a known shortcoming of using traceroute to infer AS-paths [42,45,57], but has limited impact on our approach. In our datasets, the IP-to-AS mapping fails for 2.5% to 3.5% of hops. Since traceroute sends more than one packet per hop, it is possible to receive replies from different IP addresses. If these IP addresses map to different ASes, they are included as an AS set. After mapping all hops we remove duplicate ASes, keeping only the first occurrence in the n-path.

4.3 AS Hegemony

We adapt AS Hegemony, a metric for quantifying AS inter-dependencies [36], to work with traceroute data and measure dependency to IXPs. We selected this metric because it is based on simple principles (i.e., using no BGP-specific heuristics such as AS relationships), it takes only paths as input data, and it has proven to be practical in various use cases [28,33,34,37].

First, we give an intuitive explanation based on a simplified example of AS Hegemony applied to n-paths in Fig. 5. Hegemony scores range from 0 to 1 and roughly represent the ratio of paths to the target AS that include the transit node. Since a n-path contains IXP identifiers, Hegemony scores are not only assigned to ASes but IXPs as well. For example, in Fig. 5 there are four paths from the probes (P_{0-3}) to the target AS. Two of these paths each pass through nodes AS B and IXP B, resulting in a Hegemony score of 0.5. To prevent biased scores caused by an uneven probe distribution, the calculation dismisses nodes close to the vantage points, which is why nodes IXP A, AS A, and AS C-E have a score of 0. A transit node (AS or IXP) with a high Hegemony score is commonly referred to as a *dependency* for the target AS (e.g., AS B and IXP B in Fig. 5), and large transit nodes may have numerous *dependent* target ASes. Even though the peering LAN of an IXP can be the target of traceroutes, we limit the target nodes for our study to ASes and include IXPs only as transit nodes. We give a precise definition of *dependency* below.

Formally, AS Hegemony is mostly based on Betweenness Centrality. For a graph $G = (V, E)$ composed of a set of nodes V and edges E, the betweenness centrality is defined as

$$BC(v) = \frac{1}{S} \sum_{u,w \in V} \sigma_{uw}(v) \tag{1}$$

where $\sigma_{uw}(v)$ is the number of paths from u to w passing through v, and S is the total number of paths. AS Hegemony adapts this method to make it more robust against sampling error incurred by the limited number of vantage points from which the graph is created. For this study we build one graph for each target AS t that consists only of n-paths towards t (similar to the local graphs of [36]). Graphs constructed this way are useful to study the dependency of the target on other nodes, which is the focus of our study.

Hence, we slightly modify the notation of the original work and define the Hegemony score of a node v in the graph of t as

$$\mathcal{H}_t(v, \alpha) = \frac{1}{n - (2\lfloor \alpha n \rfloor)} \sum_{j=\lfloor \alpha n \rfloor + 1}^{n - \lfloor \alpha n \rfloor} BC_{(j)}(v) \tag{2}$$

where

$$BC_{(j)}(v) = \frac{1}{S} \sum_{w \in V} \sigma_{jw}(v) \tag{3}$$

is the BC value computed with paths from only one viewpoint j, n is the total number of viewpoints, $\lfloor . \rfloor$ is the floor function, and $0 \leq 2\alpha < 1$ is the ratio of disregarded viewpoints such that the top and bottom $\lfloor \alpha n \rfloor$ viewpoints with the highest/lowest number of paths passing through the node are ignored. As recommended in the original work, we set α to 0.1.

Note that the change in notation—$\mathcal{H}_t$ compared to $\mathcal{H}$ in the original work— only indicates the difference in paths that are used for the calculation. In the original work, $\mathcal{H}$ is used in the context of *global* graphs, which include all paths from vantage points to *any* target AS, whereas $\mathcal{H}_t$ only includes paths going towards AS t. The computation is the same, only the input is different.

Definition: In accordance with past work [37], we consider dependencies with a Hegemony score lower than 0.1 as marginal and only report dependencies with a higher score. Therefore, for the purposes of this work, a node t has a *dependency* on node v if $\mathcal{H}_t(v) \geq 0.1$.

Table 3. The ten ASes with most dependents in BGP compared to traceroute and Spearman's rank correlation for all AS ranks. The rank correlation is calculated between BGP and the respective traceroute dataset.

ASN	Name	Rank			Dependencies		
		BGP	Ark	Atlas	BGP	Ark	Atlas
3356	Level 3	1	= 1	= 1	27,026	28,886	23,811
1299	Arelion	2	= 2	= 2	21,866	26,308	18,805
174	Cogent	3	= 3	= 3	19,394	19,405	13,334
6939	Hurricane Electric	4	= 4	= 4	18,883	13,636	13,035
2914	NTT-GIN	5	↓ 7	↓ 10	5819	3615	2904
3257	GTT	6	= 6	↓ 7	5456	4794	3705
6461	Zayo	7	↑ 5	↓ 8	4905	6129	3568
9002	RETN	8	↓ 10	↓ 9	3859	2777	3029
6453	Tata Communications	9	= 9	↓ 11	3345	3161	2573
52320	GlobeNet	10	↓ 12	↓ 14	2890	2375	2012
Spearman's ρ for all ranks						0.86	0.84

As explained in Sect. 4.1, in our datasets the number of probes (i.e., vantage points) per target AS may vary and a low number of probes is likely to produce uncertain Hegemony scores. For this reason we avoid unreliable Hegemony scores by studying only scores that have been computed from paths collected by probes from at least 10 different ASes.

Finally, all reported dependencies should be treated as estimates based on the traceroutes captured within the specified interval. However, as described in Sect. 4.1 we confirmed that results are stable over time at least in close temporal proximity. Furthermore a dependency on an upstream system is based on the visible path usage within the interval. It does not imply that a failure of the upstream leads to a complete disconnect of the dependents as there might be backup connections available that are normally on standby and thus not visible in traceroute. Nonetheless, as motivated in Sect. 2 we expect that an outage at the upstream has some negative impact on its dependents.

5 BGP Cross-Validation

To cross-validate our methodology with previous work and get an understanding of how dependencies derived from traceroute data compare to the ones computed from BGP data, we inspect the AS dependencies from both approaches. We fetched BGP-based Hegemony results from the publicly available archive [6] for the timestamp 2022-09-19T00:00.

The BGP dataset contains 262,817 dependencies on 10,243 transit ASes, whereas using traceroute data from Ark (Atlas) we found 227,136 (180,480) dependencies on 6970 (6145) transit ASes. This difference stems mainly from

Table 4. Dependency Categories

	Ark			Atlas		
Type	Category	Count	Pct.	Category	Count	Pct.
AS	Low	3876	55.61%	Low	3440	55.98%
	Medium	2985	42.83%	Medium	2616	42.57%
	High	109	1.56%	High	89	1.45%
	Total	6970	100%	Total	6145	100%
IXP	Low	114	53.52%	Low	107	48.86%
	Medium	94	44.13%	Medium	104	47.49%
	High	5	2.35%	High	8	3.65%
	Total	213	100%	Total	219	100%

our conservative thresholds on the minimum number of probe ASes, and because some routers do not reply to traceroute probes. Comparing the top ten transit ASes with the largest number of dependents in Table 3 shows that the rankings derived from BGP and traceroute are largely the same, with slight differences in the absolute number of dependents. If we inspect the top 100 (1000) ASes, we see an overlap of 80% (80%) with an average difference of 54 (28) dependents for ASes that are contained in both BGP and traceroute for Ark. The overlap is the same for Atlas (81% and 79%) although the average difference of dependents increases slightly (95 and 50). Finally, we compare the overall order of AS rankings using Spearman's rank correlation. There are 6420 ASes with dependents in both BGP and Ark, and 5704 ASes for BGP and Atlas. A correlation of $\rho = 0.86$ for BGP/Ark and $\rho = 0.84$ for BGP/Atlas reveals that there is a strong correlation between the order of ASes in terms of number of dependents.

There can be small differences between the control (BGP) and data (traceroute) plane [30], as well as the aforementioned caveats of traceroute. Overall, however, the sets of ASes and their order are very similar and although the number of dependents is not exactly the same, the approach of computing AS Hegemony on traceroute data produces AS dependencies similar to past work. Thus, we expect the IXP dependency results to be sensible.

6   Comparing Transit ASes and IXPs

We now focus only on the results we have obtained with the traceroute datasets and put the role of IXPs in perspective by comparing dependency results of IXPs and transit ASes. For this comparison we look at the distribution of two properties: (1) The *number* of dependents relying on ASes and IXPs respectively and (2) the *strength* of the dependencies as indicated by the Hegemony score. For Ark (Atlas) there are 6970 (6145) ASes and 213 (219) IXPs with dependents in our results (see "Total" rows in Table 4), corresponding to $\approx$ 61% (54%) of

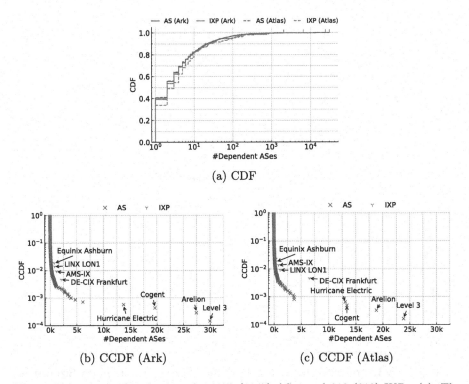

(a) CDF

(b) CCDF (Ark)   (c) CCDF (Atlas)

Fig. 6. Dependency distributions for 6970 (6145) ASes and 213 (219) IXPs. (a): The relative distributions are similar for ASes and IXPs. (b) & (c): There are some large ASes with significantly more dependents. This observation is present, although less pronounced, for IXPs as well, with four large IXPs standing out.

the 11,439 transit ASes[2] and $\approx$ 27% of the 803 IXPs with at least two members listed in PeeringDB, which is a first indication that networks are relying more on transit ASes rather than IXPs to reach the wide Internet.

The overall distribution of the number of dependents is shown in Fig. 6a. Even though the number of points in each CDF differ by one order of magnitude, the shapes are remarkably similar. Around 40% of ASes and IXPs have only a single dependent, and around 80% have less than 10, meaning that the vast majority of networks have rather small number of dependents. However, the tail of the distribution reveals some ASes and IXPs with a large number of dependents (highlighted in Figs. 6b and 6c). In case of ASes, four large Tier 1 providers have several times more dependents than the remaining distribution, emphasizing the still important role of these networks in the Internet. This effect is also present for IXPs, with four IXPs standing out. From these numbers one may think that these large IXPs have similar properties to the Tier 1 providers, but this is not the case, as Hegemony scores for IXPs are significantly lower.

---

[2] Number of ASes with a customer cone > 1 according to [3].

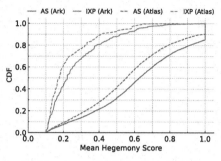

(a) Hegemony Distribution (CDF)

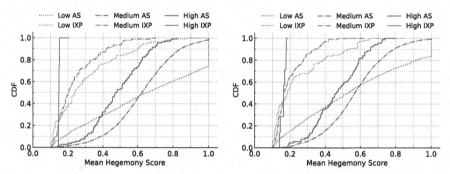

(b) Hegemony Distribution (by Size) Ark (c) Hegemony Distribution (by Size) Atlas

Fig. 7. Hegemony distributions for 6970 (6145) ASes and 213 (219) IXPs. (a): IXPs have weaker dependencies than ASes. (b) & (c): Splitting the CDF by number of dependents (Low ≤ 2; Medium ≤ 180; High > 180) reveals that strong dependencies are concentrated in *Low* ASes/IXPs.

The distribution of mean Hegemony scores in Fig. 7a highlights an important disparity between the strength of the dependencies between ASes and IXPs. The dependencies on IXPs are a lot weaker, with a median value of 0.22 (0.18) compared to 0.63 (0.55) for ASes. This means that a smaller number of paths are going through IXPs, which reveals that IXPs are usually used for a limited number of destinations as opposed to transit ASes that provide routes to the whole Internet. This agrees with the commonly accepted role of IXPs in the topology (see Fig. 2). In particular, 14.8% (9.7%) of ASes have a mean Hegemony score of 1, indicating that all their dependents rely fully on them (e.g., a single homed network with all its paths passing through a single upstream AS).

To understand the differences between these distributions in more detail, both ASes and IXPs are classified into categories according to their number of dependents. We take inspiration from [32] and define three categories: *Low* (≤ 2 dependents), *Medium* (≤ 180), and *High* (> 180). Therefore, in the following, the terms *Low IXP* (*High IXP*) refer to an IXP with a low (high) number of dependents. We use this term to distinguish from *Small IXP* (*Large IXP*), which is an IXP with a small (large) number of *members*. The resulting category sizes are shown in Table 4; The relative distribution of ASes is almost the same for Ark and Atlas, whereas a slight trend towards *Low* IXPs is visible for Ark.

The distributions of the six categories are shown in Figs. 7b and 7c which clearly show that the ASes and IXPs with a mean Hegemony score of 1 are almost exclusively those having only a single or two dependents. Conversely, an increasing number of dependents corresponds to weaker average Hegemony scores. This is also expected, as *Low* ASes are usually small Internet service providers (ISPs) with a few local single-homed customers, whereas larger ASes are likely to serve other large multi-homed ASes. Although the strength of dependencies is overall weaker for IXPs, we can assume the same is also true for IXPs.

In summary, while transit ASes have generally more dependents, there are some IXPs that separate themselves from the rest, possibly indicating a progression from their traditional role. However, the strength of dependencies on IXPs still remains relatively low, especially compared to transit ASes.

7   IXP Characterization

We now focus only on IXPs and characterize them based on two major factors: Their *topological* and *geographical* footprints. The topological footprint describes the role of an IXP in the Internet topology, based on its number of dependents. The geographical footprint refers to the physical location of the IXP and its dependents.

First, we take a look at the visibility of IXPs in traceroute (Sect. 7.1) to clarify the relationship between the presence of IXPs in traceroute and their number of dependent networks. Then, we inspect the connection between the number of members and dependents (Sect. 7.2). We comment on the general geographic footprint of IXPs (Sect. 7.3) and finally introduce a metric called *Regionality* (Sect. 7.4) to quantify the relationship between the location of an IXP and its members or dependents.

Since the results of the Ark and Atlas datasets are very similar, we limit the discussion and plots from now on only to the results obtained with the Ark dataset.

7.1   Topology: IXP Visibility in Traceroute

The study of IXP dependencies based on traceroute data comes with the limitation that we can only infer dependencies for an IXP if we see it in traceroute. This raises two questions: (1) What is the general visibility of IXPs and their members in our data and (2) does the visibility of an IXP imply the presence of dependents?

We see that a majority of IXPs is visible and that there is a relationship between the size of the IXP and its visibility. In addition, the majority of visible IXPs does not have any dependents. We found that over 57% of IXPs with at

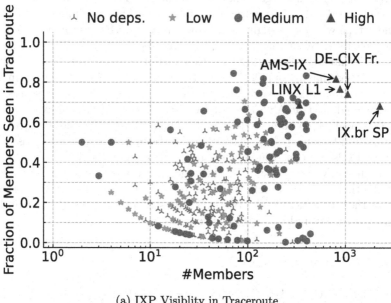

(a) IXP Visiblity in Traceroute

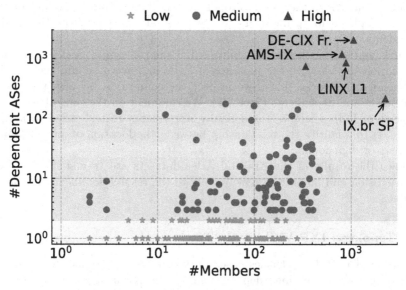

(b) IXP Dependents vs. Members

Fig. 8. Data for 205 IXPs with dependents and 259 IXPs without. Excludes eight IXPs with dependents but no members seen. (a): Large IXPs with many members enjoy good visibility. (b): The number of members and dependents are not strongly connected. (Color figure online)

least two members in PeeringDB are visible in our dataset, i.e., we see traceroute responses from within their peering LAN.

To investigate the relationship between the size of an IXP (in terms of its members) and its visibility, we count for each IXP how many members are present in traceroute. For a better comparison of IXPs with different sizes, we compute the number of members seen in traceroute as a fraction. Figure 8a shows the number of members per IXP against the fraction of members seen in traceroute. We can see that an increasing number of members usually translates into an increase in the fraction of visible members. In particular, large IXPs with around a thousand members have at least 68% of members visible in traceroute.

Next, to answer if all visible IXPs have dependents, we visualize IXPs with different symbols, based on their dependency category (Table 4). There are 213 IXPs with dependents in our dataset, however an even larger number of 259 IXPs are visible, but have no dependents. These are mostly smaller IXPs with a median number of 33 members of which a median fraction of 0.22 are visible in traceroute. From this figure it is apparent that members at large IXPs have more paths going through the IXP peering LAN than members at smaller IXPs.

In summary, for large IXPs we usually observe numerous dependent ASes, but for the majority of IXPs a more expected pattern is observed: the members are visible in traceroute, however only in a limited number of paths which result in a marginal dependency.

7.2   Topology: Member and Dependent Relationship

To understand the relationship between the number of members and dependents better, we rearrange the points of Fig. 8a to show the absolute number of dependents in Fig. 8b. There is a general trend that seems to link the number of members to the number of dependents: The median number of members for *Low* IXPs is 40, followed by 146 for *Medium*, and 814 for *High* IXPs. This is intuitive: Each member of an IXP possibly connects to several more ASes and therefore increases the chance of incurring a dependency.

However, even though there is a trend, for almost all IXP sizes there are also examples of IXPs with low and medium number of dependents. In an extreme case, the largest IXP in terms of members is IX.br São Paulo with 2246 members, but only 215 dependents. This is a clear difference to the likes of DE-CIX Frankfurt (1050 members; 2055 dependents) or AMS-IX (800 members; 1187 dependents). This reveals that the size of the IXP is not the only factor that drives the number of dependents and it also suggests that IXP may be used differently by their members, which is something we investigate more in Sect. 7.4.

7.3   Geography: Geographic Footprint of IXPs

Dependencies give us a better view of the topological footprint of an IXP in the Internet. We can also leverage these results to investigate the geographical footprint of IXPs and enhance information from PeeringDB by mapping the dependents of an IXP to countries. Precise geolocation is not trivial [56], which is why we employ a conservative approach to locate ASes. We take all announced prefixes of an AS and lookup their assigned country based on NRO stats files [48]. An AS is mapped to a country only if all its originated prefixes geolocate to the same country. If an AS announces prefixes that map to different countries, we do not geolocate it to a particular country. Instead, we treat this AS as an *international* network.

We find new countries for 48 IXPs, i.e., IXPs that have dependents in countries that are not already covered by their listed members. The most extreme case is AMS-IX, which already connects members from 63 different countries, but we see dependencies in 43 additional countries, increasing the geographical footprint by 68%. The median increase for all 48 IXPs with additional countries is 35%, revealing the hidden reach that is not obvious from simple membership data.

7.4 Geography: IXP Regionality

Based on the countries of members and dependents, we can also formulate a metric we call *Regionality*. It simply represents the fraction of members (or dependents) that are in the same country as the IXP. Regionality allows us to quickly asses, in a coarse manner, if an IXP is used to reach ASes from the local region, or if it is operating on an international scale.

First, we take a look at all IXPs and plot the regionality based on their members in Fig. 9a. Since there is a large overlap of points, we show the distribution of IXPs with green bars, labeled with a secondary y-axis on the right side. In general, regionality based on members is balanced, with a median value of 0.5. The distribution reveals that 50 IXPs (6% of 803 IXPs with members) have a regionality of 1, i.e., all members are in the same country as the IXP. These IXPs are mostly small, with a median of four members. The largest IXP with a regionality of 1 is UNY-IX, which connects 20 members (mostly universities), all from Indonesia.

The regionality based on dependents, shown in Fig. 9b, is usually higher than the one based on members: 121 IXPs (57% of 213 IXPs with dependents) have a regionality of 1. If we consider both IXPs members *and* dependents, still 6 IXPs (3%) are entirely local, and 111 IXPs (52%) have international members, but only national dependents. Overall, there is a surprising balance of national and international members, but usually ASes that depend on an IXP are solely operating in the same region as the IXP.

However, we observe interesting differences when comparing the regionality of IXPs with a high number of dependents. For four *High* IXPs there is a clear shift towards international dependents. DE-CIX Frankfurt with 1050 members and a regionality of 0.24 moves to 2055 dependents with a regionality of 0.07. A similar trend is visible for LINX LON1 (878 members, 0.31 regionality → 857 dependencies, 0.15 regionality), AMS-IX (800, 0.13 → 1185, 0.07), and Equinix Ashburn (339, 0.44 → 749, 0.09). One exception is IX.br São Paulo, which has the same regionality of 0.89 for both its 2246 members and 215 dependents.

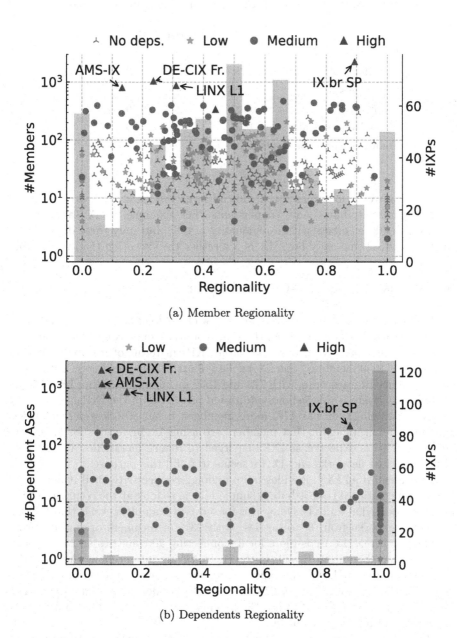

(a) Member Regionality

(b) Dependents Regionality

Fig. 9. Regionality distribution of IXPs based on the location of (a) their members, and (b) their dependents. Green bars show the distribution of points, labeled with the right y-axis. Contains data for (a) 803 IXPs with at least two members and (b) 213 IXPs with dependents. (Color figure online)

Table 5. Properties of DE-CIX Frankfurt and IX.br São Paulo.

IXP	DE-CIX Frankfurt	IX.br São Paulo
Members	1050	2246
... visible in traceroute	778	1532
Dependents	2055	215
Member regionality	0.24	0.89
Dependent regionality	0.07	0.89
Countries with dependents	94	16

It is also worth mentioning that not all large European IXPs are extremely international and have many dependents. For example, EPIX.Katowice in Poland has 406 members with a regionality of 0.83, but only three dependents. In the grand scheme, very large IXPs are rather the exception than the norm.

8   A Case Study: DE-CIX and IX.br

In this final section of the analysis we take a closer look at two IXPs and show that numerous dependencies from the same country can be connected to an IXP by a single member. We choose two large IXPs in terms of members: DE-CIX Frankfurt (1050 members) and IX.br São Paulo (2246 members). Both enjoy good visibility in traceroute, with 778 and 1532 members present for DE-CIX and IX.br respectively. Table 5 shows additional properties of the IXPs.

Even though IX.br has 47% more members, it has 89% less dependencies. This may be an indicator that members are using IX.br mostly for local connectivity. This is expected as IXPs emerged to reduce hierarchies and connect physically close networks and IX.br seems to fulfill this purpose.

To confirm if an IXP provides more regional connectivity, or if it developed into an international transit hub, a simple idea is to look at the countries of the members located at an IXP. Doing this for our two examples reveals that DE-CIX connects networks from 68 countries, with 23% of members originating from Germany, whereas IX.br is more local, connecting 20 countries and a majority of 89% of members from Brazil. However, by taking into account the countries of dependents as well, we can expand our view to reveal connections that are deeper in the topology. For DE-CIX this reveals 442 dependents in 34 countries not seen in neither PeeringDB nor the looking glass, whereas IX.br only has 11 dependents in nine new countries.

Dependencies also provide a different view on the countries reached via the IXPs. Figure 10 shows the ten countries with the most dependents for DE-CIX and IX.br. The country code ** is introduced by our conservative geolocation: It represents international ASes that can not be assigned to a single country. For DE-CIX (Fig. 10a) the country with the most dependents is Russia (331 dependents), even though only 36 members are located there. Even more pronounced

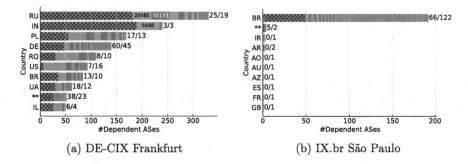

(a) DE-CIX Frankfurt   (b) IX.br São Paulo

Fig. 10. Number of dependent ASes per country for two large IXPs. The green hatched bars show dependents that are shared between members, whereas orange and purple bars represent one member each. The label shows the number of members that share dependents and the number of singular members (i.e., orange and purple bars). The country code ** marks dependents that can not be attributed to a single country. Not shown are 723 dependents from 85 countries for (a) and seven dependents from seven countries for (b). (Color figure online)

is India: There is no member that we can exclusively geolocate to India, but there are 240 dependents. The use of dependencies reveals that even though DE-CIX is located in Germany, it is a common mean to reach many Indian ASes. In contrast, looking at the dependency locations of IX.br (Fig. 10b) only reinforces the impression that it is used for regional connectivity: 89% of dependents are in Brazil, the same country as the IXP.

In the final step, we characterize individual members by analyzing through which members the dependents are reached, hence discovering if there are major networks at IXPs responsible for many dependencies. The orange and purple color bars in Fig. 10 represent one member each. The green hatched bars show dependent ASes that are reached via more than one member. Shared dependencies are caused by traceroutes to different prefixes of an AS that are forwarded over separate members of the IXP. Next to each bar is a label that describes the number of members that share dependents, and the number of members with unique dependencies. For example, for Russian dependents at DE-CIX there are 25 members that share 181 dependents and 19 members with a total of 150 dependents.

Coming back to the Indian dependents of DE-CIX, we can now see that 45 are reached over AS9498/Bharti Airtel, which is the only member registered in India. Another observation is that the majority of dependents is connected by multiple members. However, AS9498 is present for all 189 shared dependents as well. Out of these, 188 are shared with AS6461/Zayo, which does not announce prefixes registered in India, but is a large Tier 1 provider. There is one dependent additionally shared with AS4637/Telstra Global.

For Russia, there are also a number of ASes with presence in Russia (AS20485/TransTeleCom, AS31133/MegaFon) connecting 38 and 34 dependents each. In contrast to the Indian dependents, however, there is no single member

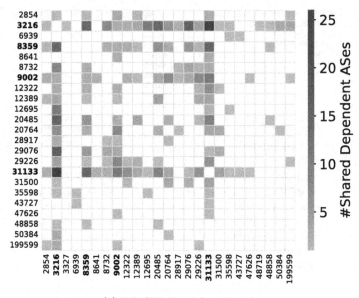

(a) DE-CIX Frankfurt, Russia

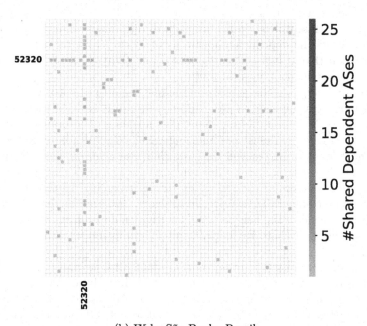

(b) IX.br São Paulo, Brazil

Fig. 11. Detailed view of member ASes with shared dependents located in (a) Russia for DE-CIX Frankfurt and (b) Brazil for IX.br São Paulo. Members that share dependents with at least ten other members are highlighted. To reduce visual noise only highlighted members are shown in (b).

responsible for most dependents, which is also apparent when looking at the shared dependents.

While there are only three members that share 189 dependents in India, the 181 dependents in Russia are shared between 25 members. Figure 11a visualizes the pairings of the individual members. Colored cells indicate shared dependents between a pair of members and the intensity of the color signifies the amount. For example, member AS3216 shares 26 dependents with AS31133. The sparseness of the heatmap shows that there are almost no members contributing to a significant number of dependents. Two exceptions are AS3216/Vimpelcom and AS31133/MegaFon, which are present in 20 and 17 pairs incurring a total of 92 and 66 dependents each. Still, the shared dependents are well distributed when compared to the Indian case.

We see that these "far away" dependencies are reached through a comparatively small number of members, however, the diversity of local members is visible: For Germany (Fig. 10a) we observe less dependents than members, and there are no members with a large number of dependents. Indeed, the median number of dependents for the 45 members with dependents in Germany is 1.

With this in mind, we can dissect the Brazilian dependents of IX.br and see that the number of dependents is a lot smaller than the number of members and over 87% of the 122 members with dependents only lead to a single dependent. This observation also holds for shared dependencies as shown in Fig. 11b. 50 dependents are shared between 66 members and 64% of members only have a single shared dependent. The absence of any major member is also apparent, as 88% share dependents with only one or two other members. The only exception is AS52320/GlobeNet, which shares 24 dependents with 20 other members and thus incurs the most dependencies out of all members. Compared to DE-CIX, however, dependents are still distributed rather well.

The comparison of two large IXPs gave us several insights: First, regional connectivity is distributed well, with less dependencies than members, and no single member incurring a large number of dependencies. Second, even large IXPs are nowadays still used to "keep local traffic local", as seen at the example of IX.br. Third, by looking at the number and locations of dependents we get a better understanding of how IXPs are used for connectivity in today's Internet and found that some large IXPs may be used as international hubs.

9   Limitations

In this section we summarize the general limitations of this study, as well as specific limitations bound to our design choices and their impact on the results.

First, we do not have a perfect view of the Internet topology. As discussed in Sect. 3, inferring the Internet topology from BGP or traceroute data is always deemed to provide a partial view of the Internet. Reasons for this include the diverse routing policies employed on the Internet and placement of vantage points [40]. Increasing the reach of measurement platforms and improving the distribution of vantage points is an ongoing research topic [17,18,51], any advances in that topic would improve this work as well. Hence, the reported dependencies should be interpreted as an *approximation* of the real world. Furthermore, by definition dependencies are derived from the most frequent routes so we expect strong dependencies to be observed even in a partial view of the Internet. Our approach can miss dependencies due to lack of visibility, nevertheless dependencies reported in this study are based on actual observations and should therefore represent a sample of the real world.

Using traceroute data to infer n-paths has some common pitfalls [42,45,57] including some related to the identification of IXPs. Some routers might be configured to not respond to traceroute probes, others might not respond from the address of the interface on which the probe was received. Both cases are particularly relevant if the affected router connects to the peering LAN of an IXP. As mentioned above, these are factors that can lead to missed dependencies. However, as discussed in Sect. 5 we expect the results to be reasonable, based on the comparison with existing approaches.

Finally, we obtain peering LAN and member information from PeeringDB. Although we do not expect every IXP to be listed in PeeringDB, we believe this is the most complete data source currently available. In addition, the peering policies of popular content providers require ISPs to maintain up-to-date PeeringDB entries [2,5,8,10], indicating that it is currently the preferred source of information by the industry. We manually confirmed that the peering LAN information for the largest IXPs is accurate and improved the member listing via the route server looking glasses where feasible. It is still possible that we miss an IXP member if they are not listed in PeeringDB and do not peer with the route server. However, this data only affects the detailed analysis in Sect. 8 for which we have route server information available thus we expect a minimal impact.

In summary, the limitations of our approach generally lead to a reduced number of dependencies. The reported dependencies are an estimate based on available data but should not be interpreted as a ground-truth view of the topology. With these limitations in mind, we demonstrated in this paper that estimated dependencies are a useful tool to study the general importance of IXPs and ASes in the structure of the Internet.

10   Related Work

There are several other works that characterize or analyze IXPs from different points of view. Prehn et al. [49] perform an analysis of the reachability benefit gained by peering at large IXPs, based on route server snapshots as well as inferred routes for bi-lateral and private peering. Giotsas et al. [39] propose a system that detects outages at IXP facilities, relying on the observation of BGP communities, and as part of their evaluation they study the impact of an outage at AMS-IX in detail. Brito et al. [23] provide an in-depth study of the IX.br peering ecosystem in Brazil based on data obtained from looking glasses at all IX.br IXPs.

Most closely related to this work, Bertholdo et al. [22] measure the coverage and representativeness of IXPs as part of their effort to forecast the impact of IXP outages. The focus of our work is not to detect outages, but more generally to provide insights about IXP usage and a long-term dataset of IXP dependency. Bertholdo et al. rely on active measurements and anycast sites deployed at large IXPs for the time of their study, whereas our results are continuously updated, as long as the measurement platforms stay active. Furthermore, they map out IXP reachability using ICMP ping replies, which enables the answer of a yes/no query, but loses path information that the traceroute data in our study retains.

11   Conclusion and Future Work

In this paper, we presented a study on IXP dependency. We gained further insights into the topological footprint of IXPs, showing that some IXPs have a number of additional dependents that are not direct members. We also investigated the geographical footprint of IXPs and found that some of them are indirectly used by ASes in many more countries than what can be inferred from PeeringDB or looking glasses. In addition, we observed that many IXPs are local, connecting to a large degree, or even exclusively, networks from the same country. Finally, for large IXPs we identified specific members that incur a large number of international dependents.

The investigation of IXP dependency opens a new avenue of research that we aim to explore in future work. An additional degree of detail can be achieved by computing per-interface dependency, that may yield further insights into how large members with multiple interfaces operate at IXPs. A different direction is the investigation of country dependencies, i.e., the role of IXPs from the viewpoint of a country. In today's geopolitical climate even internet infrastructure might become a target, making the knowledge of dependency especially valuable.

Public Dataset and Reproducibility. To empower network administrators and facilitate future research, we periodically update our results and make them publicly available at https://internethealthreport.github.io/ixp-dependency. On this website, we also publish the analysis code and data to aid in reproducibility of our work. Since all our results are based on open data, users can also run their own analysis on different time windows if they desire.

Finally, we expanded the data pipeline used to analyze the IXP outages in Sect. 2 to allow a general analysis of any AS or IP prefix and publish the code in a separate repository [52].

Acknowledgments. We thank the reviewers for their feedback. We would also like to thank Emile Aben from the RIPE NCC for fruitful discussions and CAIDA for giving us access to their dataset.

References

1. Alice-LG - Your friendly looking glass. https://github.com/alice-lg/alice-lg
2. AWS: Settlement Free Peering Policy. https://aws.amazon.com/peering/policy/
3. CAIDA AS Rank. http://as-rank.caida.org/
4. The CAIDA UCSD IPv4 Routed /24 Topology Dataset - 2022–09–01 - 2022–09–30. https://www.caida.org/catalog/datasets/ipv4_routed_24_topology_dataset/
5. Cloudflare Peering Policy. https://www.cloudflare.com/peering-policy/
6. IHR Archive. https://ihr-archive.iijlab.net/
7. LINX LON1 Outage - March 2021. https://web.archive.org/web/20221206083420/https://www.linx.net/incidents-log/
8. Peering with Meta. https://www.facebook.com/peering/
9. PeeringDB. https://www.peeringdb.com/
10. Prerequisites to Peer with Google. https://peering.google.com/#/options/peering
11. University of Oregon Route Views Project. http://www.routeviews.org/
12. Follow-up on previous incident at AMS-IX platform, May 2015. https://web.archive.org/web/20160327075404/https://ams-ix.net/newsitems/195
13. Outage on Amsterdam peering platform, November 2023. https://www.ams-ix.net/ams/outage-on-amsterdam-peering-platform
14. Aben, E.: Measuring More Internet with RIPE Atlas, January 2016. https://labs.ripe.net/author/emileaben/measuring-more-internet-with-ripe-atlas/
15. Aben, E.: Does The Internet Route Around Damage? - Edition 2021, April 2021. https://labs.ripe.net/author/emileaben/does-the-internet-route-around-damage-edition-2021/
16. Ahmed, A., Shafiq, Z., Bedi, H., Khakpour, A.: Peering vs. transit: performance comparison of peering and transit interconnections. In: International Conference on Network Protocols (ICNP), pp. 1–10. IEEE (2017). https://doi.org/10.1109/ICNP.2017.8117549
17. Alfroy, T., Holterbach, T., Pelsser, C.: MVP: Measuring Internet Routing from the Most Valuable Points. In: Internet Measurement Conference (IMC), pp. 770–771. ACM (2022). https://doi.org/10.1145/3517745.3563031
18. Appel, M., Aben, E., Fontugne, R.: Metis: better atlas vantage point selection for everyone. In: Network Traffic Measurement and Analysis Conference (TMA). IFIP (2022)
19. Arnold, T., et al.: Cloud provider connectivity in the flat internet. In: Internet Measurement Conference (IMC), pp. 230–246. ACM (2020). https://doi.org/10.1145/3419394.3423613
20. Bajpai, V., Eravuchira, S.J., Schönwälder, J.: Lessons learned from using the RIPE atlas platform for measurement research. ACM SIGCOMM Comput. Commun. Rev. 45(3), 35–42 (2015). https://doi.org/10.1145/2805789.2805796
21. Bajpai, V., Eravuchira, S.J., Schönwälder, J., Kisteleki, R., Aben, E.: Vantage point selection for IPv6 measurements: benefits and limitations of RIPE atlas tags. In: IFIP/IEEE Symposium on Integrated Network and Service Management (IM), pp. 37–44. IEEE (2017). https://doi.org/10.23919/INM.2017.7987262
22. Bertholdo, L.M., Ceron, J.M., Granville, L.Z., van Rijswijk-Deij, R.M.: Forecasting the impact of IXP outages using Anycast. In: Network Traffic Measurement and Analysis Conference (TMA). IFIP (2021)
23. Brito, S.H.B., Santos, M.A.S., Fontes, R.R., Perez, D.A.L., Rothenberg, C.E.: Dissecting the largest national ecosystem of public Internet eXchange Points in Brazil. In: Karagiannis, T., Dimitropoulos, X. (eds.) PAM 2016. LNCS, vol. 9631, pp. 333–345. Springer, Cham (2016). https://doi.org/10.1007/978-3-319-30505-9_25

24. Böttger, T., et al.: Shaping the Internet: 10 Years of IXP Growth (2018). https://doi.org/10.48550/ARXIV.1810.10963
25. Böttger, T., Cuadrado, F., Tyson, G., Castro, I., Uhlig, S.: Open connect everywhere: a glimpse at the internet ecosystem through the lens of the Netflix CDN. ACM SIGCOMM Comput. Commun. Rev. **48**(1), 28–34 (2018). https://doi.org/10.1145/3211852.3211857
26. Chang, H., Jamin, S., Willinger, W.: Inferring AS-level internet topology from router-level path traces. In: Scalability and Traffic Control in IP Networks, vol. 4526, pp. 196–207. SPIE (2001). https://doi.org/10.1117/12.434395
27. Chatzis, N., Smaragdakis, G., Feldmann, A., Willinger, W.: There is more to IXPs than meets the eye. ACM SIGCOMM Comput. Commun. Rev. **43**(5), 19–28 (2013). https://doi.org/10.1145/2541468.2541473
28. Cho, S., Fontugne, R., Cho, K., Dainotti, A., Gill, P.: BGP hijacking classification. In: Network Traffic Measurement and Analysis Conference (TMA), pp. 25–32. IEEE (2019). https://doi.org/10.23919/TMA.2019.8784511
29. Dang, T.K., Mohan, N., Corneo, L., Zavodovski, A., Ott, J., Kangasharju, J.: Cloudy with a chance of short RTTs: analyzing cloud connectivity in the internet. In: Internet Measurement Conference (IMC), pp. 62–79. ACM (2021). https://doi.org/10.1145/3487552.3487854
30. Del Fiore, J.M., Merindol, P., Persico, V., Pelsser, C., Pescapé, A.: Filtering the noise to reveal inter-domain lies. In: Network Traffic Measurement and Analysis Conference (TMA), pp. 17–24. IEEE (2019). https://doi.org/10.23919/TMA.2019.8784618
31. Dhamdhere, A., Dovrolis, C.: The internet is flat: modeling the transition from a transit hierarchy to a peering mesh. In: International Conference on emerging Networking EXperiments and Technologies (CoNEXT), pp. 185–198. ACM (2010). https://doi.org/10.1145/1921168.1921196
32. Dhamdhere, A., Dovrolis, C.: Twelve years in the evolution of the internet ecosystem. IEEE/ACM Trans. Networking **19**(5), 1420–1433 (2011). https://doi.org/10.1109/TNET.2011.2119327
33. Du, B., Testart, C., Fontugne, R., Akiwate, G., Snoeren, A.C., kc claffy: Mind your MANRS: measuring the MANRS ecosystem. In: Internet Measurement Conference (IMC), pp. 716–729. ACM (2022). https://doi.org/10.1145/3517745.3561419
34. Fontugne, R., Ermoshina, K., Aben, E.: The internet in crimea: a case study on routing interregnum. In: IFIP Networking Conference (Networking), pp. 809–814. IEEE (2020)
35. Fontugne, R., Pelsser, C., Aben, E., Bush, R.: Pinpointing delay and forwarding anomalies using large-scale traceroute measurements. In: Internet Measurement Conference (IMC), pp. 15–28. ACM (2017). https://doi.org/10.1145/3131365.3131384
36. Fontugne, R., Shah, A., Aben, E.: The (thin) bridges of AS connectivity: measuring dependency using AS hegemony. In: Beverly, R., Smaragdakis, G., Feldmann, A. (eds.) PAM 2018. LNCS, vol. 10771, pp. 216–227. Springer, Cham (2018). https://doi.org/10.1007/978-3-319-76481-8_16
37. Gamero-Garrido, A.: Transit influence of autonomous systems: country-specific exposure of internet traffic. Ph.D. thesis, University of California, San Diego, USA (2021). https://www.escholarship.org/uc/item/0hg720zn
38. Gamero-Garrido, A., Carisimo, E., Hao, S., Huffaker, B., Snoeren, A.C., Dainotti, A.: Quantifying nations' exposure to traffic observation and selective tampering. In: Hohlfeld, O., Moura, G., Pelsser, C. (eds.) PAM 2022. LNCS, vol. 13210, pp. 645–674. Springer, Cham (2022). https://doi.org/10.1007/978-3-030-98785-5_29

39. Giotsas, V., Dietzel, C., Smaragdakis, G., Feldmann, A., Berger, A., Aben, E.: Detecting peering infrastructure outages in the wild. In: Conference on Applications, Technologies, Architectures, and Protocols for Computer Communications (SIGCOMM), pp. 446–459. ACM (2017). https://doi.org/10.1145/3098822. 3098855

40. Gregori, E., Improta, A., Lenzini, L., Rossi, L., Sani, L.: On the incompleteness of the as-level graph: a novel methodology for BGP route collector placement. In: Internet Measurement Conference (IMC), pp. 253–264. ACM (2012). https://doi. org/10.1145/2398776.2398803

41. Henthorn-Iwane, A.: Understanding Internet Exchanges via the DE-CIX Outage, April 2018. https://www.thousandeyes.com/blog/network-monitoring-de-cix-outage

42. Hyun, Y., Broido, A., kc claffy: On third-party addresses in traceroute paths. In: Passive and Active Network Measurement Workshop (PAM) (2003). https:// catalog.caida.org/paper/2003_3rdparty

43. Hyun, Y., Broido, A., kc claffy: Traceroute and BGP AS Path Incongruities (2003). https://catalog.caida.org/paper/2003_asp

44. Lodhi, A., Larson, N., Dhamdhere, A., Dovrolis, C., kc claffy: Using PeeringDB to understand the peering ecosystem. ACM SIGCOMM Comput. Commun. Rev. **44**(2), 20–27 (2014). https://doi.org/10.1145/2602204.2602208

45. Mao, Z.M., Rexford, J., Wang, J., Katz, R.H.: Towards an accurate AS-level traceroute tool. In: Conference on Applications, Technologies, Architectures, and Protocols for Computer Communications (SIGCOMM), pp. 365–378. ACM (2003). https://doi.org/10.1145/863955.863996

46. McQuistin, S., Uppu, S.P., Flores, M.: Taming anycast in the wild internet. In: Internet Measurement Conference (IMC), pp. 165–178. ACM (2019). https://doi. org/10.1145/3355369.3355573

47. Nomikos, G., Dimitropoulos, X.: traIXroute: detecting IXPs in traceroute paths. In: Karagiannis, T., Dimitropoulos, X. (eds.) PAM 2016. LNCS, vol. 9631, pp. 346–358. Springer, Cham (2016). https://doi.org/10.1007/978-3-319-30505-9_26

48. Number Resource Organisation: NRO Extended Allocation and Assignment Reports. https://www.nro.net/about/rirs/statistics/

49. Prehn, L., Lichtblau, F., Dietzel, C., Feldmann, A.: Peering only? Analyzing the reachability benefits of joining large IXPs today. In: Hohlfeld, O., Moura, G., Pelsser, C. (eds.) PAM 2022. LNCS, vol. 13210, pp. 338–366. Springer, Cham (2022). https://doi.org/10.1007/978-3-030-98785-5_15

50. RIPE Ncc Staff: RIPE atlas: a global internet measurement network. Internet Protocol J. **18**(3), 2–26 (2015)

51. Sermpezis, P., Prehn, L., Kostoglou, S., Flores, M., Vakali, A., Aben, E.: Bias in internet measurement platforms. In: Network Traffic Measurement and Analysis Conference (TMA), pp. 1–10. IEEE (2023). https://doi.org/10.23919/TMA58422. 2023.10198985

52. Tashiro, M.: Atlas traceroute outage inspector. https://github.com/m-appel/atlas-traceroute-outage-inspector

53. Tashiro, M., Fontugne, R., Fukuda, K.: Accompanying website and data. https:// internethealthreport.github.io/ixp-dependency/

54. Wagner, D., et al.: United we stand: collaborative detection and mitigation of amplification DDoS attacks at scale. In: Proceedings of the 2021 ACM SIGSAC Conference on Computer and Communications Security (CCS), pp. 970–987. ACM (2021). https://doi.org/10.1145/3460120.3485385

55. Wichtlhuber, M., et al.: IXP Scrubber: learning from blackholing traffic for ml-driven DDoS detection at scale. In: Conference on Applications, Technologies, Architectures, and Protocols for Computer Communications (SIGCOMM), pp. 707–722. ACM (2022). https://doi.org/10.1145/3544216.3544268

56. Winter, P., Padmanabhan, R., King, A., Dainotti, A.: Geo-locating BGP prefixes. In: Network Traffic Measurement and Analysis Conference (TMA), pp. 9–16. IEEE (2019). https://doi.org/10.23919/TMA.2019.8784509

57. Zhang, Y., et al.: A framework to quantify the pitfalls of using traceroute in AS-level topology measurement. IEEE J. Sel. Areas Commun. **29**(9), 1822–1836 (2011). https://doi.org/10.1109/JSAC.2011.111007

You Can Find Me Here: A Study of the Early Adoption of Geofeeds

Rahel A. Fainchtein[1,2(✉)] and Micah Sherr[1]

[1] Georgetown University, Washington, DC, USA
raf3272@georgetown.edu
[2] The Johns Hopkins University Applied Physics Laboratory, Laurel, MD, USA

Abstract. IP geolocation is a popular mechanism for determining the physical locations of Internet-connected devices. However, despite its widespread use, IP geolocation is known to be inaccurate, especially for devices in less industrialized nations. In 2020, *geofeeds* were standardized by the IETF, providing a mechanism for owners of IP addresses (i.e., autonomous systems) to self-report the physical locations of IP blocks under their control. Assuming IP address owners accurately report these locations, geofeeds conceptually have the potential to enable "groundtruth" location data. This short paper takes a first look at the roll-out of geofeeds. We examine the opt-in rates of geofeeds by autonomous systems, and surmise the use of geofeed data by two major IP geolocation providers. Over the course of our 14-month data collection efforts (August 2022–October 2023), the number of IP addresses covered by geofeeds has increased tenfold; however, the adoption rate is still low—less than 1% of the IPv4 address space is covered by geofeeds. We find that the rollout is also uneven, with more industrialized nations opting into geofeeds at rates higher than those of less industrialized ones. Moreover, our comparison of geofeed data to locations reported by commercial IP geolocation services suggests that these commercial services may be beginning to incorporate geofeed data into their resolutions. We discuss the implications of our findings, including the potential that uneven adoption rates may further disenfranchise Internet users in less industrialized nations.

Keywords: IP geolocation · geoblocking · geofeeds

1 Introduction

Determining users' geographic locations has become a source of increased interest to various entities. Inferred location information is regularly used to determine the initial language that should be shown to a user, enable location-based advertising, provide locally relevant news and other geographically-tailored information, enforce usage rights governing copyrighted material, identify potentially fraudulent transactions, restrict access to gambling and other services that have regional restrictions [39] and determine the applicability of laws (e.g., GDPR

P. Richter et al. (Eds.): PAM 2024, LNCS 14538, pp. 228–245, 2024.
https://doi.org/10.1007/978-3-031-56252-5_11

and CCPA), among other uses. Various means of ascertaining or inferring users' locations have become increasingly prevalent across the Internet. In particular, *IP-geolocation*[1], or the estimation of geographic location based on a machine's IP address, has become one of the most common approaches.

Despite the lack of an inherent mapping between an IP address and a geographic location, using IP-geolocation has the distinct advantage of being a technique from which an online user cannot easily opt out. Unlike other sources of users' location information such as HTML headers or mobile phones' GPS coordinates, the IP protocol does not allow a user to make a request without sharing their source address.[2]

In practice, IP-geolocation that supports *geoblocking*, or blocking access to content based on a user's inferred location, and other forms of location-based website customization is generally performed by commercial IP-geolocation services. Though not the only reason, this is due in part to popular websites' and web services' widespread reliance on content distribution networks (CDNs) [9], and CDNs' pervasive use of commercial IP-geolocation services to support ready-made IP-geolocation based offerings, such as CDN-based geofiltering, to their customers [3,6,7,12,21].

Despite the ubiquity of geolocation and geoblocking, commercial geolocation services have been found (1) to be largely unreliable when it comes to geolocating Internet infrastructure (e.g., servers and/or routers) [13,41] and (2) to underrepresent, and more frequently, to mis-locate Internet vantage points in less industrialized nations [37]. Moreover, significant anecdotal evidence suggests that the mis-location or incorrect flagging of IP addresses as VPNs or other geoblock evasion tools is not limited to these applications or vantage points, and that it happens frequently across the Internet (cf., regular and extensive postings in the NANOG listserv complaining about erroneous geolocation of service providers' IP addresses [5]).

Introduced as a means of correcting the issue of mis-location, self-published geolocation feeds or *geofeeds*, were designed to allow network operators such as autonomous systems (ASes) to specify the geographic locations of their IP addresses. The syntax and semantics of geofeeds are codified in an Internet standard [25], which we summarize in the following section. Conceptually, the idea of geofeeds is simple: rather than infer IP geolocation based on heuristics or error-prone triangulation methods, owners of IP addresses announce the geographic locations of their IPs. Further Internet standards govern how these geofeeds can be found and how ASes can update their geofeed records to prevent them from becoming stale [38]. Ideally, geofeeds could serve as "groundtruth" location information, with the important caveat that some IP address owners may have incentives to purposefully report incorrect locations—for example, to support services that attempt to bypass geoblocking [41].

---

[1] For ease of exposition, we will often use the shorthand *geolocation* to refer to IP-based geolocation.

[2] A user could always use a means of obscuring their IP address such as Tor [16], a VPN, SmartDNS services [18], or a proxy. However, using these technologies requires technical sophistication and imposes performance and usability bottlenecks [17,34].

Geofeeds were standardized in 2020 and began seeing some adoption shortly thereafter. However, to our knowledge, geofeeds have not been studied in the literature. This paper presents the first work towards advancing our understanding of how geofeeds have been adopted. More concretely, this paper attempts to answer the following two research questions:

- **RQ1:** To what extent have geofeeds been adopted by "IP owners"?
- **RQ2:** Is there evidence that suggests that commercial IP-geolocation providers use geofeeds?

Towards answering the above research questions, we performed a measurement study over a 14 month period (August 2022 through October 2023) in which we collected geofeed records and measured their coverage of the IPv4 address space. During this period, we compared geofeed information to two popular IP geolocation services to gauge their level of agreement with geofeed data. We posit that our collection of historical geofeed information may be of independent interest to network researchers, and thus we make our data available at https://github.com/GUSecLab/geofeed-measurement.

Our results show that while geofeed adoption is limited to date (comprising roughly 0.8% of the IPv4 address space), its adoption rate is rapidly increasing—the number of covered IP addresses increased tenfold during our 14-month study. We find that adoption rates are not universal, and that less industrialized countries often (but not always) have smaller adoption rates; this is especially concerning given that countries with less Internet infrastructure experience higher rates of geoblocking by websites based in regions where Internet infrastructure is more readily available [40]. Finally, our results suggest that commercial IP geolocation services may be incorporating geofeed information into their offerings; at the very least, commercial geolocation results tend not to contradict information from geofeeds. Overall, the commercial providers' country-level agreement with geofeeds steadily improved over the course of our measurement period.

2 Background and Related Work

The mechanisms for IP-geolocation can generally be separated into passive and active approaches. Passive IP geolocation techniques rely on querying and parsing data from WHOIS [20] and/or other publicly accessible sources to learn location information. Active approaches, on the other hand, use empirical measurement methods such as multilateration from different Internet vantage points to determine the bounded geographical region in which an IP address must reside [11,19,27,41].

In general, active probing approaches tend to more accurately reflect the state of IP addresses' allocations at time of measurement than passive ones. However, they still pose significant drawbacks including the potential for interference due to high levels of cross traffic and/or network congestion, and regional variation in rates of targets' responsiveness to ICMP and traceroute messages, which are most commonly used for probing [10,36].

In light of these drawbacks, both researchers and industry have turned to more passive geolocation approaches. In particular, for use-cases in which web servers must ascertain incoming connection requests' geographic locations in real time, many rely on commercial IP-geolocation services. Although the exact geolocation methodologies used by commercial IP-geolocation services are often proprietary, previous work has shown that their level of accuracy is inconsistent across different geographic regions and is prone to errors [28,33,37]. Muir et al. and Poesse et al. independently infer that these services, which assemble a database of IP address to geographic location mappings, are likely based off of publicly available resources such as WHOIS, which have been found to have high rates of errors [33,37]. Errors in these databases are often caused by the staleness of source records, sources' lack of data granularity, and their lack of data authentication [33]. In more detail, Dainotti et al. and Richter et al., who evaluate system logs as sources of geolocation information, note that datasets originating in system logs, network flow logs, and/or large-scale network traces must be collected from Internet vantage points that can observe high volumes of traffic, and often contain numerous spoofed addresses, which must then be identified and filtered out [14,36].

Despite the potential obstacles to building accurate IP-geolocation databases, Gharaibeh et al. [28], who measure commercial IP-geolocation services' ability to accurately locate Internet routers, find high rates of country-level interservice agreement across six commercial IP-geolocation services. However, they highlight that these high rates of agreement do not translate into similar rates of accuracy. Specifically, the commercial datasets show between 77.5% - 89.4% country-level accuracy over the routers included within their respective databases—a significantly lower country-level accuracy than these services respectively advertise [28]. Gharaibeh et al. further caution that these services' country-level accuracy varies widely across different countries and regions.[3] For these reasons, Gharaibeh et al. recommend against the use of commercial IP-geolocation for the identification of routers or Internet infrastructure [28].

RFC 8805 [25] introduces self published geolocation information feeds, or *geofeeds*, as a means by which network operators such as ASes or Internet Service Providers (ISPs) can share the actual geolocation data of the IP addresses and prefixes they control. RFC 8805 defines a geofeed file to be a comma separated value (CSV) file in which each entry contains either a single IP address or range of addresses and its corresponding city and country-level geographic information.

RFC 9092 [38] expands on this by centralizing the location to which network operators can publish the URLs of their geofeeds. This enables geofeed consumers, such as commercial IP-geolocation providers, to easily find them. In more detail, RFC 9092 defines a mechanism through which network operators can register their geofeed URL with their respective Regional Internet Registries (RIRs), National Internet Registries (NIRs), or Local Internet Reg-

---

[3] For example, while most commercial providers showed over 90% accuracy in identifying routers in the U.S., most providers showed between 20% and 39% accuracy when locating routers in Canada [28].

istries (LIRs) and in so doing, add them to their WHOIS database entries. As part of this update, RFC 9092 proposes the expansion of the Routing Policy Specification Language (RPSL) used by Internet Registries to specify registrant information, to include a new geofeed field which holds the URL of the registrant's geofeed [38].

3   Data Collection and Methodology

To answer the research questions from Sect. 1 ("to what extent have geofeeds been adopted by IP owners" and "is there evidence that suggests they are used by commercial IP-location providers?"), we performed a 14-month data collection effort during which we collected all published geofeeds. In what follows, we detail our methodology and data and the limitations of our approach.

3.1   Geofeed Measurement Methodology

To collect geofeed information, we used the open-source geofeed finder [29] tool. The geofeed finder queries current WHOIS records to locate geofeed URLs, pulls the geofeeds' contents, and verifies their integrity in accordance with the requirements set by RFC 8805 [25] and RFC 9092 [38].

Using the tool, we initially queried the geofeed records in April 2022, and, starting in August of that year, pulled updated geofeed records every 13–16 days[4] over the course of a 14 month period (August 2022 - October 2023). We chose to pull (approximately) biweekly to incur only negligible load on WHOIS services.

As of the time of writing, our collection of geofeed data is still ongoing. Our database is effectively a collection of temporal snapshots, each of which reflects the Internet-wide deployment of geofeeds at a moment in time. We anticipate this may be of use to other network and security researchers (e.g., to assess the trustworthiness of geofeeds or to detect equivocation in geofeed records), and make our analysis tools and data available at https://github.com/GUSecLab/geofeed-measurement.

Ethics. We accessed only publicly available information (geofeeds) that are published (publicly) by ASes. The geofeed finder tool accesses bulk WHOIS records for each major RIR and caches the results to minimize the load incurred by repeated querying. As noted above, we further reduce the load incurred by our study by performing the geofeed queries only once every two weeks.

3.2   Limitations

Geofeed-Finder Version Changes. The software version used between April 2022 through January 2023 was deprecated and became unusable during the measurement period and we therefore had to upgrade on February 1, 2023. In June

---

[4] Measurements were initially pulled manually once every two weeks and were later automated to run on the 13th and 28th of each month.

2023 and September 2023 we once again had to upgrade the geofeed-finder tool since the previous version again became deprecated. While we do not believe that these version changes would significantly affect our results, we were unable to re-pull past geofeeds using the newer software.

Assumption of Geofeed Reliability. In our measurements of geofeeds, we assume the geofeed entries we obtain from the geofeed finder [29] accurately depict the geographic regions to which its publishers (or rather the network operators) allocate the IP addresses under their control.

Additionally, geofeed information is pulled from WHOIS, and is subject to spoofing attacks. As RFC 9092 explains, malicious network operators could exploit the weak or missing authentication of numerous RPSL repositories to spoof `inetnum:` entries and set them to point to geofeed files that contain inaccurate location information [38].

Authenticating geofeeds can be straightforwardly addressed by requiring that all network operators register and publish geofeed files that are digitally signed with their private RPKI keys. Unfortunately, since RPKI is not universally applied, this is unlikely to occur in the near term.

However as a potential stop-gap solution, RFC 8805 and RFC 9092 require geofeed consumers to perform additional checks on geofeed records before consuming them. These checks include verifying that network operators actually control the IP addresses included in their geofeed records, ensuring all consumed geofeeds are transmitted using HTTPS, and that their geofeed parsers process the data in a consistent way [25, 38]. In keeping with the standard, we note that the geeofeed finder performs these checks by default and that we intentionally did not configure it to skip them.

4   RQ1: Geofeed Adoption by Network Operators

The expansion of geofeed coverage requires network operators to actively opt-into using geofeeds, and to accurately update them when they reallocate addresses to new geographic regions. Network operators who want their geofeed URLs to be published within their WHOIS (`inetnum:`) entries can register them with their respective Internet Registries. In this section, we investigate how and where networks operators have opted in and the extent to which different geographic locations are represented within the geofeeds.

In measuring geofeed adoption (**RQ1**), we sought to answer the following more specific research questions:

1. At what rate are network operators registering and publishing new geofeeds?
2. What is the coverage of geofeed records across the Internet?
3. How has this coverage changed over time? and
4. Where are the IP ranges listed within these geofeeds geographically located? Are they evenly distributed or concentrated within a few geographic regions?

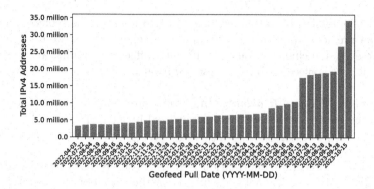

Fig. 1. Number of IPv4 addresses covered by geofeeds.

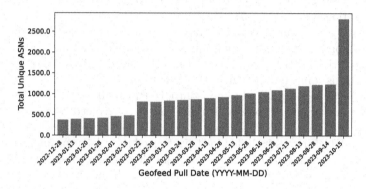

Fig. 2. Unique ASNs that publish geofeeds.

4.1 Geofeed Adoption Has Increased Tenfold in About a Year

Overall, we find network operators' adoption of geofeeds slowly but steadily grew over the course of the observation period. As shown in Fig. 1, geofeeds' IPv4 space coverage grew more than tenfold from 3.22M IPs on April 2, 2022 to 34.3M IPv4 addresses on October 15, 2023. Figure 2 shows similar patterns across the unique ASNs identified in each geofeed pull.

While the number of IPv4 addresses is monotonically increasing (with a few exceptions), there are discernible "bursts" in which large numbers of IPs become covered (see, for example, July 2023 in Fig. 1). This unevenness is largely due to a relatively small number of ASes with large IP blocks opting into publishing geofeeds. Until October 2023, the number of participating ASes has grown more linearly, as can be seen from Fig. 2.

While there has been significant growth in geofeed opt-in, geofeeds' coverage over the Internet address space remains minimal. In particular, as of October 15, 2023, the 34.3M IPv4 addresses announced within the geofeeds only account for roughly 0.80% of the IPv4 address space, or roughly 0.93% of all allocated IPv4 addresses [35]. Similarly, the number of unique ASNs identified increased

Table 1. Geofeed representation by continent.

Continent	Number of IPs	Percent of Gfeed
Europe	13,872,160	40.5%
North America	11,668,093	34.1%
Oceania	7,072,881	20.7%
Asia	725,212	2.61%
South America	214,273	1.91%
Africa	42,664	0.18%
Antarctica	26	0.000076%

Fig. 3. Percentage of in-country IPv4 addresses covered by geofeeds.

sevenfold from 375 ASNs in December 2022 to 2,805 ASNs in October 2023, but this only equates to 2.4% of the ASNs allocated [35].

4.2 Adoption Rates Vary Significantly by Geographic Region

Despite geofeeds' overall limited opt-in to date, we observe that network operator opt-in for geofeeds varies widely by geographic region. Figure 3, which provides a heatmap of the total IPv4 addresses associated with each country within the geofeeds, shows a strong concentration of the geofeed IPv4 addresses geolocated to wealthier and more industrialized countries that have more Internet infrastructure available.

This is particularly well exemplified by the breakdown of geofeed IPs by location in April 2022 - where IPv4 addresses geolocated to the United States account for about 73.7% of all geofeed IPv4 addresses. While by October 2023 numerous additional countries held more substantial proportions of the total geofeed IPv4 addresses, the vast majority (about 32.6M, or 95.3%) of geofeed IPv4 addresses were located in Europe, Oceania and North America combined. In stark contrast, only 62k IPv4 addresses, or 0.18% of those published in the October 2023, geofeeds were geolocated to Africa. Moreover, among the 20 least represented countries, twelve are located in Africa, and that no countries see an increase in the total geofeed IPv4 addresses geolocated to them.

Assessing the regional breakdown of representation by continent, as given in Table 1, further highlights this trend. Here we find that continents with lower

Fig. 4. Total ASNs included in the November 10, 2023 Geofeed Results by country. Note that the coloring is uses a logarithmic scale.

proportions of industrialized countries, or of countries with strong Internet hosting infrastructure, are less represented within the geofeed results.

To account for additional factors we also assess the breakdown of country-level representation in geofeeds normalized by IPv4 address allocation as reported by the NRO [35] and each country's total Internet users as estimated by the CIA World Factbook [8]. Heatmaps of these normalized breakdowns can be found in Fig. 9 and Fig. 10 of Appendix B. Overall we observe a similar correlation between a country's representation within the geofeed results in the normalized results, but note a few key outliers. In particular, we highlight that despite its immense Internet presence, China is the third least represented country in the geofeeds after normalizing by IPv4 address allocation and the twelfth least represented after normalizing by total Internet users. However, while China do not appear to follow the same trend, we suspect additional factors may be contributing to the limited rates at which Chinese IP owners have opted into publishing geofeeds.

AS Opt-in Rates. In addition to looking into the rate of growth over the IPv4 address space, we also sought to gain more insights into the organizations that publish them. In more detail, we wanted to ascertain where the ASes that opted into publishing geofeeds were geographically located and the types of organizations to which they pertained. Here, we consider a snapshot of geofeeds from November 2023, and use Stanford ASdb [32] from May 2023 to classify ASes.

Figure 4 shows a global heatmap of the geographic distribution of ASes that opted into publishing geofeeds. Similar to Fig. 10, we see that most of the ASes are concentrated in the "Global North" and that countries located in Central and South America, Africa and much of the Middle East are not represented. Additionally, we note that the United States' total opt-in of 1, 763 ASes vastly exceeds that of any other country.

When it came to the types of organizations opting into publishing geofeeds, the majority of ASes that opt in appear to be Internet Service Providers (ISPs). Table 2a shows the breakdown of the top ten most represented categories of ASes that participate in geofeeds as determed by ASdb [32]; we further detail the subcategories for "Computer and Information Technology" in Table 2b. As shown in Table 2a, roughly 1, 927 ASes, or 72.7% of the 2, 652 covered by the ASdb,

Table 2. Categorical Breakdowns of ASes

Category	N.ASNs	%ASNs
Computer & Info. Tech.	1927	72.7%
Other	451	17.0%
Service	446	16.8%
Retail,Wholesale & E-comm.	251	9.5%
Finance & Insurance	237	8.9%
Media,Publishing & Broadcast	226	8.5%
Construction & Real Estate	170	6.4%
Education & Research	101	3.8%
Manufacturing	91	3.4%
Government & Public Admin.	80	3.0%

(a) Categories of ASes that publish geofeeds.

Subcategory	No. ASNs
Internet Service Provider (ISP)	1634
Hosting and Cloud Provider	389
Software Development	380
Computer and Network Security	68
Technology Consulting Services	64
Phone Provider	56
Other	20
Search	15
Satellite Communication	2

(b) Breakdown of ASes in *Computer and Information Technology* category.

are identified as Computer and Information Technology organizations. Moreover, $1,634$ or 84.3% of these ASes are denoted as ISPs—accounting for 61.6% of the ASdb covered ASes overall. Given the motivation for introducing/standardizing geofeeds noted in RFC 8805 [25], this is not entirely surprising.

In an effort to gain additional insight into ASes' motivations for opting-into publishing geofeeds, we also examine the geographic distribution of ISPs across the ASNs that publish geofeeds. Figure 11 of Appendix B shows a heat-map of the geographic distribution of ISPs. Note that coloring here is in logarithmic scale to show the full variance. Here once again we see an absence of most countries in South America, Africa and the Middle East and the largest concentration of ISPs in the United States. Figure 12 of Appendix B shows a heat-map of the proportion of each countries' ASes that are ISPs. Among the countries from which ASes opted to publish geofeeds, a larger proportion of the ASes in countries with fewer geofeed ASes were ISPs.

Given geofeeds' intended role of preempting IP ranges' geographic mislocation by commercial IP-geolocation services, this discrepancy could further contribute to existing regional disparities in users' Internet accessibility and QoS if it continues to perpetuate. We discuss this in more detail in Sect. 6.

5   RQ2: Evidence of Commercial Adoption of Geofeeds

To study geofeeds' impact on the accuracy of commercial IP-geolocation services (**RQ2**), we compare geolocation estimates from two of the most popular commercial IP geolocation services [4], Maxmind-GeoIP2 and IPgeolocation.io, to the geolocation information given in the geofeeds. Since it is supplied directly from the owners of its covered IP addresses, we consider the geofeed data as "ground truth" and evaluate the degree to which the commercial IP-geolocation services agree with it. We show the geofeed fetch dates and those of corresponding commercial database (DB) accesses for Maxmind and IPgeolocation.io in Table 3 in Appendix A.

We performed the following steps to assess the agreement between the geofeeds and the commercial IP geolocation datasets:

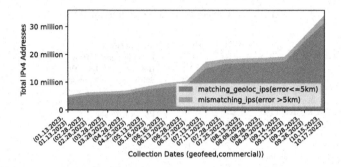

Fig. 5. Maxmind overlap with geofeed and overall accuracy.

1. We identified pairings of geofeed and commercial DB records where the IPv4 addresses referenced in their respective CIDR prefixes overlapped.
2. We compared the location named in each pairing's geofeed record with the one named in the commercial DB's estimate.[5]
3. In cases where the location names did not match, we then performed reverse-geocoding on the geofeed location names to ascertain their approximate geographic coordinates. Since Maxmind and IPgeolocation.io both reported using the Geonames reverse geocoding database [1] for this task [22,30], we decided to use it as well to maintain consistency.[6]
4. Using the geofeed locations' estimated geographic coordinates, we then computed the approximate geodesic distance [2,24] between them and the (corresponding) commercial entries' location estimates.

Upon completing these steps, we then assessed the overall agreement on both the country and city levels across all IPv4 addresses that were included in both the geofeed result and the contemporary commercial DB pull.

Results. The agreement between (1) geofeeds and (2) Maxmind-GeoIP2 and IPgeolocation.io could suggest that these services may consult geofeeds when updating their (respective) IP-geolocation DBs. As shown in Figs. 5 and 7, there are very high rates at which both commercial providers provided geolocation estimates for the corresponding geofeed's IPv4 addresses and their high accuracy rates on the geolocation of these addresses. Both commercial providers covered 99% – 99.9% of their contemporary geofeeds' IPv4 addresses. Moreover, their country and city-level accuracy for geofeed IPs roughly met or significantly surpassed their respective self-reported accuracy rates.

---

[5] To account for locales having numerous names or versions of the same name (e.g., the city name for Đakovo, Croatia could also be spelled Djakovo or Dakovo), we computed the normalized Damerau-Levenshtein distance [15] between the two location names and asserted that to match, the result had to be less than 0.5.

[6] To account for locations having multiple names or spellings, we used fuzzy matching with tokenized Levenshtein distance to find many of the named locations.

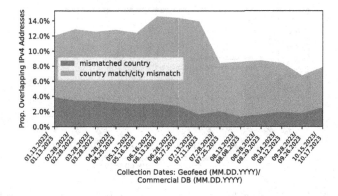

Fig. 6. Maxmind inaccuracy rates compared to geofeed results.

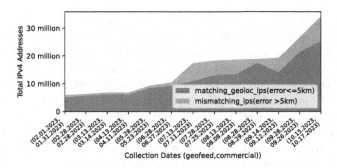

Fig. 7. IPgeolocation.io's overlap with geofeeds and overall accuracy.

At the country level, the observed agreement between geofeed results and commercial estimates was about 96% and 98% for Maxmind-GeoIP2 and IPgeolocation.io respectively, and very close to their self-reported accuracy rates of 99% (Maxmind) and 99.9% (IPgeolocation.io) [23, 31]. As shown in Figs. 6 and 8, city-level agreement between geofeed results and commercial estimates ranged from 85.1%–93.1% (mean = 88.5%) for Maxmind and between 63.0%–92.7% (mean = 81.7%) for IPgeolocation.io. It is worth noting that both providers' average rates of city level geofeed agreement exceed their self-reported accuracy rates of 66% within a 50km radius for Maxmind-GeoIP2 and 75% for IPgeolocation.io [23, 31].

6   Discussion

Our findings indicate a potentially increasing correlation between a country's level of industrialization and its overall representation within the geofeed results. If network operator opt-in to geofeeds becomes the norm in more industrialized locations, our observations indicate that the accuracy with which commercial IP-geolocation providers would be able to locate a given IPv4 Internet vantage point could become increasingly correlated with the extent to which the

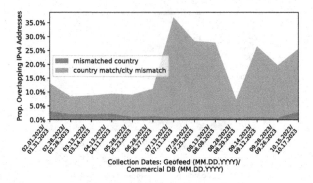

Fig. 8. IPgeolocation.io inaccuracy rates compared to geofeed results.

country housing it is industrialized. This is particularly concerning in light of existing works showing that Internet connections originating in less industrialized countries face higher rates of geoblocking [40] and that if given the option, websites/host servers will likely geofilter traffic in cases where doing so is not actually necessary [9,26]. Since websites and online services frequently rely on commercial IP-geolocation service responses to dictate who can access them and how they behave once accessed, this would translate into a growing discrepancy in the accuracy with which web hosts would be able geolocate Internet vantage points based on their rates of industrialization. Moreover, it implies that less industrialized countries could sustain further degradation to their overall Internet access and QoS as a result.

We are continuing to collect geofeed records, and are in the process of preparing an open (free) repository to house historical geofeed information[7]. We believe that this will be a valuable resource both for researchers interested in geofeeds in particular, and more generally, for those wishing to understand how network operators opt-in to new Internet standards.

Acknowledgments. We thank the anonymous reviewers and shepherd for their invaluable feedback and suggestions. This work is partially funded by the National Science Foundation through grants 1925497 and 2138078, and by the Callahan Family Chair fund. The opinions and findings expressed in this paper are those of the authors and do not necessarily those of any employer or funding agency.

---

[7] See https://github.com/GUSecLab/geofeed-measurement.

A   Geofeed and Commercial IP Fetch Dates

Table 3 lists the dates of fetches for the geofeeds and the corresponding dates of the commercial IP datasets that were used for comparison.

Table 3. Mapping of pull dates for geofeed results and matched commercial DB pulls. Pairings were selected to minimize the time between the geofeed and commercial pull dates (or vice versa).

Gfeed Date	Maxmind Date		Gfeed Date	IPgeoloc. Date
2023-01-13	2023-01-13			
2023-02-28	2023-02-28		2023-02-01	2023-01-31
2023-03-28	2023-03-28		2023-02-28	2023-02-28
2023-04-28	2023-04-25		2023-03-13	2023-03-14
2023-05-13	2023-05-16		2023-04-13	2023-04-11
2023-06-16	2023-06-13		2023-05-28	2023-05-23
2023-06-28	2023-06-27		2023-06-28	2023-06-27
2023-07-13	2023-07-11		2023-07-13	2023-07-11
2023-07-28	2023-07-25		2023-08-13	2023-08-08
2023-08-13	2023-08-08		2023-08-28	2023-08-29
2023-08-28	2023-08-29		2023-09-14	2023-09-12
2023-09-14	2023-09-12		2023-09-28	2023-09-26
2023-09-28	2023-09-26		2023-10-15	2023-10-17
2023-10-15	2023-10-17			

B   Country's Representation Within the Geofeed Results

Table 4 presents a breakdown of the top ten most and bottom 20 least represented countries within the geofeed results before normalization.

Figure 9 provides a breakdown of countries' representation within the geofeeds normalized by their respective number of Internet users [8] and Fig. 10 shows geofeeds normalized by each country's IPv4 address allocation. Additionally, Fig. 11 provides a country-wise breakdown of the total ASes categorized as ISPs by the ASdb in the November 10, 2023 geofeed results and Fig. 12 denotes the proportion of ISPs amongst each represented country's ASes in the same geofeed data.

Table 4. Top ten most *(top)* and bottom 20 least *(bottom)* represented countries.

Country	Continent	IPs (Apr22)	% Gfeed (Apr22)	IPs (Oct23)	% Gfeed (Oct23)
United States	North America	2,374,878	73.75%	9,919,174	29.0%
Sweden	Europe	4,683	0.145%	7,106,676	20.8%
Australia	Oceania	5,208	0.162	6,992,481	20.43%
Canada	North America	158,476	4.92%	1,597,552	4.67%
Russia	Europe	16,000	0.497%	1,568,923	4.58%
Germany	Europe	29,815	0.926%	844,017	2.47%
United Kingdom	Europe	88,158	2.74%	691,188	2.02%
Denmark	Europe	184,138	5.72%	632,484	1.85%
Italy	Europe	15,549	0.483%	630,185	1.84%
Netherlands	Europe	87,242	2.71%	477,869	1.40%
Djibouti	Africa	10	0.000 311%	6	0.000 023%
Chad	Africa	10	0.000 311%	6	0.000 018%
Mauritania	Africa	10	0.000 311%	6	0.000 018%
Nauru	Oceania	8	0.000 248%	6	0.000 018%
Sudan	Africa	8	0.000 248%	6	0.000 018%
Senegal	Africa	8	0.000 248%	6	0.000 018%
Sao Tome and Principe	Africa	8	0.000 248%	6	0.000 018%
Holy See (Vatican City)	Europe	8	0.000 248%	6	0.000 018%
Marshall Islands	Oceania	6	0.000 186%	6	0.000 018%
Niger	Africa	6	0.000 186%	6	0.000 018%
Tonga	Oceania	6	0.000 186%	6	0.000 018%
Samoa	Oceania	6	0.000 186%	6	0.000018%
Dominica	North America	8	0.000 248%	4	0.000012%
Mali	Africa	8	0.000 248%	4	0.000012%
Nicaragua	North America	8	0.000 248%	4	0.000012%
Burundi	Africa	6	0.000 186%	4	0.000012%
Comoros	Africa	6	0.000 186%	4	0.000012%
Togo	Africa	6	0.000 186%	4	0.000012%
Uganda	Africa	6	0.000 186%	4	0.000012%
Cuba	North America	6	0.000 186%	2	0.000 006%

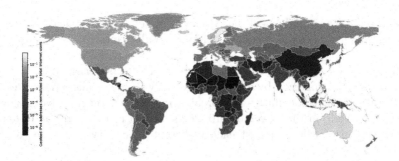

Fig. 9. Countries' IPv4 address representation within the geofeeds normalized by number of Internet users [8].

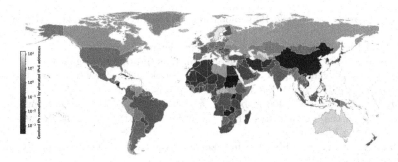

Fig. 10. Countries' IPv4 address representation within the geofeeds normalized by their IPv4 address allocations.

Fig. 11. Total number of ISPs in each country within the Geofeed Results for November 10, 2023 as categorized by the Stanford ASdb.

Fig. 12. Proportion of each country's ASNs that were categorized as ISPs by the Stanford ASdb in the November 10, 2023 Geofeed Results.

References

1. Geonames. https://download.geonames.org/export/dump/
2. Geopy documentation. https://geopy.readthedocs.io/en/latest/
3. IP geolocation database: Fastly Support. https://support.fastly.com/hc/en-us/community/posts/360078589732-IP-geolocation-database
4. CDN Comparison - Most Popular CDNs of 2021 (2021). https://www.experte.com/website/cdn

5. Seclists.org - re: Google IP geolocation (2021). https://seclists.org/nanog/2021/Apr/67

6. Digital Element (2022). https://www.digitalelement.com

7. Geoguard (2022). https://www.geocomply.com/products/geoguard/

8. Central Intelligence Agency: CIA world factbook. https://www.cia.gov/the-world-factbook/field/internet-users/country-comparison/

9. McDonald, A., et al.: 403 forbidden: a global view of CDN geoblocking. In: Proceedings of the Internet Measurement Conference 2018. IMC 2018. Association for Computing Machinery (2018)

10. Bano, S., et al.: Scanning the internet for liveness. SIGCOM Comput. Commun. Rev. 48(2), 2–9 (2018)

11. Wong, B., Stoyanov, I., Sirer, E.G.: Octant: a comprejensive framework for the geolocalization of internet hosts. In: 4th USENIX Symposium on Networked Systems Design & Implementation, NSDI 2007. USENIX Association (2007)

12. Cloudflare: Configuring Cloudflare IP Geolocation (2021). https://support.cloudflare.com/hc/en-us/articles/200168236-What-does-Cloudflare-IP-Geolocation-do-. Accessed 6 Dec 2021

13. Iordanou, C., Smaragdakis, G., Poese, I., Laoutaris, N.: Tracing cross border web tracking. In: Proceedings of the Internet Measurement Conference 2018, IMC 2018. Association for Computing Machinery (2018)

14. Dainotti, A., et al.: Estimating internet address space usage through passive measurements. SIGCOMM Comput. Commun. Rev. 44(1), 42–49 (2014)

15. Damerau, F.J.: A technique for computer detection and correction of spelling errors. Commun. ACM 7(3), 171–176 (1964). https://dl.acm.org/doi/10.1145/363958.363994

16. Dingledine, R., Mathewson, N., Syverson, P.: Tor: the second-generation onion router. In: USENIX Security Symposium (USENIX) (2004)

17. Fainchtein, R.A., Aviv, A.J., Sherr, M.: User perceptions of the privacy and usability of smart DNS. In: Proceedings of the 38th Annual Computer Security Applications Conference, ACSAC 2022, pp. 591–604. Association for Computing Machinery (2022). https://dl.acm.org/doi/10.1145/3564625.3567978

18. Fainchtein, R.A., Aviv, A.J., Sherr, M., Ribaudo, S., Khullar, A.: Holes in the geofence: privacy vulnerabilities in "smart" DNS services. In: Proceedings on Privacy Enhancing Technologies (PoPETS) (2021)

19. Gueye, B., Ziviani, A., Crovella, M., Fdida, S.: Constraint based geolocation of internet hosts. In: Proceedings of the 2004 Internet Measurement Conference, IMC 2004. Association for Computing Machinery (2004)

20. Internet Corporation for Assigned Names and Numbers: About WHOIS (2022). https://whois.icann.org/en/about-whois

21. IPGeolocation: ip-geolocation-api-jquery-sdk (2022). https://www.jsdelivr.com/package/npm/ip-geolocation-api-jquery-sdk

22. ipgeolocation.io: IP geolocation API and IP lookup documentation. https://ipgeolocation.io/documentation.html

23. ipgeolocation.io: IP Geolocation FAQs. https://ipgeolocation.io/faq.html

24. Karney, C.F.: Algorithms for geodesics. J. Geodesy 87, 43–55 (2013)

25. Kline, E., Duleba, K., Szamonek, Z., Moser, S., Kumari, W.: A format for self-published IP geolocation feeds. Informational 8805, RFC-Editor (2020)

26. Kumar, R., Virkud, A., Raman, R.S., Prakash, A., Ensafi, R.: A large-scale investigation into geodifferences in mobile apps. In: 31st USENIX Security Symposium (USENIX Security 2022). USENIX Association (2022). https://www.usenix.org/conference/usenixsecurity22/presentation/kumar

27. Laki, S., Mátray, P., Hága, P., Sebők, T., Csabai, I., Vattay, G.: Spotter: a model based active geolocation service. In: 2011 Proceedings IEEE INFOCOM (2011)
28. Gharaibeh, M., Shah, A., Huffaker, B., Zhang, H., Ensafi, R., Papadopoulos, C.: A look at router geolocation in public and commercial databases. In: Proceedings of the Internet Measurement Conference 2017, IMC 2017. Association for Computing Machinery (2017)
29. Massimo Candela: geofeed-finder (2022). https://github.com/massimocandela/geofeed-finder
30. Maxmind: Geoip2 and geolite city and country databases. https://dev.maxmind.com/geoip/docs/databases/city-and-country
31. Maxmind: Geolocation accuracy. https://support.maxmind.com/hc/en-us/articles/4407630607131-Geolocation-Accuracy
32. Ziv, M., Izhikevich, L., Ruth, K., Izhikevich, K., Durumeric, Z.: ASdb: a system for classifying owners of autonomous systems. In: ACM Internet Measurement Conference (IMC) (2021)
33. Muir, J.A., Oorschot, P.C.V.: Internet geolocation: evasion and counterevasion. ACM Comput. Surv. **42**(1), 1–23 (2009)
34. Namara, M., Wilkinson, D., Caine, K., Knijnenburg, B.P.: Emotional and practical considerations towards the adoption and abandonment of VPNs as a privacy-enhancing technology. Proc. Priv. Enh. Technol. (PoPETS) **2020**(1), 83–102 (2020)
35. NRO: Delegated-extended-file. https://ftp.ripe.net/pub/stats/ripencc/nro-stats/latest/nro-delegated-stats. Accessed 15 Oct 2023
36. Richter, P., Smaragdakis, G., Plonka, D., Berger, A.: Beyond counting: new perspectives on the active IPv4 address space. In: Proceedings of the 2016 Internet Measurement Conference, IMC 2016. Association for Computing Machinery (2016)
37. Poese, I., Uhlig, S., Kaafar, M.A., Donnet, B., Gueye, B.: IP geolocation databases: unreliable? ACM SIGCOMM Comput. Commun. Rev. **41**(2), 53–56 (2011)
38. Kumari, W., Bush, R., Candela, M., Housley, R.: RFC 9092 Finding and Using Geofeed Data. RFC Proposed Standard 9092, Internet Engineering Task Force (IETF) (2021)
39. Trimble, M.: The future of cybertravel: legal implications of the evasion of geolocation. Fordham Intell. Prop. Media Entertain. Law J. **22**, 567 (2012)
40. Tschantz, M.C., Afroz, S., Sajid, S., Qazi, S.A., Javed, M., Paxson, V.: A bestiary of blocking: the motivations and modes behind website unavailability. In: 8th USENIX Workshop on Free and Open Communications on the Internet (FOCI 2018). USENIX Association (2018). https://www.usenix.org/conference/foci18/presentation/tschantz
41. Weinberg, Z., Cho, S., Christin, N., Sekar, V., Gill, P.: How to catch when proxies lie: verifying the physical locations of network proxies with active geolocation. In: ACM SIGCOMM Conference on Internet Measurement (IMC) (2018)

Transport Protocols

Promises and Potential of BBRv3

Danesh Zeynali[1]([⊠]), Emilia N. Weyulu[1], Seifeddine Fathalli[1],
Balakrishnan Chandrasekaran[2], and Anja Feldmann[1]

[1] Max-Planck-Institut für Informatik, Saarbrücken, Germany
{dzeynali,eweyulu,fathalli,anja}@mpi-inf.mpg.de
[2] Vrije Universiteit Amsterdam, Amsterdam, The Netherlands
b.chandrasekaran@vu.nl

Abstract. The Bottleneck-Bandwidth and Round-trip (BBR) congestion control algorithm was introduced by Google in 2016. Unlike prior congestion-control algorithms (CCAs), BBR does not rely on signals that are weakly correlated with congestion (e.g., packet loss and transient queue delay). Instead, it characterizes a path using two parameters, bottleneck bandwidth and round-trip propagation time, and is designed to converge with a high probability to Kleinrock's optimal operating point [34]. Essentially, in stable state, BBR maximizes throughput while minimizing delay and loss. Google has used BBR for a significant fraction of its network traffic both within its datacenters and on its WAN since 2017 [15]. BBR's interaction dynamics with Cubic, the widely used CCA in the Internet, has received intense scrutiny: Some studies observed BBR to be unfair to Cubic, or generally loss-based CCAs. Google, to its credit, has diligently revised BBR's design to address the criticisms. This paper focuses on characterizing the promises and potential of the third, and most recent, revision of BBR—introduced to the public in July 2023. We empirically evaluate BBRv3's performance across a range of network scenarios, e.g., considering different buffer sizes, round-trip times, packet losses, and flow-size distributions. We show that despite the improvements and optimizations introduced in BBRv3, it struggles to achieve an equitable sharing of bandwidth when competing with Cubic, the widely used CCA in the Internet, in a wide range of network conditions.

Keywords: Congestion control · BBR · fairness

1 Introduction

Bottleneck Bandwidth and Round-trip (BBR) is a relatively new congestion control algorithm (CCA) that takes a proactive approach in detecting congestion on a network path. It is designed to enable a sender to converge with a high probability to Kleinrock's optimal operating point [34], which maximizes throughput while minimizing both delay and loss. To this end, BBR estimates the bottleneck bandwidth and round-trip propagation time of a path, and paces the sender appropriately to avoid building any queue along the path. It has fast replaced Cubic for *all* TCP flows on Google's B4 WAN [9,13]; for context, Google's WAN

ⓒ The Author(s), under exclusive license to Springer Nature Switzerland AG 2024
P. Richter et al. (Eds.): PAM 2024, LNCS 14538, pp. 249–272, 2024.
https://doi.org/10.1007/978-3-031-56252-5_12

traffic makes up 13.85% of all Internet traffic [41]. Since BBR runs purely on the sender side, a sample of Google's edge-to-end-user traffic (i.e., content served on google.com and youtube.com) has been delivered using BBR from as early as 2016 [9]. More recently, Google announced that they use BBR(v3) for *all* internal WAN traffic and public Internet traffic served from google.com [8].

It is quite challenging to design a CCA that works reasonably well in a wide range of network conditions. Traffic characteristics, round-trip times, and bottleneck buffers—to name a few parameters—may differ substantially from one network to another. Unsurprisingly, though Google designed BBR by analyzing traces of world-wide network traffic [13], several independent studies and reports have reported it to be highly unfair to other CCAs in the Internet [2,7,17,26,28, 42,43,49,50]. In particular, its incompatibility with Cubic, one of the widely used loss-based CCAs in the Internet, has received much scrutiny [2,17,28]. Google, to its credit, has been diligently evolving BBR to address the concerns raised, and its efforts recently culminated with the release of BBRv3, in 2023 [12]. We focus on the performance and fairness claims (or "promises") of this most recent version of BBR in this work.

BBR builds a model of the network path based on the bottleneck bandwidth and round-trip propagation time measured from each `ACK`. BBRv1 used this model to pace the sender at a rate equal to the estimated bottleneck bandwidth, while keeping the in-flight data quite close to the bandwidth-delay product (BDP). Google reported that BBRv1 achieves high throughput under random packet losses as high as 15% and maintains small queues *regardless* of buffer size [9]. In-depth evaluations revealed, however, BBRv1 to be extremely aggressive when competing with loss-based CCAs and unfair in shallow buffer scenarios [7,26,42,50]. Besides, studies also observed increased retransmission rate [7,26,42], high RTT unfairness and queue occupancy [7,26,49], and ACK aggregation issues in WiFi and cellular networks [11]. BBRv2 was released in 2019 to address these issues; chief among its changes was the inclusion of loss as a congestion signal. It reacted to explicit congestion notifications (ECNs) and optimized the congestion-window (`cwnd`) update logic. Despite the inter-CCA and RTT fairness improvements that Google reported [11,14], independent evaluations showed it suffering from low link utilization and being unfair to loss-based CCAs in deep buffer scenarios [30,37,45]. BBRv3, the most recent release introduced in July 2023, claimed to address these concerns. In particular, BBRv3 (a) claimed to offer quick bandwidth convergence to fair shares both with and without loss or ECN signals and (b) boasted of optimizations to minimize queuing delays and packet losses both during and shortly after slow start (i.e., `STARTUP`) [8].

Thoroughly evaluating a CCA to determine whether it falls short of its promises and, most importantly, along what dimensions and how, is an arduous task. The environment (e.g., a datacenter or private WAN) in which the CCA is originally designed, or for which it was specifically developed, may introduce implicit assumptions (for instance, about network conditions or traffic scenarios), which may not hold in the environment where the CCA is eventually deployed (e.g., public Internet). The literature has several examples of CCAs whose behavior in real-world network conditions significantly deviated from that observed in the controlled environments where they were designed and tested (e.g., [20,40,51]). In case of BBR, the conflicting observations between Google's internal evaluations and the various external evaluations—of BBRv1 and BBRv2—clearly attest to the challenges in accurately evaluating its performance. We bridge this conflict by designing a set of experiments—based on first principles—that unequivocally demonstrate whether BBRv3 holds its promises and where there is potential for improvement. Along the way, we outline a systematic and principled approach for evaluating a CCA in practice.

In this work, we empirically analyze the performance of BBRv3 in a wide range of network conditions. In particular, we investigate its claims of quick (throughput) convergence to fair shares in deep and shallow buffer scenarios, and of its improved compatibility (compared to BBRv1 and BBRv2) with loss-based CCAs. An accurate evaluation of these claims has substantial implications for BBR's deployment in the public Internet, since Google is transitioning more and more of its end-user facing traffic to use BBR. Consequently, we evaluate BBR in network scenarios where both long-lived (i.e., elephant) and short-lived (i.e., mouse) flows compete for bandwidth on a shared link. Our choice of using different sizes of flows is based on prior work that demonstrated that while short-lived flows contribute most packets to Internet traffic, long-lived flows contribute most bytes [4,56].

We summarize our contributions as follows.

⋆ We present a first independent empirical evaluation of BBRv3, Google's newest version of BBR, across a range of network conditions and justify the rationale behind our choice of evaluation settings. We focus our evaluation, in particular, on BBRv3's promises to (a) share bandwidth equitably with other loss-based CCAs, particularly in deep buffer scenarios, and (b) assure fairness when contending for throughput with flows that experience different RTTs, a common case in the public Internet where BBRv3 is increasingly being deployed.

⋆ Our evaluations show that BBRv3's throughput unfairness towards loss-based CCAs, i.e., Cubic, is nearly identical to BBRv1's behavior and is exacerbated in shallow buffers. We find that BBR's bias towards long-RTT flows persists in BBRv3, with the unfairness magnified when the difference in RTTs of competing flows is significant. Cubic, the widely used CCA in the Internet, in comparison, offers better throughput for flows with short RTTs than long RTTs.

⋆ We release our network testbed configuration, data sets, and scripts for experiment orchestration and analyses [54].

2   Background

BBR enables a sender to maximize delivery rate while minimizing delay and loss, i.e., converge to Kleinrock's optimal operating point [34]. To this end, it employs a sequential probing state machine that periodically alternates between probing for higher bandwidths (by increasing the delivery rate) and testing for

Table 1. An overview of the key changes between the three BBR versions.

Life cycle phases	Property	BBRv1	BBRv2	BBRv3
Startup	cwnd_gain	$2/ln\,2$ (~ 2.89)	$2/ln\,2$ (~ 2.89)	2.00
		$2/ln\,2$ (~ 2.89)	$2/ln\,2$ (~ 2.89)	2.77
	Max. cwnd	3xBDP	-	-
	inflight_hi	-		max(est. BDP, last cwnd)
	Exit	send. rate <25% for 3 consec. RTTs	loss/ECN rate >= thresh. (8)	loss/ECN rate >= thresh. (6)
Drain			0.35	
	Exit		cwnd <= 1xBDP	
ProbeBW	Phases	8 fixed gain cycles	{Cruise, Refill, Up, Down}	{Cruise, Refill, Up, Down}
	*	Cycle=RTprop	cwnd limits={inflight_hi,inflight_lo}	-
	cwnd_gain	-	cwnd_gain(Up)=2.0	cwnd_gain(Up)=2.25
	pacing_gain	[1.25,0.75,1,1,1,1,1,1]	pacing_gain(Down)=0.75	pacing_gain(Down)=0.90
	Exit	cwnd>= (pacing_gain x BDP) or loss	loss/ECN rate >= thresh	loss/ECN rate >= thresh.
ProbeRTT	Frequency	10 s	5 s	5 s
	cwnd	4	BDP/2	
	Duration	200 ms + RTprop	-	-

lower RTTs (by draining the bottleneck queue) of a path. It then uses these
bandwidth and RTT measurements to build a path model that determines various congestion control parameters of a TCP implementation such as cwnd and
pacing rate [9]. Since its introduction in 2016, BBR has underwent three major
iterations, and Table 1 summarizes the key differences between these versions.

BBRv1. The first version of BBR used four phases: *Startup, Drain, ProbeBW*
(or *Probe Bandwidth*), and *ProbeRTT* [9]. The Startup phase grows the sending
rate exponentially, similar to NewReno, Vegas, and Cubic, but it uses a window increase factor (i.e., cwnd_gain) of $2/ln\,2$. Once the bottleneck bandwidth
estimate "plateaus" (i.e., three attempts to double the delivery rate results in
increasing it by less than 25%), it exits the Startup phase. To drain the queue
that the Startup may have built, BBRv1 then enters the Drain phase, by reducing its to 0.75. A BBR flow spends the majority of its time in the ProbeBW
phase, where it probes for bandwidth via *gain cycling*. Essentially, BBRv1 cycled
through a sequence of eight values for -5/4, 3/4, 1, 1, 1, 1-where a gain higher
than one indicates a probe for higher bandwidth and a gain lesser than one represents the attempt to drain any queue built earlier. With the average of the
eight values being one, the approach allowed ProbeBW to maintain an average
pacing rate that is equal to the estimated bandwidth. BBRv1 continuously sampled the bottleneck bandwidth during this phase. Every 10 s, BBRv1 stopped
the ProbeBW phase and entered the ProbeRTT phase. It reduced its cwnd to
four packets for as long as 200 ms and one round-trip. The low rate drains the
bottleneck queue and allows the sender to sample the minimum propagation
RTT of the path; it is only in this phase that BBR updates its minimum RTT
estimate. Several studies revealed, however, that BBRv1 was extremely aggressive when competing with loss-based CCAs, and highly unfair in shallow buffer
scenarios [7, 26, 28, 42, 50].

BBRv2. Google introduced BBRv2 in 2019 to alleviate the problems with
BBRv1 [13,14]. BBRv2 split the ProbeBW phase into four new sub-phases:
Down, Cruise, Refill, and *Up*. Unlike BBRv1, it reacted to loss or ECN sig-

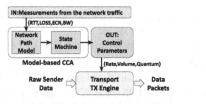

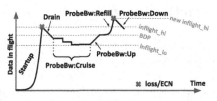

(a) *BBRv3's System Architecture*   (b) *Congestion control phases of BBRv3*

Fig. 1. An overview of (a) BBRv3's high-level implementation architecture & (b) the life cycle of the CCA showing how it transitions phases of congestion control.

nals to facilitate an equitable sharing of bandwidths with widely used CCAs such as Cubic and NewReno [14]. In BBRv2, the Startup phase ends not only when the bandwidth estimate "plateaus," but also if loss or ECN mark rate exceeds a threshold (i.e., 2%). It capped the maximum in-flight data volume to the maximum congestion window observed, prior to entering the Drain phase. During ProbeBW, BBRv2 picks the maximum bandwidth measured in the last two ProbeBW attempts instead of the last 10 RTTs as in the case of BBRv1. BBRv2 maintained three different values to bypass the issue of 2xBDP in-flight cap, which was identified in prior work as the primary source of unfairness in BBRv1 [50]: 1.25 for Probe:Down, 0.75 for ProbeBW:Up, and 1 for both ProbBW:Cruise and ProbeBW:Refill. BBRv2 also replaced the 8-phase cycle for ProbeBW with an adaptive probing time, i.e., a value picked at random between 2–3 s, for improving compatibility with Cubic and NewReno.

BBRv3. BBRv3 was introduced in July 2023 at the 117th IETF meeting [8]. Figure 1 illustrates both the high-level implementation architecture and the life cycle of the CCA, showing how it transitions between the different congestion control phases. BBRv3 is a minor revision of BBRv2, and it addresses two key performance issues of BBRv2. First, an implementation change caused BBRv2 to prematurely exit the ProbeBW phase that in turn prevented it from sharing bandwidth equitably with BBRv1 or loss-based CCAs such as Cubic [8]. The issue resulted in under-utilization of the link even after the link was no longer congested. BBRv3, hence, continues probing for bandwidth until (a) the loss rate or ECN mark rate is below a set threshold (i.e., 2%) or (b) the bandwidth saturates even if the delivery rate is not restricted by the `inflight_hi` threshold. Second, the choice of parameter values (e.g., `cwnd_gain` and) used in the ProbeBW phase made BBRv2 highly unfair: Especially in deep buffer scenarios if the sender received no loss or ECN signals, it caused the sender to be unfair to competing flows [8]. To mitigate these fairness concerns, Google adjusted several parameters, e.g., `cwnd_gain`, , and `inflight_hi`, used in the different congestion control phases, which per their report resulted in improving the CCA's performance [8].

3   Methodology

We empirically evaluate the performance of the three versions of BBR and compare them to that of Cubic using a custom network testbed. The testbed consists of six Dell R6515 blade servers, each with 16 cores and 128 GiB of RAM. We installed one or two Broadcom NetXtreme BCM5720 25 GbE NICs, as required, on each server and used 25 Gbps DACs for interconnecting the servers and four APS Networks BF6064X-T switches (as shown in Fig. 2). We configured the servers to run Linux kernel v5.4 (Debian 10). We used two VMs on one of the servers to evaluate different versions of BBR implementations using the same machine: One VM ran BBRv2 with Linux kernel v5.13.12 from [22], while the other ran BBRv3 with Linux kernel v6.4.0 from [23]. We did not enable ECN support in our testbed, and so neither BBRv2 nor BBRv3 benefited from ECN in our evaluations. Since BBRv3 promises quick (bandwidth) convergence to fair share even without loss or ECN signals [8], we assume such a scenario in our setup and leave the evaluations in the presence of ECN to future work.

To evaluate under a wide range of network conditions, we varied the capacity of the bottleneck link (in red in Fig. 2) and one-way delays as needed for the different experiments using the Linux traffic control (`tc`) utility. Specifically, we used `netem` [47] on an intermediate node, designated as the network latency emulator (NLE), between the end hosts to avoid issues with TCP small queues [31,38]. We

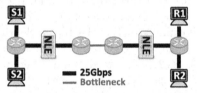

Fig. 2. Network testbed for evaluating performance of CCAs in a single bottleneck setup. (Color figure online)

also used `tc-tbf` [1] on the NLE to configure the bottleneck bandwidth and buffer size. Unless otherwise stated, we added half of the configured delay before the bottleneck and half after the bottleneck. The base RTT between sender-receiver pairs in the testbed, without any added delay, was 1.5 ms on average.

To emulate traffic representative of real-world network conditions, we generated workloads by using flow sizes from a MAWI trace [32] downloaded on January 5, 2023. We extracted the flows using Zeek [29] and scaled up the inter-arrival times by a factor of 5 to account for the difference in link capacities between the MAWI infrastructure and our testbed. The flow sizes in this data set followed the Pareto distribution, while the inter-arrival times followed the Lognormal distribution. We then used Harpoon [44] to generate traffic using samples from these empirical distributions. Unless otherwise stated, we repeated each experiment three times and reported the statistics across the three runs.

4   Evaluation

We now evaluate the three versions of BBR and Cubic in a wide range of network conditions. Our goal is to ascertain the ability of each CCA to share the bandwidth in a fair or equitable manner with other flows-regardless of whether the

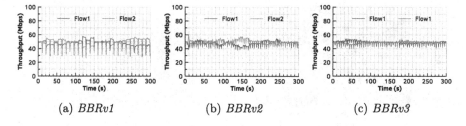

(a) *BBRv1*   (b) *BBRv2*   (c) *BBRv3*

Fig. 3. Throughput achieved by two similar, synchronous (i.e., starting at the same time) flows when competing for bandwidth on a bottleneck with a deep buffer of size 16×BDP.

contending flows use the same CCA or a different one. To this end, we evaluate fairness in two broad settings: *similar* and *dissimilar* flows. Similar flows use the same CCA and experience the same RTT, but may vary from one another in size or arrival times (at a bottleneck link). Dissimilar flows, in contrast, differ from one another based on one or more factors, e.g., choice of CCAs and RTTs experienced by the flows.

4.1 Similar and Synchronous Flows

We begin our evaluation with a simple scenario where two similar flows, i.e., using the same CCA and experiencing the same RTT (of 100 ms), contend for bandwidth on a bottleneck (refer Fig. 2). We start both flows *at the same time* and let them run for a duration of 300 s and plot the throughput experienced by the flows as a function of time in Fig. 3. Overall, all BBR variants achieve an equitable bandwidth share when competing with a similar and synchronous flow. BBRv3 significantly reduces the throughput oscillations and allows the flows to converge much quicker than either of the earlier two versions. We repeated this experiment by varying the bottleneck queue size from one-fourth to 16 times the BDP, doubling the queue size once for each experiment. Although not shown here, our inferences hold across all these settings.

Figure 4a indicates whether the flows experience high retransmissions when competing with another similar, synchronous flow.[1] The heatmap reports the percentage of retransmissions (i.e., ratio of the aggregate number of retransmitted packets to the total number of packets delivered by both flows) experienced by the two flows; higher values indicate higher retransmissions, and, hence, lower values (in green) imply better throughput or utilization. Per this figure, although BBRv1 experiences high retransmissions when competing with another BBRv1 flow started at the same time in low buffer settings, across all other settings, the CCAs converge quickly without incurring much loss. This observation of high retransmissions when using BBRv1 in shallow buffers is in line with observations made by prior work [7,26,42]: They are due to BBRv1' aggressive probing

---

[1] We omit the results for 8 × BDP and 16 × BDP as we see virtually no retransmissions in such settings.

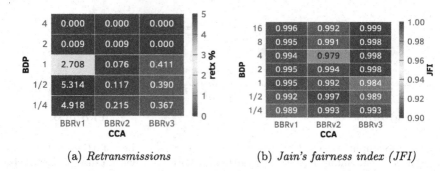

(a) *Retransmissions*   (b) *Jain's fairness index (JFI)*

Fig. 4. (a) Retransmissions experienced by and (b) Jain's fairness index (JFI) of two similar, synchronous flows competing for bandwidth on a bottleneck link as a function of bottleneck queue size.

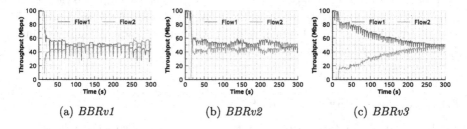

(a) *BBRv1*   (b) *BBRv2*   (c) *BBRv3*

Fig. 5. Throughput achieved by two similar but staggered flows (i.e., second flow starts 15 s after the first) when competing for bandwidth on a bottleneck with a deep buffer of size 16×BDP.

behavior and its indifference to loss. The Jain's fairness index (JFI) for the flows in Fig. 4b, however, shows that all three versions equitably share the bottleneck with a similar and synchronous flow, regardless of bottleneck buffer size; BBRv3 shows only a marginal improvement, if any, over the prior two versions.

Takeaways. BBR achieves an equitable sharing of bandwidth with similar synchronous flows, and BBRv3 address the well-documented issues of aggressiveness and unfairness in BBRv1.

4.2 Similar But Staggered Flows

We now repeat the earlier evaluation, but with one change: We *stagger* the flows so that the second flow starts 15 s after the first. In the Internet flows may arrive at a bottleneck at random times, when other contending flows on the link have already started or reached their stable state. The staggering of flows simply emulates this typical traffic condition.

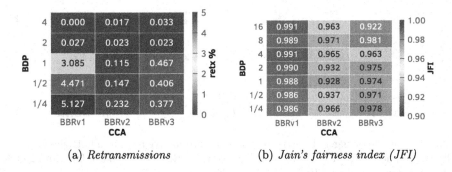

(a) *Retransmissions*   (b) *Jain's fairness index (JFI)*

Fig. 6. (a) Retransmissions experienced by and (b) JFI of two similar but staggered flows (i.e., second one starts 15 s after the first flow) competing for bandwidth on a bottleneck link as a function of bottleneck buffer size.

Per Fig. 5, BBR implementations do not converge quickly to an equitable share when flows do not start at the same time—quite unlike the case of similar and synchronous flows (Sect. 4.1). For instance, when a BBRv3 flow joins 15 s later at a bottleneck link with a 16×BDP buffer, it takes *more than 4 minutes* for it to achieve an equitable bandwidth sharing. Such large buffers are not uncommon in the internet: Router manufacturers may (by default) provide large buffers [19], and administrators may configure larger buffers on transcontinental links to cope with the high RTTs [16] or improve video QoE [46].

We observe that when flow starts are staggered by an interval of 15 s, the flows experience higher retransmissions (Fig. 6a) than when they are started at the same time.[2] The heatmap in the plot reports, as in Sect. 4.1, the percentage of retransmissions experienced by the two flows; higher values (in yellow and red) indicate higher retransmissions. BBRv1 in particular suffers high retransmissions in shallow buffer settings, again owing to its aggressive probing behavior and indifference to losses. A key change in BBRv2 (compared to BBRv1) was the addition of using loss as a congestion signal; this change enables it to reduce the loss rates in shallow buffer settings and avoid unnecessary retransmissions [10]. BBRv2 experiences, as a result, the lowest retransmissions of all three implementations. BBRv3 inherits BBRv2's changes and, as a consequence, experiences low retransmissions, which matches Google's claims about BBRv3 [8]. We observe that BBRv3 experiences more retransmissions than BBRv2 in shallow buffer settings, but the former achieves better fairness than the latter across a range of buffer sizes (Fig. 6b), with the exception of the largest buffer size (of 16-times BDP). BBRv1, which does not use packet loss to infer congestion, leads to higher fairness than BBRv2 and BBRv3, both of which take loss into consideration. These observations could partly be explained by BBRv3's less aggressive behavior compared to BBRv1 (compare BBRv3's `cwnd_gain` and `pacing_gain` to those of BBRv1 in Table 1).

---

[2] As before, we omit the results for 8 times BDP and 16 times BDP as we see virtually no retransmissions in such settings.

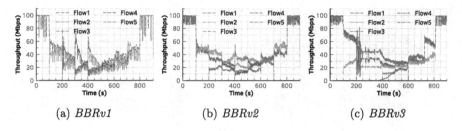

Fig. 7. When we stagger the arrivals and departures of five flows at a bottleneck link of 100 Mbps and buffer size 32×BDP by 100 s, (a) BBRv1 flows achieve fair throughput shares faster than (b) BBRv2 and (c) BBRv3.

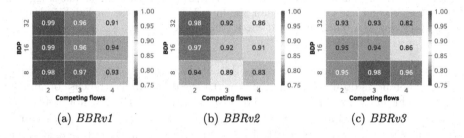

Fig. 8. When we stagger the arrivals and departures of five flows at a bottleneck link of 100 Mbps by 100 s, (a) BBRv1 flows achieve better shares of throughput than (b) BBRv2 and (c) BBRv3.

Takeaways. While BBR's refinements seem to allow it reduce losses, with recent versions taking losses into account to control their probing, even the most recent version of BBR struggles to achieve high fairness when flow arrivals are staggered by a few seconds. This observation has crucial implications for BBRv3's adoption in the Internet, since in the public Internet arrivals of competing flows might often be staggered with respect to one another.

4.3 Co-existence in Deep Buffer Scenarios

To evaluate how quickly different CCAs converge to fair bandwidth share, we run a staggered-flow experiment (similar to that of HPCC [35]), where we introduce five flows, one after another. Again, the flows are similar and we add a new flow to the testbed every 100 s until we reach five concurrent flows, and then remove one flow every 100 s until we have only one left. This experiment enables us to compare and contrast how quickly different CCAs react to dynamic changes in traffic conditions and converge to the fair share of the bottleneck (100 Mbps). In this evaluation, we specifically focus on deep buffer scenarios to verify Google's claim that BBRv3 can equitably share bandwidth in such conditions [8].

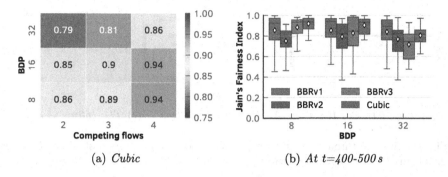

(a) *Cubic*   (b) *At t=400-500 s*

Fig. 9. (a) Cubic offers improved fairness as the number of flows increases, and (b) when all five flows compete at the bottleneck with a deep (32×BDP) buffer, BBRv3 has the worst fairness than any other CCA.

Figure 7 shows the timelines of flows in the staggered-flow experiment in a deep-buffer (i.e., 32×BDP) scenario for all three BBR versions. Per this figure, BBRv3 struggles to achieve a fair share between the flows; when all five flows compete at the bottleneck, BBRv3 performs the worst compared to both the previous versions. BBRv1 flows converge quickly to fair share both when new flows arrive and old ones leave; its quick convergence to fair share is perhaps largely due to its aggressive probing behavior, which can efficiently discover bandwidth changes. The average JFI across three runs (Fig. 8) shows that BBRv3 performs better than BBRv2, but poorer than BBRv1. Cubic, in contrast to BBRv3, performs poorly with a small numbers of flows, although it improves with increasing number of flows (Fig. 9a). Unlike Cubic, BBRv3's performance degrades with increasing number of flows. If we analyze fairness during the period when all five flows are competing for bandwidth (Fig. 9b), BBR typically performs poorer than Cubic on average, exhibiting large variations in performance. Particular in deep-buffer settings, BBRv3 performs worst compared to both Cubic and earlier versions of BBR, perhaps because of its less aggressive choice of probing parameters.

Takeaways. While BBRv3's intra-protocol fairness in deep buffer scenarios is better than that of BBRv2, its fairness is poorer than that of BBRv1 and seems to worsen as the number of flows increases (in deep-buffer scenarios). BBRv3 choice of less aggressive probing parameters compared to BBRv1 seems to be the reason behind the observed behavior.

4.4 Dissimilar Flows: RTT Fairness

Evaluations concerning fairness of CCAs in prior work (e.g., [7,50]) usually consider flows with similar RTTs. Flows in the Internet typically have different RTTs, which make it challenging in terms of fairly sharing bandwidth when such flows interact at a bottleneck link, even if they all use the same CCA. The RTT dictates a CCA's reaction to bandwidth limitations or to other flows, since

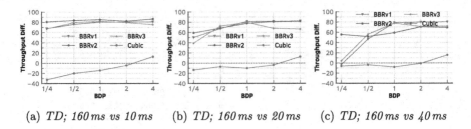

(a) *TD; 160 ms vs 10 ms*   (b) *TD; 160 ms vs 20 ms*   (c) *TD; 160 ms vs 40 ms*

Fig. 10. Average throughput difference (TD); 160 ms flow starts first, then 15 s later the (10 ms, 20 ms, 40 ms) flow starts.

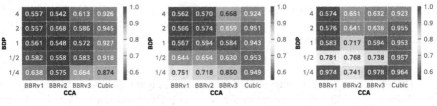

(a) *JFI; 160 ms vs 10 ms*   (b) *JFI; 160 ms vs 20 ms*   (c) *JFI; 160 ms vs 40 ms*

Fig. 11. Average Jain's fairness index (JFI); 160 ms flow starts first, then 15 s later the (10 ms, 20 ms, 40 ms) flow starts.

the signals typically used by a sender (e.g., packet loss or delay) for determining how much it can send and/or how fast, must traverse the path from the bottleneck to the receiver, which then echoes it back to the sender.

With this experiment, we evaluate the bandwidth share when flows using the same CCA traverse different routing paths, thus experiencing different RTTs, and sharing a common bottleneck along the way. We run two flows using the same CCA, where the first flow is our base flow with a fixed RTT of 160 ms and the second flows experiences a different RTT—one of 10, 20, 40, 80 ms, each constituting a different experiment. In the first experiment scenario, the base flow, 160 ms, starts first and the second flow joins after 15 s (Fig. 10, Fig. 11 and Fig. 12). In the second scenario, the base flow joins 15 s after the flow with the shorter RTT (Fig. 13, Fig. 14 and Fig. 15). These scenarios help us characterize how the different CCAs behave when the short (or long) RTT flow joins the network, while the other flow has already reached a steady state; we can safely assume a flow has finished slow start after 15 s.[3] Specifically, we calculate the throughput difference between the base flow and the second flow, as follows: $BaseFlow_{AvgTput} - SecondFlow_{AvgTput}$. A positive value implies that the base flow obtains the majority of the bandwidth, while a negative value indicates that the second flow receives higher bandwidth than the first. Additionally, we also compute the Jain's fairness index to quantify the CCA's fairness.

---

[3] We do not disturb a flow while in slow start to ensure that it does not exit slow start prematurely, which would result in link underutilization.

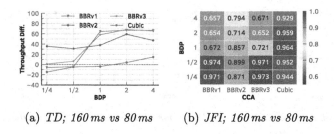

(a) *TD; 160 ms vs 80 ms*   (b) *JFI; 160 ms vs 80 ms*

Fig. 12. Average throughput difference (TD) and Jain's fairness index (JFI); 160 ms flow starts first, then 15 s later the 80 ms flow starts.

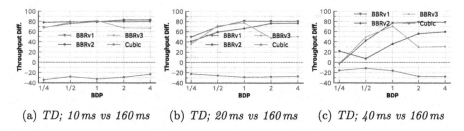

(a) *TD; 10 ms vs 160 ms*   (b) *TD; 20 ms vs 160 ms*   (c) *TD; 40 ms vs 160 ms*

Fig. 13. Average throughput difference (TD); short RTT flow (10 ms, 20 ms, 40 ms) starts first, then 15 s later the 160 ms flow starts.

When we start the long-RTT flow first, all versions of BBR favor the long-RTT flow (Fig. 10); it receives much higher bandwidth than the second flow. This bias towards the long-RTT flow (starting first) diminishes a bit when the difference in flow RTTs decreases (Fig. 10c); BBRv2 and BBRv3 (which is largely similar to BBRv2) perform much better than BBRv1 when RTT differences between the base flow and second flow decreases (Fig. 12), perhaps owing to their less aggressive design. These observations also hold if we start the short-RTT flow first and then the long-RTT (or base) flow (Fig. 13 and Fig. 15). Our inferences are in agreement with prior work that demonstrated BBR favoring long-RTT flows over short-RTT flows [26,49], which is quite different from what has been observed in case of AIMD mechanisms [6,25]; our results confirm that BBRv3's behavior does not vary substantially from BBRv2 with respect to preferring long-RTT flows over short-RTT flows. Cubic, unlike BBR, favors the second (short-RTT) flow over the base (long-RTT) flow, even though the second flow starts after the base flow, across almost all buffer settings.

All BBR versions exhibit high RTT unfairness when the RTT difference between the base and second flow is significant, regardless of which flow starts first (Fig. 11, Fig. 12, Fig. 14, and Fig. 15). Unlike BBR, Cubic achieve high fairness across all settings, regardless of how we size the bottleneck buffer. BBR's bias towards long-RTT flows is less pronounced in shallow buffers (if the RTTs of the flows do not differ substantially), where the short-RTT flow is able to compete for a better bandwidth share with the long-RTT flow.

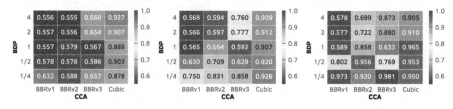

(a) *JFI; 10 ms vs 160 ms*   (b) *JFI; 20 ms vs 160 ms*   (c) *JFI; 40 ms vs 160 ms*

Fig. 14. Average Jain's fairness index (JFI); short RTT flows (10 ms, 20 ms, 40 ms) start first, then 15 s later the 160 ms flow starts.

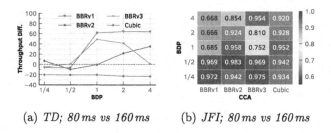

(a) *TD; 80 ms vs 160 ms*   (b) *JFI; 80 ms vs 160 ms*

Fig. 15. Average throughput difference (TD), 80 ms flow starts first, then 15 s later the 160 ms flow starts.

Fairness is improved for all BBR versions if the short RTT flow starts first, as it is able to grow its cwnd before the long RTT flow starts. Additionally, the smaller the gap between the two flow's RTT values, the better the fairness as both flows are able to estimate the bottleneck bandwidth and RTT at the same rate (Fig. 12 and Fig. 15). When BBR flows with different RTTs compete for bandwidth, the short-RTT flow is likely to observe the increase in queuing faster than the long-RTT flow (since the rate at which a sender can observe such signals depend on the RTT). Furthermore, since BBR determines the delivery rate based on such signals, the short-RTT flow may consistently slow down in response to any observed queuing before the long-RTT flow reacts. When flows eventually synchronize, short-RTT flows regain some of the bandwidth share, but the situation reverts to benefitting the long-RTT flow again as they probe for bandwidth.

Takeaways. BBR's bias towards long-RTT flows is well-known, and our evaluations confirm that BBRv3 improvements or optimizations do not change the status quo. BBR offers poor fairness across flows that differ substantially in RTT, which might be typical in the Internet. Cubic, the widely used CCA in the Internet, unlike BBR, offers higher fairness than BBR in nearly all our evaluations scenarios with flows with different RTTs.

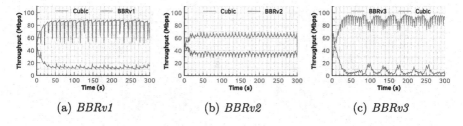

Fig. 16. Throughput of a BBR flow when competing for bandwidth with a Cubic flow on a bottleneck link with a 1×BDP buffer.

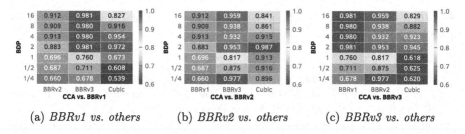

Fig. 17. Jain's fairness index (JFI) of two flows using different CCAs and competing on a bottleneck with a 1×BDPbuffer.

4.5   Dissimilar Flows: Inter-CCA Fairness

We now evaluate BBRv3's ability to share bandwidth equitably when competing with flows using CCAs other than BBRv3. With more than 40% of current Internet traffic estimated to be delivered using BBR [36], it is quite important to characterize how BBRv3 behaves when competing with non-BBRv3 flows already prevalent in the Internet. Such an inter-CCA characterization is also timely and crucial for network operators and generally the networking community, since Google intends to submit BBRv3 soon for inclusion in the Linux kernel [8]. To characterize BBRv3 flows' ability to co-exist with non-BBRv3 flows, we run two (co-existing) long-lived flows, each using a different CCA; we start these flows at the same time. We set the RTT to 100 ms and the bandwidth to 100 Mbps, and we vary the bottleneck buffer size as a function of BDP.

BBRv1 has long been reported to be extremely unfair to loss-based CCAs such as Cubic [7,26,49,50]. Figure 16b, hence, simply confirms this well-established claim. BBRv2 seems to fare well than BBRv1 (Fig. 16b), since unlike the former, the latter takes packet loss into consideration. BBRv2 improves upon BBRv1 with respect to its ability to share bandwidth with loss-based CCAs, even allowing Cubic to obtain more than its share of fair bandwidth when competing with BBRv2 flows. BBRv3, which Google claims will quickly converge to fair share, performs even slightly worse than BBRv1 (Fig. 16c). Even if flows experience same RTTs, BBRv3, in its current form, offers no room for Cubic flows to co-exist; any RTT differences between the flows may only exacerbate this situation.

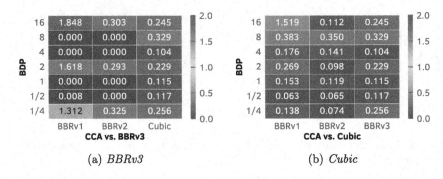

Fig. 18. Retransmissions when (a) a BBRv3 flow and (b) a Cubic flow compete against flows using other CCAs.

Figure 17 shows the Jain's fairness index for the competing flows to characterize BBR's inter-CCA fairness. In shallow-buffer scenarios, BBRv1 is quite unfair to all others. No other CCA, not even other versions of BBR, is able to obtain a fair share when competing with BBRv1 (Fig. 17a); increasing bottleneck buffer sizes, nevertheless, seems to alleviate this situation substantially. This behavior is presumably due to BBRv1 only backing off when its large in-flight data cap (3×BDP) is exceeded (refer Table 1), ignoring packet loss unlike BBRv2 and BBRv3. Unlike BBRv1, BBRv2 performs quite well (with high JFI values) across all bottleneck buffer settings (Fig. 17b) primarily because of its ability to reach to packet loss. It can equitably share bandwidth with Cubic, making it safer than BBRv1 for deployment in the public Internet where the latter is quite prevalent. BBRv3, despite being only a minor revision of BBRv2, performs quite poorly, especially against Cubic (Fig. 17c). In deep-buffer settings, Cubic is able to send more data into the network before experiencing congestion (i.e., packet loss); naturally, it obtains a higher bandwidth compared to shallow-buffer settings and, as a result, the fairness index improves.

Overall, while the design of BBRv3 (which it inherits from BBRv2) represents a substantial progress (in creating a fair and safe CCA), the performance tweaks [8] or optimizations (refer Table 1) that Google has introduced in BBRv3 are exactly the opposite. With regards to Google's claims about reduced packet loss, we observe frequent retransmissions (Fig. 18) when BBRv3 competes against Cubic, comparable almost to those when BBRv1 competes against Cubic in both deep and shallow-buffer settings.

Thus far we focused on a scenario where a single BBR flow competes with a single Cubic flow for bandwidth on a bottleneck. Previous studies showed that even when competing with several Reno or Cubic flows a single BBRv1 flow was able to grab most of the link bandwidth [40,50]. We revisit this evaluation where we pit a single BBR flow against several Cubic flows. More specifically, we conduct a series of experiments where we vary the number of BBR flows as well as competing Cubic flows from 1 through 5, and characterize the fairness (measured via JFI) across the competing flows in each experiment (Fig. 19). As

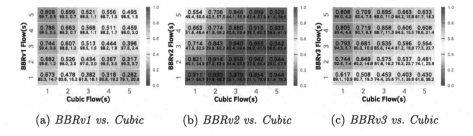

Fig. 19. JFI when 1–5 Cubic flows compete against 1–5 (a) BBRv1, (b) BBRv2 and (c) BBRv3 flows.

before, we set the link bandwidth to 100 Mbps, the RTT to 100 ms, and the buffer size to 1×BDP(i.e., 1250 KB). We start all the flows at the same time and run them for 360 s. Figure 19 shows the JFI of the experiments with the three BBR versions competing against Cubic. The top value in each cell is the mean JFI value over time, concatenated over three experiment runs, while the bottom value show the mean throughput shares of BBR and Cubic.

In Fig. 19a, JFI values become smaller (i.e., fairness worsens) as we move from top to bottom or right to left. This observation confirms the observations from prior work that even a single BBRv1 flow can outcompete multiple Cubic flows [40,50]. BBRv2's design completely reverses this behavior (Fig. 19b); when we increase the number of Cubic flows fairness improves, emphasizing once again that we can safely deploy BBRv2 in the public Internet. BBRv3, in contrast, resurrects BBRv1's aggressive behavior (Fig. 19c); it offers lower fairness than BBRv2, although the Cubic flows seem to be able to obtain a higher bandwidth when competing against BBRv3 than when competing against BBRv1.

Takeaways. While BBRv2 makes significant improvements towards achieving equitable bandwidth sharing when competing against loss-based CCAs, BBRv3 seems to undo most, if not all, such improvements. BBRv3 does not equitably share bandwidth with loss-based CCAs such as Cubic, and its behavior in some instances is even worse than that of BBRv1. Despite its ability to react to packet loss, it remains highly unfair to Cubic flows, in shallow buffers.

4.6   Dissimilar Flows: Real-World Workloads

Until now, we used a small, fixed number of (long-lived) flows in our evaluations. Now, we turn to using realistic traffic workloads to quantify BBR's performance in real-world network conditions. Specifically, we use a distribution of flows comprising both short-lived (i.e., mouse) and long-lived (i.e., elephant) flows. We sample the size of these flows from an empirical distribution of flow sizes observed in the Internet (Fig. 20a). The CDF in Fig. 20a depicts the flow size distribution from a MAWI trace (refer Sect. 3). We use the Harpoon [44] traffic generator to sample the flow sizes and connection times from this trace data. We fixed the random seed used in the sampling to ensure that the sampled

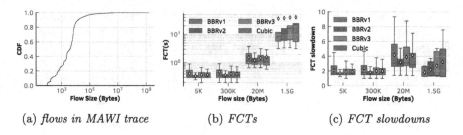

(a) *flows in MAWI trace*   (b) *FCTs*   (c) *FCT slowdowns*

Fig. 20. (a) Distribution of flow sizes in the MAWI trace; Flow completion times (FCTs) and FCT "slowdown" for various flow sizes across different CCAs.

distribution of flow sizes remains the same across the evaluations of all CCAs; we can then compare the performance of the same set of flows across different CCAs and determine which CCA performs the best. We conduct two distinct experiments using the topology shown in Fig. 2 with the bottleneck bandwidth set to 100 Mbps, RTT to 100 ms, and the buffer size to BDP. In the first, we set all flows to use the same CCA, and in the second, we configure half of the flows to use one of the BBR versions and the other half to use Cubic. We then analyze the flow completion times (FCTs) as well as the FCT "slowdowns" [53] computed by normalizing the measured FCT by the theoretically optimal FCT obtained by taking into account the flow size, the bandwidth, and the RTT.

When All Flows Use the Same CCA. In case of BBRv1, the FCTs of short flows, i.e., flows smaller than 300 KB, are comparatively longer than those of the long flows (Fig. 20b). The FCT slowdowns for the longest flows in Fig. 20c when compared to those of the smaller flows clearly show that BBRv1 prioritizes long flows over their shorter counterparts. BBRv2, in contrast, offers lower FCT for short flows than for long flows. Lastly, BBRv3 offers smaller FCT slowdowns for short flows than for long flows, but its FCT slowdowns are consistently higher than those of BBRv2.

When Flows are Split Equally Between Two CCAs. To evaluate how BBR behaves when competing with Cubic (similar to the earlier evaluations in Sect. 4.5) in realistic traffic conditions, we configure half of the flows in the workload to use one of the BBR versions and the other half to use Cubic. As before, we plot the FCTs and FCT slowdowns of the flows grouped into buckets of different sizes in Fig. 21. The FCTs and FCT slowdown values corresponding to the experiment where BBRv1 flows compete with Cubic (Fig. 21a and Fig. 21d) are not surprising; BBRv1 is quite unfair to Cubic, as amply demonstrated in Sect. 4.5, and its ability to seize bandwidth aggressively from Cubic flows result overall in substantially smaller FCTs and FCT slowdowns for BBRv1 flows than Cubic flows, regardless of flow size. BBRv2 is far less aggressive to Cubic than BBRv1 (Fig. 21b and Fig. 21e). Short flows of both CCAs experience similar FCT slowdowns, while long flows using BBRv2 fare better than those using Cubic. BBRv3's performance is similar to that of BBRv2, except in case

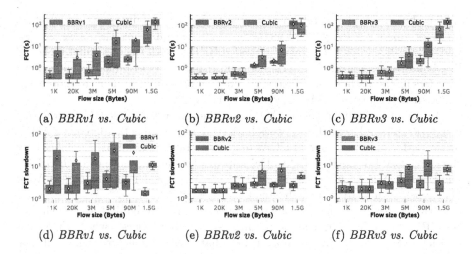

Fig. 21. Flow completion times (FCTs) and FCT "slowdowns" for flows of varying sizes split between two CCAs.

of long flows. (Fig. 21c and Fig. 21f) Long flows using Cubic experience higher FCTs and FCT slowdowns when competing against BBRv3 than against BBRv1.

Takeaways. The evaluations confirm the highly aggressive and unfair behavior of BBRv1 towards loss-based CCAs such as Cubic. BBRv2's design significantly improves that status quo, making Cubic flows achieve nearly their fair share when competing with BBRv2 flows. While BBRv3 behaves similar to BBRv2 for short flows allowing both Cubic and BBRv3 flows to experience similar FCT slowdowns, long flows using BBRv3 experience much smaller FCT slowdowns than those using Cubic.

5   Related Work

There is an extensive body of prior work on congestion control in the Internet. Google's BBR is a relatively new addition and its design intelligently combines several good ideas from the literature. Several independent studies have examined BBR's performance in various scenarios and compared it with that of other CCAs, partly perhaps because of how quickly Google has been transitioning large volumes of traffic to use BBR [8]. Below, we briefly review these prior work.

Many prior work such as [7,26,42,49,50] conducted comprehensive evaluations of BBRv1, focusing on its interactions with other well-known and widely used CCAs, e.g., NewReno, Cubic, and Vegas. Past evaluations of BBRv1 considered both similar and dissimilar flows (i.e., flows with varying RTTs or using different CCAs). Some investigated BBRv1's performance in both shallow and deep buffer scenarios [7,26,50], and some others analyzed the impact of extremely long delays, which are typical in satellite networks [18]. Prior studies identified several shortcomings with BBRv1, including unfairness to loss-based CCAs in shallow buffers, frequent retransmissions, high RTT unfairness as well as high queue occupancy. The scope of virtually all such evaluations was, however, limited to long-lived flows. Hurtig et al. tested BBRv1 with various buffer sizes and link bandwidths and used a workload comprising a mix of bulk as well as short transfers [27], but they used fixed sizes (instead of sampling them from observed traffic distributions) for long-lived and short-lived flows.

Active queue management (AQM) techniques are designed for mitigating congestion [3], and several prior work have studied the impact of deploying AQMs on the performance of different CCAs (e.g., [24]). In the case of BBR, studies have shown that AQMs such as FQ-CoDel improve the performance of both BBRv1 and BBRv2 in deep buffer scenarios [21,33,55]. We consider the analyses of AQM deployments on BBRv3 as orthogonal to this work.

BBRv2 uses ECN signals to detect queuing, and Tahiliani et al. [48] showed that BBRv2 reduces queue occupancy at the bottleneck, when ECN was enabled. Multiple studies demonstrated that BBRv2 has lower link utilization than BBRv1 owing to its conservative behavior during bandwidth probing and that both versions were unfair to loss-based CCAs in deep buffer scenarios [30,37,45,52]. We did not evaluate the benefits of ECN for BBRv3 in this study, but we leave that for future work.

Some recent work also attempted to address the BBR's shortcomings. Bi et al. [5], for instance, focused on BBRv1's frequent retransmissions issue. They proposed dynamically adjusting the in-flight data cap based on the estimate bottleneck buffer size from RTT samples as well as packet losses. BBRv2+ used path delay information for tuning the aggressiveness of bandwidth probing [52]. They used Mahimahi [39] for evaluating BBRv2+ in emulated WiFi and LTE networks. While we do not propose solutions for addressing the shortcomings in BBRv3, we hope our comprehensive evaluations and detailed analyses will pave the way for designing and validating different solutions.

6   Concluding Remarks

The bottleneck bandwidth and round-trip propagation time (BBR) algorithm is a relatively new congestion control algorithm (CCA). BBR's design eschews the typical congestion signals (e.g., transient queue delays and losses) used in the vast majority of prior work. It measures instead bottleneck bandwidth and round-trip times on each ACK and paces the sender to retain the delivery rate close to the bottleneck bandwidth and avoid any queue build up. Several studies, however, demonstrated this initial design to be highly unfair to loss-based CCAs such as Cubic. Google responded to the criticisms by evolving the design and releasing newer versions of BBR. BBRv3, released in July 2023, is the most recent version in the evolution of BBR.

Given the increasing volume of traffic that Google has been transitioning to use BBR and its current efforts to include BBRv3 in the Linux kernel, we turned our attention to performing a systematic and rigorous evaluation of BBRv3 in a range of realistic network conditions and traffic scenarios. Specifically, we checked whether Google's claims of BBRv3's fairness towards other CCAs hold water in our evaluations. While BBRv3 has evolved substantially compared to the earlier versions, in our evaluations BBRv3 struggles to achieve an equitable bandwidth sharing with competing flows. Even when competing with similar flows (i.e., flows using BBRv3) a small difference in arrival times causes BBRv3 to incur substantial delays in bandwidth convergence. Despite the revisions, optimizations, and bug fixes, BBRv3's highly competitive behavior stifles Cubic on a bottleneck link, particularly in shallow buffer settings. These results have crucial implications for BBRv3's adoption and deployment in the public Internet. We release our testbed configuration and scripts for running and analyzing the experiments as open source artifacts [54], and we hope our efforts encourage the community to think about an objective template or framework for evaluating modern CCAs.

References

1. Kuznetsov, A.N., Hubert, B.: TC-TBF(8) - Linux man page (2023). https://linux. die.net/man/8/tc-tbf. Accessed 1 Oct 2023
2. Mishra, A., Zhang, J., Sim, M., Ng, S., Joshi, R., Leong, B.: Conjecture: existence of nash equilibria in modern internet congestion control. In: Proceedings of the 5th Asia-Pacific Workshop on Networking, APNet 2021 (2022)
3. Baker, F., Fairhurst, G.: IETF Recommendations Regarding Active Queue Management. RFC 7567 (2015)
4. Bauer, S., Jaeger, B., Helfert, F., Barias, P., Carle, G.: On the evolution of internet flow characteristics. In: Applied Networking Research Workshop (ANRW) (2021)
5. Bi, P., Xiao, M., Yu, D., Zhang, G.: oBBR: optimize retransmissions of BBR flows on the internet. In: USENIX Annual Technical Conference (ATC) (2023)
6. Brown, P.: Resource sharing of TCP connections with different round trip times. In: IEEE International Conference on Computer Communications (INFOCOM) (2000)
7. Cao, Y., Jain, A., Sharma, K., Balasubramanian, A., Gandhi, A.: When to use and when not to use BBR: an empirical analysis and evaluation study. In: ACM Internet Measurement Conference (IMC) (2019)
8. Cardwell, N., et al.: BBRv3: algorithm bug fixes and public internet deployment. Technical report, Internet Engineering Task Force (IETF) (2023). https:// datatracker.ietf.org/meeting/117/materials/slides-117-ccwg-bbrv3-algorithm-bug-fixes-and-public-internet-deployment-00
9. Cardwell, N., Cheng, Y., Gunn, C.S., Yeganeh, S.H., Jacobson, V.: BBR: congestion-based congestion control. ACM Queue 14(5), 20–53 (2016)
10. Cardwell, N., et al.: BBR congestion control: IETF 100 update: BBR in shallow buffers. Technical report, Internet Engineering Task Force (IETF) (2017). https://www.ietf.org/proceedings/100/slides/slides-100-iccrg-a-quick-bbr-update-bbr-in-shallow-buffers-00.pdf
11. Cardwell, N., et al.: BBR congestion control work at google IETF 101 update. Technical report, Internet Engineering Task Force (IETF) (2018). https:// datatracker.ietf.org/meeting/101/materials/slides-101-iccrg-an-update-on-bbr-work-at-google-00

12. Cardwell, N., et al.: BBR Congestion Control: Fundamentals and Updates (2023). https://research.cec.sc.edu/files/cyberinfra/files/BBR%20-%20Fundamentals%20and%20Updates%202023-08-29.pdf
13. Cardwell, N., Cheng, Y., Yeganeh, S.H., Swett, I., Jacobson, V.: BBR Congestion Control. Internet-Draft draft-cardwell-iccrg-bbr-congestion-control-02, Internet Engineering Task Force (IETF) (2022). https://datatracker.ietf.org/doc/draft-cardwell-iccrg-bbr-congestion-control/02/
14. Cardwell, N., et al.: BBR v2: a model-based congestion control IETF 105 update. Technical report, Internet Engineering Task Force (IETF) (2019). https://datatracker.ietf.org/meeting/105/materials/slides-105-iccrg-bbr-v2-a-model-based-congestion-control-00
15. Cardwell, N., Yuchung, C.: TCP BBR congestion control comes to GCP - your Internet just got faster (2017). https://cloud.google.com/blog/products/networking/tcp-bbr-congestion-control-comes-to-gcp-your-internet-just-got-faster/. Accessed 04 Feb 2024
16. Chandrasekaran, B., Smaragdakis, G., Berger, A., Luckie, M., Ng, K.C.: A server-to-server view of the internet. In: ACM CoNEXT (2015)
17. Claypool, S.: Sharing but not Caring - Performance of TCP BBR and TCP CUBIC at the Network Bottleneck (2019)
18. Claypool, S., Chung, J., Claypool, M.: Comparison of TCP congestion control performance over a satellite network. In: Passive and Active Measurement (PAM) (2021)
19. Intel®: Intel® Tofino 6.4Tbps, 4 pipelines (2017). https://www.intel.com/content/www/us/en/products/sku/218643/intel-tofino-6-4-tbps-4-pipelines/specifications.html. Accessed 01 Oct 2023
20. Dong, M., et al.: PCC Vivace: online-learning congestion control. In: USENIX Symposium on Networked Systems Design and Implementation (NSDI) (2018)
21. Fejes, F., Gombos, G., Laki, S., Nádas, S.: Who will save the internet from the congestion control revolution? In: Workshop on Buffer Sizing (2019)
22. Google: TCP BBR v2 Alpha/Preview Release (2021). https://github.com/google/bbr/tree/v2alpha. Accessed 01 Oct 2023
23. Google: TCP BBR v3 Release (2023). https://github.com/google/bbr/tree/v3. Accessed 01 Oct 2023
24. Grazia, C.A., Patriciello, N., Klapez, M., Casoni, M.: A cross-comparison between TCP and AQM algorithms: which is the best couple for congestion control? In: International Conference on Telecommunications (2017)
25. Ha, S., Rhee, I., Xu, L.: CUBIC: a new TCP-friendly high-speed TCP variant. ACM SIGOPS Oper. Syst. Rev. **42**(5), 64–74 (2008)
26. Hock, M., Bless, R., Zitterbart, M.: Experimental evaluation of BBR congestion control. In: IEEE International Conference on Network Protocols (ICNP) (2017)
27. Hurtig, P., et al.: Impact of TCP BBR on CUBIC traffic: a mixed workload evaluation. In: International Teletraffic Congress (2018)
28. Huston, G.: BBR TCP (2017). https://labs.ripe.net/author/gih/bbr-tcp/
29. ICSI: Zeek: An Open Source Network Security Monitoring Tool (2022). http://www.zeek.org. Accessed 20 Sept 2023
30. Ivanov, A.: Evaluating BBRv2 on the dropbox edge network. In: Netdev, The Technical Conference on Linux Networking (2020)
31. Corbet, J.: TCP small queues (2012). https://lwn.net/Articles/507065/. Accessed 01 Oct 2023
32. Kenjiro, C., Koushirou, M., Akira, K.: Traffic data repository at the WIDE project. In: USENIX Annual Technical Conference (ATC) (2000)

33. Kfoury, E.F., Gomez, J., Crichigno, J., Bou-Harb, E.: An emulation-based evaluation of TCP BBRv2 Alpha for wired broadband. Comput. Commun. **161**, 212–224 (2020)
34. Kleinrock, L.: Power and deterministic rules of thumb for probabilistic problems in computer communications. In: IEEE International Conference on Communications (1979)
35. Li, Y., et al.: HPCC: high precision congestion control. In: Annual Conference of the ACM Special Interest Group on Data Communication on the Applications, Technologies, Architectures, and Protocols for Computer Communication (SIGCOMM) (2019)
36. Mishra, A., Sun, X., Jain, A., Pande, S., Joshi, R., Leong, B.: The great internet TCP congestion control census. Proc. ACM Meas. Anal. Comput. Syst. **3**(3), 1–24 (2019)
37. Nandagiri, A., Tahiliani, M.P., Misra, V., Ramakrishnan, K.K.: BBRvl vs BBRv2: examining performance differences through experimental evaluation. In: IEEE International Symposium on Local and Metropolitan Area Networks (LANMAN) (2020)
38. Cardwell, N.: BBR evaluation with netem (2017). https://groups.google.com/g/bbr-dev/c/8LYkNt17V_8. Accessed 01 Oct 2023
39. Netravali, R., et al.: Mahimahi: accurate record-and-replay for HTTP. In: USENIX Annual Technical Conference (ATC) (2015)
40. Philip, A.A., Ware, R., Athapathu, R., Sherry, J., Sekar, V.: Revisiting TCP congestion control throughput models & fairness properties at scale. In: ACM Internet Measurement Conference (IMC) (2021)
41. Sandvine: The Global Internet Phenomena Report January 2023. Technical report, Sandvine Corporation (2023). https://www.sandvine.com/hubfs/Sandvine_Redesign_2019/Downloads/2023/reports/Sandvine%20GIPR%202023.pdf?hsCtaTracking=3cbc04da-fd44-481b-ad03-811d23b7b2c5%7C131df09f-dbdd-41a0-9dce-aac8879403ff
42. Scholz, D., Jaeger, B., Schwaighofer, L., Raumer, D., Geyer, F., Carle, G.: Towards a deeper understanding of TCP BBR congestion control. In: IFIP Networking (2018)
43. Shah, A.: BBR Evaluation at a Large CDN (2019). https://edg.io/tw/resources/technical-article/bbr-evaluation-at-a-large-cdn/
44. Sommers, J., Kim, H., Barford, P.: Harpoon: a flow-level traffic generator for router and network tests. In: ACM SIGMETRICS International Conference on Measurement and Modeling of Computer Science, vol. 32, no. 1 (2004)
45. Song, Y.J., Kim, G.H., Mahmud, I., Seo, W.K., Cho, Y.Z.: Understanding of BBRv2: evaluation and comparison With BBRv1 congestion control algorithm. IEEE Access **9**, 37131–37145 (2021)
46. Spang, B., Walsh, B., Huang, T.Y., Rusnock, T., Lawrence, J., McKeown, N.: Buffer sizing and video QoE measurements at Netflix. In: Workshop on Buffer Sizing (2019)
47. Hemminger, S., Ludovici, F., Pfeifer, H.P.: tc-netem(8) - Linux manual page (2023). https://man7.org/linux/man-pages/man8/tc-netem.8.html. Accessed 01 Oct 2023
48. Tahiliani, M.P., Misra, V.: A principled look at the utility of feedback in congestion control. In: Workshop on Buffer Sizing (2019)
49. Turkovic, B., Kuipers, F.A., Uhlig, S.: Interactions between congestion control algorithms. In: Network Traffic Measurement and Analysis Conference (TMA) (2019)

50. Ware, R., Mukerjee, M., Seshan, S., Sherry, J.: Modeling BBR's interactions with loss-based congestion control. In: ACM Internet Measurement Conference (IMC) (2019)
51. Yan, F.Y., et al.: Pantheon: the training ground for Internet congestion-control research. In: USENIX Symposium on Networked Systems Design and Implementation (NSDI) (2018)
52. Yang, F., Wu, Q., Li, Z., Liu, Y., Pau, G., Xie, G.: BBRv2+: towards balancing aggressiveness and fairness with delay-based bandwidth probing. Comput. Netw. **206**, 108789 (2022)
53. Zapletal, A., Kuipers, F.: Slowdown as a metric for congestion control fairness. In: SIGCOMM Workshop on Hot Topics in Networking (HotNets), HotNets 2023 (2023)
54. Zeynali, D., Weyulu, E.N., Fathalli, S., Chandrasekaran, B., Feldmann, A.: Promises and Potential of BBRv3: Testbed configuration and evaluation artifacts (2024). https://dzeynali.gitlab.io/
55. Zhang, H., Zhu, H., Xia, Y., Zhang, L., Zhang, Y., Deng, Y.: Performance analysis of BBR congestion control protocol based on NS3. In: International Conference on Advanced Cloud and Big Data (CBD) (2019)
56. Zhang, Y., Breslau, L., Paxson, V., Shenker, S.: On the characteristics and origins of internet flow rates. In: Annual Conference of the ACM Special Interest Group on Data Communication on the Applications, Technologies, Architectures, and Protocols for Computer Communication (SIGCOMM) (2002)

QUIC Hunter: Finding QUIC Deployments and Identifying Server Libraries Across the Internet

Johannes Zirngibl[(✉)](ORCID), Florian Gebauer, Patrick Sattler(ORCID),
Markus Sosnowski(ORCID), and Georg Carle(ORCID)

Technical University of Munich, Munich, Germany
{zirngibl,gebauer,sattler,sosnowski,carle}@net.in.tum.de

Abstract. The diversity of QUIC implementations poses challenges for
Internet measurements and the analysis of the QUIC ecosystem. While
all implementations follow the same specification and there is general
interoperability, differences in performance, functionality, but also security (*e.g.*, due to bugs) can be expected. Therefore, knowledge about
the implementation of an endpoint on the Internet can help researchers,
operators, and users to better analyze connections, performance, and
security. In this work, we improved the detection rate of QUIC scans to
find more deployments and provide an approach to effectively identify
QUIC server libraries based on `CONNECTION_CLOSE` frames and transport
parameter orders. We performed Internet-wide scans and identified at
least one deployment for 18 QUIC libraries. In total, we can identify
the libraries with 8.0 M IPv4 and 2.5 M IPv6 addresses. We provide a
comprehensive view of the landscape of competing QUIC libraries.

1 Introduction

Based on UDP, the new QUIC protocol [17] can be implemented in user space
and has thus seen wide attention from various implementors [16]. Several operators (*e.g.*, Cloudflare [5]), as well as open source teams, started to implement
QUIC libraries during the standardization process. They regularly update their
implementations to follow new developments and improve their library.

Even though all libraries follow the same standard, implementation differences are to be expected. Related work has shown that these differences affect
functionality [24,36] and performance [18,42,47]. They can drastically influence scans, *e.g.*, during deployment detection as shown in this work, and future
research. It is important to differentiate between effects due to the network, the
protocol specification, and implementation specifics. The assessment of performance and bottlenecks of QUIC connections on the Internet [4] or new QUIC
features [19,33] could be improved considering the involved libraries. Therefore,
means to properly scan and identify QUIC libraries and an overview of their
deployment on the Internet are essential. Our key contributions in this work are:

(*i*) We analyze current QUIC scanning approaches and propose a new ZMap
approach to identify more deployments. We evaluate the current state of QUIC
deployments and analyze the importance of Server Name Indication (SNI) values.

© The Author(s), under exclusive license to Springer Nature Switzerland AG 2024
P. Richter et al. (Eds.): PAM 2024, LNCS 14538, pp. 273–290, 2024.
https://doi.org/10.1007/978-3-031-56252-5_13

(ii) We propose an approach to identify QUIC libraries based on error messages and transport parameters. We conducted Internet-wide scans and found at least one deployment for 18 libraries respectively, and 12 different libraries in one Autonomous System (AS).

(iii) We developed a test environment for scanners and our library identification approach. We published all tools to evaluate future changes of QUIC libraries and scan configurations and to update our approach to identify libraries in case of changes: https://github.com/quic-hunter/libraries

2 Background

QUIC combines functionality from different layers, *e.g.*, transport functionality, but also security through Transport Layer Security (TLS) [17]. It is used on top of UDP and implemented in user space. This has led to many QUIC libraries. The QUIC working group lists more than 24 different libraries [16], of which 16 are tested by the QUIC Interop Runner [36].

The QUIC handshake combines the transport handshake with a TLS handshake and exchanges various information. QUIC restricts TLS to version 1.3 but adds a new `quic_transport_parameters` extension to TLS [41]. This extension allows the peers to exchange transport parameters during the QUIC handshake. These include values like maximum timeouts or limits on the amount of data that may be sent in this connection [17].

Furthermore, relying on TLS allows QUIC clients to send a domain as SNI value during the handshake, indicating the requested service. SNI is part of the TLS 1.3 standard and allows a server with multiple domains to select the correct certificate for authentication. Similarly, TLS offers an extension called Application-Layer Protocol Negotiation (ALPN), which allows the negotiation of an application layer protocol during the handshake (*e.g.*, `h3` to request Hypertext Transfer Protocol (HTTP) version 3). The client sends a list of supported and requested values, while the server selects an offered value or terminates the connection early with an error.

In case of an error, QUIC peers should send a `CONNECTION_CLOSE` frame and terminate the connection. This frame may contain an error code to explicitly indicate the associated error if there was one. Interestingly, the frame may include an arbitrary reason phrase provided by the peer and encoded as a string [17].

We rely on information exchanged during the `CONNECTION_CLOSE` frame and QUIC handshake to identify implementations (see Section 6).

3 Related Work

Differences in implementations and their behavior during communications have been used by Sosnowski et al. [39,40] and Althouse et al. [3] to differentiate TLS/TCP deployments or to analyze operating systems and TCP behavior [23, 37]. In contrast, we focus on QUIC libraries and specific features independent of the used TLS library and deployment configurations.

QUIC deployments and their behavior have been analyzed at different stages of the standardization phase [32,48] and since the release of RFC 9000 [26,27]. Zirngibl et al. [48] developed and published a ZMap module to detect QUIC implementations and the QScanner. The QScanner is a stateful QUIC scanner based on quic-go [1]. It allows conducting complete RFC 9000 [17] conform QUIC handshakes and HTTP/3 requests. It extracts QUIC and TLS properties, X.509 certificates, and HTTP headers. According to the QUIC Interop Runner [36], quic-go can conduct handshakes with all other implementations. Zirngibl et al. identify widespread deployment mainly driven by large Content Delivery Networks (CDNs) and show differences in configured parameters and used versions. However, they did not analyze which QUIC libraries are actually used by found deployments. We base our work on their tools, show an increase in deployments compared to their findings, and provide a methodology to identify the library of found deployments.

Nawrocki et al. [27] evaluated the behavior of different deployments with a focus on certificates and their conformance to amplification limits during the handshake. They show differences between QUIC deployments. However, they did not focus on specific library differences and their identification but on the interplay between QUIC and certificate (chain) sizes. Mücke et al. [25] evaluate QUIC deployments but focus on specific hyper giants and do not focus on an identification of libraries in general. Furthermore, Marx et al. [24] have analyzed libraries and showed the impact of different draft interpretations on the implementations, e.g., due to congestion control mechanisms. Gbur and Tschorsch [9] have evaluated QUIC libraries focusing on security aspects in local tests. Other works on QUIC mainly focused on interoperability [30,36] and performance [18,28,34,38,42,43,45–47].

While most of these works showed differences in QUIC libraries and their impact on specific features, none analyzes the impact of these differences on scans and provides means to identify libraries on the Internet. To the best of our knowledge, there is no published test environment for QUIC scanners and no methodology to identify deployed QUIC libraries.

4   Test Environment

QUIC scanners are typically built on a single library and assume the correct implementation of the QUIC protocol as defined by the RFCs. However, due to the number of available implementations, some implement standards incorrectly, interpret parts of it differently or miss some functionality. While the QUIC Interop Runner [36] covers a variety of test cases between libraries, no test environment was available for scanners. Therefore, we developed a local test environment to evaluate QUIC libraries and their behavior to various requests. It allows for ethical evaluations without interfering with the network and existing deployments in case of unexpected behavior in edge-case scenarios.

The environment is based on Docker and isolates different servers from the scanners (see Fig. 1). Each implementation is running in its own Docker container

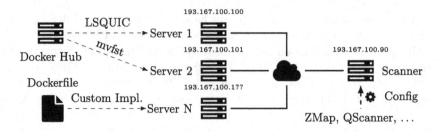

Fig. 1. Test environment Docker setup. Each server implementation is hosted within its own container and thus isolated. Public (*e.g.*, from the QUIC Interop Runner) or self-built containers can be used.

and is reachable via an individual IP address. An additional container executes scanners, *i.e.*, ZMap and the QScanner. While individual containers can be added, we include all 16 existing server implementations of the QUIC Interop Runner [36] as of October 2023 (see Appendix Table 5 for a complete list). The library developers themselves mainly provide and regularly update them. Our test environment supports general QUIC handshakes and HTTP/3 requests.

We used this environment *(i)* to test different scanners and configurations to improve QUIC scans (Sect. 5) and *(ii)* to develop an approach to identify QUIC libraries (Sect. 6). Furthermore, we publish this environment [49] to allow others to reproduce our findings and update our identification approach in the future in case of library changes. Updated QUIC servers can easily be integrated using new and up-to-date containers published by the library maintainers or built individually. Other researchers can use it to test scanners or scan configurations.

Besides our local environment, we collected a set of servers explicitly announced as test servers or operated by the developers of specific libraries. They allow us to verify findings with real deployments on the Internet and to analyze additional libraries where no QUIC server is available for the QUIC Interop Runner (*e.g.*, google.com for Google Quiche [10]). While only little information about a QUIC library by Akamai is available, we confirmed with Akamai that they maintain their own library originally forked from Google Quiche.

5   Scanning for QUIC Deployments

Scanning for QUIC deployments is often a two-step process: *(i)* identifying targets with a stateless scan and *(ii)* evaluating the capabilities of targets with a stateful scan completing a handshake. We deployed this approach on large scale, improved the relevant components, and evaluated the state of QUIC servers on the Internet.

We conducted Internet-wide scans to analyze current QUIC deployments, focusing on used libraries. Our approach follows scan approaches based on ZMap to identify potential targets and Domain Name System (DNS) resolutions to find potential SNI values, followed by stateful QUIC scans (see Fig. 2).

We seeded our DNS scans with more than 400 M domains, *e.g.*, from the Centralized Zone Data Service (CZDS), a list of country-code TLD (ccTLD) domains and domains extracted from Certificate Transparency Logs. We resolved all domains to A and AAAA records for IPv4 and IPv6 addresses.

For IPv4, we seeded ZMap with the entire address space. Regarding IPv6, we used the IPv6 Hitlist [8,51] and added IPv6 addresses extracted from AAAA records. The latter ensures that we include IPv6 addresses of large CDNs in our dataset. Zirngibl et al. [51] have shown that IPv6 prefixes of CDNs, *e.g.*, Fastly and Cloudflare, often appear aliased and are filtered by the regular hitlist service to prevent biases. Therefore, additionally relying on AAAA records besides the Hitlist implements suggestions by the operators regarding proper usage [51]. We used the QScanner [48] for the stateful scan. We conducted a QUIC handshake to collect transport parameters and used *h3* as ALPN value. After a successful handshake, we sent an HTTP request to collect HTTP header information.

In this work, we do not rely on HTTPS DNS resource records which could indicate QUIC support via an HTTP/3 ALPN value [35]. Zirngibl et al. [50] have shown in March 2023 that the records are mostly used by Cloudflare so far. Furthermore, we do not use Alt-Svc HTTP headers from TLS over TCP scans, an otherwise recommended approach to negotiate HTTP/3 support [44]. On one side, they would require additional Internet-wide scans using TCP, on the other side, they are impacted by missing SNI values as well and not necessarily reveal additional targets. Our approach solely relies on QUIC probes sent out using ZMap and is independent of other scans.

5.1 ZMap: Version Negotiation

The first important step is a ZMap scan, designed to effectively evaluate on a large scale whether a target IP address is offering a service on a given port [7]. While TCP-based protocols are identified based on the 3-way handshake (sending a SYN packet and expecting a SYN-ACK), the UDP-based QUIC protocol requires a meaningful payload during the first flight. Previous work [32,48] relied on a payload that triggers a Version Negotiation (VN) by the server, *i.e.*, sending a QUIC packet with an unsupported version. The QUIC standard [17] explicitly reserves versions following the pattern 0x?a?a?a?a to be used to trigger a VN.

In the following, we focus on the most recent module by Zirngibl et al. [48]. It sets a reserved version and a valid size but omits most of the remaining information, *e.g.*, a valid Client Hello. Servers should first parse the version field and directly send a VN in case of an unsupported version [17], allowing

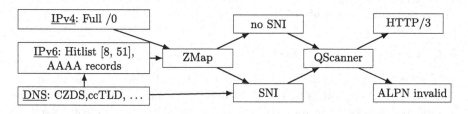

Fig. 2. Scan setup to identify QUIC deployments and used libraries. The ALPN **invalid** scan is explained in Sect. 6. Ethics are covered in Sect. 7.

Table 1. Found QUIC deployments based on ZMap with three different probes in October 2023.

	VN		Initial		Initial-VN	
IP	Addr	ASes	Addr	ASes	Addr	ASes
v4	9.2 M	7.5 k	9.3 M	8.7 k	11.9 M	8.7 k
v6	460.7 k	2.7 k	483.6 k	2.9 k	7.9 M	2.9 k

Table 2. Successful handshakes based on the QScanner. For SNI, IP addresses with at least one successful domain are counted.

	No SNI		SNI		Total	
IP	Addr	ASes	Addr	ASes	Addr	ASes
v4	522.6 k	6.0 k	411.9 k	3.9 k	876.6 k	7.8 k
v6	118.4 k	2.4 k	2.1 M	1.3 k	2.2 M	2.8 k

to identify QUIC servers in a stateless manner. We tested this module in our test environment and found that three implementations do not respond to the probe, namely Amazon's s2n-quic, LSQUIC and aioquic. They try to parse the entire initial packet first, only check the version afterward and do not respond to the existing module. Therefore, deployments based on these libraries are not detected by the ZMap module and are missed by related work.

In contrast, sending a QUIC initial packet including a valid Client Hello results in a response by all three implementations in our test environment. However, it triggers a handshake and key exchange, thus creating state on the server. To reduce state during ZMap scans, we extracted a valid initial packet from a QUIC communication as raw bytes, but manually set a reserved version. This extracted and customized packet can be used as pre-defined payload in combination with the existing UDP ZMap module. It triggers a VN which can be implemented without state on the server (cf. [17]) and works with all tested libraries. We have published the required configuration and payload along with our test environment [49].

We compared the three possibilities within an Internet-wide scan: *(i)* a VN with zero bytes, *(ii)* a QUIC initial with version 1, and *(iii)* a QUIC initial with a reserved version. Table 1 shows results from a scan during October 2023. The approaches with zero bytes or a proper initial packet result in similar sets of identified deployments. However, our newly proposed approach with a valid QUIC initial and a reserved version identified 2.6 M more IPv4 and 7.4 M IPv6 targets. These targets are operated by few ASes, mainly Amazon. While s2n-quic responded to initial packets with a correct version in our test environment, Amazon deployments do not respond but probes time out. This is due to missing SNI values as shown in the next section.

Key take-away: Properly selecting a QUIC probe during ZMap scans can drastically influence the number of identified deployments. Our test environment helps to identify high-quality probes and can be used in the future to adapt scans to potential library or protocol changes.

5.2   The Importance of SNI

Servers often host multiple domains on the same IP address. The client can add the desired domain as SNI to the Client Hello during the TLS handshake. Therefore, the server can use the correct certificate and authenticate itself. In case no SNI is provided, the server can *(i)* serve a default certificate, *(ii)* respond with an error, or *(iii)* time out the connection attempt.

Analyzing uniquely identified deployments by the third ZMap approach (see Table 1) reveals that implementations require a proper QUIC initial packet, respond with a version negotiation in case of an incorrect version, but do not respond to a QUIC initial without SNI. Amazon owns most of these addresses. Thus, we searched for a domain hosted by them and conducted a handshake with 1 k IP addresses revealed by ZMap and the domain set as SNI. In this scenario, the handshake is successful with 97.7 % of the addresses. Missing values result in timeouts and not necessarily QUIC errors that can be analyzed. This indicates the importance of SNI values during QUIC handshakes.

To further investigate this, we scanned all identified QUIC deployments with the QScanner without SNI values and all addresses we could map to a domain based on DNS with SNI. The latter set covers fewer IP addresses because we could not map domains to all addresses. For IPv4, ZMap discovers 11.8 M addresses that react to our new probe. Using the QScanner, handshakes with 522.6 k addresses without SNI are successful (see Table 2). Considering the scan with SNI values 601.9 k addresses were tested. At least one handshake with 411.9 k (68.4 %) addresses was successful.

As indicated by the total (836.2 k), the overlap of successful addresses between SNI and no SNI scans is small. Out of the 522.6 k IPv4 addresses with a successful handshake without SNI, we could map 63.1 k to a domain. The handshake with an SNI was also successful for 58.0 k (91.0 %) out of these addresses. In contrast, only 14.1 % out of 411.9 k addresses with a successful SNI handshake were also successful without an SNI value. Without SNI, they often resulted in generic TLS errors or timeouts. This shows the importance of SNI for many deployments.

We used addresses from AAAA records besides the IPv6 Hitlist during our scans. Therefore, we can identify more QUIC-capable targets than the hitlist (7.9 M compared to 320 k). Similarly to IPv4, scans without SNI resulted in more timeouts. For SNI, the increased number of IPv6 addresses compared to IPv4 was mostly due to Amazon which often responds with eight AAAA records compared to at most four A records per domain. The distribution of IPv6 addresses is more biased toward a few ASes. 73.7 % of addresses were within Amazon (AS16509), the main contributor to fully responsive prefixes [51].

Comparing these results to previous findings by Zirngibl et al. [48] shows a significant increase in found QUIC deployments (from 2.1 M to 11.8 M), their AS distribution (from 4.7 k to 8.1 k) and the number of successful handshakes (from 148.2 k to 503.1 k). The comparison is made based on IPv4 ZMap scans and handshakes without SNI, but the same effects can be seen for IPv6 and scans with SNI. Two deployments mostly dominate the new addresses. *(i)* Akamai (AS16625) with 5.6 M addresses, a 20-fold increase, and *(ii)* Amazon (AS16509) with 2.2 M addresses not mentioned in 2021 [48]. The deployment by Amazon is not necessarily a new deployment, but only detected now due to the different ZMap probe. In comparison, the deployment by Akamai could also be detected with the previously existing ZMap QUIC module and is thus new [12].

Key take-away: Scanning with or without SNI drastically influences results. SNI values are essential with some operators, especially CDNs hosting multiple domains on the same IP address, to guarantee successful handshakes. In some cases, e.g., Amazon, incorrect or missing SNI values result in timeouts. This leads to incorrect conclusions regarding the existence of QUIC deployments.

6 Library Identification

As shown in Sect. 5 and by related work, different QUIC libraries show different behavior even though they implement the same standards. Based on these differences, we developed an approach to actively identify QUIC libraries.

6.1 Identification Methodology

Our goal was to identify libraries with few packets and a high success rate. Therefore, we used our test environment to evaluate different scanner configurations (*e.g.*, different TLS parameters) and the individual behavior of server implementations. Our tests resulted in an approach relying on QUIC-specific properties, namely CONNECTION_CLOSE frames and transport parameters. Appendix Table 5 provides information which methodology identifies which library.

Table 3. Example error messages in response to the ALPN value `invalid`. The first column indicates who formats this exact error message. Full list: [49].

	Implementation	Code	Message
Scanner	quiche, quic-go	0x178	tls: no application protocol
	XQUIC	0x178	ALPN negotiation failed. Server didn't offer any protocols
Server library	LSQUIC	0x178	no suitable application protocol
		0x150	TLS alert 80[a]
	NGINX	0x178	handshake failed
	Quant	0x178	(frame type: 0x6): PTLS error 120 (NO_APPLICATION_PROTOCOL)
	Quinn	0x178	peer doesn't support any known protocol
	Haskell QUIC	0x178	no supported application protocols

[a]LSQUIC checks SNI before ALPN and sends this error if SNI is required/incorrect.

Error Message. The CONNECTION_CLOSE frame can provide a detailed error message, *i.e.*, a string without a specified structure. We expect that individual deployments do not change this behavior, and the respective string is specific for a library. We identified an unusual ALPN value as a reliable method to trigger an error during the handshake. ALPN values are simple strings without limitations and thus allow us to send *invalid*, a value we argue is highly unlikely used.

We found that nine implementations send a unique error message as response to unknown ALPN values. Table 3 shows error messages of some implementations in our test environment and from public servers. While all libraries indicate the same error, they send different text formats and slightly different content.

Seven implementations do not send a specific error message, and the QScanner outputs a message from quic-go internally. Interestingly, XQUIC continues with the handshake but does not include an ALPN extension, resulting in the QScanner terminating the connection. The mvfst container image does not send an error but only indicates an error in internal logs. However, testing against `facebook.com` results in a unique error message. The same error is visible in the server logs in our local environment but most likely not sent due to a different configuration. LSQUIC checks the SNI value first and ALPN second. However, both error messages are unique compared to others in our experience and identify LSQUIC. We saw matching error messages for the remaining implementations with a server in our local environment and a test server on the Internet.

We verified the respective messages are created within the published code and found that messages have not been changed within the last three to five years for most libraries. For example, the error message within LSQUIC has not been updated for at least five years as of January 2024 [22]. Thus, we expect them to remain stable in the future as well.

Table 4. Examples of transport parameter [13] orders and TLS extensions [14] to identify QUIC libraries. The last two randomize their order. Full list: [49].

Impl	Ext	Transport Par.	Impl	Ext	Transport Par
s2n-quic	43-51	4-6-7-8-0-f	quiche	51-43	0-3-4-6-7-8-a-b-f
	51-43	4-6-7-8-0-f	NGINX	51-43	4-8-6-7-3-b-a-0-f-2
LSQUIC	51-43	4-6-7-8-0-f-2		43-51	4-8-6-7-3-b-a-0-f-2
HAProxy	43-51	0-2-f-3-4-6-7-8	Google Q	51-43	set(0, 2, 3, 4, 6, 7, 8, f)
mvfst	43-51	0-6-7-4-8-a-3-2-f	Akamai Q	43-51	set(0, 2, 3, 4, 6, 7, 8, f)

Transport Parameters. Besides the error message usable for nine libraries, we use the order of transport parameters. Our test environment reveals that most implementations send specific transport parameters in a particular order. The explicit transport parameters are implemented and set by individual QUIC libraries and are not necessarily part of the TLS library, *e.g.*, BoringSSL. We create an identifier for each QUIC library representing the parameters and their order. We remove their values as they can be more easily configured. In 2021, on- and off-net deployments of Facebook and Google sent the same set of parameters but with different values [48]. Table 4 shows examples for different libraries.

While the order of most implementations is stable, we found that four libraries randomize the order of a constant set (*e.g.*, Quant [31] and Google Quiche [11]). However, the set alone can not be used as an identifier. One permutation of Google Quiche and Akamai QUIC collides with Quinn and HAProxy respectively. Nevertheless, the latter libraries do not randomize the order. Therefore, a second handshake can be used to check whether permutations are visible or the identifier remains stable. Furthermore, for some implementations, the set of transport parameters and their order is the same, *e.g.*, for XQUIC and

Haskell QUIC. Therefore, we add the order of the *key share* and *supported versions* extensions from the received Server Hello. Both extensions must be present in TLS 1.3, and thus do not depend on a deployment-specific configuration.

Additional Considerations. During the development of our approach, we tested the following features but excluded them: Additional TLS parameters could be used. However, QUIC relies solely on TLS 1.3, thus a simplified feature set compared to TCP/TLS stacks. No specific features from earlier TLS versions and only four instead of hundreds of ciphers can be used [15, 41]. Furthermore, features are often unique to the TLS library. Some libraries are shared by implementations and information is not necessarily unique. Furthermore, information can be hardware (*e.g.*, preferred cipher suites) or configuration dependent (*e.g.*, supported groups). While this can be used as information to differentiate specific deployments, it can not be used to identify libraries. Different QUIC features are not visible during the initial handshake (*e.g.*, the acknowledgement frequency or a path MTU discovery) or not necessarily static. For example, we find 48 different configurations of transport parameter values across all quic-go deployments but all with the same order. We leave an extension to our approach to future work.

Key take-away: QUIC libraries send different error messages or transport parameter orders and can therefore be identified. While these identifiers can change in the future, our published test environment can be used to identify new error messages testing against updated server implementations.

6.2   Library Classification on the Internet

We updated our scans (see Sect. 5) and used the QScanner with two configurations: *(i)* sending a valid h3 ALPN and *(ii)* sending invalid. We focused on the classification of libraries per IP address and expect a consistent QUIC deployment on a reachable target.

Stability of Identified Libraries. We verified this assumption based on the stability of our identification. Some targets can have multiple identifications due to multiple domain names mapping to a single IP address. Within a single scan, we saw no inconsistent libraries per IP address, even though up to 100 domains were used as SNI values for each IP address. Furthermore, we evaluate the stability of our identification over nine months comparing our library identification of four scans, one from April, July, October and December 2023. 6.6 M IPv4 targets were visible in all four scans and were identified in at least one. 6.3 M were identified in all four scans; for 99.99 % of them, the identified library was consistent. It shows that the identification is consistent and stable and not influenced by network or timing events, *e.g.*, caching. Only for 215 IPv4 addresses changes were visible. They are distributed across 53 different ASes and consist of different library combinations. We argue that our identification is stable and not influenced by network or timing effects. Changes are due to actual deployment changes. For the remaining evaluation, we focused on the scan from October 2023.

Resolving Collisions. For 462 IPv4 addresses, the order of transport parameters either matches HAProxy/Quinn or the respective permutation of Akamai

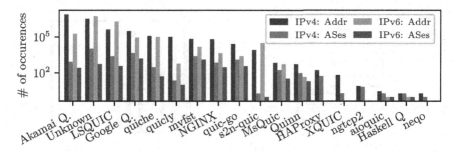

Fig. 3. Libraries on the Internet based on both scans (with/without SNI) and our approach. Handshakes are not necessarily successful with all targets.

QUIC/Google Quiche, which randomize the order (see Table 4). However, for 146 (31.6 %) targets, the *Error Message*-based approach identified the library as Quinn and directly resolved the collision (see Table 3). For the remaining 316 targets indicating a collision between HAProxy and Akamai QUIC, we tried to conduct three additional handshakes and succeeded for 172. The remaining targets were not responsive anymore because the scans were conducted one week later. Given the randomization, it is highly unlikely that multiple consecutive handshakes result in the same order. Thus, for 171 targets, the order remained consistent, and we identified the library as HAProxy. One target randomized the order during all three scans and was classified as Akamai QUIC.

Approach Effectiveness. In the IPv4 scan without SNI, we could identify the library for 7.9 M targets based on the *Error Messages* and 519.7 k based on the transport parameters. This shows the utility of the first approach. We could identify a majority of target libraries because no successful handshake is required. As shown in Sect. 5, many targets hosted by CDNs require a valid SNI, *e.g.*, Akamai. However, they terminate with a usable *Error Message* in case of an invalid ALPN value. While the *Error Messages* approach identifies libraries on more targets, the transport parameter approach allows the identification of more distinct libraries. It identified the library for 167.2 k previously unknown targets. For 352.5 k targets, both approaches resulted in a matching classification, and in total 8.0 M (67.1 %) targets could be classified. Using a domain as SNI allowed identifying libraries for 433.4 k targets. In this scenario, fewer results are based on the *Error Messages* (289.8 k) than the transport parameters (411.4 k). Combining both the results from the scan with and without SNI slightly improved the results, allowing us to identify the library on 8.2 M targets, 68.0 % of initially identified deployments from ZMap.

The unknown category consists of 3.9 M IPv4 addresses. However, 2.2 M (56.7 %) are hosted by Amazon and 658.2 k (17.2 %) by Cloudflare. For both, scans without the correct SNI resulted in a timeout or a generic TLS error and due to load balancing, we can only map domains to few IP addresses. We tested 1 k random IP addresses from Amazon with a valid SNI again (see Sect. 5), can conduct handshakes with 977 targets and identified the library as s2n-quic. Therefore, we could identify more libraries, but opted to not use the same SNI

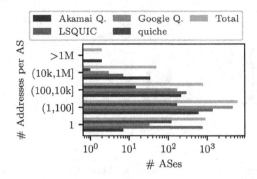 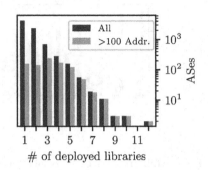

Fig. 4. Distribution of identified libraries in IPv4 targets across ASes. Note the log x-axis.

Fig. 5. Number of distinct libraries within ASes. Note the log y-axis.

with multiple millions of targets within the same provider for ethical reasons. The remaining targets with unknown libraries mostly run into timeouts thus no information is available (another 5.8 %), result in generic TLS errors or can not provide a certificate (*e.g.*, for scans without SNI). We argue that for most of these targets, a valid SNI and thus a successful handshake results in required information to identify the library based on our approach.

Deployed Libraries. Figure 3 shows the classification for the IPv4 and IPv6 scans, including the number of visible ASes. We found all libraries at least once, but Kwik. Figure 4 shows the distribution of libraries across ASes. Most ASes contain between 1 and 100 QUIC deployments we can identify, but ASes with more than 100 or even 10 k deployments are visible. The most visible implementation for IPv4 is the library from Akamai, which is also the most present operator based on IP addresses deploying QUIC in general. It is the only library with more than 1 M deployments in two ASes each (both operated by Akamai itself). However, it is only visible in 864 ASes, compared to the libraries of other large so-called hyper giants [20], *e.g.*, Google (4.7 k ASes) and Facebook (2.5 k ASes). Interestingly, quic-go (1.3 k ASes) and LSQUIC (2.5 k ASes) show the largest distribution across different networks besides the libraries of hyper giants. They are used for production-ready QUIC servers in Caddy and LiteSpeed. Therefore, deployments based on these products can easily use QUIC, *e.g.*, [2,21].

Figure 5 shows up to 12 libraries within a single AS. In most ASes only one (4.2 k, 54.3 %) or two (2.3 k, 30.1 %) implementations are visible. Within Amazon (AS16509) (66.9 % s2n-quic, 23.7 % LSQUIC) and Digital Ocean (AS14061) (93.3 % LSQUIC, 3.9 % quic-go) the highest variety of implementations is visible. Thus, identifying an AS operator does not necessarily reveal the used library. Amazon develops its own library, but visible servers also rely on different QUIC libraries. Our methodology is required to correctly identify an implementation.

HTTP Server Header. We compare our identification to HTTP Server headers. The header should represent the HTTP implementation, but QUIC libraries often directly include HTTP/3. However, the value is only available for 699.2 k IPv4 addresses, 79.8 % of targets with a successful QUIC handshake and 8.5 %

of targets we can identify a library of. Thus, it is no replacement for our approach, and we only used it to cross-check our identification. Our scans show that if available, the Server header value often matches or relates to the identified library. Thus, for most targets relying on Akamai QUIC, the Server header is *AkamaiGHost*, while *gvs* is used with Google Quiche. Appendix Table 6 shows two prominent header values for the top 10 libraries. We mainly focused on deployments outside the AS of the respective developers and found the same results supporting the correctness of our approach. However, the value does not always reveal the library and is only available after a successful handshake,

Key Take-away: *Our approach is stable and works for the majority of targets. Compared to a more incomplete approach based on HTTP Server headers, our error message-based approach succeeds because no successful handshake is required. We find deployments for 18 different QUIC libraries on the Internet and 12 different libraries within a single AS, showing the QUIC ecosystem diversity.*

7 Conclusion

We analyzed QUIC deployments and used server libraries on the Internet. We evaluated QUIC scanning approaches and are able to detect previously unseen deployments based on a new ZMap scan approach. Furthermore, we developed an effective approach based on *Error Messages* and the order of transport parameters to identify QUIC libraries. Eighteen different libraries are in use with at least one target on the Internet, and up to 12 libraries are visible within a single AS. We can identify the library used by more than 8.0 M IPv4 and 2.5 M IPv6 addresses. *Network analysts and researchers need to be aware of this and consider potential differences based on different QUIC stacks.*

Impact on Research. The variety of seen QUIC implementations shows that key goals of the standardization have been met, and libraries can be quickly developed and deployed. However, this diversity potentially increases the complexity of the network and might influence research regarding performance and security. Our library identification could extend recent studies, *e.g.*, to evaluate the impact of libraries on performance [4], to analyze the spin bit [19] or to evaluate ECN in QUIC [33] instead of relying on more incomplete HTTP server headers.

Test Environment. We presented and published [49] an environment for testing scanners against different QUIC libraries. During the development of our scan and library identification methodology, we mainly limited ourselves to this environment to reduce the impact on the network and deployed QUIC servers. The environment helps to easily test scanners against various implementations without impacting real-world deployments. It can easily be used in the future to adapt our approach to potential library changes.

Malicious Use. Our identification approach can expose vulnerable deployments, thereby offering more effective means to identify exploitable systems. We have contacted developers of QUIC libraries about our findings and the potential to identify their specific implementations.

Ethics. During our Internet-wide scans, we follow community standards [6,7,29]. We scan at a limited rate, use a local blocklist based on opt-out requests, and clearly identify our measurement infrastructure in WHOIS, RDNS, and via a hosted website on the machines. We have received no complaints.

Acknowledgements. The authors would like to thank the anonymous reviewers and our shepherd Robin Marx for their valuable feedback. This work was partially funded by the German Federal Ministry of Education and Research under the project PRIMEnet, grant 16KIS1370.

A   Full List of Test Servers

Table 5. Functional servers available in our test environment (Env). GH indicates a Github repository. The listed domains can additionally be used as test servers for respective libraries on the Internet. We confirmed with Akamai that they maintain their own library forked from Google Quiche. The last two columns indicate which methodology can be used to identify the respective library (see Sect. 6). The transport parameter (TP) order allows identifying more libraries but requires a successful handshake.

Implementation		Env	Domain	ALPN	TP
quic-go	GH: quic-go/quic-go	√	*interop.seemann.io*		√
ngtcp2	GH: ngtcp2/ngtcp2	√	*nghttp2.org*		√
Quant	GH: NTAP/quant	√	*quant.eggert.org*	√	√
mvfst	GH: facebookincubator/mvfst	√	*www.facebook.com*	√	√
quiche	GH: cloudflare/quiche	√	*cloudflare-quic.com*		√
Kwik	GH: ptrd/kwik	√		√	√
picoquic	GH: private-octopus/picoquic	√	*test.privateoctopus.com*		√
aioquic	GH: aiortc/aioquic	√	*quic.aiortc.org*	√	√
Neqo	GH: mozilla/neqo	√			√
NGINX	quic.nginx.org/	√	*quic.nginx.org*	√	√
MsQuic	GH: microsoft/msquic	∼ᵃ	*[*].sharepoint.com*		√
XQUIC	GH: alibaba/xquic	√			√
LSQUIC	GH: litespeedtech/lsquic	√	*www.litespeedtech.com*	√	√
HAProxy	GH: haproxytech/quic-dev	√	*www.haproxy.org*		∼ᵇ
Quinn	GH: quinn-rs/quinn	√			∼ᶜ
s2n-quic	GH: aws/s2n-quic	√	*[*].cloudfront.net*	√	√
Haskell Q.	GH: kazu-yamamoto/quic		*mew.org*		√
Google Q.	GH: google/quiche		*google.com*	√	∼ᶜ
Akamai Q.			*akaquic.com*	√	∼ᵇ

ᵃ The container only supports hq-interop handshakes but no h3.
ᵇ The Transport parameter order of HAProxy can collide with one permutation of Akamai QUIC (see Sect. 6).
ᶜ The Transport parameter order of Quinn can collide with one permutation of Google Quiche (see Sect. 6).

Table 5 lists all QUIC servers integrated in our local test environment introduced in Sect. 4. We use already available Docker images for each implementation provided to the QUIC Interop Runner [36]. Furthermore, it lists QUIC targets on the Internet used besides our local environment to extend and verify our insights. These targets are either listed as test servers for implementations by the Internet Engineering Task Force (IETF) working group [16] or official company pages by the developers of libraries. The table further shows which methodology can be used to identify each library. While the identification based on ALPN values can only be done for nine libraries, it does not require a successful handshake. This is especially helpful for deployments that require an SNI value as shown in Sect. 5 and Sect. 6.

B Overview about seen HTTP Server Header Values

Table 6 shows the two most common HTTP Server header values for each implementation and IPv4 target. The header can only be collected for targets with successful QUIC handshakes and a successive HTTP request. The analysis combines results from the scan without and with SNI. For the latter, different server headers can be received and are combined as comma separated list.

Table 6. Most common HTTP Server header value for top 10 implementations. Note that the header is only available after successful handshakes and HTTP requests. An asterisk indicates aggregated values containing the leading substring.

| Impl | Target | HTTP Server Header | | |
		Value	Targets	%
Google Quiche	213 034	gvs 1.0	109 571	51.43
		gws	39 821	18.69
LSQUIC	194 953	LiteSpeed	193 411	99.21
		MCP_VCLOUD_LIVE	283	0.15
quiche	121 756	cloudflare	104 973	86.22
		nginx	9126	7.50
quicly	91 602	Varnish	88 923	97.08
		Cloudinary	822	0.90
NGINX	48 875	nginx	28 160	57.62
		GreyWS	4906	10.04
quic-go	12 526	Caddy	11 325	90.41
		nginx	426	3.40
s2n-quic	7509	AmazonS3	1640	21.84
		CloudFront	1071	14.26
mvfst	5317	proxygen[*]	5316	99.98
		gunicorn, proxygen[*]	1	0.02
Akamai QUIC	2376	Akamai[*]	1653	69.57
		TLB	87	3.66
MsQuic	927	Microsoft[*]	805	86.84
		Kestrel, Microsoft[*]	52	5.61

References

1. A QUIC implementation in pure Go (2023). https://github.com/quic-go/quic-go
2. A2 Hosting: The Best LiteSpeed Web Server Hosting Solution (2023). https://www.a2hosting.com/litespeed-hosting/
3. Althouse, J., Smart, A., Nunnally, Jr., R., Brady, M.: Easily Identify Malicious Servers on the Internet with JARM (2020). https://engineering.salesforce.com/easily-identify-malicious-servers-on-the-internet-with-jarm-e095edac525a
4. Bauer, S., Sattler, P., Zirngibl, J., Schwarzenberg, C., Carle, G.: Evaluating the benefits: quantifying the effects of TCP options, QUIC, and CDNs on throughput. In: Proceedings of the Applied Networking Research Workshop, Association for Computing Machinery (2023). https://doi.org/10.1145/3606464.3606474
5. Cloudflare: quiche (2023). https://github.com/cloudflare/quiche
6. Dittrich, D., Kenneally, E., et al.: The Menlo Report: Ethical principles guiding information and communication technology research. US Department of Homeland Security (2012)
7. Durumeric, Z., Wustrow, E., Halderman, J.A.: ZMap: fast internet-wide scanning and its security applications. In: Proceedings of USENIX Security Symposium (2013)
8. Gasser, O., et al.: Clusters in the expanse: understanding and unbiasing IPv6 hitlists. In: Proceedings of ACM International Measurement Conference (IMC) (2018). https://doi.org/10.1145/3278532.3278564
9. Gbur, Y., Tschorsch, F.: QUICforge: client-side request forgery in QUIC. In: Proceedings of Network and Distributed System Security Symposium (NDSS) (2023). https://doi.org/10.14722/ndss.2023.23072
10. Google: QUICHE (2023). https://github.com/google/quiche
11. Google: Randomization of QUIC Transport Parameter Order (2023). https://github.com/google/quiche/blob/main/quiche/quic/core/crypto/transport_parameters.cc#L832
12. Herrera, J.C.: Deliver Fast, Reliable, and Secure Web Experiences with HTTP/3 (2023). https://www.akamai.com/blog/performance/deliver-fast-reliable-secure-web-experiences-http3
13. IANA: QUIC Transport Parameters (2023). https://www.iana.org/assignments/quic/quic.xhtml#quic-transport
14. IANA: Transport Layer Security (TLS) Extensions (2023). https://www.iana.org/assignments/tls-extensiontype-values/tls-extensiontype-values.xhtml
15. IANA Registry: TLS Cipher Suites (2023). https://www.iana.org/assignments/tls-parameters/tls-parameters.xhtml#tls-parameters-4
16. IETF QUIC Working Group: Implementations (2023). https://github.com/quicwg/base-drafts/wiki/Implementations
17. Iyengar, J., Thomson, M.: QUIC: A UDP-Based Multiplexed and Secure Transport. RFC 9000 May 2021. https://doi.org/10.17487/RFC9000
18. Jaeger, B., Zirngibl, J., Kempf, M., Ploch, K., Carle, G.: QUIC on the highway: evaluating performance on high-rate links. In: IFIP Networking Conference (Networking) (2023)
19. Kunze, I., Sander, C., Wehrle, K.: Does it spin? On the adoption and use of QUIC's spin bit. In: Proceedings of ACM International Measurement Conference (IMC) (2023). https://doi.org/10.1145/3618257.3624844
20. Labovitz, C., Iekel-Johnson, S., McPherson, D., Oberheide, J., Jahanian, F.: Internet Inter-Domain Traffic. ACM SIGCOMM Computer Communication Review (2010). https://doi.org/10.1145/1851275.1851194

21. Lapiene, A.: Improving Website Performance with LiteSpeed (2019). https://www. hostinger.com/blog/introducing-litespeed
22. LSQUIC: LSQUIC ALPN error (2024). https://github.com/litespeedtech/lsquic/ blame/master/src/liblsquic/lsquic_mini_conn_ietf.c#L2157
23. Lyon, G.F.: Nmap Network Scanning: The Official Nmap Project Guide to Network Discovery and Security Scanning (2009)
24. Marx, R., Herbots, J., Lamotte, W., Quax, P.: Same standards, different decisions: a study of QUIC and HTTP/3 implementation diversity. In: Proceedings of the Workshop on the Evolution, Performance, and Interoperability of QUIC (2020)
25. Mücke, J., et al.: Waiting for QUIC: On the Opportunities of Passive Measurements to Understand QUIC Deployments (2022). https://arxiv.org/abs/2209.00965
26. Nawrocki, M., Hiesgen, R., Schmidt, T.C., Wählisch, M.: QUICsand: quantifying QUIC reconnaissance scans and DoS flooding events. In: Proceedings of ACM International Measurement Conference (IMC) (2021). https://doi.org/10.1145/ 3487552.3487840
27. Nawrocki, M., Tehrani, P.F., Hiesgen, R., Mücke, J., Schmidt, T.C., Wählisch, M.: On the interplay between TLS certificates and QUIC performance. In: Proceedings of ACM International Conference on emerging Networking Experiments and Technologies (CoNEXT), November 2022. https://doi.org/10.1145/3555050. 3569123
28. Nepomuceno, K., et al.: QUIC and TCP: a performance evaluation. In: 2018 IEEE Symposium on Computers and Communications (ISCC) (2018)
29. Partridge, C., Allman, M.: Addressing ethical considerations in network measurement papers. Commun. ACM (2016)
30. Piraux, M., De Coninck, Q., Bonaventure, O.: Observing the evolution of QUIC implementations. In: Proceedings of the Workshop on the Evolution, Performance, and Interoperability of QUIC (2018)
31. Quant: Randomization of QUIC transport parameter order (2023). https://github. com/NTAP/quant/blob/main/lib/src/tls.c#L857
32. Rüth, J., Poese, I., Dietzel, C., Hohlfeld, O.: A First Look at QUIC in the Wild. In: Proceedings Passive and Active Measurement (PAM) (2018)
33. Sander, C., Kunze, I., Blöcher, L., Kosek, M., Wehrle, K.: ECN with QUIC: challenges in the wild. In: Proceedings of ACM International Measurement Conference (IMC) (2023). https://doi.org/10.1145/3618257.3624821
34. Sander, C., Kunze, I., Wehlre, K.: Analyzing the influence of resource prioritization on HTTP/3 HOL blocking and performance. In: Proceedings Network Traffic Measurement and Analysis Conference (TMA) (2022)
35. Schwartz, B.M., Bishop, M., Nygren, E.: Service binding and parameter specification via the DNS (SVCB and HTTPS Resource Records). RFC 9460, November 2023. https://doi.org/10.17487/RFC9460, https://www.rfc-editor.org/info/ rfc9460
36. Seemann, M., Iyengar, J.: Automating QUIC interoperability testing. In: Proceedings of the Workshop on the Evolution, Performance, and Interoperability of QUIC (2020)
37. Shamsi, Z., Nandwani, A., Leonard, D., Loguinov, D.: Hershel: single-packet OS fingerprinting. IEEE/ACM Trans. Netw. (2016). https://doi.org/10.1145/2637364. 2591972
38. Shreedhar, T., Panda, R., Podanev, S., Bajpai, V.: Evaluating QUIC performance over web, cloud storage, and video workloads. IEEE Transactions on Network and Service Management (2022)

39. Sosnowski, M., Zirngibl, J., Sattler, P., Carle, G.: DissecTLS: a scalable active scanner for TLS server configurations, capabilities, and TLS fingerprinting. In: Proceedings of Passive and Active Measurement (PAM) (2023). https://doi.org/10.1007/978-3-031-28486-1_6

40. Sosnowski, M., et al.: Active TLS stack fingerprinting: characterizing TLS server deployments at scale. In: Proceedings of Network Traffic Measurement and Analysis Conference (TMA) (2022)

41. Thomson, M., Turner, S.: Using TLS to Secure QUIC. RFC 9001, May 2021. https://doi.org/10.17487/RFC9001

42. Tyunyayev, N., Piraux, M., Bonaventure, O., Barbette, T.: A high-speed QUIC implementation. In: Proceedings of the 3rd International CoNEXT Student Workshop (2022)

43. Volodina, E., Rathgeb, E.P.: Impact of ack scaling policies on QUIC performance. In: 2021 IEEE 46th Conference on Local Computer Networks (LCN) (2021). https://doi.org/10.1109/LCN52139.2021.9524947

44. Web Almanac: Negotiating HTTP/3 (2021). https://almanac.httparchive.org/en/2021/http#negotiating-http3

45. Wolsing, K., Rüth, J., Wehrle, K., Hohlfeld, O.: A performance perspective on web optimized protocol stacks: TCP+TLS+HTTP/2 vs. QUIC. In: Proceedings of the Applied Networking Research Workshop (2019)

46. Yang, X., Eggert, L., Ott, J., Uhlig, S., Sun, Z., Antichi, G.: Making QUIC quicker with NIC offload. In: Proceedings of the Workshop on the Evolution, Performance, and Interoperability of QUIC (2020). https://doi.org/10.1145/3405796.3405827

47. Yu, A., Benson, T.A.: Dissecting performance of production QUIC. In: Proceedings of the Web Conference (2021). https://doi.org/10.1145/3442381.3450103

48. Zirngibl, J., Buschmann, P., Sattler, P., Jaeger, B., Aulbach, J., Carle, G.: It's over 9000: analyzing early QUIC deployments with the standardization on the horizon. In: Proceedings of ACM International Measurement Conference (IMC) (2021)

49. Zirngibl, J., Gebauer, F., Sattler, P., Sosnowski, M., Carle, G.: Test Environment and Identification Tools (2023). https://github.com/quic-hunter/libraries

50. Zirngibl, J., Sattler, P., Carle, G.: A first look at SVCB and HTTPS DNS resource records in the wild. In: 2023 IEEE European Symposium on Security and Privacy Workshops (EuroS&PW), pp. 470–474 (2023)

51. Zirngibl, J., Steger, L., Sattler, P., Gasser, O., Carle, G.: Rusty clusters? Dusting an IPv6 research foundation. In: Proceedings of ACM International Measurement Conference (IMC) (2022). https://doi.org/10.1145/3517745.3561440

User Privacy

Trust Issue(r)s: Certificate Revocation and Replacement Practices in the Wild

David Cerenius[1], Martin Kaller[1], Carl Magnus Bruhner[1(✉)], Martin Arlitt[2], and Niklas Carlsson[1]

[1] Linköping University, Linköping, Sweden
`carl.magnus.bruhner@liu.se`
[2] University of Calgary, Calgary, Canada

Abstract. Every time we use the web, we place our trust in X.509 certificates binding public keys to domain identities. However, for these certificates to be trustworthy, proper issuance, management, and timely revocations (in cases of compromise or misuse) are required. While great efforts have been placed on ensuring trustworthiness in the issuance of new certificates, there has been a scarcity of empirical studies on revocation management. This study offers the first comprehensive analysis of certificate replacements (CRs) of revoked certificates. It provides a head-to-head comparison of the CRs where the replaced certificate was revoked versus not revoked. Leveraging two existing datasets with overlapping timelines, we create a combined dataset containing 1.5 million CRs that we use to unveil valuable insights into the effect of revocations on certificate management. Two key questions guide our research: (1) the influence of revocations on certificate replacement behavior and (2) the effectiveness of revocations in fulfilling their intended purpose. Our statistical analysis reveals significant variations in revocation rates, retention rates, and post-revocation usage, shedding light on differences in Certificate Authorities' (CAs) practices and subscribers' decisions. Notably, a substantial percentage of revoked certificates were either observed or estimated to be used after revocation, raising concerns about key-compromise instances. Finally, our findings highlight shortcomings in existing revocation protocols and practices, emphasizing the need for improvements. We discuss ongoing efforts and potential solutions to address these issues, offering valuable guidance for enhancing the security and integrity of web communications.

1 Introduction

Trust is paramount for secure communication on the web. To uphold the trust that we communicate with the correct service, HTTPS (HTTP over TLS), the dominant protocol for delivering web content, relies on X.509 certificates. At a high-level, each of these certificates binds a public key to the identity of the owner(s) of that key; this serves as a guarantee that the identity of an otherwise anonymous party (domain) is as claimed. However, maintaining the continued trustworthiness of these certificates requires not only their proper issuance and

P. Richter et al. (Eds.): PAM 2024, LNCS 14538, pp. 293–321, 2024.
https://doi.org/10.1007/978-3-031-56252-5_14

management, but also their timely revocation in case of compromise, fraudulence, or misuse. Two essential aspects of maintaining the integrity and security of web communications are therefore to (1) revoke certificate that are no longer trusted and (2) replace them with new, trustworthy certificates.

In this paper, we present the first data-driven characterization of the certificate replacements (CRs) of revoked certificates, in which we provide a head-to-head comparison of the CRs associated with revoked vs. non-revoked certificates. By taking advantage of two existing and complementing datasets with overlapping collection periods, we first create a combined dataset consisting of 1.5 million CRs and their associated revocation statuses. Using this dataset, we then compare the CRs for which the replaced certificate was revoked versus those for which it was not revoked and provide new insights into the effects that revocations have on certificate management. To help guide the research, we aimed to address two previously not answered questions:

- What effect(s) do revocations have on certificate replacement behavior?
- How effectively are replacements preventing post-revocation usage?

In our analysis, we use statistical comparisons of several properties to identify differences in the characteristics of revoked and non-revoked certificates. Our study reveals statistically significant discrepancies that can be attributed to differences in the certificate management practices seen across the issuing Certificate Authorities (CAs). For example, the revocation rates vary from a fraction of a percent to over 17% for individual CAs that partially can be mapped to differences in their revocation requirements. We also found that the retention rates varied significantly among CAs, indicating that the CA's handling of revocations and overall satisfaction with their services affect subscribers' decisions.

In addition, a notable percentage of certificates were either directly observed to have been used (meaning actively provided as part of an HTTPS handshake, collected in one of our datasets) after revocation or estimated to have been used after revocation. For example, 7% of the revoked certificates were observed after their revocations when preferably a reissued or otherwise replacing certificate should be used instead. Using the replacing certificate as an indicator of a certificate's actual lifetime, we estimated that at least 24% of the revoked certificates in our dataset were used despite their revoked status, with the periods of illegitimate advertisement ranging from a few days to multiple years. The extent of post-revocation usage varied by CA, validation types, and revocation reasons. Perhaps most concerning was that certificates with "Key Compromised" as the revocation reason had the highest observed post-revocation usage, raising concerns about how these possible key-compromise instances were handled.

Finally, to provide concrete guidance, we also use our findings and insights to highlight some of the current problems with the existing revocation protocols and practices, we also provide a discussion of ongoing efforts and possible solutions to address some of these issues.

The remainder of the paper is organized as follows. Section 2 introduces the necessary background on X.509 certificates and current revocation practices. Section 3 describes the datasets and the methodology used to combine the datasets. In Sect. 4 we present our results, aimed at addressing the above guiding questions. We then discuss our findings, highlight problems with existing revocation protocols and practices, and discuss possible improvements in Sect. 5. Finally, Sect. 6 presents related work, before Sect. 7 concludes the paper.

2 Certificates and Their Lifetime

X.509 Certificates: The X.509 standard defines the public key certificates used by TLS (and hence also HTTPS) to verify the legitimacy of the public keys used as part of the Public-Key Infrastructure (PKI) specified in RFC 5280 [4]. This RFC covers (among other things) certificate format, semantics, and standardized fields like serial numbers, issuer details, signatures, and validity periods, along with various extensions.

Certificate Issuer: An X.509 certificate may either be self-signed or issued by a certificate authority (CA). As the term suggests, self-signed certificates can be generated by anyone as they are issued, received, and signed by the same entity (for instance a web domain) without third-party involvement [38,47]. Consequently, all major web browsers will reject these certificates as there is no way to validate them [38]. The more common approach is to utilize CAs, where a CA is a third-party entity/organization that issues, signs, and acts as a guarantor for the certificate's validity. CAs are also able to issue certificates to themselves in which case they are regarded as self-issued [4].

Validation Type: While not part of the X.509 PKI specification, the standard-defining CA/Browser Forum defines three types of SSL/TLS certificates [7,9]:

- **Domain Validation (DV):** Issued as soon as ownership of the domain in question has been demonstrated (usually through e-mail validation).
- **Organization Validation (OV):** In addition to the domain, the issuing CA validates other information to verify the legitimacy of the organization.
- **Extended Validation (EV):** Similar requirements to OV certificates but with a much stricter vetting process (generally requiring more time).

A certificate in one of these categories is identified by an Object Identifier (OID) of the corresponding type in the `certificatePolicies` extension [4,9].

Validity Period: The validity period of a certificate is the time span between the `notBefore` and `notAfter` timestamps, inclusive, defined in the certificate [4]. A CA is only required to maintain information about a certificate's status during this time. The set validity period varies depending on the CA and validation type. However, the general trend across CAs is that validity periods are getting shorter. For example, over the last few years the CA/Browser Forum Baseline Requirements (BR) [9] has gone from capping validity for new certificates at 39 months (~1186 days) in 2015 to 398 days in 2020 [6], with intentions in 2023 to further reduce down to 90 days in the future [45].

Certificate Replacements: To ensure that the certificates used by a domain (or web server) are valid and up-to-date, certificates must regularly be replaced.

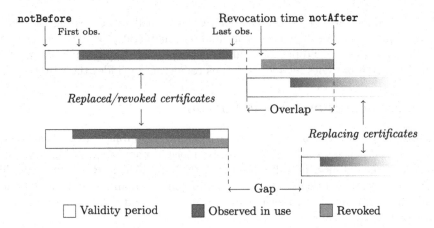

Fig. 1. Validity overlap and gap. Definitions are the same with or without a revocation.

When a certificate is replaced by another certificate, a certificate replacement (CR) occurs. While replacements generally happen near the end of a certificate's validity period [5], some replacements are done with some margin ahead of the certificate expiry while others are made after expiry. We define a validity *overlap* as the intersection of the new certificate's validity period with that of the previous one. Similarly, we say that a validity *gap* occurs (see Fig. 1) if there is a discontinuity in the two validity periods. Having validity overlap is a good practice (often simplified and facilitated by automation) that is important to guarantee availability of a service, since a validity gap will result in an invalid period impacting service access (serving as a mismanagement indicator [5]).

For the analysis in this paper, we use the CRs identified by Bruhner et al. [5]. Focusing on certificates observed in use via large-scale scans, they define a CR as a relation between a pair of observed certificates, where the IP address, port number, and `subjectCN` (entity name, including cases of so-called wildcard subdomains) of the certificates match, thus capturing them being valid for the same entity and usage. Additionally, to form a CR, the replacing certificate must begin and end its validity period later than the begin and end, respectively, of the replaced certificate's validity period, allowing for both overlaps and gaps as defined above. For full details, we refer to the paper by Bruhner et al. [5].

Certificate Revocations: There are several reasons that the trust in a certificate must be revoked before it expires. For example, if a certificate's private key is compromised or an integral information field warrants modification, the issuing CA might be obliged to revoke (invalidate) the certificate in question [4]. There are currently two main methods of revocation (both having some shortcomings and later improvements that we will discuss in 5):

- **Certificate Revocation List (CRL):** As per the original X.509 PKI certificate RFC [4], a CRL issuer (typically a CA) publishes lists of revoked certificates, available through a link under the `cRLDistributionPoints` extension of the certificate. This link can be used to download the CRL and ascertain the presence of the serial number associated with a given certificate.

- **Online Certificate Status Protocol (OCSP):** Within the X.509 PKI, OCSP, defined in a separate RFC [37], provides real-time revocation information on an on-request basis [37]. In contrast to CRLs, updated every 24 h by CAs, OCSP servers always deliver up-to-date revocation details without the need to fetch an entire list of serial numbers (which might contain several hundred thousand entries), and certificate statuses are generally removed within seven days of certificate expiry [23].

Certificate Transparency (CT): Since 2018, both Google and Apple [10] require CAs to add all issued certificates (regardless of type) to one or more append-only logs [26]. The main goal of CT is to combat misissuance of certificates by allowing the public to audit them. The logs can be operated by anyone as long as one follows the specified standards; however, the largest ones are almost exclusively run by CAs or browser vendors [40]. As of today, there is no widely implemented revocation transparency solution. Instead, CRLs (when available) are the most reliable source for revocation times and revocation reasons.

3 Dataset Creation

This section describes the originating datasets and how they were merged and refined to create a combined dataset that fits the purpose of our analysis.

3.1 Original Datasets

This paper leverages complementing features of two existing datasets with overlapping collection periods. The first dataset contains a large number of observed *certificate replacements* [5], capturing the replacing certificate and relative timing of when a certificate was replaced. The second dataset contains all *certificate revocations* with certificates that were revoked before their expiry and that had an expiry date between March 2 and April 1, 2020 [23].

Replacement Dataset [5]: The replacement set was derived from publicly available Rapid7 logs collected as part of Project Sonar [35,36]. In particular, the certificates observed in weekly/biweekly scans of port 443 across the full IPv4 address space were used to reconstruct (artificial) certificate replacement (CR) relations. This dataset spans from Oct. 2013 to July 2020, and contains 129 million CRs.

Revocation Status Dataset [23]: The revocation status set was compiled using Certificate Transparency (CT) logs to check for any certificates expiring within the period of March 2 to April 1, 2020. The day before expiry (and periodically for 120 days afterwards in case of revocation) OCSP statuses were collected and saved for every certificate. In total, this dataset contains 49 million certificates out of which 1.08 million (2.18%) were revoked.

3.2   Creation of a Combined Dataset

For our analysis, we created a combined dataset that includes both certificate replacement and revocation information for a large set of certificates expiring between March 2 and April 1 (2020). This is made possible by recognizing that the CRs collected by Bruhner et al. [5] includes the CRs for a large set of the 49 million certificates that Korzhitskii and Carlsson [23] collected revocation status information about (all with expiry during the period above). First, we considered all CRs (from the set of 129 million CRs) for which the replaced certificate expired between March 2 and April 1, 2020 (and for which we therefore had access to accurate revocation information in the 49 million certificates of the revocation status set). This corresponded to 6 million CRs (as illustrated in Fig. 2a), to which we appended the data of the revocation status set.

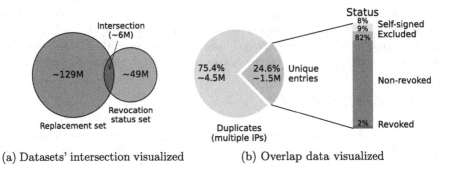

(a) Datasets' intersection visualized   (b) Overlap data visualized

Fig. 2. Overview of the dataset analyzed in this paper.

Next, we removed all duplicate CRs (i.e., those that differed only in the IP addresses where the certificates were observed), after which we were left with 1.5 million certificates (as illustrated in Fig. 2b). We then removed self-signed certificates (as those are not included in the revocation status set)—noting that these certificates have been found to make up the majority of invalid certificates on the internet [11]—as well as all certificates for which the OCSP queries did not offer either a status **revoked** or **good** (we denote these "Excluded", also including a mix of timeouts as well as the **unknown** and **unauthorized** responses). With this, we were left with 1.2 million unique CRs for our combined dataset.

3.3   Augmenting with Revocation Times and Revocation Reasons

As the revocation status set did not provide revocation times or reasons, we augmented the dataset by collecting more than 300,000 complete CRLs from the roughly 2,400 distribution points (gathered by Korzhitskii et al. [23]).

CRLs usually contain multitudes of revoked serial numbers and their associated revocation times/reasons. This posed a bit of a challenge as there was no mapping between the CRL distribution point URL and CA. This led to every

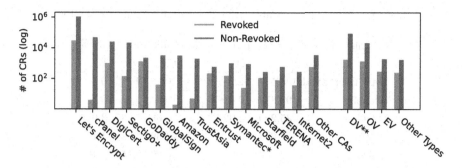

Fig. 3. Total number (in logarithmic scale) of CRs per CA and type.

serial number having to be individually searched for among the approximately 250 GB of CRLs available to us. In total, the revocation times and reasons for 3,768 certificates ($\approx$ 10% of all revocations, as explained below) were successfully obtained and are used for the analysis of revocation time in Sect. 4.7. Notably, this does not include data for Let's Encrypt, constituting 89% of all revocations, as they did not support CRL until September 2022 [17], and TrustAsia that did not operate their own root or CRL before August 2020 [46].

3.4 Limitations

Neither of the two used datasets are perfect. First, the replacement set contains only certificates found via IPv4 scans of port 443. While broader scans (e.g., more ports) could have increased the observed lifetimes, we note that most HTTPS servers use port 443. Second, the Project Sonar scans are conducted relatively infrequently (biweekly) and occasionally miss certificates. Since this affects the granularity with which we can estimate the observed lifetimes of certificates, we report both observed and approximated lifetime values, the latter being a calculated approximation explained in Sect. 4.7. Third, the scans may also miss many certificates found in CT logs, potentially causing us to miss some certificates of interest. However, this dataset has the advantage that it captured certificates in use (not only certificates with some intended validity period), helping us focus on certificates observed in the wild. Fourth, the dataset is from 2020. As noted, several changes in the certificate landscape have since happened and, at that time, Let's Encrypt did not use CRLs, preventing timing analysis of their certificate revocations (possible for most other revoked certificates).

3.5 Ethical Statement

This paper does not pose any ethical issues. By using datasets collected for prior works, we limit the extra load faced by servers. Furthermore, the measurements used here (e.g., IP scans, OCSP status requests, and CRLs) are expected to contribute only a small portion of the overall load typically seen by the servers. Finally, all data were collected from public infrastructures using public protocols.

Table 1. Selected certificate authorities sorted by number of CRs.

Issuing CA	# of CRs	Revocation rate (%)	Validation type (%)		
			DV	OV	EV
Let's Encrypt	1,106,587	2.75	100	0	0
cPanel	98,819	0.01	100	0	0
DigiCert	35,299	2.92	22.69	73.35	3.91
Sectigo+	28,663	0.50	94.39	4.48	1.13
GoDaddy	7,756	17.07	96.29	2.15	1.13
GlobalSign	4,916	0.81	41.33	56.79	1.77
Amazon	3,259	0.06	100	0	0
TrustAsia	2,080	0.24	99.90	0.10	0
Entrust	1,640	13.48	0	83.11	16.89
Symantec*	1,188	12.96	56.90	42.93	0
Microsoft	1,030	2.43	0	0	0
Starfield	888	12.61	97.07	1.91	1.01
TERENA	705	11.77	0	76.45	23.55
Internet2	652	5.83	0	100	0
Other CAs	59,051	1.01	1.66	2.71	0.19

4   Characterization Results

4.1   Summary of Dataset

Figure 3 shows the total number of revoked and non-revoked CRs for all CAs with at least 500 CRs with roots approved certificates. Here, we say that a certificate is root approved if it was validated by all three major browser vendors' trust stores at the time of the collection (Apple, Microsoft, and Mozilla/NSS; Chrome had not yet released its own root store at the time [44]). As a reference point, we also included an "Other" category that contained all other CRs. To simplify the reading going forward, Sectigo, including certificates issued under their old Comodo brand, will be denoted as *Sectigo+*; Symantec, including certificates issued by GeoTrust (when they were still under the Symantec PKI), will be denoted as *Symantec**; and DV certificates, excluding certificates issued by Let's Encrypt (as explained in the next section), will be denoted *DV***.

We note that Let's Encrypt dominates the dataset, accounting for approximately 83% of the total number of CRs and 89% of all revocations. No other CA comes close in terms of pure quantity. Part of the high Let's Encrypt numbers are due to their 90-day validity policy and widespread use of their ACME client (Certbot) that simplify both replacement and revocations, but also a mass-revocation event that took place around the time of the data collection.

Note: To simplify reading, we use the name of the CA to refer to certificates issued by that CA. Nevertheless, we stress that it is ultimately the subjects that are responsible for the certificate's usage, including many types of revocations.

4.2 Revocation Rates

Table 1 summarizes the revocation rates of certificates of all root approved CAs with at least 500 CRs. To simplify comparisons of CAs, we also include a breakdown of each CA's share of DV, OV, and EV certificates observed in the CRs.

Big Differences in CAs' Revocation Rates: While the overall revocation rates are similar to those observed in prior works (e.g., [19,23,29,48]), and revocations typically are relatively rare (all things considered), we observe big differences between the revocation rates of individual CAs, with revocation rates ranging from a fraction of a percent (Amazon and cPanel) to 17% (GoDaddy).

At this time, it should also be noted that part of the higher-than-average revocation rate seen for Let's Encrypt (2.75%) is due to a mass revocation event that took place in March 2020. This event was triggered by a Certification Authority Authorization (CAA) rechecking bug [28] (when the revocation data was collected) but did not affect the security of the users. As Let's Encrypt only offers DV certificates, this results in DV certificates being the primary validation type. For this reason, we excluded Let's Encrypt from the DV category when presenting data as they would otherwise essentially be identical.

From the table, it is also apparent that most of the CAs with fewer CRs (Starfield, Symantec, Internet2, and TERENA) have noticeably higher revocation rates in general compared to the larger CAs (e.g., Let's Encrypt or DigiCert). This is consistent with a similar study on revoked certificates, retrieved from CT Logs, by Halim et al. [19]. This phenomenon could in part be explained by smaller CAs having different customer bases (the same study found for example that a majority of Starfield's revocations was due to domain owners ceasing operations). While this pattern does not match the lower revocation rates observed for the "Other" category, we note that this category also contains certificates that are not validated by the major root stores and other certificates that for which we saw more irregular behaviors.

Influence of Revocation Policies: Another factor that appears to affect the relative revocation rates seen with different CAs is their revocation policies. While all CAs are expected to follow the CA/Browser Forum Baseline Requirements (BRs) [9], we have found (in a not yet published related work) that there are differences in who can request revocations, revocation procedures, and revocation reasons. Of special note here is Amazon, who has the second-lowest revocation rates of the reported CAs but also has (1) the most stringent requirements for who can request revocation (exclusively the subscriber) and (2) the most unaccommodating revocation procedures (no round-the-clock support for Certificate Problem Requests and no publicly readily available revocation instructions). At the other end of the spectrum, we have found that Starfield states that

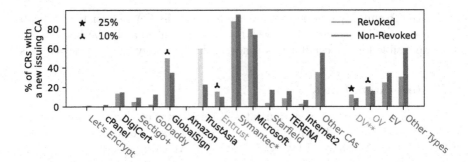

Fig. 4. Percentage of CRs with a different issuing CA for the replacing certificate. A transparent bar/box denotes five or fewer datapoints. The black symbols signify the degree of Z-test bias for the revoked population and a colored CA/type-name indicates a Fisher bias in the respective direction that the color represents.

they will revoke a certificate if the subscriber fails to pay any invoice, possibly contributing to their higher-than-average revocation rates.

4.3   Issuer Changes and CA Retention Rates

The decision of whether a subscriber chooses to remain with their current CA or to switch to a new one when replacing their certificate can reveal a lot about revocation procedures and CA satisfaction. To investigate to what degree customers are more or less likely to change CAs when revoking their certificate, we next look at the percentage of CRs where the replacing certificate was issued by a different CA than the CA that issued the replaced certificate of a CA. Figure 4 summarizes these results.

Statistical Tests and Visual Annotations: For these results and some of the later results, we used different forms of statistical testing to reveal statistically significant biases and enhance the data representation in certain graphs. As far as sample sizes allowed, we used single-tailed, two-proportion Z-tests to compare revoked ratios with non-revoked (times alternating constants, $(1.1/1.25/2)$). When an insufficient number of data points were available for those tests, we applied binomial tests as a complement, with n and k being taken from the revoked population and the "true" proportion p coming from the non-revoked population. Both of these tests use a significance level of 90% and will be presented as a range of symbols in the bar charts depending on the degree of bias. This was also coupled with Fisher's exact test at a 95% significance level as a definitive indicator of bias between revoked and non-revoked samples.

Big Differences in Retention Rates: We see a massive spread in the joint averages between CAs as Let's Encrypt, cPanel, and Amazon seem to have virtually no subscribers leaving them while Microsoft and Symantec both have noticeably lower retention rates. Symantec's case can, just as Bruhner et al. [5]

theorized, be explained by Google over this time period implementing a plan to distrust all Symantec issued certificates [18].

Mostly Small Effect of Revocations: At an aggregate level, we observe that there is not much of a difference between the revoked and non-revoked ratios. If anything, there is even a small bias towards the non-revoked CRs switching their issuing CA. The deviating CAs are GlobalSign and Entrust who both display a slight partiality of 10 percent in the revoked direction (even though GlobalSign is missing the Fisher bias). As for the types, revoked DV certificates having poorer CA retention rates could simply be explained by low validation requirements leading to an easy switch in case of subscriber dissatisfaction.

4.4   Validity

Figure 5 shows a box-and-whisker plot of the validity period of revoked certificates compared with non-revoked (divided by CA and type). While the validity periods vary greatly among CAs, some offer a diverse range of validity periods, while others (e.g., Let's Encrypt) offer only one. We note that for the CAs with variable validity periods, the revoked certificates typically had significantly longer validity periods than the non-revoked. For cPanel, two out of the four revoked certificates (transparent since too few samples) had a validity period of a year but were revoked immediately, suggesting they may have been misissued.

It is also worth noting that the revoked certificates in our dataset were issued before validity periods were capped at 398 days in 2020. The above trend is particularly evident when examining larger CAs such as DigiCert, Sectigo, or GoDaddy as well as DV and OV type certificates. EV certificates breaking this tendency could be explained by the rigorous validation requirements leading to a more homogeneous subscriber group, especially compared to that of DV certificates.

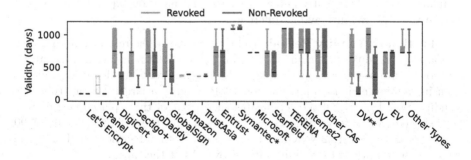

Fig. 5. Validity time measured in days per CA and type. The plotlines in this box-and-whisker plot are capped at the 10th and 90th percentile, with the box representing the 25th to 75th percentile, and a black line marking the median.

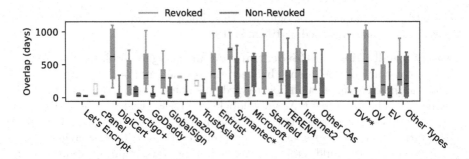

Fig. 6. Overlap in validity time for CRs measured in days, per CA and type.

4.5   Overlap

The degree of overlap between the two certificates in a CR captures to what extent the subscriber (or the CA in case of automated replacements, e.g., with Let's Encrypt and cPanel) desires a safety margin. Figure 6 compares the overlaps of revoked and non-revoked certificates. As perhaps expected, with the exception of Microsoft, the revoked certificates exhibit significantly higher levels of overlap compared to their non-revoked counterparts. This trend is primarily due to revocations frequently happening at the start of a certificate's validity period [19].

We expect that part of the reason for Microsoft diverging is that most of their non-revoked certificates have a (seemingly) static 2-year validity period and a median overlap of 600 days, meaning that most of their **good** certificates were only used for a few months before being replaced without getting revoked afterwards (considering Microsoft's low (2.43%) revocation rate).

Of the other CAs, some CAs stand out more than others when it comes to divergence in overlap for revoked vs. non-revoked CRs, with DigiCert and Symantec being particularly noteworthy. As for validation types, both DV and OV certificates also display big differences.

Implication of Validity Period: To better visualize the relationship between overlap and validity, we include Fig. 7 which shows heat maps with these statistics for both non-revoked and revoked CRs, respectively. Per definition (and as seen in the figure) it is impossible for a CR to have a larger overlap than the validity period of any of the certificates (here that of the replaced certificate). As expected, we observe distinct heat zones within the validity periods of 90 days, 180 days, 1 year, 2 years, and 3 years for both categories of CRs. These were common options for validity offered by CAs at the time.

Early Revocations and Late Replacements of Non-revoked Certificates: Comparing the figures more closely, we note that non-revoked CRs exhibit strong heat patterns at the bottom along the x-axis, indicating minimal overlap, whereas the revoked CRs show a more prominent middle diagonal (especially for certificates with longer validity) but minimal heat at the bottom. The strong

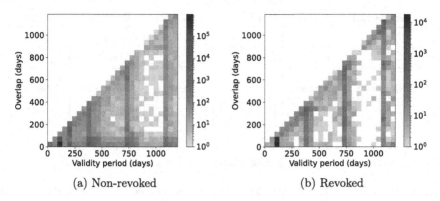

(a) Non-revoked   (b) Revoked

Fig. 7. Heat map of the relationship between validity and overlap. Heat colors are represented on a logarithmic scale, with white indicating an absence of data.

middle diagonal signifies very early replacements (implying early revocations), matching early revocation patterns previously reported by Halim et al. [19], for example. As a corollary to this, we note the lack of instances (heat) at the bottom along the x-axis, which is reasonable considering that a revocation rarely happens at the very end of a certificate's validity as making revocations that late would serve little to no practical purpose.

Per-CA Analysis: The CDFs presented in Fig. 8 further corroborate our findings that revoked CRs exhibit earlier overlap than non-revoked ones. Here, for each CA, we show CDFs of the normalized overlap (i.e., overlap divided by validity period) for both revoked and non-revoked CRs. As we noted in Fig. 6, DigiCert and Symantec (together with GoDaddy, Entrust, and Starfield) show the greatest disparity. Microsoft once again stands out as the sole CA with a significantly earlier overlap for non-revoked CRs than revoked ones. This supports the theory of how they only use their good certificates for a short while before replacing them. Specifically, observing the dotted lines in the CDF, half of Microsoft's non-revoked certificates have overlap just 17% into their validity period while the revoked ones reach the 50 percent mark at 78% into their validity. Also contrasting the rest, Let's Encrypt and Sectigo show very little difference between revoked and non-revoked CRs, which could potentially be an indicator of certificate misuse. We have already established that a revocation generally occurs early on in a certificate's lifetime, which should mean that revoked certificates also get replaced early on (the case for most of our CAs). This indicates that revoked CRs, like non-revoked ones with late replacements, may imply subscribers disregarding their certificate's revoked status.

Mass Revocation Event: Given that all certificates in our dataset expire between March 2nd and April 1st, coinciding with Let's Encrypt's mass revocation event in early March, it is of high interest to scrutinize the conduct of Let's Encrypt certificates during this period. Interestingly, most of their subscribers with revoked certificates still used the default automated renewal period [27]

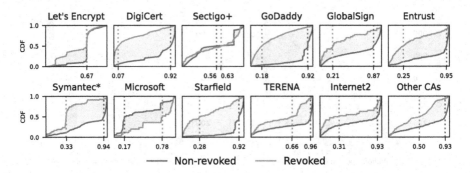

Fig. 8. Normalized CDFs of how far into the replaced certificate's validity overlap begins per CA. The dotted lines mark 50 percent of the respective population. cPanel, Amazon, and TrustAsia have been excluded due to lack of data.

after two-thirds of the validity period has passed (orange CDF), something we see is even more rigorously followed for non-revoked certificates (blue CDF). Based on this, we can draw the conclusion that most certificates revoked in the event were already scheduled for replacement anyway, meaning the revocation had minimal effect on the replacement behavior of these certificates. Furthermore, given that 96.6% of our revoked Let's Encrypt certificates were part of the event, it is not surprising that the revoked and non-revoked CDFs are relatively homogeneous.

4.6   Gaps

Gaps are much more frequently observed in non-revoked compared to revoked CRs. This is shown in Fig. 9, where we show statistics for the top CAs and the different revocation types. It is worth noting that DigiCert, GoDaddy, and Starfield exhibit an especially high rate of gaps among their certificates. The visibly obvious exception to this trend is cPanel. However, as seen by the transparent color of the revoked bar for cPanel, there is not enough data to draw any conclusions for cPanel. In particular, cPanel only has four revoked certificates (out of which one has a gap).

While it is rare for replacements with revoked certificates to contain gaps, it seems that when a gap does exist, it tends to be larger than in non-revoked CRs. This is illustrated in Fig. 10, where we show the distribution of the gapped CRs. Interestingly, Let's Encrypt demonstrates the most substantial disparity between the two groups, which could be a mismanagement indicator for revoked certificates. As we have already established, revocations typically occur early in a certificate's validity period, which affords the subscriber ample time to obtain a replacement. Therefore, if a revoked certificate is replaced too late (resulting in a gap) it is more likely to be forgotten for a longer time period compared with non-revoked ones, as gaps in those CRs typically arise from the subscriber missing the expiry date. This always results in warnings to users that tend to result in the issue quickly being resolved.

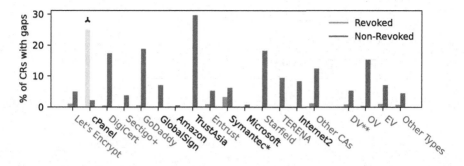

Fig. 9. Percentage of CRs with gaps in validity time per CA and type.

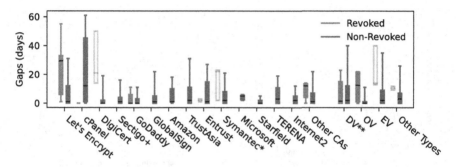

Fig. 10. Gaps measured in days per CA and type.

4.7 Revocation Time Analysis

To understand how quickly revoked certificates were replaced in practice, we compared the revocation times with the period over which each revoked certificate was used, which we call its *lifetime*.

Revocation Times: Using the CRL data, we were able to extract revocation times for every revoked certificate in our dataset except for those issued by Let's Encrypt and TrustAsia as explained in Sect. 3.3. This resulted in a set of 3,768 revoked certificates ($\approx$ 10% of all revocations) with recorded revocation times and reasons. We next describe two lifetime estimates.

Lifetime Estimation: The time period between the beginning of a certificate's validity and the last time the certificate was observed in the Project Sonar scans is what we from hereon will call its *observed lifetime*. The observed lifetime is a conservative estimate of the actual lifetime due to the limitations in the originating scans in terms of frequency and responses, which gives a considerable error margin. To improve the potentially late discovery of new certificates, we use a certificate's `notBefore` date instead of the first observation since our main focus is to compare the end of the lifetime against the revocation time, meaning an accurate beginning of lifetime does not affect the comparison.

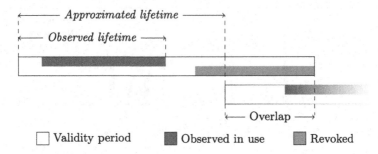

Fig. 11. Revoked certificates, with possible discrepancy between observed and approximated lifetime illustrated.

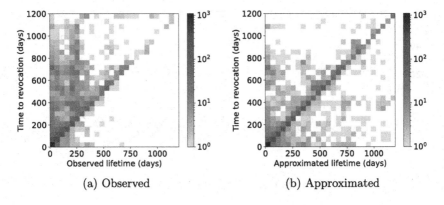

(a) Observed   (b) Approximated

Fig. 12. Time to revocation and measured lifetime (days).

We also introduce a second way to calculate the lifetime of a certificate. We call this the *approximated lifetime*. This is the time between the replaced and replacing certificates' notBefore timestamps (as can be noted in Fig. 1). In the majority of cases, the replacing certificate is at its earliest advertised on its notBefore date [11], meaning the replaced certificate was in all likelihood used up to that point. As a result, the approximated lifetime should be a better but still conservative estimate of the certificate's actual lifetime.

The problem of observation inaccuracy is demonstrated in Fig. 11 where the revocation, in this case, takes place after the last observation making it seem as if the certificate never was illegitimately used. However, taking the replacing certificate into account makes it clear that the original certificate was indeed used despite being revoked.

Revocations in Relation to Their Lifetime Estimates: To capture this relationship, Fig. 12 shows heat maps of (a) the observed lifetime against the revocation time and (b) the approximated lifetime against the revocation time. First, there is noticeable diagonal observed at $x = y$, where the revocation time and lifetimes are equal. In the observed lifetimes (Fig. 12a) the majority of certificates are, however, located above this diagonal, meaning that the time to revocation is greater than the observed lifetime of the certificate. This implies that they were revoked sometime after the end of their lifetime. Still, there are some certificates under the $x = y$ diagonal, meaning those were observed to be used after being revoked. Specifically, out of the 3,768 revoked certificates, 281 were observed to be used after they were revoked, including 256 for over a day, 170 for more than a week, and 90 for more than a month after revocation.

Examining the approximated lifetime (Fig. 12b), we observe a noticeable shift, indicating that many more certificates were likely used after revocation. Here, the $x = y$ diagonal is also more distinct, implying that a greater number of certificates were replaced in close proximity to their revocation times. Out of the 3,768 revoked certificates, 941 were approximated to be used after revocation with a threshold of at least one hour to increase accuracy. Among those, 824 were approximated to be used for more than a day, 500 for more than a week, and 311 for more than a month after revocation.

Our initial expectation was that most certificates would have a similar end-of-life time and revocation time, with the replaced certificate being revoked shortly after its subsequent replacement. However, a large portion of the certificates have an observed lifetime of less than 200 days while the time to revocation exceeds 200, 400, or even 600 days. When considering the approximated lifetime on the other hand, this pattern of revoking the certificate months/years after its replacement becomes much less pronounced and the diagonal becomes more prominent instead. It is also worth noticing that a great number of the certificates were observed only once, which might be the reason we see this behavior of late revocations in relation to the lifetime. With this in mind, our belief that the approximated lifetime gives a better estimate of the actual lifetime compared with the observations is strengthened.

Here, it should be noted that also the approximated lifetime sometimes underestimates the lifetime. For example, out of the 281 certificates observed after revocation, 78 had a replacement certificate that could have been used instead. In those cases, despite that there appear to have been a new certificate issued that eventually were used, the subscriber kept advertising the revoked certificate for some time period after the revocation, leaving the valid replacement idle, before finally switching. For these cases, both lifetime estimates are underestimating the actual lifetime of the replaced certificate.

Normalized Revocation-to-Lifetime Comparisons: To allow capture of the relative timings, Fig. 13 shows a normalized heat map, where we normalize both the lifetime estimates and the revocation periods with the validity periods of the revoked certificates. Comparing with the non-normalized versions, we observe that the diagonal line now becomes more prominent using both lifetime measurements. This is due to the shorter validity certificates contributing along the whole line instead of just at the bottom. A phenomenon which also becomes more apparent is that there are quite a few certificates in the approximated lifetime graph (Fig. 12b) that have had a lifetime equal to their validity yet were revoked very early on. As it seems quite unlikely for the subscriber to revoke their

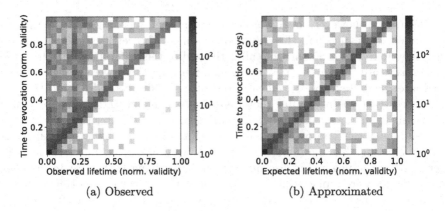

Fig. 13. Time to revocation and measured lifetime (normalized).

own certificate and then did not try to replace it, two probable explanations are that these certificates (i.e., that still are used after revocation) were involuntarily revoked, meaning that the subscriber might not have been aware of the event, or that the subscriber somehow failed to replace them (at least on the observed machines).

Post-revocation Usage: To summarize the above results, 7.2% of the certificates have been observed while 24% have been approximated to be used after revocation (observed rate and approximated rate, respectively). When dividing these numbers into different categories however, such as issuing CA, validation types, or revocation reasons (see Fig. 14), significant individual variation is revealed. Specifically, Microsoft had no observed revocation usage, while Sectigo, GoDaddy, and GlobalSign had an observed rate of at least 9%. Another interesting pattern is the degree of variation between the observed rate and the approximated rate. For example, Symantec shows the greatest difference with the next to lowest observed rate overall at 1.3%, but the highest approximated rate at 50.6%. In this case, the observed rate is inaccurate due to the fact that most of the Symantec issued certificates were observed just once.

As earlier theorized, if involuntary revocations are the contributing factor to certificates being used despite being revoked, then Microsoft is worth looking into as it has the lowest observed and approximated rate of all included CAs. One thing to note is that Microsoft does not issue certificates to the public[1], meaning one could say that they technically do not issue third-party certificates. While looking at Microsoft's policies regarding revocations, it becomes apparent that only they themselves (per their policy, as they solely issue certificates to affiliated domains) can request a revocation, indicating that involuntary revocations should not happen. This would furthermore strengthen the hypothesis that certificates that were used after revocation were also involuntarily revoked.

---

[1] From our data, Microsoft has only issued certificates to themselves or affiliated organizations, such as MSN or Skype etc.

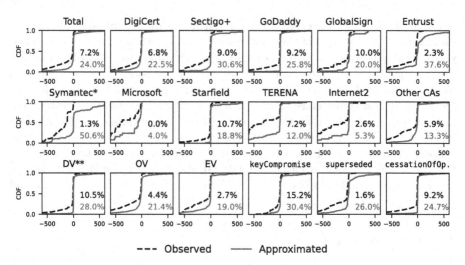

Fig. 14. Individual CDFs of lifetime minus (−) the revocation time. This corresponds to placing the revocation instance to take place at $x = 0$, meaning that all certificates where $x \geq 1$ were used for more than a day after being revoked. The exact proportions are represented by the percentages displayed in each graph. In addition to per-CA and per-type breakdowns, we also include CDFs for three noteworthy revocation reasons.

Late Post-usage of Certificates with Potentially Compromised Key: The revocation category with the highest observed rate is, worryingly enough, the case of key compromises. The vast majority of these were issued by Digi-Cert and their intermediates such as Encryption Everywhere and RapidSSL. Encryption Everywhere stands out as they are responsible for the biggest share of key compromises (mostly wildcard DV certificates) while also offering a service where third parties (primarily hosting providers) can upsell and distribute DigiCert certificates [13].

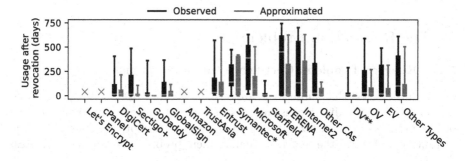

Fig. 15. Days of usage after revocation measured by observed/approximated lifetime per CA and type. The × implies that no revocation times are available.

Time Certificates Were Advertised After Being Revoked: As shown in Fig. 15, the exact amount of time certificates were advertised after being revoked varies greatly depending on the issuing CA. In the aggregate, the observed lifetime measurement displays a longer period of revocation usage compared to the approximated lifetime. This once again highlights that the approximated lifetime is a discernibly conservative measurement and suggests that the actual lifetime is often greater than the approximations. One surprising pattern is seen for Microsoft, Terena, and Internet2 which have some of the lowest overall revocation rates, yet some of the longest actual revocation usage. When looking at the validation types, it is clear that DV (10 days) has a significantly shorter median usage period compared to OV (30 days) and EV (20 days), which could simply be due to the, in general, shorter validity periods.

4.8   Key Takeaways

In this section, we have characterized and analyzed certificate replacements and corresponding revocations. We see big differences in CAs' revocation rates (0–17%) and statistical testing of the data shows big differences in retention rates, however seemingly unrelated to revocation ratios.

For CAs with variable validity periods, we see that revoked certificates typically had significantly longer validity periods than non-revoked. Naturally, the former show a significantly higher degree of overlap compared to the latter and the data further shows that revocations often occurring early on in a certificate's lifetime. The per-CA analysis found that for CAs more prominently using automated solutions, there is only a very limited difference in overlap between revoked and non-revoked certificates. This suggests a risk of mismanagement in cases of automation. Non-revoked certificates exhibit a higher frequency of gaps, while the (few) cases of revocations with gaps tend to result in larger gaps.

The revocation time analysis reveals both cases of certificates being revoked after their lifetime and those being used after being revoked. Our approximations suggests that 24% of revoked certificates are used after revocation. Worryingly, key compromises are the most common category observed in use after revocation.

5   The Revocation Problem

5.1   Observed Problem: Certificate (mis)management

Our results suggest that subscribers are mismanaging revoked certificates. While we believe that the direct consequences of using these revoked certificates are benign in most circumstances, it sets a bad standard and puts users at risk. This section looks closer at the certificate management problem of revoked certificates.

Certificates Used Despite Being Revoked: We have found the usage of revoked certificates to be a relatively widespread phenomena with a total average of 7% (observed) or 24% (approximated) of revoked certificates being used after the revocation. One explanation could be that subscribers revoke certificates but do not immediately replace them, meaning that certificates will be advertised despite being revoked. Perhaps the subscriber is lacking competence, or it could simply be that no replacement certificates have been prepared beforehand (and getting one issued is a slow process—especially for EV certificates). Although the idea of subscribers revoking their own certificates without preparing replacements first might seem strange, it is reasonable in cases of, for instance, key compromises where swift action is necessary.

Another, perhaps more probable, explanation is involuntary revocations. Since almost all CAs reserve the right to revoke certificates for different reasons without the subscribers' consent, this means that subscribers might not even be aware of these events. Even when subscribers are made aware of such events, the same issues with lacking competence and/or lead time might prevent subscribers from swiftly replacing certificates even if the CA tries to facilitate the process. One possible way to increase transparency and help improve best practices is to complement the revocation reasons included in CRLs with information about who requested the revocation.

Used Well After Revocation: Thus far, we have discovered that usage after revocation is not a rare (however unwanted) event for revoked certificates. Assuming most of them were involuntarily revoked could explain, but not justify, the certificates being advertised for a few days, since it can take a while to obtain a replacement. The problem becomes clear when considering that the majority of certificates approximated to be used after revocation were advertised for more than a week (53%) and many for more than a month (33%).

Comparing with Gaps and Overlaps: An interesting parallel can be drawn with the gaps in validity time found in the non-revoked CRs since serving an expired certificate should be comparable with serving a revoked one: both are examples of mismanagement. Gaps are not as frequent a phenomenon as usage after revocation but still relatively common (especially if disregarding Let's Encrypt and cPanel with their automated replacement services). Comparing Fig. 10 and 15 we see that gaps typically only last a day or two while revocation usage is much longer on average. We believe that the primary reason for this discrepancy is the fact that for the former case, all major web browsers display warnings informing the user that the domain in question cannot be trusted if it advertises an expired certificate [1]. This motivates subscriber to replace the expired certificate since they in all likelihood wish their website to appear trustworthy.

The same cannot be said for revoked certificates, even though—similar to an expired certificate—a revoked certificate should also be considered invalid (untrustworthy). The difference comes down to the fact that many browsers, including Chrome, Edge and almost all mobile browsers, to a large extent do not check the revocation status of a certificate at all [29,31,32,43]. As a result, most end-users (Chrome and Edge together accounting for about 70% of the global browser market share [41,42]) trying to access a website with a revoked certificate will receive no warning, leaving the user oblivious to the fact that they were served a non-trustable certificate, and leading to the subscriber not being aware/not caring (compared to expiry) that their certificate is revoked.

In contrast to gaps and uses after revocation, overlaps signal a better certificate management as an increased overlap in the case of revocations implies that at least some effort has been given to introduce a replacing certificate earlier than in the case of non-revocation. Consequently, examples like the average management of certificates from Let's Encrypt and Sectigo where the differences in overlap between revoked and non-revoked certificates are not that prominent instead implies a mismanagement of certificate replacements.

The Solution at Brief: Given the mismanagement that we see in our data, we argue that there is need for improvement in terms of automation regarding revocation events. We discuss a possible solution in Sect. 5.3.

5.2   Evolution of Revocation Protocols and Current Trends

In addition to mismanagement of revocations, it is evident from our findings that revocations are not being respected. This can largely be attributed to CRL and OCSP not being well suited for the internet in their current forms. To provide some context before we suggest how to address the certificate replacement problem associated with revoked certificates, we next discuss some related trends and on-going improvements to the revocation protocols themselves.

Challenges with Current Revocation Protocols: It might seem strange that browser vendors would choose to disregard revocation checking when, for instance, a compromised certificate can have quite dire consequences. The reality of the situation, however, is that both CRLs and OCSP have flaws that make them less than ideal for the modern internet landscape [25]. First, both protocols add delay when making HTTPS requests (especially CRLs since they can be several MBs in size), and since speed is a big selling point for web browsers, this becomes a rather undesirable trait. Second, each of the two has a single point of failure, meaning that if a CRL distribution point or an OCSP server becomes unavailable, a large number of certificates will be affected. Finally, CRLs are usually updated in set time intervals (e.g., every 24 h) meaning the protocol can be quite ineffective or slow against certificate compromises, and OCSP, that is designed to improve upon some of the weak points of CRLs (less overhead and always up-to-date revocation statuses), has privacy concerns since CAs are able to monitor browsing habits by checking which domains have their revocation statuses requested (by domain visitors contacting their OCSP responders).

Revocation Protocol Improvements: One of the most widely deployed revocation protocol improvements as of today is OCSP stapling, which tackles some of the inherent flaws of the regular OCSP by being push-based instead of pull-based [12]. This means that the client (browser) no longer has to request the revocation status of a certificate as it will automatically be fetched and presented by the server, leading to less overhead and fewer privacy concerns for the user. OCSP stapling still has limitations, however, as the server will not pre-fetch any intermediate certificates in a certification chain, unless the "multi-stapling" extension is enabled [34], leading to additional OCSP server requests regardless. More importantly, clients will usually accept a certificate as valid if they are unable to verify its revocation status via CRL/OCSP, also known as a "soft-fail". The consequence of this is that a potential MITM attacker, possessing a compromised (and revoked) certificate, could simply intercept any outgoing OCSP requests or incoming staples, effectively forcing the client to accept the revoked certificate as valid. To combat this significant vulnerability, the OCSP Must-Staple extension was added, which if enabled in a certificate requires an OCSP staple to be included in the TLS handshake or the connection will be terminated, also known as a "hard-failure". However, during a 2018 study Chung et al. [12] found that only a very small fraction of certificates supported the extension and that none of the major browsers except Mozilla checked if the OCSP staple was included. Other recent studies have confirmed that Firefox supports OCSP Must-Staple, but Chrome does not [24].

Today, most major browsers use a proprietary push-based protocol for revocations. However, such sets typically only cover a very small fraction of all revocations on the web. Improved coverage has been achieved by using a CRL/OCSP aggregator that collects certificates from CT logs and IP scans and then searching through available CRLs and making status requests from OCSP responders [25]. By using various filters and compression techniques, CRLite [25] reduces the size of the complete list of active revocation statuses to a ~10 MB download, with daily ~0.5 MB updates to keep revocations fresh. Mozilla incorporated CRLite into their nightly build of Firefox in 2020, replacing OCSP statuses [21]. With the mandatory use of CT logs, Mozilla is able to rely solely on these (without IP scans), reducing the revocation delay to six hours. Other similar solutions include Chrome's CRLSets [43] and Firefox's OneCRL [32].

The Rebirth of CRL: After having declined steadily since 2015 [16], CRL has regained new interest from CAs and browsers with the introduction of solutions like CRLite and CRLSets. In Sept. 2022, Let's Encrypt announced that they would begin supporting CRLs to be able to facilitate the on-going transition of browsers adopting browser-summarized CRLs [17]. In July 2023, the CA/Browser Forum decided to require CRLs (from previously being optional) and instead making OCSP optional [8]. This means that the tables have turned in favor of CRL leaving OCSP behind – at least for now.

Trend Towards Shorter Validity Periods: Certificates with long validity periods pose a greater security risk in general compared to short-lived ones. If, for instance, a private key is compromised during the first month of a one-year certificate, clients will be vulnerable to MITM attacks for the remaining 11 months while a 90-day certificate would only leave them exposed for 2 months.

The concept of short-lived certificates has been widely discussed and advocated for [39]. This is also evident in recommendations by the CA/Browser Forum, which have shifted from stipulating a maximum validity of three years to one year. Furthermore, similar to when Apple announced that they would only accept certificates with a validity time of 398 days (as compared with the then-standard 825 days) [2], Google in 2023 announced that they intended to propose a reduction of certificate validity from 398 days to 90 days [45]. Even though this initiative is yet to be taken in the CA/Browser Forum, the BR has since then introduced a short-lived certificate with a maximum of 10 days validity starting March 15, 2024, that will be reduced to 7 days starting March 15, 2026 [8]. We note that this trend also likely will push subscribers to use automated certificate management solutions.

5.3   Suggested Solution: Automation of Certificate Management

The Automatic Certificate Management Environment (ACME) protocol [3] offers automation solutions for certificate issuance, verification, and revocation. However, despite its automation capabilities, some clients (e.g., EFF's Certbot for Let's Encrypt certificates) still require manual intervention for reissuance outside regular intervals [33]. As evident from our results, this can result in post-revocation usage of revoked certificates and otherwise late certificate replacements of these certificates. To address these issues, we argue that automated solutions must better incorporate reissuances when a certificate is revoked.

Notification of Subscribers and Automated Reissuance: Our data, showcasing certificate mismanagement, as evident in validity gaps and post-revocation usage, for example, calls for enhanced automation, particularly concerning revocation events. Initiating revocation events should ideally involve the CA or the subscriber, with a preference for the CA to notify the subscriber promptly when revoking a certificate at their discretion. In the case that the CA does not provide such notification, the subscriber would be dependent on the monitoring of CRLs and/or OCSP. Subscriber-initiated revocations should be accompanied by immediate reissuance requests if necessary.

Collaboration Between CAs and ACME Providers: Based on our findings, we recommend collaborative efforts between CAs and ACME client providers to bolster automated responses to revocation events. This collaboration aims to prevent the use of revoked certificates, enhance the robustness of revocation handling, and ultimately improve the secure availability of websites online while safeguarding users.

Enhancing certificate management through automation and collaboration is pivotal for addressing the challenges associated with certificate mismanagement. By automating processes, encouraging shorter validity periods, and strengthening responses to revocation events, we can mitigate risks, bolster security, and ensure the trustworthiness of web communications.

6   Related Works

Certificate Replacements: Previous studies on certificate replacements are relatively scarce with the more prominent ones focusing on mass revocation events like Heartbleed. Heartbleed was discovered in 2014 and is a bug found in an older version of OpenSSL which made it possible to extract sensitive data from the affected servers [14]. This prompted several studies to be conducted on certificates during this event, including the works by Zhang et al. [48] who analyzed certificate management by looking at reissues (replacements) and revocations, and Liu et al. [29] who focused only on revocations and CRL/OCSP characteristics. Omolola et al. found that at least 28% of domains affected by the Let's Encrypt mass revocation and with a history of regular reissuance managed to reissue their certificates within a week [33]. Perhaps most closely to ours is the work by Bruhner et al. [5]. In this paper, we make use of a specific subset of the certificate replacement relationships that they identified, extracted, and analyzed. In contrast to them, and other prior work, we focus on the relative comparison of certificate replacement relationships (e.g., gaps, overlaps, etc.) of revoked vs. non-revoked certificates. This is achieved by augmenting the replacement set with the revocation data of Korzhitskii et al. [23], enabling us to analyze the intersection of observed certificates and announced revocations. A recent work by Ma et al. [30] looks at certificate *invalidations* during a certificate's lifetime. This includes certain revocations (key compromises) but also changes in domain registrant or managed TLS certificates that do not necessarily trigger revocations, even if resulting in stale certificates. Furthermore, Ma et al. focus on certificate invalidations, irrespective of whether the certificate is actively in use or replaced. In contrast, our work relies solely on certificates observed in use with corresponding revocation status data available.

Network Scans: The certificate replacements used here were all based on data from Rapid7's network scans. Before the launch of ZMap [15] (the scanner used by Rapid7), collecting data on TLS certificates was a more tedious and rather resource-intensive task. Nevertheless, comprehensive studies were made despite this. For example, Holz et al. [20] conducted longitudinal passive and active scans on popular HTTPS domains at the time and found several causes for concern in the Web PKI landscape, particularly in broken certification chains and subject names. Durumeric et al. conducted a similar study using ZMap, scanning the IPv4 address space on port 443 (HTTPS) for over a year and retrieving roughly 42 million unique certificates. Their statistics included issuing CAs, validity periods, encryption types, and revocation reasons.

Revocations: There has been plenty of works in other areas of certificate revocations as well. Zhu et al. [49] looked at the performance of the OCSP protocol in practice and found improvements in latency and wider deployment compared to a few years prior. Kim et al. [22] studied the revocation process itself and found a handful of security threats such as CAs being slow to revoke, inaccurate "effective" revocation dates, and missing/unavailable CRL distribution points or OCSP servers. Others have studied how the status of revoked certificates sometimes change after the certificate have expired [23] or focused on the relative timing and reason of revocations [19]. However, neither of these studies considered the replacing certificate.

Reduced Validity Time: As discussed in Sect. 5.2, there is a push for short-lived certificates. Motivated by observations from their study of certificate replacements, Bruhner et al. [5] introduced the concept of "parent and child" certificates that allow for key re-usage, allowing them to use one-week certificates without introducing substantial overhead to the existing PKI. Further motivation was provided by the aforementioned study by Ma et al. [30], which estimated that a reduction of validity time of certificate from the current 398 days to (the now forthcoming) 90 days would be able to reduce the overall prevalence of staleness with over 75%, also noting that automation is a double-edge sword both enabling further reductions in certificate lifetime but at the same time presenting a risk of automatic issuance of soon-to-be stale certificates. However, in general, these trends motivate the need for good automation solutions that can provide timely reissuance both during normal conditions and when certificates are revoked. As highlighted by our results, current automation solutions do not yet appear to be satisfactory in the case that a certificate is revoked.

7   Conclusion

This paper presents the first comprehensive comparative characterization of certificate replacements of revoked certificates. Our study uncovers the complexities of certificate management in web security, delivering critical contributions and insights, including the effects revocations have on replacement behavior. Our analysis revealed significant disparities in certificate management practices among Certificate Authorities (CAs), with varying revocation rates and retention rates, demonstrating the need for standardized practices. While we have showed that certificate replacements help prevent post-revocation usage by resulting in notably longer overlaps, we alarmingly find a substantial post-revocation usage of certificates, with 7% directly observed and an estimated 24% of cases. This raises questions about the effectiveness of current revocation mechanisms and the effectiveness of replacements. To address these challenges, we advocate for enhanced automation in managing revocation events. We propose a collaborative approach between CAs and ACME client providers, emphasizing proactive notification and immediate reissuance upon revocation to bolster web security. In summary, our research offers a comprehensive understanding of certificate replacement dynamics and calls for automation and cooperation to reduce risks, strengthen security, and maintain trust in web communications.

Acknowledgments. This work was partially supported by the Wallenberg AI, Autonomous Systems and Software Program (WASP) funded by the Knut and Alice Wallenberg Foundation.

References

1. Akhawe, D., Felt, A.P.: Alice in Warningland: a large-scale field study of browser security warning effectiveness. In: Proceedings of the USENIX Security Symposium, pp. 257–272. USENIX Security 2013, USENIX Association, Washington, D.C. (2013). https://www.usenix.org/conference/usenixsecurity13/technical-sessions/presentation/akhawe

2. Apple: About upcoming limits on trusted certificates (2020). https://support.apple.com/en-us/102028

3. Barnes, R., Hoffman-Andrews, J., McCarney, D., Kasten, J.: Automatic Certificate Management Environment (ACME). RFC 8555 (2019). https://doi.org/10.17487/RFC8555

4. Boeyen, S., Santesson, S., Polk, T., Housley, R., Farrell, S., Cooper, D.: Internet X.509 Public Key Infrastructure Certificate and Certificate Revocation List (CRL) Profile. RFC 5280 (2008). https://doi.org/10.17487/RFC5280

5. Bruhner, C.M., Linnarsson, O., Nemec, M., Arlitt, M., Carlsson, N.: Changing of the guards: certificate and public key management on the internet. In: Proceeding of Passive and Active Measurement Conference, pp. 50–80. PAM 2022, Virtual (2022). https://doi.org/10.1007/978-3-030-98785-5_3

6. CA/Browser Forum: Ballot SC31: Browser Alignment (2020). https://cabforum.org/2020/07/16/ballot-sc31-browser-alignment/

7. CA/Browser Forum: Guidelines for the Issuance and Management of Extended Validation Certificates (2022). https://cabforum.org/wp-content/uploads/CA-Browser-Forum-EV-Guidelines-1.8.0.pdf

8. CA/Browser Forum: Ballot SC-063 v4: Make OCSP Optional, Require CRLs, and Incentivize Automation (2023). https://cabforum.org/2023/07/14/ballot-sc-063-v4make-ocsp-optional-require-crls-and-incentivize-automation/

9. CA/Browser Forum: Baseline Requirements for the Issuance and Management of Publicly-Trusted Certificates Version 2.0.1 (2023). https://cabforum.org/wp-content/uploads/CA-Browser-Forum-BR-v2.0.1.pdf

10. Certificate Transparency: Our Successes. https://certificate.transparency.dev/community/#successes-grid

11. Chung, T., et al.: Measuring and applying invalid SSL certificates: the silent majority. In: Proceedings of the Internet Measurement Conference, pp. 527–541. IMC 2016, ACM, Santa Monica, CA (2016). https://doi.org/10.1145/2987443.2987454

12. Chung, T., et al.: Is the web ready for OCSP must-staple? In: Proceedings of the Internet Measurement Conference, pp. 105–118. IMC 2018, ACM, Boston, MA (2018). https://doi.org/10.1145/3278532.3278543

13. DigiCert: DigiCert Encryption Everywhere Partner Program (2020). https://www.digicert.com/content/dam/digicert/pdfs/guide/partner-program-guide-en.pdf

14. Durumeric, Z., et al.: The matter of Heartbleed. In: Proceedings of the Internet Measurement Conference, pp. 475–488. IMC 2014, ACM, Vancouver, BC, Canada (2014). https://doi.org/10.1145/2663716.2663755

15. Durumeric, Z., Wustrow, E., Halderman, J.A.: ZMap: fast internet-wide scanning and its security applications. In: Proceedings of the USENIX Security Symposium, pp. 605–620. USENIX Security 2013, USENIX Association, Washington, D.C. (2013). https://www.usenix.org/conference/usenixsecurity13/technical-sessions/paper/durumeric

16. Farhan, S.M., Chung, T.: Exploring the evolution of TLS certificates. In: Proceeding of Passive and Active Measurement Conference, pp. 71–84. PAM 2023, Virtual (2023). https://doi.org/10.1007/978-3-031-28486-1_4

17. Gable, A.: A New Life for Certificate Revocation Lists - Let's Encrypt (2022). https://letsencrypt.org/2022/09/07/new-life-for-crls.html
18. Google Security Blog: Chrome's Plan to Distrust Symantec Certificates (2018). https://security.googleblog.com/2017/09/chromes-plan-to-distrust-symantec.html
19. Halim, A., Danielsson, M., Arlitt, M., Carlsson, N.: Temporal analysis of X.509 revocations and their statuses. In: 2022 IEEE European Symposium on Security and Privacy Workshops, pp. 258–265. EuroS&PW 2022, Genoa, Italy (2022). https://doi.org/10.1109/EuroSPW55150.2022.00032
20. Holz, R., Braun, L., Kammenhuber, N., Carle, G.: The SSL landscape: a thorough analysis of the x.509 PKI using active and passive measurements. In: Proceedings of the Internet Measurement Conference, pp. 427–444. IMC 2011, ACM, Berlin, Germany (2011). https://doi.org/10.1145/2068816.2068856
21. Jones, J.: Design of the CRLite Infrastructure (2020). https://blog.mozilla.org/security/2020/12/01/crlite-part-4-infrastructure-design/
22. Kim, D., Kwon, B.J., Kozák, K., Gates, C., Dumitraş, T.: The broken shield: measuring revocation effectiveness in the windows code-signing PKI. In: Proceedings of the USENIX Security Symposium, pp. 851–868. USENIX Security 2018, USENIX Association, Baltimore, MD (2018). https://www.usenix.org/conference/usenixsecurity18/presentation/kim
23. Korzhitskii, N., Carlsson, N.: Revocation Statuses on the Internet. In: Proceeding of Passive and Active Measurement Conference, pp. 175–191. PAM 2021, Virtual (2021). https://doi.org/10.1007/978-3-030-72582-2_11
24. Larisch, J., et al.: Hammurabi: a framework for pluggable, logic-based X.509 certificate validation policies. In: Proceedings of the Conference on Computer and Communications Security, pp. 1857–1870. CCS 2022, ACM, Los Angeles, CA (2022). https://doi.org/10.1145/3548606.3560594
25. Larisch, J., Choffnes, D., Levin, D., Maggs, B.M., Mislove, A., Wilson, C.: CRLite: a scalable system for pushing all TLS revocations to all browsers. In: 2017 IEEE Symposium on Security and Privacy, pp. 539–556. S&P 2017, IEEE, San Jose, CA (2017). https://doi.org/10.1109/SP.2017.17
26. Laurie, B., Langley, A., Kasper, E., Messeri, E., Stradling, R.: Certificate Transparency Version 2.0. RFC 9162 (2021). https://doi.org/10.17487/RFC9162
27. Let's Encrypt: Integration Guide. Internet Security Research Group (2016). https://letsencrypt.org/docs/integration-guide/
28. Let's Encrypt: 2020.02.29 CAA Rechecking Bug (2020). https://community.letsencrypt.org/t/2020-02-29-caa-rechecking-bug/114591
29. Liu, Y., et al.: An end-to-end measurement of certificate revocation in the web's PKI. In: Proceedings of the Internet Measurement Conference, pp. 183–196. IMC 2015, ACM, Tokyo, Japan (2015). https://doi.org/10.1145/2815675.2815685
30. Ma, Z., et al.: Stale TLS certificates: investigating precarious third-party access to valid TLS keys. In: Proceedings of the Internet Measurement Conference, pp. 222–235. IMC 2023, ACM, Montreal QC, Canada (2023). https://doi.org/10.1145/3618257.3624802
31. Microsoft: Microsoft Edge - Policies (2023). https://learn.microsoft.com/en-us/deployedge/microsoft-edge-policies
32. Mozilla: CA/Revocation Checking in Firefox (2021). https://wiki.mozilla.org/CA/Revocation_Checking_in_Firefox#OneCRL

33. Omolola, O., Roberts, R., Ashiq, M.I., Chung, T., Levin, D., Mislove, A.: Measurement and analysis of automated certificate reissuance. In: Proceeding of Passive and Active Measurement Conference, pp. 161–174. PAM 2021, Virtual (2021). https://doi.org/10.1007/978-3-030-72582-2_10

34. Pettersen, Y.N.: The Transport Layer Security (TLS) Multiple Certificate Status Request Extension. RFC 6961 (2013). https://doi.org/10.17487/RFC6961

35. Rapid7: Open Data: SSL Certificates. https://opendata.rapid7.com/sonar.ssl/

36. Rapid7: Project Sonar. https://www.rapid7.com/research/project-sonar/

37. Santesson, S., Myers, M., Ankney, R., Malpani, A., Galperin, S., Adams, D.C.: X.509 Internet Public Key Infrastructure Online Certificate Status Protocol - OCSP. RFC 6960 (2013). https://doi.org/10.17487/RFC6960

38. Sectigo: What is a Self-Signed Certificate (2021). https://sectigo.com/resource-library/what-is-a-self-signed-certificate

39. Sheffer, Y., Lopez, D., de Dios, O.G., Pastor, A., Fossati, T.: Support for Short-Term, Automatically Renewed (STAR) Certificates in the Automated Certificate Management Environment (ACME). RFC 8739 (2020). https://doi.org/10.17487/RFC8739

40. SSLmate: Certificate Transparency Log Growth. https://sslmate.com/labs/ct_growth/

41. Statcounter GlobalStats: Browser Market Share Worldwide (2023). https://gs.statcounter.com/browser-market-share

42. Statista: global market share held by leading internet browsers from January 2012 to January 2023 (2023). https://www.statista.com/statistics/268254/market-share-of-internet-browsers-worldwide-since-2009/

43. The Chromium Projects: CRLSets. https://www.chromium.org/Home/chromium-security/crlsets/

44. The Chromium Projects: Chrome Root Program Policy, Version 1.4 (2023). https://www.chromium.org/Home/chromium-security/root-ca-policy/

45. The Chromium Projects: Moving Forward, Together (2023). https://www.chromium.org/Home/chromium-security/root-ca-policy/moving-forward-together/

46. TrustAsia: TrustAsia CA Certificate Practice Statement (CPS) V1.1 (8 2020). https://repository.trustasia.com/repo/cps/TrustAsia-Global-CP-CPS_EN_V1.1.pdf

47. Yee, P.E.: Updates to the Internet X.509 Public Key Infrastructure Certificate and Certificate Revocation List (CRL) Profile. RFC 6818 (2013). https://doi.org/10.17487/RFC6818

48. Zhang, L., et al.: Analysis of SSL certificate reissues and revocations in the wake of Heartbleed. Commun. ACM **61**(3), 109–116 (2018). https://doi.org/10.1145/3176244

49. Zhu, L., Amann, J., Heidemann, J.: Measuring the latency and pervasiveness of TLS certificate revocation. In: Proceeding of Passive and Active Measurement Conference, pp. 16–29. PAM 2016, Heraklion, Greece (2016). https://doi.org/10.1007/978-3-319-30505-9_2

SunBlock: Cloudless Protection for IoT Systems

Vadim Safronov[1]([✉])(iD), Anna Maria Mandalari[2](iD), Daniel J. Dubois[3](iD), David Choffnes[3](iD), and Hamed Haddadi[1](iD)

[1] Imperial College London, London, UK
{v.safronov,h.haddadi}@imperial.ac.uk
[2] University College London, London, UK
a.mandalari@ucl.ac.uk
[3] Northeastern University, Boston, USA
d.dubois@northeastern.edu, choffnes@ccs.neu.edu

Abstract. With an increasing number of Internet of Things (IoT) devices present in homes, there is a rise in the number of potential information leakage channels and their associated security threats and privacy risks. Despite a long history of attacks on IoT devices in unprotected home networks, the problem of accurate, rapid detection and prevention of such attacks remains open. Many existing IoT protection solutions are cloud-based, sometimes ineffective, and might share consumer data with unknown third parties. This paper investigates the potential for effective IoT threat detection locally, on a home router, using AI tools combined with classic rule-based traffic-filtering algorithms. Our results show that with a slight rise of router hardware resources caused by machine learning and traffic filtering logic, a typical home router instrumented with our solution is able to effectively detect risks and protect a typical home IoT network, equaling or outperforming existing popular solutions, without any effects on benign IoT functionality, and without relying on cloud services and third parties.

1 Introduction

Internet of Things (IoT) devices are increasingly popular, pervasive, and promise a wide range of functionality including remote health monitoring, adaptive climate and lighting, automated control of various appliances and assets within smart spaces. The heterogeneity of IoT device types, functionality, and their applications lead to major security and privacy threats for smart home users. IoT devices are manufactured all over the world, send data globally, may be updated over-the-air, and use a myriad of third-party software libraries [47]. A single vulnerability in one part of the IoT supply chain can have broad security and privacy impacts for IoT users. For example, compromised IoT devices can compromise user privacy, *e.g.,* exposing sensitive user activities on personal computers by reading power consumption from a compromised smart plug [27], among many other serious threats described in recent literature [32,48,49,51]. Also, the combination of IoT device sensors with Internet connectivity poses substantial risks of personally identifiable information (PII) exposure [47].

P. Richter et al. (Eds.): PAM 2024, LNCS 14538, pp. 322–338, 2024.
https://doi.org/10.1007/978-3-031-56252-5_15

To address such risks, several IoT protection solutions have been proposed so far, but they pose several issues, including their lack of completeness. Evidence from prior research [39] suggests that popular IoT protection solutions fail to accurately detect and mitigate a significant proportion of threats, particularly those available with basic subscriptions. Moreover, most IoT protection solutions largely rely on cloud-based ML models for detecting attacks. Such cloud-based models necessarily require vendors to collect personal and sensitive data from the networks they protect, and this itself poses the risk of such data being shared with third-parties, used for purposes beyond threat detection, and even being compromised by attacks on cloud infrastructure. In contrast, implementing IoT protection solutions locally can enhance user privacy, obviating the need to disclose personal and potentially sensitive data to other parties outside the local network. Such an edge protection approach can also improve robustness and stability of operations by eliminating the dependence on cloud services. However, a key open question is how feasible such locally run solutions are, and how well they work compared to cloud-based ones.

In this paper, we investigate the possibility of using threat detection and prevention algorithms on a home router, as well as measure quantitative implications on the router's memory (RAM), processing power (CPU), bandwidth (BW), and whether consuming these resources has any impact on the smooth operation of IoT devices and applications. Specifically, we demonstrate the feasibility of a completely local IoT protection solution, named SunBlock, which combines existing rule-based traffic filtering tools and machine-learning libraries to provide a resource-efficient prototype combining both intrusion detection (IDS) and intrusion prevention (IPS) systems. SunBlock operates on a typical home router, thus improving user privacy without the need for end users to share potentially sensitive data with cloud-based IDS/IPS solutions as well as bypassing the expense of their premium subscriptions. We conclude this paper by exposing our SunBlock prototype to a set of various IoT threats, demonstrating that it can detect a spectrum of threats more than twice as large as that detected by commercial IoT protection solutions [39]. The paper's code is available online [17].

Goals. The paper targets two main research questions (RQs) detailed below. *RQ1: How can we replace commercial cloud-based safeguards by a threat detection and prevention software running locally on a home router?* We address this by designing a new cloudless threat detection/prevention approach (Sect. 3) and implementing it on popular off-the-shelf router hardware (Sect. 4).
RQ2: What is the performance of our solution in terms of overhead and threat detection capability? We address this by establishing a rigorous evaluation methodology (Sect. 5) and performing an extensive evaluation (Sect. 6) to evaluate: (*i*) the overhead of running AI and rule-based IDS locally in terms of router memory, processing power, and bandwidth; (*ii*) how successfully our cloudless solution detects popular attacks compared to existing cloud-based IoT security solutions.

Non-goals. The following topics are not the focus of this paper.
Novel ML/AI algorithms for anomaly detection. We assess existing ML methods

for their feasibility to run on constrained devices performing IPS functions. *Classification of end-user traffic, such as smartphones, tablets and PCs.* The main focus of the paper is on protecting smart home IoT devices.

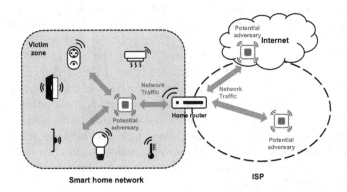

Fig. 1. Threat model diagram. Victim zone is a smart home with connected IoT devices. A potential adversary can analyze traffic and conduct privacy/security attacks from smart home, ISP and wider zones, such as the Internet.

2   Threat Model

In this paper we investigate the problem of protecting a typical home network from threats deriving from its IoT devices. We focus on instrumenting the home router providing connectivity to the IoT devices with existing algorithms (*i.e.*, combining IDS/IPS functions with a classic rule-based approach) to investigate the feasibility of running anomaly detection at the edge. This paper is not about proposing novel ML/AI algorithms or about surveying and comparing different AI/ML models for IoT anomaly detection, as done in previous studies [33,34,55].

Our threat model (Fig. 1) assumes a typical smart home deployment, with a home router connected to the Internet (WAN interface) creating and providing connectivity to a local smart home network ((W)LAN interface), where IoT devices are deployed. In this setting, we assume the victim to be a user of IoT devices, and the adversary any entity that can gain network access either from the WAN side (*e.g.*, an attacker in the ISP network or the Internet) or the (W)LAN side (*e.g.*, a compromised IoT device). In both cases the adversary can abuse network access and capture network data (such as traffic rates, protocols used, source/destination IP addresses, *etc.*) that can result in security and privacy threats for the victim. For example, network data can be used to conduct analyses to infer victim's sensitive data (*e.g.*, user activities [47]), and assess and exploit vulnerabilities [44]. The threats we focus on in this paper are the following:

Security: anomalous traffic, anomalous upload as well as various flooding (*e.g.,* DoS) and scanning attacks (e.g. port-scanning).

Privacy: PII exposure, unencrypted network/application data.

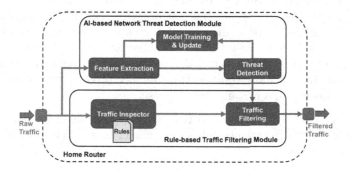

Fig. 2. SunBlock architecture running on a home router.

3 System Design

In this section we propose the design of SunBlock, *i.e.,* an approach for detecting IoT threats at a home router without relying on the cloud. Figure 2 shows the architecture of our system. SunBlock runs on a home router and is composed of: (*i*) a rule-based traffic filtering module; and (*ii*) an AI-based network threat detection module. Raw IoT traffic traversing the home router is inspected against a defined set of IPS rules [26], the features are extracted and fed to the trained threat detection model. Both rule-based and AI threat detection steps are performed in parallel and described in detail below.

3.1 Rule-Based Traffic Filtering Module

This module is responsible for blocking unwanted or potentially harmful traffic while allowing safe and necessary traffic to pass, thereby enhancing the overall security of the network. This module is composed of the following components.

Traffic Inspector: As network packets arrive, they are inspected against a defined set of rules at various levels: IP (*i.e.,* the source and destination IP addresses are checked), transport level (TCP or UDP source and destination ports), and/or at the application level (where the actual content of the packets is inspected, if the HTTP protocol is used, for example).

Traffic Filtering: Based on the set of pre-defined rules, allowed traffic passes further, while all the inspected traffic matching the blocking rules is dropped.

3.2 AI-Based Network Threat Detection Module

AI anomaly detection identifies irregular traffic patterns that could indicate potential security threats. The module consists of the following components.

Feature Extraction. Similar to rule-based traffic filtering, the first step includes collecting and processing raw network data, including information about source and destination IP addresses, port numbers, packet sizes, time durations, *etc.* The collected data is then transformed into a set of features, which are measurable properties or characteristics of the observed network traffic. These could include rate of data transmission, number of connections to a specific server, or frequency of a certain type of packet.

Model Training. An ML model is trained locally on the extracted dataset of network features. At the training phase, the model learns what 'normal' network traffic looks like.

Threat Detection. SunBlock uses the trained model for comparing live incoming network traffic to the 'normal' patterns learned during training. If the live traffic deviates significantly from normal patterns, SunBlock reports a threat.

Model Update. To support high threat detection accuracy, the model continues to learn and refine its understanding of what constitutes normal behavior.

4 Implementation

This section answers our first research question by describing a SunBlock prototype, demonstrating that IoT protection can run at the edge, on a home router.

4.1 Hardware

To demonstrate our approach, we use an off-the-shelf middle-range home router: a LinkSys WRT3200ACM [8]. The reason for this choice is its popularity and support for OpenWrt [12], a Linux-based OS targeting embedded devices. Due to the router's limited flash memory (256 MB), we use a USB stick to allocate 4GB and 512 MB partitions for AI libraries/dependencies and swap space, respectively.

4.2 Rule-Based Traffic Filtering

We use Snort3 [15] as a rule-based IDS/IPS. The reason for this choice is the extensive support for rule-based detection techniques, deep packet inspection and various customization options, making it flexibly well-suited for IoT threat prevention use cases. We prefer Snort3 over other solutions like Fail2ban [4], Zeek [21], and Suricata [18] due to its comprehensive rule-based detection techniques, extensive customization options, and flexibility. Other tools have either narrower focus (*e.g.,* Fail2Ban focuses on log-based IDS/IPS) or require more scripting overhead to match Snort3's functionality. Besides utilizing the Snort3 community rules [16], we enhanced them by adding blocking logic for DoS, scanning attacks, and unencrypted HTTP traffic.

We configure Snort3 to run in NFQ IPS mode, which allows it to operate as an inline IPS. In this mode, Snort3 intercepts network traffic using Netfilter [10], a packet filtering and manipulation framework in the Linux kernel. In NFQ IPS inline mode, Snort3 receives network packets before they reach their target, thus allowing the system to react promptly to any suspicious traffic.

Upon receiving packets, SunBlock performs packet inspection by applying the pre-defined rules serving as criteria for identifying and blocking security and privacy threats. The inspection process involves protocol decoding, traffic analysis, and pattern matching against the defined rule set. Based on the results of the inspection, SunBlock applies rule-based actions. It determines if a packet matches any rules in its rule set and takes actions accordingly, such as dropping the packet or blocking the entire malicious traffic flow.

4.3   AI-Based Network Threat Detection

For our threat detection model, we utilize the netml library [11,55], a robust tool designed for feature extraction and threat detection in network traffic traces.

While the netml library is primarily intended for powerful machines with ample RAM and CPU resources, we successfully adapt it to be used on home routers. As netml is initially dedicated to x86 architectures, we adapt it for the ARMv7l architecture, commonly used in modern Wi-Fi routers and other embedded networked systems with limited resources. This portability enhances SunBlock's accessibility and flexibility, allowing it to run on a wider range of router configurations. We incorporate netml into a Docker image based on Debian version 10. The resulting image is open-source and accessible online [17]. After a series of deployment installations and tests, we selected the following versions of netml dependencies, a combination of which allows for the successful running of ML anomaly detection logic on the ARMv7l architecture: numba = 0.56.0, netaddr = 0.8.0, numpy = 1.22.0, pandas = 1.5.3, pyod = 1.0.9, scapy = 2.4.5 and scikit-learn = 0.24.1.

For anomaly detection tasks, SunBlock employs the One-Class Support Vector Machine (OCSVM) model in unsupervised mode with the packet interarrival time (IAT) feature. The OCSVM model is recognized for its outlier detection capabilities, lightweightness and efficacy [38,46,50]. The precision of the netml-based OCSVM implementation, used by SunBlock, has been extensively evaluated by the netml authors on various datasets, showing high precision for IoT anomaly classification tasks when using the IAT feature [55]. The Area Under the ROC Curve (AUC) metric is 0.95 for detecting infected devices, 0.96 for detecting novel devices, and 0.81–0.97 for detecting abnormal device activity. The chosen OCSVM configuration has been wrapped into a real-time threat detection logic having the following characteristics:

- Our system is configured to capture batches of 200 packets[1], thus capturing and classifying network traffic every batch.
- Our model is set up to learn from the most recent 7 days of network traffic. This period is chosen based on research indicating a decrease in model accuracy beyond a week without retraining [34].
- Upon detection of a threat, SunBlock uses iptables [7] for blocking malicious sources of traffic.

5   Evaluation Methodology

In this section we describe how we assess the performance of SunBlock in terms of overhead and threat detection capability. We first describe the IoT testbed we use for analyzing SunBlock, then how we emulate the threats, and finally describe the experiment setting and the evaluation metrics.

5.1   Evaluation Testbed

To assess the efficacy of SunBlock, we build an IoT testbed that emulates a typical smart home setting. According to previous research [31] that examined smart home traffic from 4,322 households, an average home tends to host around 10 IoT devices. Based on this number, and considering popular IoT device models and categories, we build our testbed using the 10 IoT devices detailed below.

- **Smart speaker:** Amazon Echo Spot, Google Home.
- **Video:** Amazon Fire TV.
- **Camera:** Yi Home Camera, Blink Home Camera.
- **Home automation:** Nest thermostat, TP-Link Kasa plug, WeMo plug, Gosund bulb, TP-Link Kasa bulb.

The IoT devices are performing daily activities within a 2.4 GHz WiFi home network in a location similar to a two-bedroom flat. We trigger the IoT device functionality by using a methodology similar to [40] for a period of one week.

5.2   Threats Emulation

For triggering the threats, we employ a Raspberry Pi Model B+ (RPi) as a threat generation node, equipped with 4 GB RAM and running a Debian image. The RPi is connected to the (W)LAN side of the home network along with the IoT devices. In order to check the SunBlock performance in realistic scenarios, the RPi used real attack scripts from an open GitHub repository [14] containing threat emulation scripts from recent research on the efficiency of IoT protection systems [39]. The threats we emulate are the following.

---

[1] We obtained this number empirically after extensive testing showing a good trade-off between ML accuracy and reaction time.

Anomalous Traffic. RPi acts on behalf of the Echo Spot device by spoofing its IP and MAC addresses. However, instead of sending typical Echo Spot traffic, the RPi injects previously captured traffic from the Google Home. We inject this traffic using tcpreplay [19], where we replace the IP and MAC addresses of the Google Home with Echo Spot's ones.

Anomalous Upload. We emulate anomalous upload behavior by making the RPi upload a video to an external unauthorized server while spoofing the IP and MAC addresses of the Yi home camera using the tcpreplay tool [19].

DoS Flooding. For SYN, UDP, DNS and HTTP flooding threats, the RPi uses suits of attacks from Kali Linux emulating a typical Mirai-infected device [23].

Privacy Script. The RPi acts on behalf of Google Home (by spoofing its IP and MAC addresses) and transmits unencrypted sensitive data, such as login details, passwords and other private data, to an external server through HTTP.

Scanning Attacks. We emulate OS and port scanning using Nmap [37]. This information can be utilized by a potential attacker to determine the most effective attack strategy for the detected OS, taking advantage of the open ports.

5.3   Experiments Description and Evaluation Metrics

Prior to executing the threat emulation scripts, we benchmark the resource utilization (CPU, RAM, and bandwidth) of the home router running SunBlock with respect to a router not running it. We continuously monitor these metrics using a Python-based script, which captures resource consumption data over a span of 3.5 h of regular IoT traffic.

To evaluate SunBlock performance, we time the training process under four distinct conditions: both modules operational, only the AI-based module active, only the Rule-based module active, and an unprotected scenario. Under each condition, the model underwent five training iterations. A background script records CPU usage, RAM (actual RAM used by the system, excluding buffers/cache), bandwidth consumption, and the start and end times of each training instance.

We conduct each attack for 100 s in 10 separate iterations. After each attack, we reset the network to its normal operational state before we start the next iteration. The RPi logs both the start and end times for each individual attack. We conduct all experiments in a home network environment equipped with the SunBlock router. We then repeat the same set of experiments in a network with the same router, but with SunBlock disabled.

To measure resource utilization of the home router, both with and without SunBlock, we execute a background Python-based script during each attack, which records the utilization of *CPU, RAM, and BW* every second.

To measure *threat prevention latency*, we execute a script to capture SunBlock's notifications, which provided timestamps and types of blocked threats. We calculate the prevention latency as the time between the start of the attack and the arrival of a SunBlock's notification indicating a blocked threat.

6   Evaluation

In this section we answer our second research question by evaluating the performance of SunBlock in terms of overhead and threat detection capability.

6.1   Performance Overheads

Table 1 shows model training performance overhead in distinct conditions: fully protected (Rule-based and AI-based enabled modes), partially protected (either Rule-based or AI-based mode is enabled), and unprotected (disabled SunBlock).

Table 1. ML training time and resource usage for various protection levels.

Protection Level	CPU (%)	RAM (MB)	swap (MB)	Training Time (s)
Rule-based & AI-based	18 ± 3	444 ± 4	296 ± 21	924 ± 253
AI-based only	26 ± 2	442 ± 6	197 ± 28	429 ± 171
Rule-based only	32 ± 4	423 ± 9	132 ± 20	180 ± 22
Unprotected	39 ± 2	410 ± 3	55 ± 1	113 ± 10

When deployed in tandem, Rule-based and AI-based modules constitute the most secure mode. Although the fully protected mode takes the longest time for training—up to 20 min—it has the lowest CPU utilization among all modes. Compared to AI-based/Rule-based only modes, the fully protected mode has increased training time by a factor of 1.5–6.5, and up to a factor of 10.5 when compared to the unprotected mode. However, the duration of fully protected training remains within an acceptable range and can be scheduled during off-peak hours to minimize disruptions.

Memory usage is also critical for a home router. During the fully protected mode, swap memory usage peaks at around 300MB, which is manageable for a typical home router equipped with sufficient flash memory (either internally or through an external USB stick). It is noticeable that swap is required only for model training and is not used in SunBlock's daily behavior. Swap should be allocated as a separate partition for its isolation from router's storage memory.

Figure 3 provides a performance comparison between the router in SunBlock's protected mode and the same router in the unprotected mode, during their routine operation without network threats. SunBlock exhibits a wider CPU utilization range compared to the unprotected router; however, the utilization peaks at only ∼15%. The median CPU utilization remains at an approximate 3%, thus maintaining a negligible impact on overall performance. SunBlock has 1.7 times higher RAM consumption than the unprotected router. While this increment is notable, the overall RAM usage remains well within the router's capacity, leaving about 30% of free RAM. The bandwidth usage is the same in both modes

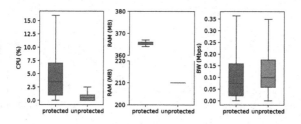

Fig. 3. Resource usage in protected vs. unprotected mode for regular IoT traffic.

due to the same traffic conditions under which both protected and unprotected modes were tested.

Figure 4 illustrates the Empirical Cumulative Distribution Functions (ECDFs) representing the times taken by SunBlock to prevent threat types listed in Sect. 5.2. It can be observed that most threats are blocked within ∼5 s. However, SunBlock requires more time to detect anomaly threats, namely ∼10 s for anomalous upload and ∼50 s for anomalous traffic.

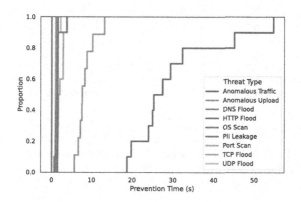

Fig. 4. ECDFs of SunBlock's prevention time per each attack.

Figures 5, 6 show RAM, CPU and BW overhead of SunBlock under a number of traffic-heavy attacks (DNS, HTTP, SYN, UDP flooding and anomalous upload), compared to an unprotected mode.

As anticipated, SunBlock exhibits an elevated CPU/RAM usage due to the operational load imposed by Rule-based and AI-based modules actively performing threat mitigation tasks. SunBlock's median CPU consumption varies between 3–40%, while the RAM usage remains fairly stable within a range of 365–375 MB. Conversely, an unprotected router exhibits significantly lower RAM/CPU usage, ∼220 MB of RAM and 1–25% of median CPU utilization.

The protective effects of SunBlock are evident in the bandwidth consumption under heavy DoS attacks. The box plots indicate a substantial bandwidth

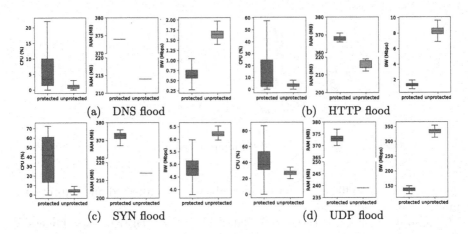

Fig. 5. Resource usage in protected vs. unprotected mode under DoS attacks.

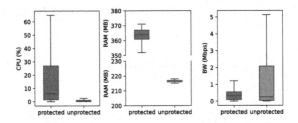

Fig. 6. Resource usage in protected vs. unprotected mode for anomalous upload.

reduction of up to ∼8 times during intense DoS attacks, with the strongest reductions during HTTP and UDP flooding. During the attacks, SunBlock maintains an adequate buffer of resources, with 50% of CPU and 30% of RAM always available.

6.2   Threat Detection Capability

Table 2 presents a comprehensive comparison of SunBlock's threat detection capability with existing IoT protection solutions. The data on threat detection capabilities of existing solutions is sourced from prior comparative research [39], which evaluated a number of most popular IoT protection solutions (Avira [20], Bitdefender [2], F-Secure [3], Fingbox [5], Firewalla [6], McAfee [9], RATtrap [13], and TrendMicro [1]) using the same threat generation scripts as our evaluation. For the sake of brevity, the table shows merged IoT threat detection results of these protection systems. A check mark against a threat means at least one system can detect it. Results show that SunBlock outperforms IoT protection solutions in terms of threat detection capabilities.

Table 2. Threats detected by existing IoT solutions vs. detected by SunBlock.

Threat	IoT Protection Systems	SunBlock
Anomalous Traffic	✗	✓
Anomalous Upload	✗	✓
SYN Flooding	✓	✓
UDP Flooding	✗	✓
DNS Flooding	✗	✓
HTTP Flooding	✓	✓
Port Scanning	✓	✓
OS Scanning	✓	✓
PII Leakage	✗	✓

7 Limitations and Future Work

Hardware. Our approach was tested on an off-the-shelf router with 512MB of RAM. We choose this since full-featured routers offered by the most popular US ISPs have more memory than that (*e.g.*, the Xfinity xFi XB6 from Comcast has 768 MB [42] and the CR1000A [53] from Verizon has 2 GB). However, some older routers and lower-tier router offerings may still have a lower amount of RAM. In such case, our approach would be slower due to requiring swap space. Future improvements involve developing a more efficient Docker image for ML anomaly detection by utilizing lighter Linux distributions such as Arch Linux, which require more custom configuration compared to Debian-based images. Additionally, it is worthwhile to monitor emerging ML/AI methods and associated compression and pruning techniques that may reduce RAM and CPU usage while maintaining high classification performance.

Zero-Day Threat Protection. Zero-day threats pose a common challenge for ML systems, as learning models require time to gather relevant training data during their first run. Shortening the initial training period can reduce exposure but might compromise accuracy, necessitating more user input for custom classification. This is not always feasible as home users are not typically security experts. SunBlock's Rule-based Traffic Filtering, functioning from day one, reduces the risk of zero-day exposure by protecting against most severe threats, such as flooding and scanning. Additionally, other security measures during the initial setup may include factory resetting all present IoT devices, ensuring they are updated with the latest software versions, and, if feasible, placing them on a separate network segment with limited Internet access.

Model Updates. Since our approach is cloudless, it does not include external (cloud-based) means of updates. The capability of our approach to learn and self-adapt partially address this limitation; however, faster updates can be achieved by allowing the periodic download of updated Snort community rules [16] and/or by building and sharing AI models in a privacy-preserving crowdsourced way (*e.g.*, as discussed in [25,56]).

Configuration. As discussed before, default parameters of our approach were chosen empirically for our prototype. However, depending on the particularities of deployment scenario and user needs, such parameters may need to be tuned to achieve the desired trade-off between false negative and false positive threat reporting. This limitation can be addressed, for example, by using a interactive ML approaches [29,54], where the user is asked to confirm what to do for each threat until the system learns how to make this decision on its own.

8   Related Work

The growing privacy and security issues in the consumer IoT domain have prompted the creation of various tools [36,40] designed to block malicious traffic originating from IoT devices. Despite the promising advances these tools represent, there remains an area for their potential improvement by incorporating AI for the detection of threats.

Other attempts [28,43,45] to shift IoT protection to the edge have limitations. Implementations of [28,45] rely solely on classic rule-based traffic filtering, which is less sensitive to anomalous traffic threats and requires additional AI-based classification. The evaluations in [28,43,45] were conducted on non-router-specific superior hardware and may not reflect consumer router performance.

There have been recent introductions of AI-based methodologies dedicated to device identification tasks at the edge [33,35,41,52]. However, they alone are insufficient for comprehensive protection against major IoT threats and would benefit from rule-based and AI-based threat detection techniques.

Numerous studies have examined IoT threats, assessing smart home vulnerabilities, attack scenarios, and defense strategies [22,24,30]. Recent research [39] introduced a methodology to assess the efficacy of current IoT protection solutions in responding to prevalent security and privacy threats. The associated threat emulation scripts and benchmarks were adopted in our study for testing the effectiveness of our prototype against popular IoT protection solutions.

9   Discussion and Conclusion

The growing ubiquity of IoT devices in residential settings is transforming our homes into sophisticated, interconnected digital environments. As such, the importance of robust and proactive protection measures for these devices is vital, ensuring not only their functionality but also the privacy and security of the vast amounts of personal data they handle.

Our research reveals that IoT threats can be rapidly mitigated on a home router, equipped with ML/AI anomaly detection and rule-based traffic filtering algorithms. Most types of threats are promptly identified and blocked within the first 5 s. Nonetheless, certain threats such as anomalous traffic and anomalous upload require a longer time due to their initial similarity with normal network behavior of other IoT devices in the network. The presented local threat detection approach eliminates the need for dependence on cloud-based IoT security solutions and thus blocks extra channels of potential PII and other user-sensitive data exposure. It is important to note that integrating ML with rule-based traffic analysis in our off-the-shelf router (which has inferior hardware with respect to full-featured routers currently offered by top ISPs in the US [42,53]) cause a slight increase in CPU utilization (up to ~15% with an average use of ~3%) and RAM consumption (by ~150 MB) during normal operation, without affecting main router functions. Our plans for further enhancements involve intensive beta testing and precise performance benchmarking against existing cloud-based security solutions.

Acknowledgements. We thank the anonymous reviewers and our shepherd Roland van Rijswijk-Deij for their constructive and insightful feedback. This work was supported by the EPSRC Open Plus Fellowship (EP/W005271/1), the EPSRC PETRAS grant (EP/S035362/1), and the NSF ProperData award (SaTC-1955227).

References

1. Asus (TrendMicro). https://www.asus.com/Content/AiProtection/. Accessed 03 Nov 2023
2. Bitdefender Box 2. https://www.bitdefender.com/smart-home/#products. Accessed 03 Nov 2023
3. F-Secure. https://www.f-secure.com/gb-en/home/products/sense. Accessed 03 Nov 2023
4. Fail2ban. https://www.fail2ban.org/wiki/index.php/Main_Page. Accessed 03 Nov 2023
5. Fingbox. https://www.fing.com/products/fingbox. Accessed 03 Nov 2023
6. Firewalla. https://firewalla.com/. Accessed 03 Nov 2023
7. iptables. https://linux.die.net/man/8/iptables. Accessed 03 Nov 2023
8. LinkSys — WRT3200ACM Data Sheet. https://downloads.linksys.com/downloads/datasheet/WRT3200ACM_WiFiRouter_EN.pdf. Accessed 03 Nov 2023
9. McAfee Secure Home Platform. https://www.mcafee.com/support/?page=shell&shell=article-view&locale=en-US&articleId=TS102712. Accessed 03 Nov 2023
10. netfilter. https://www.netfilter.org/. Accessed 03 Nov 2023
11. netml. https://github.com/noise-lab/netml. Accessed 03 Nov 2023
12. OpenWrt. https://openwrt.org/. Accessed 03 Nov 2023
13. RATtrap. https://www.myrattrap.com/. Accessed 03 Nov 2023
14. Safeguards study: threat simulation scripts. https://github.com/IoTrim/safeguards-study. Accessed 03 Nov 2023
15. Snort 3. https://www.snort.org/snort3. Accessed 03 Nov 2023
16. Snort3 community rules. https://snort.org/downloads/community/snort3-community-rules.tar.gz. Accessed 03 Nov 2023

17. SunBlock project page. https://github.com/SunBlock-IoT/SunBlock_router. Accessed 11 Jan 2023

18. Suricata. https://suricata.io/. Accessed 03 Nov 2023

19. Tcpreplay Official Site. https://tcpreplay.appneta.com/. Accessed 03 Nov 2023

20. TP-Link HomeShield (Avira). https://www.tp-link.com/us/homeshield/. Accessed 03 Nov 2023

21. Zeek. https://zeek.org/. Accessed 03 Nov 2023

22. Alrawi, O., Lever, C., Antonakakis, M., Monrose, F.: SoK: security evaluation of home-based IoT deployments. In: 2019 IEEE Symposium on Security and Privacy (SP), pp. 1362–1380 (2019). https://doi.org/10.1109/SP.2019.00013

23. Antonakakis, M., et al.: Understanding the Mirai Botnet. In: 26th USENIX Security Symposium (USENIX Security 2017), Vancouver, BC, pp. 1093–1110. USENIX Association (2017). https://www.usenix.org/conference/usenixsecurity17/technical-sessions/presentation/antonakakis

24. Babun, L., Denney, K., Celik, Z.B., McDaniel, P., Uluagac, A.S.: A survey on IoT platforms: communication, security, and privacy perspectives. Comput. Netw. **192**, 108040 (2021). https://doi.org/10.1016/j.comnet.2021.108040. https://www.sciencedirect.com/science/article/pii/S1389128621001444

25. Briggs, C., Fan, Z., Andras, P.: A review of privacy-preserving federated learning for the internet-of-things. In: Federated Learning Systems: Towards Next-Generation AI, pp. 21–50 (2021)

26. Chakrabarti, S., Chakraborty, M., Mukhopadhyay, I.: Study of snort-based IDS. In: ICWET 2010, pp. 43–47. Association for Computing Machinery, New York (2010). https://doi.org/10.1145/1741906.1741914

27. Conti, M., Nati, M., Rotundo, E., Spolaor, R.: Mind the plug! Laptop-user recognition through power consumption. In: Proceedings of the 2nd ACM International Workshop on IoT Privacy, Trust, and Security, IoTPTS 2016, pp. 37–44. Association for Computing Machinery, New York (2016). https://doi.org/10.1145/2899007.2899009

28. Dua, A., Tyagi, V., Patel, N., Mehtre, B.: IISR: a secure router for IoT networks. In: 2019 4th International Conference on Information Systems and Computer Networks (ISCON), pp. 636–643 (2019). https://doi.org/10.1109/ISCON47742.2019.9036313

29. Dudley, J.J., Kristensson, P.O.: A review of user interface design for interactive machine learning. ACM Trans. Interact. Intell. Syst. (TiiS) **8**(2), 1–37 (2018)

30. He, W., et al.: SoK: context sensing for access control in the adversarial home IoT. In: 2021 IEEE European Symposium on Security and Privacy (EuroS&P), pp. 37–53 (2021). https://doi.org/10.1109/EuroSP51992.2021.00014

31. Huang, D.Y., Apthorpe, N., Li, F., Acar, G., Feamster, N.: IoT inspector: crowdsourcing labeled network traffic from smart home devices at scale. Proc. ACM Interact. Mob. Wearable Ubiquitous Technol. **4**(2) (2020). https://doi.org/10.1145/3397333

32. Karale, A.: The challenges of iot addressing security, ethics, privacy, and laws. Internet Things **15**, 100420 (2021). https://doi.org/10.1016/j.iot.2021.100420. https://www.sciencedirect.com/science/article/pii/S2542660521000640

33. Kolcun, R., et al.: Revisiting IoT device identification. In: Bajpai, V., Haddadi, H., Hohlfeld, O. (eds.) 5th Network Traffic Measurement and Analysis Conference, TMA 2021, Virtual Event, 14–15 September 2021. IFIP (2021). http://dl.ifip.org/db/conf/tma/tma2021/tma2021-paper6.pdf

34. Kolcun, R., et al.: The Case for Retraining of ML Models for IoT Device Identification at the Edge. arXiv preprint (2020). https://arxiv.org/abs/2011.08605

35. Kotak, J., Elovici, Y.: IoT device identification using deep learning. In: Herrero, Á., Cambra, C., Urda, D., Sedano, J., Quintián, H., Corchado, E. (eds.) CISIS 2020. Advances in Intelligent Systems and Computing, vol. 1267, pp. 76–86. Springer, Cham (2021). https://doi.org/10.1007/978-3-030-57805-3_8

36. Lastdrager, E., Hesselman, C., Jansen, J., Davids, M.: Protecting home networks from insecure IoT devices. In: NOMS 2020-2020 IEEE/IFIP Network Operations and Management Symposium, p. 1–6. IEEE Press (2020). https://doi.org/10.1109/NOMS47738.2020.9110419

37. Lyon, G.F.: Nmap network scanning: the official Nmap project guide to network discovery and security scanning. Insecure. Com LLC (US) (2008)

38. Mahdavinejad, M.S., Rezvan, M., Barekatain, M., Adibi, P., Barnaghi, P., Sheth, A.P.: Machine learning for internet of things data analysis: a survey. Digit. Commun. Netw. **4**(3), 161–175 (2018). https://doi.org/10.1016/j.dcan.2017.10.002. https://www.sciencedirect.com/science/article/pii/S235286481730247X

39. Mandalari, A., Haddadi, H., Dubois, D.J., Choffnes, D.: Protected or porous: a comparative analysis of threat detection capability of IoT safeguards. In: 2023 2023 IEEE Symposium on Security and Privacy (SP) (SP), pp. 3061–3078. IEEE Computer Society, Los Alamitos (2023). https://doi.org/10.1109/SP46215.2023.00151. https://doi.ieeecomputersociety.org/10.1109/SP46215.2023.00151

40. Mandalari, A.M., Dubois, D.J., Kolcun, R., Paracha, M.T., Haddadi, H., Choffnes, D.: Blocking without Breaking: Identification and Mitigation of Non-Essential IoT Traffic (2021)

41. Meidan, Y., et al.: ProfilIoT: a machine learning approach for IoT device identification based on network traffic analysis. In: Proceedings of the Symposium on Applied Computing, SAC 2017, pp. 506–509. Association for Computing Machinery, New York (2017). https://doi.org/10.1145/3019612.3019878

42. Modems, A.: Comcast Infinity xFi XB6 Review (2023). https://approvedmodems.org/xfinity-xfi-xb6-review/. Accessed 03 Nov 2023

43. Palmese, F., Redondi, A.E., Cesana, M.: Feature-sniffer: enabling IoT forensics in OpenWrt based Wi-Fi access points. In: 2022 IEEE 8th World Forum on Internet of Things (WF-IoT), pp. 1–6. IEEE (2022)

44. Paracha, M.T., Dubois, D.J., Vallina-Rodriguez, N., Choffnes, D.: IoTLS: understanding TLS usage in consumer IoT devices. In: Proceedings of the Internet Measurement Conference (2021)

45. Patel, N., Mehtre, B., Wankar, R.: A snort-based secure edge router for smart home. Int. J. Sens. Netw. **41**(1), 42–59 (2023). https://doi.org/10.1504/IJSNET.2023.128505. https://www.inderscienceonline.com/doi/abs/10.1504/IJSNET.2023.128505

46. Razzak, I., Zafar, K., Imran, M., Xu, G.: Randomized nonlinear one-class support vector machines with bounded loss function to detect of outliers for large scale IoT data. Future Gener. Comput. Syst. **112**, 715–723 (2020). https://doi.org/10.1016/j.future.2020.05.045. https://www.sciencedirect.com/science/article/pii/S0167739X19313913

47. Ren, J., Dubois, D.J., Choffnes, D., Mandalari, A.M., Kolcun, R., Haddadi, H.: Information exposure for consumer IoT devices: a multidimensional, network-informed measurement approach. In: Proceedings of the Internet Measurement Conference (IMC) (2019)

48. Sadek, I., Rehman, S.U., Codjo, J., Abdulrazak, B.: Privacy and security of IoT based healthcare systems: concerns, solutions, and recommendations. In: Pagán, J., Mokhtari, M., Aloulou, H., Abdulrazak, B., Cabrera, M. (eds.) ICOST 2019.

LNCS, vol. 11862, pp. 3–17. Springer, Heidelberg (2019). https://doi.org/10.1007/978-3-030-32785-9_1

49. Setayeshfar, O., et al.: Privacy invasion via smart-home hub in personal area networks. Pervasive Mob. Comput. **85**, 101675 (2022). https://doi.org/10.1016/j.pmcj.2022.101675

50. Shorman, A., Faris, H., Aljarah, I.: Unsupervised intelligent system based on one class support vector machine and Grey Wolf optimization for IoT botnet detection. J. Ambient Intell. Humaniz. Comput. **11**, 2809–2825 (2020). https://doi.org/10.1007/s12652-019-01387-y

51. Swessi, D., Idoudi, H.: A survey on internet-of-things security: threats and emerging countermeasures. Wirel. Pers. Commun. **124**(2), 1557–1592 (2022). https://doi.org/10.1007/s11277-021-09420-0

52. Thompson, O., Mandalari, A.M., Haddadi, H.: Rapid IoT device identification at the edge. In: Proceedings of the 2nd ACM International Workshop on Distributed Machine Learning, DistributedML 2021, pp. 22–28. Association for Computing Machinery, New York (2021). https://doi.org/10.1145/3488659.3493777

53. Verizon: VerizonRouter CR1000A Datasheet (2023). https://www.verizon.com/supportresources/content/dam/verizon/support/consumer/documents/internet/verizon-router_datasheet.pdf. Accessed 03 Nov 2023

54. Wu, X., Xiao, L., Sun, Y., Zhang, J., Ma, T., He, L.: A survey of human-in-the-loop for machine learning. Futur. Gener. Comput. Syst. **135**, 364–381 (2022)

55. Yang, K., Kpotufe, S., Feamster, N.: A Comparative Study of Network Traffic Representations for Novelty Detection. arXiv preprint (2020). https://arxiv.org/abs/2006.16993v1

56. Zhou, C., Fu, A., Yu, S., Yang, W., Wang, H., Zhang, Y.: Privacy-preserving federated learning in fog computing. IEEE Internet Things J. **7**(11), 10782–10793 (2020)

Author Index

P. Richter et al. (Eds.): PAM 2024, LNCS 14538, pp. 339–340, 2024.
https://doi.org/10.1007/978-3-031-56252-5

Printed in the United States
by Baker & Taylor Publisher Services